PHILIP AUGUSTUS
KING OF FRANCE
1180–1223

THE MEDIEVAL WORLD
Editor: David Bates

JUSTINIAN
John Moorhead

CHARLES THE BALD
Janet Nelson

CNUT
M.K. Lawson

MEDIEVAL CANON LAW
James A. Brundage

THE FORMATION OF THE ENGLISH COMMON LAW
John Hudson

WILLIAM MARSHAL
David Crouch

KING JOHN
Ralph V. Turner

PHILIP AUGUSTUS
Jim Bradbury

INNOCENT III
Jane Sayers

THE FRIARS
C.H. Lawrence

THE WESTERN MEDITERRANEAN KINGDOMS 1200–1500
David Abulafia

ENGLISH NOBLEWOMEN IN THE LATER MIDDLE AGES
Jennifer C. Ward

BASTARD FEUDALISM
Michael Hicks

. . . . .

PHILIP AUGUSTUS

King of France
1180–1223

Jim Bradbury

LONGMAN
London and New York

Addison Wesley Longman Limited
Edinburgh Gate,
Harlow, Essex CM20 2JE, United Kingdom
and Associated Companies throughout the world.

Published in the United States of America by Addison Wesley Longman, New York.

First published 1998

ISBN 0–582–06058–3 CSD
ISBN 0–582–06059–1 PPR

British Library Cataloguing in Publication Data

A catalogue entry for this title is available from the British Library

Library of Congress Cataloging-in-Publication Data

A catalogue entry for this book is available from the Library of Congress

Set by 35 in 11/12pt Baskerville
Produced by Longman Singapore Publishers (Pte) Ltd.
Printed in Singapore

TO JANE AND GUNAR, HANNAH AND FRANCES

CONTENTS

LIST OF GENEALOGICAL TABLES AND MAPS

. . . . .

EDITOR'S PREFACE

Philip Augustus is undeniably a king whose reign is of central importance for the development of the history of western Europe. Heir to a kingdom of France in which the king's power was equalled by several territorial princes, and which was dramatically overshadowed by the rulers of the Angevin Empire, Philip succeeded in both destroying the Angevin Empire and consolidating royal power to the extent that, in his last years, and under his successors, the French kings not only dominated their own kingdom, but emerged as rulers of the most prestigious monarchy in western Europe. His great moments of triumph were undoubtedly the ejection of King John from almost all of his territories of the Angevin Empire and the famous victory at the battle of Bouvines in 1214. But his achievement is much more than a military one, since monarchy was consolidated and royal government placed on a sound legal and administrative basis.

Philip's reign has long been the focus of scholarly enquiry. The celebrated *Registers* were first published in the second half of the nineteenth century, his charters have now all been edited and the major literary sources are all in print. Historians of the highest calibre have devoted their attention to the reign, from Léopold Delisle in the nineteenth century, to the major volume celebrating the octocentenary of Philip's accession, which contained essays by numerous leading French medievalists, and to John Baldwin's monumental study of Philip's government and the republication of the *Registers*. Yet surprisingly no one has ever attempted to produce a study which synthesizes and comments on the extensive historical literature. Equally surprisingly, Philip's character and achievements have remained both unappreciated and obscure for an English-speaking readership. Attention has often been focused much more heavily on Philip's colourful Angevin contemporaries, above all on Richard the Lionheart and his flawed brother John, and on such powerful contemporary figures as Pope Innocent III. But the man who was arguably more successful than any of them is frequently seen as somehow lucky, sneaky or dull.

Jim Bradbury's book sets out to do justice to Philip as a man and a king and to redress the balance of assessment in relation to his contemporaries. Philip's well-known skill and resourcefulness in the basic tasks of government are emphasized. Much more originally, the narrative of events and the contemporary sources are tellingly utilized to underline Philip's considerable abilities as a soldier and a leader. The contrast between his moderation and basic humanity and the strident and downright unpleasant behaviour of Richard the Lionheart on the Third Crusade and in the great conflict for possession of the Angevin Empire, is persuasively set out. Philip also emerges as a religious and often principled king in the long-standing Capetian tradition. Above all what emerges from Jim Bradbury's book is a picture of a very high intelligence, a remarkable capacity to assess realistically the situations he faced, and a determination to succeed which frequently crossed over the boundary into ruthlessness.

Best known as a historian of warfare in the medieval period, Jim Bradbury here ranges across the wider range of politics, culture and religion. His book is a very welcome addition to the Medieval World series for the way in which it sets out to achieve a personal, yet balanced and evaluative assessment of a major medieval king.

David Bates

PREFACE

The idea to write this book came in a rather unusual manner which, since the completion of it has taken up several years of my life, seems worth recording. As long ago as 1989, when I was contemplating a new subject to work on, I heard about the plans for a Longman series on 'The Medieval World' through a friend, David Crouch, and wondered about approaching the academic editor, David Bates. I have long had an interest in the counts of Anjou, and suggested a contribution on that subject, but as an American historian had already been asked to provide a work on one of the counts, this project was not viable. However, I was keen to tackle a biography, or something at least which seemed of less wide scope than my books on *The Medieval Archer* and *The Medieval Siege*. Over a pleasant lunch with David Bates and Andrew MacLennan, Philip Augustus emerged as a subject. I have been working on it ever since.

I can smile now, a little wryly perhaps, at the initial expectation that this would be a more restricted project. The vast amount of material available on Philip – the lengthy life by Alexander Cartellieri, the volumes of *Actes*, the almost interminable poem by William the Breton, the enormous modern volume of papers on the reign edited by R-H. Bautier, and so on – hardly make for a quick study. Everything on Philip seems to be vast and long.

But I had not set out to spend my life researching the reign. Since my aim was an overall view, the wise approach seemed to be to use the work done by various modern scholars. My main object has been to turn this material into something of manageable length and approach for intelligent readers who have only a certain amount of background information. It is intended, in other words, to be only an introduction to the reign. A biography is not really possible, in the modern sense of the word, since the available material is not of a kind to allow that, but I have aimed to concentrate on the life of Philip and his personal contribution, though the outcome is inevitably about the 'reign' as much as it is about the 'life'.

Those who wish to examine the reign in greater depth will find more narrative detail in the volumes of Alexander Cartellieri, and more research into original records in the work of Professor John W. Baldwin. However, I do not apologize for this attempt at a relatively brief book on the reign. I taught undergraduates this topic for many years and was often struck by the difficulty of suggesting an introductory work on what is after all one of the major reigns in European history. Few undergraduates or casual readers would have the energy, even if they had the linguistic ability, to tackle Cartellieri; and Baldwin's work, though invaluable and in English, concentrates on government and is very detailed. These two works also perhaps typify the divide in most existing works on Philip Augustus, between those which concentrate on the narrative sources, as Cartellieri, and those who focus on the administrative records, as Baldwin. This present book is an attempt to marry these approaches.

The completion of this book was delayed because I suffered a heart attack in the autumn of 1993, when in the middle of working on it. As a result of that, I gave up my work at West London Institute of Higher Education, as it then was, to concentrate on writing. While I was stretched on a hospital bed, I received a number of welcome letters and cards. But one in particular was relevant to this book; it was from John Gillingham, wishing me a speedy recovery so that I could get on with the book on 'that horrible man', Philip Augustus.

In a hospital bed one has plenty of time to muse. John Gillingham of course was teasing, and had his allegiance to Richard the Lionheart in mind, but it spurred me to crystallize thoughts which had been revolving in my head about Philip Augustus for some time. I realized that I violently disagreed with that tongue-in-cheek, but also I suspect heartfelt, condemnation. The result is that in this book I have tried not only to present Philip as an important king, a view with which most people would agree, but also as an admirable man, with which most people have disagreed. Philip's merits, far more than Richard's, it seems to me, are of the kind that the modern age should find meritorious.

I owe thanks to a number of people, none of whom can be blamed for the errors and omissions which are bound to exist. Firstly to the editors: David Bates and Andrew MacLennan, for their initial enthusiasm, for their constant encouragement, for their perceptive criticisms of the first draft, and especially for their kind concern and tolerance during the period of delay. David Bates has been a most careful and conscientious commentator and, but for him, there would be far more errors and faults than survive. I should also like to thank Bill Jenkins for seeing it through the press.

I did most of the reading for this book in London: in the library of the Institute of Education, which is my favourite place to work, except for home, and to whose staff I owe gratitude for their help over many years; in the British Library, whose move to new premises and away from the blue dome of the Reading Room I do not relish; and in Senate House, to whose staff I owe a debt for making special arrangements to allow me books on loan during the course of one year, notably the Cartellieri volumes.

I have, as so often, been sustained by help and inspiration from various people, including those I have met in London Institute of Historical Research seminars. As I have mentioned most of those who organize the early medieval seminars in previous prefaces, I would wish here to add to the list Michael Clanchy, whose work on Abelard, as presented through these seminars, is an enormous inspiration to anyone working on the period, and who also was able to put me in touch with Professor Baldwin. Brenda Bolton, Bernard Gauthiez and Cyril Edwards have also given assistance or encouragement through their work or their comments.

My thanks as always need to go to my wife, Ann, who continues to work daily for an accountant in order to keep me in the style to which I am accustomed (i.e. near but not actual poverty). Before this book was ever thought of, Ann and I spent a holiday in Normandy during which we visited the great castle of Château-Gaillard. While I spent the day, a beautiful clear sunny day, tramping around every inch of the site, Ann sat and sketched it for a water-colour painting. I could not bear to see that painting go, so I acquired it from her, and it still hangs on the wall, an effective means of recalling two sorts of past: personal and historical. I think my fondness for Philip Augustus began there. It's odd how life and history tend to become so entwined, but who would have it otherwise?

Jim Bradbury
Selsey 1997

A NOTE ON THE SOURCES

NARRATIVE SOURCES

The major narrative sources for the reign are the works emanating from the abbey of St-Denis. The first of these is the history by the monk Rigord. He tells us that he had come to Paris from southern France and was a physician, but otherwise we know little of him. He had started on his great work, the *Gesta Philippi Augusti* (generally known as the *Vie* or *Life*), before entering monastic life.[1] Rigord was not an official historian, but he had access to royal archives, and for example was able to copy into his chronicle the 'Testament' made before Philip went on the Third Crusade. The first version of Rigord's work was finished by 1196 and dedicated to Philip. He then made two further versions, extending his work first to 1200 with a dedication to Prince Louis, and then to 1206 at about which time he died. We treat the work of Rigord as being favourable to the king, and certainly it is more friendly than the Anglo-Norman chronicles; but it is also critical, not least of Philip's association with Agnes de Méran.

The second and greater source for the reign was the work of William the Breton, who began by continuing the *Life* of Philip Augustus left by Rigord. William was a priest, not a monk at St-Denis, but he worked in that abbey and used its

1. The major edition of the works of Rigord and William the Breton is the *Oeuvres de Rigord et de Guillaume le Breton*, ed. H-F. Delaborde, SHF, vols 210, 224 (Paris, 1882–85). The *Gesta*, the combined work of Rigord and William the Breton, is sometimes referred to as the 'Vie' or 'Life of Philip Augustus', and is abbreviated as 'Vie' in the footnotes here.

resources. He came from Brittany and became a chaplain at the royal court, where he developed a close relationship with the king. William accepted ambassadorial tasks for his master, which included representing him before the papacy over the king's marriage problem. William the Breton also became tutor to Philip's illegitimate son, Philip Charlot. This implies a more tolerant attitude to what the papacy regarded as the king's adultery than that held by Rigord. His relationship with the king also meant that William was an eyewitness to many of the major events of the reign. He was at both the siege of Château-Gaillard and the battle of Bouvines, when he chanted psalms behind the king during the conflict. William both continued Rigord's account up to Bouvines and abbreviated it with additions in a second version, which he later took on to 1220. After his death another writer added further material. This prose history work is the *Gesta Philippi*, again commonly called the *Vie* or *Life*.

William the Breton also wrote an even fuller account of the events of Philip's reign in the poem known to us as the *Philippide*. He says it took three years to write and two to correct, though it seems actually to have taken somewhat longer. The first version was finished in about 1222, the second by 1226. He first intended to write the work in ten books, but needed twelve before he was finished. It is a poem in epic style, subject to a certain amount of poetic licence and exaggeration, but it contains a wealth of detail, which often brings the period vividly to life. William the Breton undoubtedly gives a version of events which favours Philip, and his contributions need to be seen in that light. But his work also provides the best information from close to the king, and should therefore be seen as the fundamental source for the reign.

Apart from these two authors, French narrative sources for the reign are disappointing. At the same time there is a wealth of historical writing on the period from Anglo-Norman chroniclers. Not surprisingly the majority of these see the reign from the point of view of the kings of England, and are basically hostile to Philip. Their quality, their weight of numbers, and probably their accessibility to English historians, have made these sources a dominant factor in our view of the reign, and it is that dominance which this book seeks to redress. If we must be careful about William the Breton because he is prejudiced in favour of Philip, we

must be equally careful about the host of works emanating
from the Plantagenet lands, and chiefly from across the Channel, which are predominantly hostile to the French king. A
brief summary of this kind is not the place to go into detail
about the 'Angevin' sources. The authors include some first-
rate writers: Roger of Howden, probably also the author of
the work once called 'Benedict of Peterborough', Roger
of Wendover, Walter Map, William of Newburgh, Richard of
Devizes, Gervase of Canterbury, Robert of Torigny, Ralph
Diceto (perhaps of Diss), Ralph of Coggeshall, Matthew Paris,
Jocelyn of Brakelond – to name only some of them. Without these works we should be far less informed of details,
especially regarding Philip's relationship with the kings of
England.

Several of these writers were in a position to gain good
information: Robert of Torigny as abbot of Mont-St-Michel,
Ralph Diceto as dean of St Paul's, Matthew Paris in the
much-visited abbey of St Alban's, while Roger of Howden
was a royal justice during the latter part of the twelfth century. We cannot dismiss all of these as simply being 'hostile',
and indeed they provide a wealth of differing viewpoints,
but nor should they be taken in preference to the source
closest to the king, the work of William the Breton. Richard
of Devizes, for example, was as strong in his praise of Richard
as was William the Breton in praise of Philip Augustus. At
least one Angevin writer was critical of the Angevin kings
for his own personal reasons of disappointment in promotion. This is Gerald of Wales, whose waspish writings,
especially his 'Instruction to Princes', can serve as a useful
antidote to more fawning attitudes. Both he and Ralph
Diceto are known to have spent time in Paris, while Roger
of Howden went on the Third Crusade. Other Angevin
writers, such as Gervase of Canterbury, were critical of Henry
II because of the killing of Thomas Becket. It is commonly
pointed out that virtually all the English narrative sources
of the time were critical of John because of his differences
with the Church, but it is rarely noted that they did not as
a result become favourable to Philip and France. With very
few exceptions, it is necessary to treat the Anglo-Norman
historians as being hostile to Philip.

There is one other valuable work worth mentioning in
this brief survey, that of Giselbert of Mons. This chronicler

gives balance to another important relationship in the reign, since he was close to the count of Flanders, and even more to the count of Hainault, and therefore illuminates events relating to Philip's first marriage, and affairs in the northern region in general. Giselbert of Mons was a canon at Namur who became chancellor to Baldwin V, count of Hainault and later count of Flanders (1191–94).

Apart from the *Philippide*, there are a number of other poetic works which are of importance for the reign. For the Third Crusade there is the poem of Ambroise, *L'Estoire de la Guerre Sainte*, and the remarkable biographical poem *Guillaume le Maréchal*. Again, though, one notes the pro-Angevin bias of both these works.

. . .

ADMINISTRATIVE SOURCES

Philip's reign saw an important growth in French administrative records, made even more noticeable by the loss of many which existed at the time but were lost after they were captured by Richard at Fréteval. Others again were lost in an eighteenth-century fire in Paris, and more during the French Revolution. As in England, the main source of information of governmental action in this period is to be found in acts, which might be subdivided into categories such as letters, writs and diplomas. In form the royal acts are fundamentally letters from the king, though of course other lords both lay and ecclesiastical issued similar documents.

The royal acts for Philip have been collected in the *Recueil*. About a quarter of those known came from the governmental collections known as registers. In the past the acts collected in the registers have been printed as part of chronological collections of all the surviving royal acts: in both Léopold Delisle's *Catalogue* and Henri-François Delaborde's *Recueil*. The printed edition of the registers edited by John W. Baldwin, the first volume of which, containing the text, has now appeared, will be a valuable addition to the printed records. This work follows the pattern of chapter headings used in the registers themselves, but does not attempt to give each register in full, since this would involve much repetition. There is also a photographic copy of Register A, edited by Delisle, which allows a clear idea of the nature of these documents in their original form, but which is unfortunately not widely available.[2]

The acts cover many aspects of government, including judicial decisions, gifts of land, grants of privileges and proclamations. Full financial and judicial records had not yet emerged, or at least if they had do not survive, though there are some fragments from our period, which allow us to see the beginnings of national archives and central records, later called the *Trésor des Chartes*. Under Louis IX (1226–70), these records began to be kept in 'the king's cupboards', but the collection had its origins at the time of Philip Augustus. There are also some vital fragments, especially concerning finance, mostly surviving because they were copied out from the archives before the 1737 fire. The work by Ferdinand Lot and Robert Fawtier on what they misleadingly called 'the first budget' contains the first of these financial fragments.

. . .

SECONDARY SOURCES

The reign of Philip Augustus has not received the degree of attention by English historians that it merits. There is one short and excellent English work on the reign, by W.H. Hutton, but it is now rather elderly. The main narrative account remains that by the German historian Alexander Cartellieri. It is said that this meticulous work so impressed the great French historian, Achille Luchaire, that he gave up the idea of writing his own account of the reign. This is not quite true, however, since Luchaire did write a history of Philip which is contained in the volumes edited by E. Lavisse, and also a work on the social history of the reign. There have been some recent additions in French, including a biography by G. Bordonove, and the valuable volume of papers edited by R-H. Bautier, which covers pretty well every aspect of the reign one could imagine. But the most important work on

2. A copy of the facsimile is held by the British Library. At the time of writing, Baldwin's edition of the registers is also not widely available, not for example in the major London libraries, and I had to use the copy in the Cambridge University library, which had wisely acquired it early. This situation will no doubt soon be remedied. There is now, as I add to this note, a copy in the Institute of Historical Education, London.

the reign in recent times is that of the American historian, John W. Baldwin. Baldwin's work concentrated on the administrative sources and is specifically focused on government, but it does contain narrative passages, and is a must for every serious student of the reign. There are also various histories of France in the period, including those by Elizabeth Hallam, Robert Fawtier and Georges Duby, all of which have useful sections on Philip.

In this brief review we shall conclude with the other major primary and secondary sources for each chapter. Chapter 1 is mainly about the reign of Louis VII (1137–80), and the most important reading for this must be the volume on the reign by Marcel Pacaut. There is a more recent and sound work on Louis VII by Yves Sassier, which unfortunately has only minimal footnotes. The great chronicler of the reign of Louis VI (1108–37), Suger, who was minister to both kings, also wrote briefly about Louis VII.

Chapter 2, on Philip's first decade, is dominated by relations with the count of Flanders and the king of England. Giselbert of Mons, for Flanders, and the numerous chroniclers of Henry II's reign (1154–89) mentioned above are significant here. The main secondary work must be Lewis Warren's *Henry II*, and there are other biographies in English by Richard Barber and John T. Appleby. John Gillingham's work on the Angevin Empire and the relevant section in his work on Richard are important.

Chapter 3, on the crusades, can be studied through various general works on the movement, such as those by Steven Runciman, Jonathan Riley-Smith and H.E. Mayer, or the volumes edited by K.M. Setton. The biography of Richard the Lionheart by John Gillingham is the major work on the reign of the king who was Philip's chief protagonist. Other readable works on that reign are the now oldish work by Kate Norgate and more recent books by Philip Henderson and Anthony Bridge. The poem by Ambroise, and the closely related prose work, the *Itinerarium*, are major sources for the Third Crusade. On the Fourth Crusade, the chronicle by Villehardouin is invaluable, and secondary works by John Godfrey and D.E. Queller are useful.

Chapter 4 on the conflict with Richard and Chapter 5 on the defeat of the Angevins under John both require the host of Anglo-Norman chroniclers, such as Roger of Howden.

There are many useful books in English on the reigns of Richard (1189–99) and John (1199–1216), including Gillingham's biography of Richard, and his collected short works on the reign, in *Richard Coeur de Lion*, which includes his brief but vital book on the Angevin Empire. There is another useful collection of papers edited by Jinty Nelson, in *Richard Coeur de Lion in History and Myth*. On both reigns the work of Kate Norgate retains its usefulness, and there are good works on John by Lewis Warren and Ralph Turner. John T. Appleby's book on *England Without Richard* fills a gap, and F.M. Powicke's great work on the loss of Normandy remains important.

Chapter 6, on the papacy, is well resourced by the papal records, including the Vatican Register for Innocent III (1198–1216). Innocent is the outstanding pope of the period and there are several English works on him, including those by L. Elliott Binns, C.H.C. Pirie-Gordon, C.R. Cheney, and Helena Tillmann's book is now available in translation. More recently there is the excellent short account by Jane Sayers. More general works which have good sections on the period include histories of the papacy by I.S. Robinson and C. Morris, while Ullmann's short history of the papacy remains useful. There are also several helpful papers on this subject in Bautier's volume.

These same works are all relevant to Chapter 7 on the Church in France. For details on the marriage problem with Ingeborg and Agnes de Méran, one still needs to use R. Davidsohn on Philip and Ingeborg, and Cartellieri's work on the reign, while John W. Baldwin has a good modern summary. Baldwin also looks at the royal administration in detail, including the work of clerics in it. The acts of Philip in the *Recueil* provide much basic information on Philip's dealings with the Church in France.

For Chapters 8 and 9 on kingship, government and administration, one must turn to Baldwin's book on Philip. There are also several useful contributions in the collection of papers edited by R-H. Bautier, including particularly that by M. Nortier. The collection of acts in the *Recueil* is fundamental to any study of Philip's government, and L. Delisle's *Catalogue* is still useful. The most important addition to the printed sources in recent times is the new edition of the registers by Baldwin, of which the first volume is now available.

Chapter 10 on Bouvines must rely primarily on the *Philip-pide*, which concentrates upon the battle as the centre of the poem. The wide-ranging French historian, Georges Duby, has written on the battle, though much of his book wanders up side-tracks. It does, though, include some interesting ideas and a very useful collection of translations of passages from various primary sources on the battle, including the Anonymous of Béthune, William the Breton, the Minstrel of Reims and Philip Mouskes. There is also the work on the battle by A. Hardengue, now reprinted. On the military background to Bouvines, the works of Philippe Contamine and J.F. Verbruggen are vital.

Chapter 11 on the last decade of the reign needs the same works on King John mentioned above, together with David Carpenter's first volume on the reign of Henry III (1216–72), which deals with the minority. These also supply information on Louis's invasion of England. On the Albigensian Crusade there is a vast literature. The *Chanson de la Croisade contre les Albigeois* is perhaps the most important primary source, and there are secondary works in English by Jonathan Sumption, Jacques Madaule (translated), Bernard Hamilton and Joseph R. Strayer, among others; in addition to the general crusading works mentioned for Chapter 3. For Louis VIII (1223–26) and Louis IX (1226–70), the general histories by Elizabeth Hallam and Robert Fawtier are helpful. An account of Louis VIII's reign is found in the same volume edited by E. Lavisse as that on Philip. There are many works on St Louis, where the chronicle by Joinville is an important primary source. In French there is the work by J. Richard, and among books on the king in English are those by W.C. Jordan and M.W. Labarge.

Chapter 1

PHILIP'S INHERITANCE

. . .

THE BIRTH OF PHILIP AUGUSTUS

In 1179 the abbot of Mont-St-Michel copied into his chronicle a prophecy made by 'a certain astrologer' that great calamities were in the offing, with signs from heaven in the form of great winds, death and disease, the eclipse of sun and moon, and 'a fearful voice which shall terrify the hearts of men'.[1] For Henry II's Angevin Empire, within which Abbot Robert lived, the following year was indeed to see events of significance for the future, not least the coronation and succession of Philip II king of France.

Saracen ambassadors to France had predicted that Philip would be a great king. This was recorded by Gerald of Wales, as a twenty-year-old student at Paris in 1165. In later days Gerald recalled one Saturday night in August when he was woken from his sleep by noise, trumpets, lights and confusion: 'through all the great city there was such a noise and clanging of bells, such a multitude of tapers kindled through all the open spaces of the town, that not knowing what such a racket and abnormal disturbance could mean, with such a blaze of light in the night, it was thought the city was

1. Robert of Torigny in J. Stevenson, ed., *The Church Historians of England*, 5 vols (London, 1853–58) IV, Pt II, p. 133; Robert of Torigny, 'Chronicle', in R. Howlett, ed., *Chronicles of the Reigns of Stephen, Henry II and Richard I*, 4 vols, RS no. 82, (London, 1884–89) IV, pp. 283–4, where it appears as a rubric, a prophecy: 'et in vento vox terribilis audietur, et terrebit corda hominum'.

threatened by a great fire'.[2] Gerald poked his head through
the window of his room to investigate. Two old women bearing torches were passing by, and he asked the cause of the
disturbance, to be told that a new prince had been born. At
last King Louis VII (1137–80), after many years of marriage,
and by this time with his third wife, had fathered a son and
heir. 'Now,' Gerald reported one of the women saying, 'we
have a king given us by God, through whom *your* kingdom
will be destroyed and damned.' This prophecy spat at him
by the old woman, says Gerald, would later come true. No
doubt this smacks of hindsight, and not a little of the bitter-
ness which he harboured for the Plantagenet rulers who
blocked his hopes of advance to the bishopric of St David's,
but Gerald had recognized the fatal effect that Philip would
have on the Angevin Empire.

In 1165 Henry II (king, 1154–89) ruled over an enormous
parcel of territories collected through inheritance, aggression, agreement and marriage, which we have come to call
the Angevin Empire. More than half of modern France was
a part of this empire. The kings of France ruled the Ile-de-
France and little more, which was still the case when Philip
succeeded to the throne in 1180. Two years later Bertran de
Born could still call Philip 'the little king of Lesser-land'.[3]
Yet, after some twenty-five years of the rule of Philip II (1180–
1223), the Angevin Empire was smashed beyond repair, and
the king of France had become unquestionably a more
powerful ruler than the king of England. The birth of Philip
Augustus was indeed a fateful event in medieval western
Europe.

Louis VII heard of his son's birth, appropriately and typically, while at matins, though the event had occurred at about
eleven o'clock the previous evening. France rejoiced and
Paris celebrated with the king. The infant was baptized the
next day in the castle chapel of St-Michel-de-la-Place and
given the exotic name Philip, after his tragically killed uncle.

2. H.E. Butler, *The Autobiography of Giraldus Cambrensis* (London, 1937)
   pp. 37–8; Gerald of Wales, *Opera*, ed. J.S. Brewer, J.F. Dimock and
   G.F. Warner, 8 vols, RS no. 21 (London, 1861–91) VIII, pp. 292–3.
3. Bertran de Born, *The Poems of the Troubadour Bertran de Born*, ed.
   W.D. Paden Jr, T. Sankovitch and P.H. Stäblein (Berkeley, CA, 1986)
   p. 114: 'Del pauc rei de Terra Menor'.

The first of the name in the family had been King Philip I (1060–1108). The unusual eastern name had been introduced into the Capetian family by Henry I's Russian-born wife, Anna of Kiev, mother of Philip I.

Louis and the whole of France thanked God with all their hearts for the birth. Louis's lack of an heir had threatened the future of the dynasty. Their luck in passing the throne from father to son had looked in danger. Louis's first wife thought that marriage to him was like being wedded to a monk, though he fathered two children by her, and two more by his second wife. However, all his first four children were daughters. One senses the growing desperation as Louis hastily made a third marriage, to Adela of Champagne, and still the male heir did not arrive – until 1165. On being told the sex of her child, the queen wept with joy. The male slant of twelfth-century attitudes was expressed by Louis VII in a charter, referring to his daughters, and also now to the birth of a child 'of a more noble sex'.[4]

. . .

PHILIP'S PARENTAGE

By 1180 the Capetian dynasty had held the throne of France for two centuries; the kings had been fertile and fortunate. Louis the Young had not expected to become king, a position reserved for his older brother Philip, but the latter suffered a riding accident in Paris in 1131. One source says a pig had run free and upset his mount, so that Philip fell and hit his head on a stone; while another records that Philip 'was chasing a squire in sport through the streets of Paris, fractured his limbs terribly, and expired the next day'.[5] At any rate Louis became the heir to Louis VI (1108–37). Still a boy, at his brother's death, he was associated in the rule of France, and crowned by Pope Innocent II (1130–43).

4. A. Luchaire in E. Lavisse, *Histoire de France depuis les Origines jusqu'à la Révolution*, III, Pt I (Paris, 1911), p. 57.
5. Suger, *Vie de Louis VI, le Gros*, ed. H. Waquet (Paris, 1929) p. 266; Orderic Vitalis, *The Ecclesiastical History*, ed. M. Chibnall, 6 vols (Oxford, 1969–81), VI, p. 240.

Louis VII married three times, first to Eleanor of Aquitaine in 1137. Eleanor's father, William X duke of Aquitaine (1126–1137), made deathbed arrangements for his daughter to marry the heir to the French crown. William had no sons, and Eleanor was his eldest daughter, so the Capetians looked set to acquire Aquitaine. Louis, aged sixteen, was sent south to claim the bride, and seems to have developed a passion for Eleanor. They produced two girls, Marie and Alice, but the marriage foundered. Louis had difficulty in accepting Eleanor's southern ways, and their liaison was rocked by a rumoured affair between Eleanor and her uncle Raymond during the Second Crusade. After attempts at reconciliation, the marriage ended in 1152. Eleanor then fled to her second husband, Henry Plantagenet, soon to become Henry II of England.

Louis's second marriage was to Constance of Castile, in 1154. If the divorce meant the loss of Aquitaine, the marriage to the Castilian princess gave Louis VII a renewed interest in southern France and an ally against the Plantagenets. Louis's main motive in divorcing Eleanor may have been her failure to produce a son, in which case he was again disappointed, since Constance bore two more daughters but no male heir.[6]

By the time of Constance's death in 1160 the situation was causing concern. Louis married Adela of Champagne within five weeks of being widowed, failing even to observe the normal period of mourning. Adela was the daughter of Theobald IV count of Blois (1102–1152), whose territories to the east and west of the Capetian lands were a potential threat. The house of Champagne was the major rival to the Plantagenets, and a useful ally for Louis. Adela's brothers played a major role in French politics: Theobald, Henry the Liberal count of Champagne (1152–81), Stephen count of Sancerre, and William Whitehands bishop of Chartres, then archbishop of Sens and later of Reims. The house of Champagne claimed descent from Charlemagne, so that Adela and Louis's son was called 'Karolide' by his foremost chronicler.[7]

6. Georges Duby, *France in the Middle Ages, 987–1460*, trans. J. Vale (Oxford, 1991) p. 183.
7. R. Fawtier, *The Capetian Kings of France*, trans. L. Butler and R.J. Adam (London, 1964) p. 60; E.M. Hallam, *Capetian France, 987–1328* (Harlow, 1980) p. 177.

. . .

THE FORMATION OF THE PRINCIPALITIES OF FRANCE

By the tenth century royal power had been sinking to a level little greater than that of the territorial princes, who had come to dominate the regions of France. From the ninth century, the Carolingian Empire had been split into three separate realms. The West Frankish monarchy had attempted to keep control in its sector by establishing favoured individuals to rule on behalf of the monarchy in the regions. These counts and dukes had some success in their regions, and the monarchy had failed to keep them subordinate. Under such men were formed virtually autonomous principalities, such as the duchies of Aquitaine and Burgundy. Even these principalities proved too large to retain political unity with ease, and some split further into counties or other lordships.

But the fragmentation of political units slowed. Like logs, flecks and weeds floating in a pond, certain more solid centres attracted the attachment of weaker neighbours. Such centres, each in their own way, formed principalities, often by an accumulation of lordships, viscounties and counties. Thus was formed, for example, Normandy, Brittany, Anjou, Blois and Flanders. There was no uniformity about this process. To an extent royal power had passed from the Carolingians to their locally appointed rulers. But the nature of the principalities depended on the method of formation of each one; they formed from below according to local conditions rather than from above by central decree. Hence the inconsistency in titles: duke, marquis, count or prince. In most cases these terms included aspects of military command, judicial powers and financial rights, but these powers had been seized rather than granted.

The vast territory of Aquitaine, the whole area south of the Loire, assumed the name of duchy, but the ducal power could not be retained by one family or one centre, and for centuries was at stake in internal conflicts. The title moved from the lords of the Auvergne to the counts of Toulouse, and then to those of Poitou. By the beginning of the Capetian period, Aquitaine was ruled by the comital family of Poitou and royal power in the region was minimal.

Like Aquitaine, Burgundy had ancient historical claims to autonomy. Burgundy had been an independent middle kingdom in the Frankish lands. But the duchy of Burgundy was a lesser unit, retained from the old middle kingdom by the ruler of the West Franks at the end of the ninth century. Richard the Justiciar, count of Autun, had established his authority in this area by military victory over the Vikings and Magyars, and by loyalty to the Carolingian monarch. This tradition of loyalty was an abiding element in the history of the duchy. Indeed in 960, through marriage, Capetian relatives took over an admittedly reduced Burgundy.

Flanders, like Burgundy, was troubled for centuries to come by its historical connections to the old middle kingdom. The memory of this past produced aspirations to a power and independence at odds with the ambitions of the West Frankish monarchy. Both Flanders and Burgundy, from historical past and geographical position, were troubled by the interest of the East Frankish as well as the West Frankish kings. The county of Flanders owed its formation partly to the opportunism of its founder, Baldwin I (862–79), who in 863 seized and married the monarch's daughter. Against the odds he withstood opposition from her father and from the Church, and with the lands now granted to him was able to establish a new powerful principality. These beginnings were consolidated and extended by the efforts of Baldwin's son and successor, Baldwin II (879–918).

Brittany also had pretensions to a greater past, with claims to have been a kingdom. As in Normandy, there had been Viking settlement, but no enduring dynasty was able to establish itself. In the 930s a descendant of the old ruling house, Alan II Barbetorte (936–52), recovered power in Brittany, becoming count of Nantes and reuniting the duchy. But Brittany failed to achieve quite the power of the other major principalities, partly because of internal division between the lords at Nantes and those at Rennes, and partly because of external threats from the neighbouring principalities of Blois, Anjou and Normandy. Brittany remained for centuries strong in tradition, but weak in terms of centralized government.

Normandy had been part of the northern area of the West Franks, once known as Neustria. In 911 the West Frankish monarch, Charles the Simple (893–929), permitted the formation of a territory ruled by a Viking leader, Rollo (911–28), partly in order to counter raids by other Scandinavians. The dynasty founded by Rollo acquired a ducal title and was to continue in power to the time of William the Conqueror and beyond. Rollo and his descendants extended their authority to the boundaries of what became Normandy, and began to absorb neighbouring counties.

Anjou and Blois also grew from relatively small and largely military foundations. Blois merged with the neighbouring county of Tours, while Anjou gradually expanded at the expense of its neighbours. Even the counties of Anjou and Blois were virtually independent of the monarchy by the beginning of Capetian rule in the late tenth century.

In a summary, such as this, one is inclined to get a false impression of a neat uniform progress, with the almost inevitable emergence of certain great principalities. The truth is that much of the development outlined above depended upon chance and events. Some territorial units, for example Maine in the north or Angoulême in the south, might in other circumstances have become as great as Anjou or Aquitaine. Nor was the development of any principality continuous and inevitable. There were numerous disputes between the emerging principalities, for example would Touraine fall to Blois or to Anjou? The exact form of the new principalities was always fluid, and future development uncertain. The only seemingly assured outcome was that *some* larger territorial blocks would be formed and become the chief powers in the regions of France.

· · ·

THE CAPETIAN DYNASTY

The Robertian or Capetian family's rise was tied to the emergence of the new West Frankish kingdom. Charlemagne had ruled over virtually all of western Europe, but his empire had been subdivided in the ninth century into three kingdoms: East Francia, the nucleus of Germany; West Francia, the nucleus of France; and Lotharingia, the middle kingdom, which failed to survive. The Robertian family supported the West Frankish Carolingian kings, and eventually replaced them.

7

One of the Capetian ancestors, Odo, became king of West Francia (889–98), and his brother was crowned as Robert I (922–23), temporarily replacing the declining Carolingians. Robert was killed in 923. His son, Hugh the Great (d.956), refused to take the crown, allowing his brother-in-law Ralph of Burgundy to gain that honour. But the Robertian family retained a strength which their rivals lacked. Louis V (986–87), the last of the Carolingian kings, died without heir in a hunting accident in 987.

Count Robert's grandson took the crown for the Robertians again in 987, this time to keep it in direct line of succession until 1328. The son of Hugh the Great is known to us as Hugh Capet, supposedly because he bore the cope or *capet* of the abbot of St Martin of Tours; an alternative explanation is that the word meant a cap which he wore. At any rate the name remained as that of his family. Adalbero, archbishop of Reims, crowned Hugh, explaining that 'the kingship is not acquired by hereditary right', a statement which would dog the Capetians in the fight to establish their dynasty.[8]

The Robertians had been powerful territorial princes, but became frail monarchs. As has been said: 'the most powerful of dukes proved the weakest of kings'.[9] They inherited responsibilities, but little power. Their role with regard to the Church gave them status above other princes, on which they had to rely. A reputation for godliness developed, and the second Capetian was known as Robert II the Pious (996–1031), but he was in debt to the Church for the crown itself. Compared to the rulers of the East Franks, the kings of France seemed insignificant. They were barely lords of their own demesne, making little mark on much of France, even less on the international scene.

It is true that the French king Henry I (1031–60) helped establish William the Conqueror as duke of Normandy, but he became disillusioned with his protégé, and twice invaded Normandy though only to be twice defeated. Philip I (1060–1108) diminished the family's pious reputation by repudiating his wife of twenty years' standing to marry Bertrade de Montfort, whom he had seized from her husband Fulk of

8. T.F. Tout, *The Empire and the Papacy, 918–1273* (London, 1924) p. 71.
9. Tout, p. 73.

Anjou. He was excommunicated by Urban II in 1094. Philip I has been condemned for 'greed, debauchery, idleness and sloth', and was fat into the bargain.[10] Nevertheless one begins to see the emergence of the Capetians as a force to be reckoned with, if only in their demesne. The twelfth century saw a remarkable advance in their fortunes. The dynasty survived until 1328, one of the great ruling families of France. Between 987 and 1328 there were fourteen long-lived kings, including some of the great figures of French history, not least St Louis (1226–70) and Philip Augustus.

. . .

TRADITIONS OF THE CAPETIAN DYNASTY

Capetian traditions meant that certain attitudes were expected of the king. Philip Augustus's approach to kingship derived from the Capetian tradition. He was bound, restricted, burdened by this past; yet at the same time it provided a mask to hide behind. The king benefited from the rights collected by his ancestors and from the alliance with the Church, but at the same time he found difficulty in establishing new claims and would be criticized unless he acted as 'the most Christian king' should. The past was a protection and a trap. It is vital to understand the traditions of the Capetian monarchy, not always quite those of other monarchies.

Medieval states gloried in past victories gained under royal commanders: the Capetians had no such tradition. For all their dogged and aggressive activity, warlike as all rulers needed to be, successful on that limited scale though they were, they had no record of major military achievement. Few Capetians before Philip had commanded a large army. When they intervened outside the demesne, they gained few successes. Louis VI did begin to alter this image, and appears to have positively enjoyed military campaigns. It is in no small way due to his efforts that the monarchy gained control over the lords in the royal demesne. Yet when he went further and invaded Normandy, he suffered humiliating defeat at the hands of Henry I of England at Brémule.

10. Tout, p. 80.

Necessarily the Capetians emphasized their religious role in order to bolster a relatively unremarkable military record. When Louis VII is criticized for his monkish behaviour and lack of military interest, we ignore the fact that he was following the normal Capetian tradition. Louis VII's greatest military effort was blessed by the Church, a holy war, a crusade. The success of the Capetians in fostering their image as religious leaders is demonstrated by the fact that even the disasters of the Second Crusade failed to make a serious dent in Louis VII's position at home.

If military triumph was not yet part of the Capetian image, being a military figurehead was. The most dramatic example of this is the taking of the oriflamme, the supposed standard of St Denis, kept in his church, and perhaps used by Charlemagne. It became the symbol of the nation at war, when ceremoniously taken up by the king. Here is a growing tradition, fostered by the abbey of St-Denis, which placed responsibility for national defence on the king. The scarlet banner was a potent rallying call throughout France. The strength of the idea was demonstrated in 1124 when Louis VI took the oriflamme against a threat from the Holy Roman Empire.[11]

Even the military image of the Capetians came to be ecclesiastical in its form, typified by crusading rather than by European conflicts. That image contained the concept of the French king as a peace-maker. Even an English chronicler, Walter Map, saw Louis VII as the 'lover of peace' and 'the peaceful king'. Suger claimed that the florets on the crown represented the bringing together of the fiefs of France, in peace under the crown.[12]

The relationship between the Capetians and the Church is central to Philip's reign. Some 'traditions' were recent in origin, but in the case of the Church they grew from a strong root. The dynasty had always depended on ecclesiastical support. Royal power, however slight, had as a base its special relationship with bishops and abbeys, and particularly those which we call 'royal'. With few exceptions, the

---

11. Hallam, p. 125; Walter Map, *De Nugis Curialium*, ed. M.R. James, C.N.L. Brooke and R.A. Mynors (Oxford, 1983) p. 443.
12. J-P. Poly and E. Bournazel, *The Feudal Transformation, 900–1200*, trans. C. Higgitt (New York, 1991) p. 193; Hallam, p. 176; Duby, p. 187; Map, pp. 461–3.

Capetians had maintained good relations with the Church, both inside and outside France. France was seen as the safest refuge for popes in difficulty in Italy.

At first the lack of conflict with the papacy sprang from the weakness of the monarchs: the early Capetians offered little threat to the ambitions of the Church at large. It was in the king's interest to present a 'godly' image. Whatever his personal failings, Robert II earned the soubriquet of 'the Pious' and established a new image as 'the holy king'. Robert was not always pious, though he did write hymns and discuss theology with his bishops. Duby accuses him of 'incest and trigamy'; he married for a third time with both previous wives still living and not discarded, a comment as much on tenth-century marriage customs as on Robert's piety. It may be that the 'holy king' was an invention, but the important point is that the image was established.[13]

If not outstandingly pious, the early Capetians were nevertheless virtuous in comparison to other royal families of the time. Philip I had, it is true, seized Bertrade de Montfort from her husband.[14] But this, and the divorce of Louis VII, were the only serious scandals in Capetian history before Philip Augustus. From fourteen Capetian kings there were few bastards, in contrast to the kings of England: Henry I of England alone had over twenty illegitimate children, more than all the Capetians put together. There was an expectation, usually fulfilled, that a Capetian would be the example for Christian kingship. The series of popes who sought protection and refuge in France is impressive, including Innocent II and Alexander III (1159–81). Before 1180 there had been no conflicts between the papacy and French monarchy to compare with the troubles with the German emperors. Royal encouragement allowed papal reform to develop firmly, and the new monasticism to flourish in France, from Cluny and Cîteaux, to Grandmont and Paris.

The royal official, Cadoc, claimed at Louis VII's coronation that consecration placed the king 'on a level with the priesthood'; it put the king above other lay lords. Touching for the king's evil was a demonstration of the powers

---

13. Duby, p. 87; J. Dunbabin, *France in the Making, 843–1180* (Oxford, 1985) p. 135.
14. Fawtier, p. 53.

entrusted by God. Guibert of Nogent wrote of seeing such a ceremony: 'I have seen as clearly as I see you now, those suffering from scrofula crowd around to be touched by him [the king], and marked by the sign of the cross, and I was there at his side'.[15]

The Capetians were long-lived monarchs who invariably produced heirs; son had followed father for two centuries, and hereditary succession was firmly established. This 'accident' was essential to Capetian power. To recognize this, one need only look at Germany, where the emperors faced difficulties because no single family managed to retain power for long; or at England where since AD 1000 for two centuries, for a variety of reasons, eldest son hardly ever followed father on the throne. This is of far greater significance than might appear, since easy succession, often through association in the throne, brought peaceful transfer from one ruler to the next without harmful disputes, as well as continuity in administration. The Capetian tradition incorporated the expectation of good relations between father and son. Contrast this with England and the troubles that came from quarrels between William the Conqueror and Robert Curthose, or Henry II with all his sons. Capetian family loyalty extended to brothers and sisters. Few Capetian siblings failed to cooperate. Robert of Dreux's rebellion in 1149 is an exception and was probably aimed against Suger rather than his brother Louis. In any case Robert of Dreux was not as great a problem to Louis as was Curthose to Rufus or Henry I, or John to Richard.

An image of French kingship was crystallizing in the years before Philip Augustus came to the throne. Some of the traditions were recent, some manufactured. Historians credit Suger, abbot of St-Denis, with a significant role in this process; his abbey produced forgeries which helped to build the royal image. The abbot focused attention on the link between monarchy and Church, and on the importance of St Denis. With Suger's guidance the third-century martyr became the patron saint of France.

One belief was more worrying: the forecast that the Capetian dynasty would end. The prophecy of St Valery may have been invented at Montreuil-sur-Mer in the 1040s, but

15. Fawtier, p. 58; Poly and Bournazel, pp. 337, 341; Dunbabin, p. 259.

it was taken seriously in the twelfth century.[16] Hugh Capet was said to have taken the saint's relics to St-Bertin, and in return was promised that his family would hold the crown for seven generations. Depending on how the counting was done, Louis VII or Philip would be the last of the line, and the crown would return to the successors of Charlemagne. The story caused anxiety in Philip's circle, and his biographers took care to explain it away. The stress given to the descent from Charlemagne of Philip's mother is not simply genealogical.

. . .

LOUIS VI (1108–1137) AND THE DEVELOPMENT OF THE FRENCH MONARCHY

The early Capetians were weak monarchs in Europe. The power of the Carolingian emperors had devolved upon a number of territorial princes, such as the dukes of Normandy and Aquitaine or the counts of Flanders and Blois. The Capetian monarch was on a par with these princes, his lands being neither the greatest in extent nor the richest. Like the princes he struggled to control his own territories, in his case focused around Paris, Orléans and Sens. The role of Louis VI the Fat has been distorted by too great a reliance on the account of Suger, but others saw his importance. Walter Map remarked that Louis was 'huge in body, but no smaller in act and thought'. Map saw Louis as advancing the reputation of the French monarchy from insignificance to significance.[17]

Control of the demesne was a gradual process, but Louis VI's campaigns against recalcitrant lords had a lasting effect. He justified his attacks as protection of the Church. Thomas de Marle's crime was to oppose the bishop of Laon. Thomas was accused of sheltering the men who killed the bishop during a local conflict, and of cutting the throat of an archdeacon and blinding opponents. Guibert of Nogent said: 'no one can tell how many expired in his dungeons'. Louis ordered Thomas to destroy a castle built without royal permission. When Thomas refused, Louis stretched out a hand

16. Fawtier, pp. 56–7; Duby, p. 206.
17. Map, p. 441.

and swore that 'he would not eat until it was taken'.[18] His expedition succeeded, but Thomas caused trouble again later, this time resulting in his wounding, capture and subsequent death in captivity. At the council of Reims Louis claimed to have acted against Thomas on behalf of the bishops.

Hugh du Puiset, 'handsome but evil', was another lord brought to heel by Louis's campaigns. He was accused of 'unspeakable crimes', and excommunicated. Hugh refused a summons to court and, in the ensuing conflict, killed Anselm de Garlande. Hugh was captured and released, but with the encouragement of Theobald of Blois opposed the king again. Louis led two further expeditions against him, before bringing him to submission. Hugh was permitted to go on pilgrimage to the Holy Land, in the course of which he died. Louis dealt in a similarly commanding manner with other lords in the demesne, with lasting benefit for the monarchy. He also improved his grip on the demesne by extending the use of prévôts to represent his interests.[19]

Walter Map wrote that when Louis VI was young he could not go outside Paris beyond the third milestone without protection, but that he determined not to allow himself to be so constrained.[20] In his early years we find him active in the Bourbonnais and Berry. Louis again claimed to be enforcing royal rights and acting on behalf of the Church. Thus Louis acted for the bishop of Clermont against William VI count of Auvergne, forcing reconciliation. He attempted to advance Capetian interests in Normandy, where the count of Anjou with his encouragement defeated Henry I of England at Alençon. However, when count and king together invaded Normandy in the following year, Louis was badly beaten at Brémule. Louis VI was humbled but not finished, and continued to harass Henry I by supporting his opponents. Louis had the virtue of persistence. Walter Map portrays him after the defeat in 1119 sitting at table, still cheerful, claiming: 'I am not disheartened, I have become hardened by frequent misfortunes'.[21]

18. J.F. Benton, *Self and Society in Medieval France: The Memoirs of Abbot Guibert of Nogent* (Toronto, 1984) pp. 199, 204; Hallam, p. 115.
19. Orderic, VI, p. 158; Suger, p. 62.
20. Map, p. 443.
21. Map, p. 457.

Louis's actions in Flanders also involved opposition to Henry I. Louis's greatest success there was to champion William Clito, the son of Robert Curthose, for the vacant countship after the murder of Charles the Good. But again his success was short-lived: Clito died within the year, and Thierry of Alsace, antagonized by Louis's support of Clito, became count. Even more potentially dangerous was the fact that Theobald IV of Blois, constantly at odds with the crown, managed in 1125 to unite Blois and Champagne, so that he now threatened the royal demesne in a pincer from east and west.

Louis VI involved himself outside the demesne more than his predecessors, even if his success was intermittent. The advance in authority is shown by the events of 1124, when Louis took up the oriflamme at St-Denis, forcing the emperor to abandon his campaign. Suger was behind that act, together with the claims that the king had no superior on earth and could do homage to no man. This may seem inflated, considering Louis's failures against powerful vassals, but it marks a growing confidence and a widening horizon. In a more practical manner, Louis VI encouraged the aspirations of certain communities by granting or confirming customs and commune status, his most famous act in this respect being the grant of the customs of Lorris. Louis saw the advantages for the crown in supporting communal aspirations against the claims of local lords or the Church.

Louis VI's increasing authority in the demesne was reflected in the nature and activities of the royal household. The great lords became less involved there, active positions being taken over by men from castellan families of the demesne, or by the urban elite of royal towns. Louis's defeat of Thomas de Marle and Hugh du Puiset in the demesne was matched by his breaking of the power of the Montlhéry, Rochefort and Garlande families within the household. The lesser figures who now peopled the household themselves posed a threat to royal power, seeking to make their offices hereditary, but Louis kept them under control. The officials nearest to the crown also began to act as a royal council.

The Church flourished under Louis VI. The royal abbey of St-Denis received favours. Louis also founded a Benedictine abbey at Montmartre and a house of the new canons regular at St-Victor. He offered refuge to popes Paschal II, who was to die at Cluny in France, and Innocent II during the schism. Louis was rewarded by Paschal II, who allowed him to end his unsuitable marriage to Lucienne de Rochefort from a relatively humble castellan family of the royal demesne.[22] France was becoming the main secular support for the new monasticism and papal reform, as well as the protector of the pope when Italy became too difficult, or the Holy Roman Emperor too pressing.

By the middle of the twelfth century France was emerging as a leading cultural and economic area of Europe, though it was far from being a unified or uniform state. It consisted of a patchwork of territorial principalities, themselves fluctuating in size and strength. The principalities, like a blanket, covered a lower level of even greater variety: of lordships, castellanies, ecclesiastical authorities, as well as urban and rural communities.

. . .

THE REIGN OF LOUIS VII (1137–1180)

The major division within France was between north and south, from a line drawn approximately along the Loire. North and south had different traditions, cultures and languages. The south was more romanized and retained the marks in culture and law; but Capetian power was slight in 'the land without a king'.[23] The north looked to the Rhine, the North Sea and the Atlantic; the south to the Pyrenees, the Alps and the Mediterranean. The south possessed greater achievements in architecture and culture, but stemming from Paris an intellectual revolution was growing in the north. People saw themselves as belonging to nations: as Normans, Aquitainians or Burgundians, for example. It has been said that there were many kingdoms in Gaul, though only one king.[24]

In the south, Aquitaine was the major political unit. The former kingdom had shaped itself into a duchy. Unlike the other major French principalities, Aquitaine formed part of

22. Hallam, p. 114.
23. Dunbabin, pp. 162–222, 295–357; Fawtier, pp. 110–36. On the 'land without a king', see Poly and Bournazel, p. 236, and M. Pacaut, *Louis VII et son royaume* (Paris, 1967) p. 20.
24. Duby, p. 30.

a Franco-Spanish political sphere. The great principality in the north was Flanders, which like Burgundy needed to keep one eye on the Empire. It became the major industrial state through its production of cloth. It was Louis VII's marriage and the link with Aquitaine which first began to bridge the divide between north and south under Capetian rule.

But France remained a kingdom made up of powerful principalities. Anjou, established under the Carolingians, had developed from a small lordship on the Loire into one of the greatest principalities, thanks to the achievements of a series of outstanding counts, including Fulk Nerra (987–1040) and Geoffrey Martel (1040–60), the ancestors of the Plantagenets. The counties of Blois and Champagne were areas of economic growth, the Champagne fairs providing the heartbeat of European trade. Through Theobald IV, Blois and Champagne were re-united from 1125 to 1152, becoming perhaps the most powerful political bloc in France and threatening the Capetian monarch trapped between them. Normandy, first established under a Viking dynasty, carried its expansionist spirit into the eleventh and twelfth centuries with the Norman Conquest of England and the creation of the Norman kingdom of Sicily. By the end of Louis VI's reign, such great and growing principalities posed a major threat to the monarchy.

At the end of an imperfect life Louis VI had declared: 'I Louis who am a sinner believe in the one true God.'[25] Suger and all those around then broke into tears. The deservedly contrite king consoled the sobbing abbot: 'Do not weep for me, my dearest friend, be glad I have been able to prepare myself.' Louis gave his son a ring, and made him promise to watch over God's church, the poor and orphans, and to guard the rights of his subjects, relying on 'the strong arm of all-powerful God, through whom kings reign'. Peter the Venerable, more distant and perhaps more honest, hoped on Louis's death 'that the sins of the fathers should not be visited on an innocent child'.[26]

Louis the Young, aged sixteen, succeeded his father in 1137 as Louis VII. His seal of this year shows him with long

25. On Louis VII, see Pacaut, and Luchaire in Lavisse; on the deathbed, Suger, pp. 274–8.
26. Pacaut, p. 39.

hair to the shoulders. Having been aimed for the Church, and educated in the cathedral school in Paris, he had become heir on his brother Philip's death in 1131. He was pious and narrow, yet clever and devious. The real Louis VII is not easy to locate under the veil of ecclesiastical praise. He appears to have been a serious Christian, chaste in his behaviour despite three marriages. His first wife, Eleanor of Aquitaine, referred waspishly to living with Louis as being like marriage to a monk. Walter Map described Louis at the siege of Nonette, when married to his third wife Adela of Champagne, as falling ill and being offered a young girl to speed his recuperation. Louis primly refused: 'if nothing else will cure me, let the Lord do his will by me, since it is better to die ill and chaste than to live as an adulterer'. His tolerance of the Jews is an admirable and unusual virtue for his day, shared by few. We have a picture of a gentle and modest ruler, noted by Map for his 'kindness and simple mildness'.[27]

His conduct was generally upright, and he probably slept sounder in his bed than Henry II. On one occasion Theobald IV count of Blois found him sleeping in the forest, alone but for two knights. He rebuked the king for risking his life, and the latter responded: 'I sleep alone and safe, because no one envies me.' Louis conducted himself quietly, living without great display. John of Salisbury says that German students in Paris mocked him for living like a citizen, in contrast to the imperial style of their own ruler. A plain life was part of the image which the Capetians chose to project. Louis once remarked that England had everything, great wealth and abundance, whereas 'we in France have only bread, wine and the enjoyment of life'.[28]

Louis VII was portrayed as the just king, harsh when occasion demanded. Once the queen's chamberlain gave offence: a young clerk had been beaten up, and the chamberlain was held responsible. The queen begged for mercy for her official, but Louis would make no concessions and had him mutilated, his arm cut off. Again, when the new palace

27. On the seal, Luchaire in Lavisse, p. 2; on the monk, Pacaut, p. 60; on Nonette, Gerald of Wales, VIII, p. 132; on kindness and mildness, Map, p. 443.
28. On sleeping alone, Map, p. 459; on students, Luchaire in Lavisse, p. 46; on bread and wine, Map, p. 451.

at Fontainebleau was being built, Louis discovered that a humble man's field had been seized for the site. He ordered that the new buildings on it be demolished, and the field returned to its owner, for which 'most men accused him of folly'. Nor were the king's own officials immune from punishment, thus Waleran d'Yèvre was banished for proven misconduct with the ladies at court: a mild king then, but a just one.[29]

The ecclesiastical portrait of Louis has led some historians to portray him as a weak king, dominated by the Church. Such a view glosses over his obstinacy and bad temper, and especially his burning to death of innocent people at Vitry. Some explain the contradictions by suggesting that he made mistakes while young – he was only sixteen in 1137 – and that 'the true Louis VII' only emerged in 1152, after his crusade and divorce. But most human beings contain inconsistencies and contradictions in their character, and though generally a tolerant and kindly man, Louis had his faults and could commit occasional acts of violence. Something of the man may be glimpsed in his letters. In one he could refer to John of Salisbury as 'my most dear friend'; and many, including John and Thomas Becket, saw him as 'the most Christian king'.[30]

. . .

LOUIS VII AND THE CHURCH

Louis VII contributed considerably to the Capetian tradition of the pious ruler, a model for his son. Yet in the early part of his reign, Louis had several difficult passages with the Church, which demonstrated some independence of ecclesiastical advice and some disregard of papal opinion. There were conflicts over Church appointments, which despite the

29. On the chamberlain and Fontainebleau, Map, p. 455; on Waleran, Map, pp. 447–51.
30. On the 'true Louis', Pacaut, p. 33; on his obstinacy, Luchaire in Lavisse, p. 41. The letter to John of Salisbury in Ralph of Diceto, *Opera Historica*, ed. W. Stubbs, 2 vols, RS no. 68 (London, 1876) p. 412; on the Christian king, see for example, J.C. Robertson, ed., *Materials for the History of Thomas Becket, Archbishop of Canterbury*, 7 vols, RS (London, 1875–85) VI, pp. 247, 408; Map, p. 443.

passing of the investiture controversy, remained a vital question in the western monarchies. The Capetians had avoided the worst of the clashes, but they expected to be consulted over elections to 'royal' bishoprics and abbeys, and to confirm such elections. Though less interfering than the German emperors or the kings of England, they expected their wishes to be taken into account.

Louis VII became embroiled in a clash with the papacy over the election of the archbishop of Bourges in 1137. Louis expressed a preference for his household official Cadoc, but the canons chose Peter de la Châtre. Louis claimed he had not been consulted and refused to confirm the election, for which he was rebuked by Innocent II, who thought Cadoc unworthy of the office. Louis 'shook with anger not a little', and swore that while he lived Peter should not become archbishop. As a result Innocent placed Louis's lands under interdict. It was not until 1144, under the more conciliatory Celestine II (1143–44), that Louis backed down and allowed Peter to take up his post, the interdict being raised.[31]

This clash became part of a conflict in which Theobald of Blois allied with the papacy against Louis. They condemned the liaison between Ralph of Vermandois and Louis's sister-in-law, Petronilla of Aquitaine. Ralph was already married but abducted the desirable Petronilla and repudiated his wife, which Louis was prepared to countenance. Louis reacted to Theobald's opposition by invading his lands, and was responsible for an act which seems out of character, and which he came bitterly to regret. The church at Vitry, in which several hundred people were sheltering, was fired. Later Louis expressed contrition, but the act was condemned, and worsened the breach with the papacy.

Possibly Louis undertook the Second Crusade in expiation of the burning of Vitry. He was able to make peace with the Church and transform his image from that of a petulant and even brutal youth. For this reason the crusade proved a positive and successful venture, though in military and crusading terms it was disastrous. The county of Edessa, one of the four Christian settlements which were established as the Kingdom of Jerusalem as a result of the First Crusade, had fallen in 1144, and the achievements of the First Crusade

31. Pacaut, p. 43; from William de Nangis.

were threatened. The papacy and St Bernard sought a response from the West, and at Vézelay in 1146 Louis VII took the cross, as did many leading French nobles. Odo of Deuil claimed that Louis went from religious zeal and desire to save the Holy Land.[32] In Germany Conrad III also responded positively, and the crusade got under way in 1147. From then on little went right. Even before they arrived in the Holy Land there were differences. The armies went their separate ways. Conrad was badly beaten at Dorylaeum, and Louis nearly suffered a similar fate at Laodicea. The survivors continued, but with confidence dented. They agreed a joint attack on Damascus in 1148, though the ruler was an amenable prince. The crusaders attacked the city from the south-east, where there were gardens, food and water, but then fatally agreed to approach instead from the opposite side, where food and water were scarce. The siege had to be abandoned. Conrad returned to the West, though Louis stayed on for six months to complete his pilgrimage, despite pleas to come back. In his absence, Suger had to cope with a rebellion led by the king's brother, Robert of Dreux. Louis's return in 1149 finally scotched this opposition, and the abortive crusade curiously left him stronger in the favour of the Church, and as king in France. The kudos gained from the act of pilgrimage was not lost on his son.

Louis's conduct from 1147 onwards made him a model king whom ecclesiastics could set on a pedestal. According to one, he was so pious 'you would think he was not a king but a man of religion'.[33] Described as like a monk in his marriage, he lived like a priest, fasting on bread and water every Friday, and living with the canons at Notre-Dame. He patronized the new orders, as well as ancient abbeys such as St-Denis. Some 177 of his charters are donations or concessions to the Church, and a further 275 confirm gifts by others.[34] He encouraged building, contributing towards the newly rising Notre-Dame. He supported reform within the Church, such as the peace movement. Proclaiming a ten-year peace at Soissons in 1155, the king declared: 'we have given our royal word that we will keep this peace unbroken'.

32. Luchaire in Lavisse, p. 11.
33. Hallam, p. 119; *Recueil des Historiens des Gaules et de la France (RHF)*, ed. M. Bouquet and L. Delisle, 24 vols (Paris, 1869–1904) XII, p. 89.
34. Pacaut, p. 80.

Louis, 'the most Christian of all princes', became a favourite son of the Church.[35] The gains from this were also noted by his son.

Underlining his devotions, Louis demonstrated a humanitarianism in advance of his age, prepared to defend the Jews by appointing a *prepositus judaeorum*. His freeing of serfs also seemed to come from conviction, one charter declaring: 'all men having a common origin were endowed from birth with a kind of natural liberty. It is given to our royal majesty to raise them anew to this liberty.'[36]

Louis posed as the champion of the Church, but there was always a political motive too. His actions and successes are too consistent to be merely the chance result of fortune and simple-mindedness. Louis championed the Church outside the demesne, beyond those areas where the Capetians had previously had an interest. He undertook expeditions to defend the Church, using his position as protector to bring local lords to heel. The pose as champion of the Church gave him justification for practically every military action which he undertook. For example, he enforced submission to the views of the Church by the lord of Le Puiset in 1144; by the counts of Clermont and Le Puy in 1163; by the count of the Mâconnais in 1166 and 1171. Louis's influence spread into Aquitaine, Languedoc, Toulouse and Burgundy. He declared: 'from our office bestowed upon us, we intend to help all the Churches established in our realms'; and on another occasion: 'we must conserve the rights belonging to God's Churches in our realm'.[37] Here were further gains which Philip would not relinquish.

The Church, threatened by local lay lords, turned to the king for aid, and in gratitude increasingly offered Louis a direct role in its estates, generally through a pariage or sharing agreement. Thus Louis extended Capetian influence in areas beyond the demesne. Churches outside the demesne were, in the words of Fawtier, 'Capetian advanced posts'.[38] If under the Carolingians all Churches had been under royal guardianship, it was a power which had often been lost to other lords. But certain bishoprics and abbeys had always

35. On Soissons, Duby, p. 188; on Christian prince, Pacaut, p. 32.
36. Luchaire in Lavisse, p. 78.
37. Pacaut, pp. 34, 94.
38. Fawtier, p. 73.

recognized themselves as under direct royal patronage; these are the 'royal' Churches. By the twelfth century there were some twenty-six royal bishoprics and about eighty royal abbeys.[39] Louis brought the southern Churches of Narbonne, Agde, Lodève and Maguelonne into a similar relationship. The friendly attitude of bishops to the crown is apparent. The bishop of Cevennes saw the king as 'our good master, our defender, and our liberator'.[40]

Louis recognized freedoms which the Church was seeking and refrained from using his powers oppressively, a tradition caused by royal weakness but transformed by Louis into deliberate policy. Capetian tact in allowing free elections to bishoprics and abbeys was contrasted to the interventionist policies of the Plantagenets. Henry II was called 'the hammer of the Church', a criticism which the killing of Becket underlined.[41] Yet Louis did not relinquish his influence, and those he favoured often succeeded in elections. Royal relatives and numerous members of Louis's household and their families became bishops. This also assisted in the formation of an amenable and co-operative panel of bishops.

Louis intervened in elections more than had been possible for his predecessors, but at the same time was praised for moderation. Louis contrasted his own actions with those of Henry II: 'I am a king as much as is the king of England, but I could not depose the lowliest clerk in my realm.' When Louis received papal letters allowing him profits from vacancies, he burned the letters with his own hand, declaring that it was better to burn evil letters than for his soul to burn in hell. This is exaggeration by Gerald of Wales, and Louis did not ignore the possibilities of profit, but the Capetians did not exploit vacancies as did the Plantagenets, and Gerald's words suggest the success of Louis's propaganda.[42]

France under Louis VII became the refuge for Eugenius III (1145–53) and Alexander III (1159–81), as well as for Thomas Becket. How could the Church fail to contrast the pious Louis with the oppressors Henry II and Frederick Barbarossa (1155–90)? Alexander III established himself as

39. Pacaut, p. 102; Fawtier, pp. 70–2.
40. Luchaire in Lavisse, pp. 62–3.
41. Gerald of Wales, VIII, p. 160: 'ecclesiae malleus'; Stevenson, V, Pt I, p. 140.
42. Luchaire in Lavisse, p. 51; Gerald of Wales, VIII, p. 133.

sole pope, and could not forget Louis's aid in time of need.
With regard to Becket, Louis had done his best to bring
about reconciliation, which earned credit from the Church.
Becket's death branded Henry II with a mark that repent-
ance could not remove.

Not that Louis was a subservient king. The political gains
he made from defence of the Church, from offering refuge
to ecclesiastics, show this. Luchaire has presented Louis as
being ruled by Alexander III when in France, and certainly
the two co-operated, but the king was strong-willed and did
not care to be opposed.[43] Louis VII was aggrieved when
Alexander III showed complaisance over Henry II's move to
have the marriage of his son Young Henry to Louis's daughter Margaret performed more quickly than was expected, as
an excuse to seize the dowry lands. Louis, however, was not
prepared to simply accept it, and showed his displeasure of
the papacy's inaction by opening negotiations with the pope's
great bugbear, Frederick Barbarossa. Nothing came of the
negotiations, but Alexander was given a sharp reminder of
whom he really depended on, and where the line had better be drawn. Alexander would later grant Louis a golden
flower, marking his special contribution to the Church.

. . .

LOUIS VII AND THE PLANTAGENETS

A discussion of Louis's relationship with the Plantagenets is
at the heart of any assessment of his reign. The question
must be asked, how great an error was his divorce from
Eleanor of Aquitaine? Luchaire saw it as 'a political fault of
the gravest kind', and Cartellieri as a 'political error which
could not be justified'. Fawtier believed 'it is by no means
clear that to repudiate Eleanor was a mistake', but this has
always been a minority view.

In 1137, when they married, Louis was sixteen and Eleanor
a little younger. The alliance had been arranged by their
respective fathers. William X duke of Aquitaine left instructions for the marriage to go ahead, and 'made the king himself heir of all his lands'. Eleanor was his eldest daughter

43. Luchaire in Lavisse, p. 41.

and heiress to Aquitaine, while the link gave opportunities to the Capetians to expand their influence in the south.[44]

But the marriage went sadly wrong. Eleanor's remark that being married to Louis was like marriage to a monk expresses her sexual dissatisfaction with the liaison. Louis was at first besotted by his beautiful wife, according to John of Salisbury and St Bernard, but the honeymoon period passed. There was no offspring for the first seven years, then two daughters, but no sons, and no further children after 1149. Problems emerged before the Second Crusade, with talk of a separation in 1143. Chroniclers noted personal incompatibility: Robert of Torigny reporting that 'a dislike had sprung up'; and Gervase of Canterbury, with more discretion than his counterparts in the modern press, that their discord was better passed over in silence.[45]

The crusade brought the strains of the marriage to public notice. Eleanor flirted with her uncle, Raymond prince of Antioch, while staying with him in the Holy Land. William of Tyre believed there was actual adultery.[46] At any rate the tension broke over the progress of the crusade, when Eleanor sided with her uncle against her husband and refused to go on. At this, Louis, not the complaisant feeble figure generally presented, seized his wife and carried her off to Jerusalem.

The crusade failed, but the marriage continued to limp along. On their way home, in Italy, Eugenius III did his best to reconcile them: 'the pope made them sleep in the same bed, which he had had decked with priceless hangings of his own; and daily, during their brief visit, he strove by friendly converse to restore love between them. He heaped gifts upon them; and when the moment for departure came, though he was a stern man, he could not hold back his tears.'[47] Perhaps

44. Luchaire in Lavisse, p. 28; A. Cartellieri, *Phillip II. August, König von Frankreich*, 4 vols (Leipzig, 1899–1922) I, p. 28; Fawtier, p. 24; and cf. W.L. Warren *Henry II* (London, 1973) p. 42; Orderic, VI, p. 482.
45. John of Salisbury, *Historia Pontificalis*, ed. M. Chibnall (Edinburgh, 1956) p. 53 and n. 1; Robert of Torigny in Stevenson p. 66; Robert of Torigny in Howlett, p. 164; Pacaut, p. 59; Gervase of Canterbury, *Opera Historica*, ed. W. Stubbs, 2 vols, RS no. 73 (London, 1879–80) I, p. 149: 'orta est quaedam discordia inter ipsum et reginam suam Alianor ex quibusdam forte quae melius tacenda sunt'.
46. William of Tyre, *A History of Deeds Done Beyond the Sea*, ed. E.A. Babcock and A.C. Krey, 2 vols (New York, 1943) II, p. 186.
47. John of Salisbury, pp. 61–2.

his efforts prolonged the marriage a little, but the personal differences proved too great. It was Louis rather than Eleanor who took the initiative to divorce, on the grounds of consanguinity. A co-operative French Church agreed, in an assembly at Beaugency in 1152.

Should Louis have kept his wife? There were fears that the desired son and heir would never be conceived, given the unsatisfactory nature of their sexual relationship. Eleanor had borne only two daughters in fifteen years of marriage. Dozens of medieval royal marriages were ended in similar circumstances. Eleanor on her release, eluding two suitors, fled to Henry Plantagenet, eleven years her junior. According to Walter Map she had 'cast her unchaste eyes' upon him.[48] There were rumours of misconduct by Eleanor when Henry and his father Geoffrey V of Anjou visited Paris in 1151, though the rumours centred on Geoffrey rather than his son, but Geoffrey had died unexpectedly in the same year. The new liaison was as much political as personal. Henry would not miss the opportunity to acquire Aquitaine through marriage. His Angevin predecessors had long been interested in Poitou.

Henry was energetic and ambitious. His father had already associated him in the rule of Normandy, and now Henry was duke of Normandy and count of Anjou. From Eleanor's point of view, the Angevin–Aquitaine connection seemed attractive, and she viewed Henry as the potential duke of Aquitaine rather than the ruler of an Angevin Empire, which in 1152 had not come into being. His hopes of obtaining England still seemed distant.

Nor could Louis have easily foreseen the emergence of the Angevin Empire. In England Stephen (1135–54) and his two sons were still alive, and when Henry switched his interests to England, Louis, angered by the marriage, tried to block Plantagenet ambitions in that direction. But in releasing Eleanor, Louis allowed the possibility that she would remarry. The Angevin Empire was an unexpected consequence, but the likelihood that Eleanor would remarry must have been clear. Could Louis have removed the possibility? Probably only by keeping Eleanor, or by placing her in a convent. Many medieval women who had been repudiated chose or

48. Map, p. 475.

accepted such a course, but it seems unlikely, given Eleanor's appetites and attitudes, that such a move could have been forced upon *her*. Louis's safeguard was that, as their overlord, his permission was necessary for a new marriage between his vassals. Both Henry and Eleanor broke this understanding of the royal role in making their hasty marriage, only two months after the divorce. Nevertheless Louis had been out-manoeuvred.[49] The error was magnified by Henry's subsequent success. In 1153 Stephen agreed to the terms of the treaty of Winchester, whereby Henry Plantagenet was accepted as Stephen's heir. The death of Stephen's son Eustace in 1153, his readiness to disinherit his second son William, followed by Stephen's own death in 1154, brought Henry with surprising rapidity to the throne of England.

Louis, who had 'always felt hatred for the king of England', was infuriated by the marriage.[50] He continued to claim Aquitaine as the 'lawful inheritance' of his daughters, though that was questionable, and the birth of a son to Eleanor and Henry would undermine any hope for his daughters. If Eleanor had seemed uncertainly fecund, the five sons and three daughters she produced for her new husband gave the lie, and probably angered Louis more than the marriage itself. Louis summoned Henry to his court for 'violating feudal custom', and declared his lands in France forfeit.[51] It was an interesting precedent, which in due course his son would employ to greater effect. Louis proceeded to invade Normandy, but his efforts failed. The Angevin Empire emerged. Henry II became an overpowerful vassal who threatened the future of Capetian France.

But, for Louis, it was not all loss. His subsequent marriages were less traumatic. When Eleanor rebelled against Henry in 1173, Louis could have been forgiven for thanking his lucky stars. Also the Plantagenets, in order to retain their acquisitions, were prepared to offer homage for their French lands more readily than had their predecessors. Henry II, in 1151 and 1169, did homage to the French king, and all his surviving sons followed suit. Louis had some success in blocking

49. J. Martindale, 'Eleanor of Aquitaine', in J.L. Nelson, ed., *Richard Coeur de Lion in History and Myth* (London, 1992) pp. 17–50, 31–2.

50. *Gesta Regis Henrici Secundi*, 'Benedict of Peterborough', ed. W. Stubbs, 2 vols, RS no. 49 (London, 1867) I, p. 34.

51. Fawtier, p. 140 and n. 1.

the Plantagenets' further ambitions. Henry claimed Toulouse, through his rights in Aquitaine. Louis opposed and
thwarted him by marching south and entering the city of
Toulouse alongside Count Raymond V (1148–94), at which
Henry backed off. Raymond expressed a new confidence in
the king of France: 'it is in you, after God, that we put all
our trust'.[52]

The south was generally turbulent, and Plantagenet rule
was never easy. The troubles there helped to undermine the
Angevin Empire in the next generation. The Capetians had
a ready-made fifth column within Aquitaine, which Louis
was able to exploit. The growth of the Angevin Empire forced
Louis into counter-moves, which helped build a stronger
Capetian position in the east of France, including a settlement with the house of Champagne. In the end Louis carried out a fairly successful programme of damage limitation,
but it is hard to deny that he had brought on his own head
the greatest of the challenges to his power.

In the long run, however, the Capetians rather than the
Plantagenets benefited most in the south. If Henry had found
Louis's Achilles' heel through his marriage, so Louis soon
detected Henry's. As Eleanor's sons grew up, each in turn
opposed his father. Partly this was from frustrated desire for
power, partly from personal antagonism: son against father,
brother against brother. As Gerald of Wales put it: 'the
enmity of those of the same family is among the worst of
human plagues'. In 1173 Eleanor sided with her older sons
against Henry, encouraged by Louis. Henry suppressed the
rising, but his new empire never quite recovered. The hostility between father and sons was not healed, even by Henry's
generosity in victory. Gerald of Wales thought the reconciliation 'more shadowy than real'.[53]

The brothers fought each other as well as their father:
Young Henry, 'shallow, vain, careless, empty-headed, incom-
petent, improvident and irresponsible', but otherwise handsome and chivalrous; Richard, unwilling to give up Aquitaine
to brother or father; Geoffrey, 'eloquent, hypocritical, a
deceiver, a schemer', a 'son of perdition'; John, his father's

52. Pacaut, p. 192.
53. Gerald of Wales, VIII, p. 165: 'umbratilique magis quam vera
concordia'.

favourite who also turned against him. Young Henry rebelled again in 1183, but shortly afterwards died. At the end of his life Henry II was humiliated by his son Richard, allied to Philip Augustus. As for Eleanor, captured when participating in the great rebellion against Henry II, she spent most of the rest of her marriage imprisoned at her husband's will.[54]

The gap between 1152, when Louis divorced Eleanor, and 1204, when his son broke the Angevin Empire by conquering Normandy, can be seen as years when the Capetian monarchy prepared itself to rule a wider territory. The growth then might have been harmed had the distraction in Aquitaine been greater. By 1204 expansion was more likely to succeed, and the divorce seems 'providential'.[55] Louis could not be expected to predict the growth of the Angevin Empire; no more should he be credited with foreseeing the long-term benefits of losing Eleanor. In short Louis made a dangerous error in 1152, not by divorcing Eleanor but by allowing her to remarry; but he did his best to repair the damage, and in the long run the situation unravelled itself in favour of the Capetians.

. . .

LOUIS VII AND THE PRINCIPALITIES

Philip Augustus owed a considerable debt to his father, not least for extending royal authority into the principalities. Louis forged links which brought the great vassals closer to a monarchy which was becoming more than one among equals, establishing the suzerainty of the Capetians. Previously the magnates had rarely attended court, only doing homage, if at all, on their borders, and providing small contingents for military service, if any. Even in the Plantagenet lands, Louis advanced the royal position. Henry Plantagenet came to Paris to give homage in return for recognition in Normandy, something previous dukes had avoided. He went again as king in 1158, acknowledging that for his French

---

54. Warren, pp. 580, 592; Roger of Howden, *Chronica*, ed. W. Stubbs, 4 vols, RS no. 51 (London, 1868–71) I, p. 297; cf. Bertran de Born, who criticizes both Young Henry and Geoffrey.
55. Fawtier, p. 24.

lands: 'I am his man'.[56] The Plantagenet sons made frequent visits to Paris to give homage. They offered Louis lands in return for recognition, weakening their grasp on vital border territories.

Even the practice of magnates having significant functions in the palace went into decline, but now a new sort of link began to be forged. The role of the magnates was altered by the emergence of large assemblies, sometimes local, sometimes broader. The assemblies at Vézelay and Étampes, in preparation for the Second Crusade, were an important step in the significance of something akin to national assemblies.[57]

Louis's resistance to Frederick Barbarossa also paid dividends: in Flanders, Champagne and Burgundy. Barbarossa saw Louis as a 'kinglet', and coveted the lands between their respective realms, threatening and cajoling his French neighbours.[58] Hostile relations developed between the kings, especially during the papal schism. Again Louis's Church policy gave him advantages. His favoured candidate for the papacy, Alexander III, carried the day, and Churches in the danger area turned to him as protector, as did some of the lesser nobility. The lord of Bresse offered himself as a vassal: 'come into this region where your presence is necessary to the churches as well as to me'.[59]

Nor was Louis easy to push against his will. Even the count of Champagne experienced the king's wrath: 'you have presumed too far, to act for me without consulting me'.[60] Louis's third marriage, to Adela in 1160, cemented his improving relations with the house of Champagne. He had transformed French policy to ally with the natural enemies of Anjou. Adela's brothers, Theobald V count of Blois, Henry the Liberal count of Champagne, Stephen count of Sancerre, and William who would be archbishop of Reims, became vital supporters of the crown; Theobald and Henry also married Louis's two daughters by Eleanor. The crown therefore did not have to face Henry II alone. When in 1173 Louis encouraged the rebellion by Young Henry, he could

56. Dunbabin, p. 262; *RHF*, XVI, p. 16.
57. Y. Sassier, *Louis VII* (Paris, 1991) p. 410.
58. Fawtier, p. 85; Saxo Grammaticus, *Pontificorum Romanorum Vitae*, ed. Watterich (Leipzig, 1862) II, p. 532.
59. Luchaire in Lavisse, p. 60.
60. Luchaire in Lavisse, p. 41.

call to his support the counts of Flanders, Boulogne, Troyes, Blois, Dreux and Sancerre.

In the south Louis attempted to improve his position through marriage agreements. His marriage to Eleanor gave him an interest in Aquitaine, which was not completely abandoned after the divorce. He married his sister Constance to Raymond V count of Toulouse in 1154. In 1162 Raymond declared: 'I am your man, and all that is ours is yours.'[61] It is true that Raymond's marriage failed, his wife complaining 'he does not even give me enough to eat', and that Raymond flirted with a Plantagenet alliance, but only to join Richard against his father. By 1176 he had returned to the Capetian fold.[62]

Louis used marriage as a prospect to cement relations with Flanders. Louis had brought Flanders into the coalition against Henry II, and now agreement was made for his son Philip to marry Isabella of Hainault, the count of Flanders' niece. The dukes of the other great eastern principality, Burgundy, were a branch of the royal family. As Fawtier has said, it was 'the only great fief over which royal suzerainty was never contested' – at least until the time of Philip Augustus.[63] At Louis VI's coronation, three princes of the realm had refused to give homage. By the accession of Philip Augustus, liege homage of the great vassals to the crown had become the expected practice.

Vassals of the princes sometimes turned directly to the king for aid rather than to their own lords. Many in the south sought Louis's protection, including the viscountess of Narbonne, who declared: 'I am a vassal especially devoted to your crown.'[64] Roger Trencavel received the castle of Minerve from Louis and did homage for it, though he was a vassal of the count of Toulouse, and the castle was not even the king's to give. William of Ypres, though a vassal of the count of Flanders, asked Louis to enfief his son Robert. Under Louis, not only were the great vassals brought closer, but Capetian influence was filtering through to a lower stratum of vassals.

61. Fawtier, p. 62; *RHF*, XVI, pp. 69–70.
62. Luchaire in Lavisse, p. 64.
63. Fawtier, p. 130.
64. Luchaire in Lavisse, p. 66.

∙ ∙ ∙

LOUIS VII AND THE TOWNS

This was a vital period of urban development, not least in the rise of Paris as the capital. The Ile-de-la-Cité began to take on its familiar face, with the building in Gothic style of the new church of Notre-Dame by Bishop Maurice. By 1177 a visitor declared: 'the choir of the church is now finished with the exception of the roof of the middle aisle . . . there will be no church to compete with it on our side of the Alps'.[65] Louis recognized privileges for the watermen, butchers and bakers of Paris. The Parisian schools began to make a wider mark in the intellectual development of Europe. Paris was growing in size, wealth and as a centre for government.

Louis gave encouragement to the commune movement and received reciprocal support from the communities, at the expense of local lords. The customs of Lorris were granted, becoming the model for rural communes in the twelfth century; they had been introduced under Louis VI, but only now became a model in the creation of other communes. Wherever royal power was weak, Louis followed a policy of intervention by whatever means might succeed. Encouragement of urban development outside the demesne became another instrument of royal expansion. The chronicle of Auxerre expressed the effect bluntly: 'all towns where a commune was established belonged to him'.[66]

∙ ∙ ∙

LOUIS VII'S ADMINISTRATION

One reason for stressing Louis VII's administration is that Suger was at its head early in the reign and wrote at some length about it. Suger saw Louis as a model royal administrator, fitted 'by nature as well as by application'.[67] Suger's death has been seen as a great blow to the administration. He was important to his royal masters and played a major role in government during Louis VII's absence on crusade, but he exaggerated his own significance. At times Suger was

65. Robert of Torigny in Howlett, p. 127.
66. Luchaire in Lavisse, p. 81; Sassier, p. 427.
67. Suger, *Vie de Louis VI, le Gros, suivie de le Histoire de Roi Louis VII*, ed. A. Molinier (Paris, 1887) p. 150.

opposed, for example by Louis VII's mother, or by the seneschal Ralph de Vermandois, and he was not always in royal favour. Virtually all commentators on Louis's reign see the later years as the most successful. The demise of Suger does not seem seriously to have damaged the effectiveness of the administration.

Our knowledge of administration is, however, incomplete, especially with regard to finance. There are arguments over the extent of Louis's income. We depend upon an unreliable and unclear account by Conon the prévôt of Lausanne, based on gossip overheard at Philip Augustus's funeral, nearly forty years after Louis's death.[68] It concerned how much money Louis had left at his death. Even if the figures were accurate, there is doubt over their meaning; whether they refer to net or gross income, to income from the demesne or in total. Of course Conon's report is important evidence, and we shall return to it, but the debate underlines the problem of evidence in this area.

By this time the higher nobility were being excluded from working offices; the great offices were in decline; the entourage had become laicized. Lesser nobility and royal clerks rather than bishops were employed. Walter the Chamberlain was thought 'more noble in his actions than in his birth', a sneer at both his humble birth and his high-handed actions.[69] Such men also provided advice; in 1158 Louis referred to 'the council of those who surround us'. Certain key figures taken from the household or entourage became regular counsellors of the king, advising on even the greatest matters of state. Such men were also employed on missions as representatives of the king. Josbert Briand, for example, acted 'in the place of the lord king' over the judgement relating to the abbey of St-Germain-des-Prés, and Thierry Galeran acted for the king in Aquitaine in 1150, presiding over a local assembly.[70] In addition Louis extended the use of prévôts as royal administrative agents, creating sixteen new prévôtés

68. Hallam, pp. 166–7; Pacaut, pp. 156–9; J.F. Benton, 'The revenue of Louis VII', *Spec*, XLII, 1967, pp. 84–91. M. Pacaut, 'Conon de Lausanne et les revenus de Louis VII', *Revue historique*, CCXXXIX, 1968, pp. 29–32.
69. E. Bournazel, *Le Gouvernement Capétien au XIIe siècle, 1108–1180* (Limoges, 1975) pp. 65–6.
70. Bournazel, p. 163; Sassier, pp. 415–16: 'loco domini regis'.

and reorganizing others. At the start of the reign there were about twenty-five prévôts, by its end perhaps forty. However, Louis opposed the development of dynasties of agents which would have diminished royal control over them, declaring that 'hereditary right is completely forbidden'.[71]

The role of the major officials was modifying, few now were great nobles. There were five major officials: the seneschal, who was a major-domo; the chancellor, who ran the secretariat; the chamberlain, with responsibility for finance; the butler, who supervised the demesne; and the constable, who had military duties. This breakdown is neater than practice, since officials were sometimes moved from one task to another. No official was indispensable. When Ralph of Vermandois died in 1152, no new seneschal was appointed for two years, and on the disgrace of the chancellor Hugh de Champfleury in 1172, no replacement was made for seven years. This was probably deliberate policy. It is worth noting that whenever a major office was left vacant, the routine of government continued without any apparent problem. During the period from 1149 to 1154, all the main officials except one were replaced, so that a new team emerged more closely linked to Louis, and more subservient.[72]

Louis's administration was loyal; he favoured trusted officials, and they and their relatives benefited from promotions and gifts. Louis rarely gave demesne lands, but often found desirable offices for loyal servants. We have seen the furore caused by his attempt to obtain the archbishopric of Bourges for the chancellor, Cadoc.[73] On that occasion, unusually, he failed. More typically we have Louis's instruction to the bishop of Paris to reserve the next benefice which became vacant for his clerk Barbedon.[74]

It was a loyal and effective household, but not without problems. Walter Map gives some interesting insights, showing conflict at court between the lay and clerical members. He relates the story of the poet Waleran d'Yèvre, who penned a verse criticizing three officials who had been 'set up over the whole of France' and were cheating Louis 'in his simplicity',

71. Luchaire in Lavisse, p. 77; Sassier, p. 425.
72. Pacaut, *Louis VII*, pp. 172–3; Sassier, pp. 406–9, refers to a policy of 'vacance'.
73. Pacaut, *Louis VII*, pp. 172–3.
74. Bournazel, p. 81.

keeping their takings and giving the king only 'what escaped them'. The three officials saw to it that Waleran was accused and banished from court. He was only restored, says Map, through the support of Henry II. The same chronicler also presents a picture of the two kings at one of their innumerable conferences, in a large field surrounded by knights. Encouraged by Henry, the poet appeared in poor clothes and won Louis's pity. So the king learned the truth and Waleran was restored, while the guilty officials were punished.[75]

Royal wealth depended on the demesne, so its administration was vital to the monarchy's health. The main areas of the demesne spread from Paris to Sens and Orléans; from the right bank of the Seine to Montereau; westwards to Dreux and Mantes; north-east to Laon and Soissons. The demesne was also extended southwards to Berry and Bourges. While Louis VI had been forced to struggle throughout his reign in order to control the demesne, Louis VII needed force to deal with difficult vassals on only a handful of occasions. He was more secure on home territory and better able to raise his sights beyond the traditional areas of crown influence. Louis's involvement beyond the demesne, as shown by his charters to Toulouse, Poitou, Gascony and the Auvergne, was not simply demonstrating a spreading royal influence, but was aiming towards further acquisitions.

. . .

WAS LOUIS VII A WEAK KING?

The general consensus of historians on Louis VII before recent times had been to condemn him as a mild, ineffectual king, lacking military ability, outmanoeuvred and outshone by the stronger and more worldly rulers around him, failing to keep Aquitaine, a slave to the Church, a monk in marriage, a simpleton in the world. He has been seen as a 'colourless nonentity', 'almost silly', 'a weak, pious and shifty king'.[76] He has been compared unfavourably with his contemporaries, Frederick Barbarossa and Henry II, with his

75. Map, pp. 447–59, where the name appears as Walter of Effia.
76. For Louis being colourless, Hallam, p. 120, though this does not fully represent her view; as almost silly or simple-minded, Cartellieri, I, p. 2; cf. C. Petit-Dutaillis, *The Feudal Monarchy in France and England*, trans. E.D. Hunt (London, 1936) p. 180; weak etc., Tout, p. 285.

predecessor Louis VI, and with his successor Philip Augustus. Views of the reign were distorted because the two short French chronicles for the early years have been overwhelmed by use of the more numerous and detailed works written in the Plantagenet lands for the later years. But modern historians, by more careful interpretation and by the use of non-narrative sources, have shown that Louis used his piety to advantage, was a successful diplomat, and 'not the feeble monarch of textbooks'.[77]

Pacaut, in defending Louis, was swimming against the tide of opinion, but rightly saw how he built and used personal power, held his own with the Plantagenets, gained ground for the monarchy with regard to his greater vassals, and re-shaped the administration to give the crown greater authority. Such achievements cannot be reconciled with the pious simpleton of popular imagination. Following Pacaut, other historians are now coming round to this viewpoint.[78]

Louis's piety was not a pose; he was genuinely devout, but he was neither stupid nor compliant. He gave less to the Church than Louis VI, but earned higher dividends. He could make a firm stand, and at one point in the crisis over Eleanor's sister Petronilla, faced out Innocent II, Theobald of Blois, and even St Bernard. A Christian life-style was essential to achieve close co-operation with the Church. His was not a passive piety; Louis was also 'the lover of justice, the defender of the weak', and respected by ecclesiastics. Divorcing Eleanor may have been a mistake, but there was no easy alternative, and Plantagenet profit was not long-lasting. After Eleanor's remarriage, Louis combated Henry II with determination, never allowing him to get the upper hand for long. Louis devised the strategy which was to destroy the Angevin Empire: he encouraged and used divisions within the Plantagenet family, worked on the jealousies and fears of other great vassals to turn them against the Angevins, and showed his son the way to eventual triumph.

Louis faced stiff opposition at home and abroad, but it is not clear that any of his rivals finally got the better of him. Barbarossa gained nothing in France, and suffered more in his relations with the Church than did Louis. Henry II,

77. Duby, p. 182; Pacaut, *Louis VII.*
78. Sassier, pp. 8–11; Duby, p. 182.

though master of the Angevin Empire, recognized Louis as his suzerain for the French lands, lost moral stature in the West over his part in the killing of Becket, and ended his life in humiliating defeat by Louis's son. As Fawtier notes, 'Louis cannot fairly be said to have had the worst of the conflict.'[79]

Louis VII was the first Capetian seriously to involve the monarchy in the south, making gains in land, prestige and influence. He presented himself as king of all the realm. In 1177 he pointed out that kings were consecrated by holy oil, so 'it followed that only they could labour to govern the people of God'. He referred to himself as 'imperator Augustus' of the Franks. Across the Channel, Ralph of Diceto saw Louis as 'transcending the majesty of his predecessors'. In this period Stephen de Tournai came close to seeing the king as emperor in his realm.[80] Louis's authority over the great vassals was stronger than that of any earlier Capetian. Far from allowing royal power to diminish, Louis considerably increased it.

Louis also controlled royal officials more firmly than had been done before. Hereditary officialdom disappeared, over-powerful officers were not allowed to become a threat. This was no accident, but consistent and determined policy to oppose hereditary office, to counter the power of officials, to select men he could trust, and to keep their loyalty. Louis made it clear that a Capetian monarch should receive homage from all vassals, however great, and owe homage to none.

It is odd that in our age when warfare is condemned, we reserve our highest praise for those in the past whose triumphs were mainly military, and thus undervalue those who triumphed by other means. If we are to appreciate the Capetians, we need to revise the values we credit in the past. Neither Louis VII nor Philip Augustus gained their main triumphs through war. Since they nevertheless achieved much, ought we not to praise them the more?

79. Fawtier, p. 143.
80. On governing the people of God see Pacaut, *Louis VII*, p. 35; on *imperator*, ibid., p. 36, from *Layettes du Trésor des Chartes*, 5 vols (Paris, 1863–1909), I and II ed. A. Teulet, I no. 141, a charter on Maguelonne; Diceto, I, p. 432; on emperor in his realm, Sassier, p. 419, quotes Stephen of Tournai: 'rex in regno suo. Vel eundem vocat regem et imperatorem'.

Louis VII brought the Capetians to a new peak: master of the royal demesne and thus of a safe income, master of the royal administration, a match for enemies and rivals. He extended royal territorial control and royal influence through the realm. Above all he presented a picture of the Christian monarch which his age could admire, which gained co-operation from the French Church and from Rome, and moral advantage over the murderer of Becket or the supporter of an anti-pope. A monk at St-Germain-des-Prés saw him as 'the most glorious King Louis'. As Fawtier has it, the Capetians 'put right before might', and they should be praised for so doing. Louis was aware of the propaganda value of bearing the oriflamme as defender of the realm, and it was Louis who adopted the symbol of the fleur-de-lys.[81]

.   .   .

LOUIS VII THE FATHER

Whatever Louis's failings in the eyes of his first wife, he later proved a good husband and father. There are no unfavourable comments on his second and third marriages, which both produced offspring. The second marriage, to Constance of Castile, added two daughters to the two by Eleanor. But there is no doubt that when his third wife, Adela of Champagne, gave birth in 1165, the God-given son became the apple of his father's eye. Louis resisted the Capetian practice of associating his son in government with him. Perhaps the security of his position made it unnecessary. Perhaps, in 1172, when Henry archbishop of Reims suggested a coronation, and with papal support, Louis thought his seven-year-old son too young.[82] Louis had no doubts that Philip should be his heir. In 1179, when ill, Louis called an assembly in Paris. There he announced his intention of having Philip crowned on the feast of Assumption, on 15 August. These plans, however, were dramatically interrupted. Philip went hunting near Compiègne. Chasing a boar, he became lost alone in the woods. Found by a charcoal-burner, Philip was led to safety, but a night in the open, two days without food,

81. On the glorious king, Duby, p. 189; on right before might, Fawtier, p. 230; on the fleur-de-lys, Duby, p. 187.
82. Sassier, p. 467.

and the shock of the whole episode, damaged his health. The prince became ill to the point where death seemed imminent. The coronation was postponed.

Now Louis conducted himself as the caring father, weeping profusely, sighing night and day, inconsolable. One night the murdered Thomas Becket appeared before him, proclaiming: 'Our Lord Jesus Christ sends me as your servant, Thomas the martyr of Canterbury, in order that you should go to Canterbury, if your son is to recover.'[83] Louis's counsellors tried to dissuade the ageing king from a journey into the lion's den, but he overrode all opposition and went, accompanied by the counts of Flanders, Guisnes and Louvain, arriving at Dover on 22 August. He was met by Henry II who, whatever his suspicions, escorted Louis to Canterbury and treated him as an honoured guest. Louis spent two days praying, 'a humble and devout suppliant', and then returned home.[84] Philip recovered rapidly and was crowned at Reims on 1 November. The episode added to Louis's pious reputation, though the journey had probably been undertaken less for prestige than from love of his son.

The Norman chronicler, Robert of Torigny, says that in 1179 there were great winds and forecasts of impending calamities.[85] The effort of the journey had been too much for the sixty-year-old monarch. He went into decline, suffering a stroke which left him paralysed and unable to speak. Philip was installed as king and immediately took an active role. Louis VII became no more than 'a spectator in the last year of the reign'.[86] His incapacity was such that his personal seal was taken away. He died in September 1180, with his fifteen-year-old son still recuperating. The father was buried at his own foundation, the Cistercian house of Barbeau. The inscription on his tomb, which Philip may well have taken to heart, read:

You who survive him are the successor of his dignity;
You diminish his line if you diminish his renown.[87]

83. *GRH2*, I, pp. 240–3.
84. Gerald of Wales, VIII, p. 159: 'humilis ac devotus'.
85. Robert of Torigny in Howlett, pp. 283–4.
86. Sassier, p. 470.
87. Sassier, p. 473: 'Huic superes tu qui superes successor honoris;/ Degener es, si degener a laude prioris'.

Chapter 2

THE YOUNG KING

. . .

THE CORONATION

Philip acceded to power before he ascended the throne.
The moment came suddenly. Until 1179 Louis VII had
resisted the coronation of his son during his own lifetime,
probably because it seemed unnecessary. It may be that the
succession hung by a fairly thin thread, the life of the young
Philip, a life that had seemed very much in the balance in
1179. But at the same time, there were no rivals to the succession, and no question about his rights. Indeed it must
be a moot point who would have succeeded had Philip's
serious illness in 1179 proved fatal. There were no brothers,
and the question of female succession had not been con-
fronted. The marriages of Philip's half-sisters by Eleanor of
Aquitaine to the counts of Champagne and Blois, and of his
half-sister Margaret by Constance of Castile to the Plantagenet
heir, Young Henry, complicated rather than resolved any
settlement.

In the event, subsequent to his father's trip to Canterbury, Philip recovered. Louis VII's own illness then precipitated the full recognition of his son. Philip was crowned in
November 1179, not in order to demonstrate his rights, but
because it was necessary for him to govern. He was crowned
by his uncle, William Whitehands, archbishop of Reims, in
the presence of many of the magnates and prelates of the
realm. Also attending were three of the sons of Henry II:
Young Henry, Richard and Geoffrey. Whatever differences
there had been between Henry and Louis, the coronation
of the new king of France was too great an event for the

Plantagenets to miss. They brought presents for him commensurate with their pride and wealth, but they were also acknowledging his overlordship for their French territories. Louis VII was too ill to attend, and the queen stayed at his bedside.

The crowd greeted Philip with shouts of 'vive le roi!', which indeed he now was, assuming full power.[1] Louis had probably suffered a stroke, since we hear that his right side was paralysed, and he lost the power of speech. Even the king's chancery seal was removed: 'in case he decided anything in the realm against the conscience of his son'.[2] Philip began at once to issue charters in his own name, without any reference to consent from his father.

Philip's marriage to Isabella had been organized by Louis VII and the count of Flanders. A marriage for her had previously been arranged with the heir to Champagne, and her father Baldwin V count of Hainault (1171–95, Baldwin VIII count of Flanders, 1191–94) was not pleased at having to break that alliance.[3] The new link, however, had its advantages for Hainault, as well as for the monarchy. Should Philip of Alsace count of Flanders (1168–91) die without children, much might come to the French crown: Artois including Arras, St-Omer, Aire and Hesdin, what Giselbert called 'the land beyond the great dyke'; there would also now be a royal interest in the lands of the count's wife, Vermandois.[4] The count of Flanders currently had no children, and this possibility was therefore quite a strong one. Though she was still only ten years old, Isabella and Philip married at Bapaume on 28 April 1180, when a new coronation ceremony was performed for the young couple.

Even from the beginning, Philip took command. He was only fourteen at the time of the first coronation, and fifteen when his father died. His mother, Adela of Champagne,

1. J.W. Baldwin, *The Government of Philip Augustus* (Berkeley, CA, 1986) p. 6.
2. Ralph of Diceto, *Opera Historica*, ed. W. Stubbs, 2 vols, RS no. 68 (London, 1876) II, p. 6: 'ne quid in regno statueret citra filii conscientiam'.
3. Baldwin became count of Flanders through his wife, and ceased to hold the title when she died in 1194, a year before his own death.
4. Giselbert of Mons, *La Chronique de Gislebert de Mons*, ed. L. Vanderkindere, Recueil des textes pour servir à l'étude de l'histoire de Belgique (Brussels, 1904) p. 130: 'terra extra Fossatum'.

was in a good position to dominate affairs. This would have been the case with many young kings. She was strong-minded, but also sister to a group of the most powerful men in the kingdom. Her brother William Whitehands was archbishop of Reims, a cardinal and papal legate, who had crowned the king; he was the most influential churchman in France. The other brothers were Henry I the Liberal, count of Champagne (1152–81); Theobald V count of Blois and Chartres (1152–90), the seneschal of France; and Stephen count of Sancerre. A younger sister, Mary, was married to Hugh III duke of Burgundy (1162–91). Their family lands surrounded the royal demesne and they could easily have held sway over a nephew less determined than Philip.

As it was, Philip quarrelled with his mother from the very moment of his marriage. Philip had apparently already taken the royal seal out of his dying father's possession in order to prevent his maternal uncles from obtaining it. None of Queen Adela's brothers had truly approved of the marriage to Isabella, and the likely hold over Philip it would present to the count of Flanders. They had attended the king's coronation but studiously avoided the wedding and coronation of the new queen. When his mother, Adela, began to fortify her own lands, Philip scented trouble, and went so far as to have her lands seized. She then fled to her brother, Theobald count of Blois, for protection.

Philip turned from his maternal relatives to another powerful magnate, Philip of Alsace count of Flanders. Perhaps to a degree, and for a short time, Philip was in the hands of this manipulative count. Philip of Alsace had held the sword at the coronation. It was he, rather than Baldwin V of Hainault, the father, who arranged the new king's marriage to Isabella of Hainault. Baldwin of Hainault was married to the count of Flanders' sister, Margaret. In the first years of the new reign the role of Philip of Flanders, uncle to the queen, was that of a guardian.

Such interweaving of relationships has great significance in the politics of the age. One might think that Philip Augustus had evaded the network of maternal Champagne relatives only to be embroiled in that of his new wife's Flemish set. But the marriage proved useful, and before many years Philip showed that he would no more be a pawn of Flanders than of Champagne. One of the several advantages that Isabella brought to him was a claim of descent from Charlemagne. This, added to the similar assertion made for his mother Adela, firmed up the Capetian position. Until now, descent from Charlemagne could be better claimed by a number of magnate houses than by the Capetians. But now William the Breton could confidently refer to Philip as *Karolide*.[5]

A second coronation had been planned for 1180, after Philip's marriage. On the advice of the count of Flanders it was brought forward to May, and occurred at St-Denis. Philip's accession was confirmed on 19 September 1180 by the death of his invalid father. Philip seems always to have respected his father, who in turn had cared much for him. Early documents granted by the young king often refer to his father fondly.[6] Louis was buried at Barbeau, and at his request gold, silver, gems, clothes and ornaments were distributed to the poor.

Philip is not a king who attracted many vivid personal portraits, either of his looks or of his character. He is therefore an elusive figure for the modern historian. However, at the moment of his accession one finds a thumbnail sketch of the young king. As a child he had been noted for rather solemn remarks and a precocious attitude, no doubt the result of an upbringing always aimed towards kingship. In young manhood he once forecast his own growth in power and in the number of men he would rule. He also would point out: 'I am only a man, but a man who is king of France.'[7]

5. See R. Fawtier, *The Capetian Kings of France*, trans. L. Butler and R.J. Adam (London, 1964) p. 56; William the Breton, in the prologue, *La Philippide, Poème*, ed. and trans. M. Guizot (Paris, 1825) p. 2; Baldwin, p. 366; E.A. Brown, 'La notion de la légitimité et la prophétie à la cour de Philippe Auguste', in R-H. Bautier, ed., *La France de Philippe Auguste, le Temps des Mutations*, Actes du Colloque International organisé par le Centre National de la Recherche Scientifique, 1980 (Paris, 1982) pp. 77–111, on pp. 81–2.
6. For example *Recueil des Actes de Philippe Auguste*, ed. H-F. Delaborde, 4 vols (Paris, 1916–79) I, no. 10, 1180, pp. 14–15, the quote on p. 15: 'karissimus pater noster Ludovicus'; no. 54, 1182, pp. 75–7, on p. 74: 'venerabilis memorie'.
7. *Recueil des Historiens des Gaules et de la France* (*RHF*), ed. M. Bouquet and L. Delisle, 24 vols (Paris, 1734–1904) 'Historia regum Francorum', XVII, p. 425: 'ego autem viribus et aetate et sapientia proficiam'; Baldwin, p. 27.

Philip was earnest, with a conventional and rather stern piety. William the Breton called him 'very pious'; and he is known to have introduced rules against swearing at court: blasphemy would result in a fine of twenty sous to be given to the poor, on pain of being thrown into the river. His somewhat puritanical piety led to early measures against corruption: merchants and prostitutes were removed from the Church of the Innocents; the expulsion of the Jews was also in part a reflection of this outlook.[8] The same rather severe view led to a cool attitude towards tournaments, which were frowned on by the Church; and a lack of any great interest in music or literature, so that he was considered 'not courteous'.[9]

If there is any truth in it, the story about the beggar could suggest humour as well as thriftiness, and even if invented, the tale shows what was thought of the king. It was said that a beggar asked him for alms in the name of his forebears. Philip asked, those on which side? The beggar replied those on the side of Adam, and the king then gave him an obol. The beggar studied the small coin and said: 'Is that all your forebears are worth?' Philip answered: 'If I gave you an obol for every ancestor by *that* line, I should not have much left'.[10]

Such physical descriptions as we have, suggest that he was 'handsome and well built', with a face that shone with pleasure, and even looked jovial. He was quite tall and fresh-faced. It is likely that his physical appearance and physique were normal, but suffered somewhat from the ravages of his crusade. He was also fond of alcohol, another trait which gave rise to later tales. It was said that when he was ill, he asked for wine, but the medics recommended he should stick to water. The king persuaded them to let him have some wine

---

8. William the Breton, *Philippide*, ed. Guizot, p. 6; and 'Philippide' in *Oeuvres de Rigord et de Guillaume le Breton*, ed. H.F. Delaborde, SHF, vols 210, 224 (Paris, 1882–85); A. Luchaire, *Social France at the time of Philip Augustus*, trans. E.B. Krehbiel (London, 1912); and see R-H. Bautier, 'Philippe Auguste: la personalité du roi', in Bautier, pp. 33–57.

9. Y. Lefèvre, 'L'Image de Philippe Auguste chez les poètes', pp. 133–44, in Bautier, p. 137; from Conon de Béthune.

10. J. Le Goff: 'Philippe Auguste dans les *exempla*', pp. 154–5, in Bautier, p. 152.

on the promise that it would be followed by water. Philip then drank down the wine, but refused the water on the grounds that he was no longer thirsty.

Philip Augustus is described as fearful for his own life, not surprising given the importance placed upon his survival, and the serious illness of 1179. He was of a nervous disposition and rather untidy. A less friendly writer said he lacked moderation, was impatient and impetuous; another that he was greedy and avaricious. The suggestion in a number of modern works that Philip had only one eye seems to be a modern myth. But we shall probably get closer to the real Philip through his acts than through contemporary comment on his looks and character.[11]

Philip's first marriage was in general a success. Isabella proved a popular and discreet wife. Giselbert, her father's chronicler, describes her as having beauty and merit, and being 'a most holy woman'.[12] There was a crisis for the marriage in 1184, when Philip temporarily sought divorce, but

11. See Baldwin, pp. 356–9, on appearance, p. 356; *RHF*, XVIII, p. 304, 'Chronicle of St Martin, Tours': 'colore rubens ... potui ciboque deditus'; A. Luchaire in E. Lavisse, *Histoire de France depuis les origines jusqu'à la Révolution*, III, Pt I (Paris, 1911) pp. 279–84; and A. Cartellieri, *Philipp II. August, König von Frankreich*, 4 vols (Leipzig, 1899–1922) IV, pp. 577–94. On being handsome, Bautier, 'Personalité', in Bautier, pp. 34–5 and n. 6, the quote is from Pagan Gastinel. S. Runciman, *A History of the Crusades*, III, The Kingdom of Acre (Cambridge, 1955), p. 35, J. Riley-Smith, *The Crusades, a Short History* (London, 1987) p. 114, and A. Bridge, *Richard the Lionheart* (London, 1989) p. 63, and others say Philip was one-eyed, but do not give a specific reference. I have been unable to find anything to support the suggestion. The reference in *Recueil*, see n. 16 below, is hardly enough to support this, and only refers to 'our watchful eye', not the right eye in particular. One possible source for the myth, if such it is, is the story in Giovanni Boccaccio, *The Decameron*, trans. R. Aldington (London, 1954) p. 61, in the fifth tale on the first day, in which appears the king of France 'Philip the One-Eyed', who prepares to leave on crusade with 'The Marquess of Monferrato'. The king falls in love with the marquess's wife, and sails on crusade from Genoa. Although fictional and not precisely historical, she hints at her coolness towards his advances by serving a meal of all hens and no cocks! This does seem to be based on Philip Augustus; but the source for the story I have not yet found. On lacking moderation is Gilles de Paris. On greed see Lefèvre in Bautier, from Peire Vidal. On wine see Le Goff in Bautier, p. 153.
12. Giselbert of Mons, p. 129; the quote, p. 154: 'mulier sanctissima'.

this was patched up. In 1187 Isabella bore Philip's only legitimate child, Louis. The occasion saw singing, dancing and rejoicing, continued by torchlight through the night: a repetition of the celebrations at Philip's own birth. Isabella died in 1190, but her son survived to inherit the throne as Louis VIII.

The position of the Champagne relatives was further eroded by a new friendship between Philip Augustus and Henry II of England, ruler of most of the lands that we know as western France. Rivalry between Plantagenets and the Capetians seemed almost inevitable in the circumstances, and much of Louis VII's reign had been spent in war over Toulouse and other disputed areas. But at the beginning of Philip's reign, Henry II adopted a new attitude, that of benevolent elder statesman. To some extent the relationship between the two monarchies was ambivalent. There were existing family ties, and new ones would be made. Eleanor of Aquitaine had been wife to Louis VII before she married Henry II; so there was a blood link between her daughters by Louis, and her children by Henry. Then Henry's son, Young Henry, married Margaret, Louis's daughter by his second wife Constance of Castile. And again, Margaret's full sister, Alice, was treated for many years as the intended wife of Richard the Lionheart. The quarrels between the Plantagenets and the Capetians in this period are virtually divisions within one extended family.

The Champagne group of royal relatives was less significant at the start of the reign than might have been anticipated; but its power was too great to be ignored for long. Henry II seemed amicable, but the grounds for difficulty between the two monarchies could not long be forgotten. The count of Flanders had won the position of guardian which he desired, but the threats to his position were many, and any sense of security proved transitory. The early reign has the air of a phoney peace, with demons waiting in the wings to make their entrance.

Not least among the instabilities was the relative weakness of the monarchy in comparison with the great princes. Bertran de Born could still sneer at Philip as 'the little king of Lesser-land', whom he saw as 'too soft' and not the leader France needed. Historians see Philip as no more than 'the king of Paris, Orléans, Bourges and Amiens', but his ambitions were not the least of the factors which would bring dramatic change after the uneasy honeymoon period.[13]

. . .

THE NEW REGIME

Naturally Philip had to settle into his new situation, and there were no major changes at first. Philip kept his father's household officials, and his father's prévôts on the demesne; he confirmed his father's acts concerning towns and communities; he re-asserted his father's policy of protecting the Church. Indeed Philip's administration was never a revolution against Louis VII's system. There would be major developments, but they were evolutionary, they grew naturally out of what was there before. Perhaps Professor Baldwin has overemphasized the degree of dependence and conservatism during the first decade.[14] By the end of the 1180s there are signs that Philip was seeking change, sometimes radical change; we do not need to wait for the crusade as a turning point.

We have seen that Philip did not placidly accept the arrangements of his father or the wishes of his mother. Before Philip the major officials had been magnates, often dominant in court and household. Theobald count of Blois, for example, was the seneschal of France. Louis VII had allied with the house of Champagne through his marriage to Adela. Philip soon broke from his mother's family, relying on the support at first of Philip of Flanders and Henry Plantagenet. For a time his mother's family left court. A reconciliation was arranged through the mediation of Henry II, but Philip had made his declaration of independence.

In fact, once the initial trouble had been sorted out, Philip did not reject his maternal family or remain on bad terms.

13. Bertran de Born, *The Poems of the Troubadour Bertran de Born*, ed. W.D. Paten, T. Sankovitch and P.H. Stäblein (Berkeley, CA, 1986) p. 115 l. 15: 'Del pauc rei de Terra Menor'; p. 379, l. 11, p. 393, l. 32: 'trop mols'. The modern quote is from Luchaire in Lavisse, p. 90.
14. Baldwin, p. 73, Philip before the Third Crusade 'had followed in his father's footsteps'; p. 101, sees 1190 to 1203 as a period of 'extraordinary innovation', with the crusade as 'a great divide'. Baldwin is, however, moderate and careful, and points out those early changes which were made.

After the reconciliation, his uncle William, archbishop of Reims, became the most influential of his advisers: 'the watchful eye of his councillors, and his right hand in business', even a 'second king'.[15] And when, in 1190, Philip made arrangements for his kingdom during his absence on crusade, his mother Adela and his uncle William of Reims were named as regents, though their powers were carefully hedged.

At his accession Philip had no choice but to tread cautiously with the most powerful magnates. The royal demesne was surrounded by magnate territories: the Plantagenets to the west and south; Flanders to the north; Champagne and Blois to the west, east and south. The Plantagenets held territory only 60 kilometres from Paris, while Champagne was 30 kilometres away. Philip escaped from too close a tutelage, but he was careful when at odds with one great vassal, to seek alliance with others. His position was made more secure with the birth of his son Louis in 1187, recognized at once, for example in the 1190 crusade arrangement, as 'our heir'.[16]

Royal administration and income were still based on the demesne, which was not a compact bloc but scattered from Compiègne and Senlis in the north, southwards through Paris and Orléans to Bourges. In the first decade Philip made acquisitions, including Montargis from Peter de Courtenay; Amiens, Montdidier and Roye in 1185; the county of Tournai in 1187. Here on the demesne the royal system of administration operated. Louis VII's system had depended primarily upon his prévôts, and Philip significantly increased their numbers from thirty-five to fifty-two by 1190. This focus on officials was rewarded by an increase in revenue of some 22 per cent by 1190, no less than 72 per cent of this income deriving from the prévôts.[17]

Again, in opposition to Baldwin's view that the crusade was the turning point, it seems clear that Philip had already inaugurated the major reform in the structure of the administration before 1190, with the introduction of the baillis by

15. Baldwin, p. 32; *Recueil*, I, no. 109, p. 137: 'karissimus avunculus noster W[illelmus], Remensis archiepiscopus, in consiliis nostris oculus vigilans, in negociis dextra manus'.
16. A.W. Lewis, *Royal Succession in Capetian France: Studies in Familial Order and the State* (Cambridge, MA, 1981) p. 82.
17. Baldwin, pp. 35, 44, 54.

1184. In the following year, the chancellor Hugh died and was not replaced; indeed there would be no new chancellor until 1185. This avoidance of a chief minister was clearly policy and shows Philip's desire to escape from the tie of former restraints. One could suggest that 1185, the year of the downfall of the count of Flanders, rather than 1190, was the first watershed in the development of Philip's administration.

The new officials, the baillis, were used to check the activities of the prévôts, reporting on their activities in Paris. They began as itinerant officials with judicial and financial functions, working in small groups on defined missions. It has been suggested that they were based on the English system of itinerant justices, but there is no certain proof, and they did not operate in the same manner. Duby thinks the model for change was the Church, but new powerful officials to check the operations of existing agents is such a common mode of change as hardly to require a model.

Our knowledge of the operation of Philip's government in this first decade is restricted by the paucity of records. The royal archives were lost during the later wars with Richard the Lionheart, and our major source for Philip's government are the new registers, which do not deal directly with the earliest period of the reign. Nevertheless it is accepted that a well-organized governmental and administrative system appeared under Philip, a system which was more centralized than had previously been the case.[18]

It was, though, still a system with serious limitations. How far the financial arrangements of France borrowed from the Anglo-Norman realm or from Flanders is unclear, and probably always will be. Those two neighbours had systems which we can see in operation, simply because their records survive. But the French system was not exactly like either, and it seems probable that all three were growing in a similar direction at the same time. The limitations of Philip's system are best illustrated by the demands for a crusade. Philip and Henry II levied a similar tax on their lands, which has become known as the Saladin Tithe. It was not popular in either realm, despite the good cause it was intended to support. In France, the Church, on being asked to bear part of

18. Fawtier, p. 174: 'a well-established governmental and administrative system appears'.

the burden, somewhat hypocritically complained that the tax was made 'at the price of the tears of widows and the poor'. It was claimed that people were 'tortured by the agents of the royal fisc'. But it seems likely that the novelty rather than the burden of the tax caused most complaints. Henry II managed nevertheless to carry it through, though he never went on crusade. Philip on the other hand, who would become a crusader, yielded to the criticisms and abandoned the Tithe, promising that 'no future exactions shall be made by reason of it or for any similar cause'.[19]

It is wise to remind ourselves that Philip's early efforts were made against a background of difficulties. The same point must be made about law and order in the kingdom. One should not overestimate the degree of order in twelfth-century Europe, otherwise one fails to appreciate the achievements of the great rulers of the period. France in the 1180s was far from stable: castellans abused their power, while powerful secular lords took lands from the Church. One associates bands of troops preying on the countryside with a later age, but they existed already in France. The *cottereaux* or *routiers*, as the roving bands of mercenaries-cum-brigands were known, were accused of taking captives for ransom, sleeping with their wives, flogging, killing, destroying holy objects and burning churches.[20]

In 1183 some disgruntled local populations, finding that central and local government seemed unable or unwilling to save them from oppression, took the law into their own hands. They formed associations, notably the followers of the carpenter Durand, wearing the uniform of a hood and hence known as *capuchons* or whitehoods. They were said to number thousands, and began a campaign of revenge against the *cottereaux*. In Auvergne they won a victory which led to the death of 3,000 brigands. In Rouergue the brigand leader, Courbaran, was hanged with 500 of his followers. But within a year the aristocracy was viewing the *capuchon* movement as a threat and accusing the whitehoods of heretical beliefs. In

19. C. Petit-Dutaillis, *The Feudal Monarchy in France and England from the Tenth to the Thirteenth Centuries* (London, 1936) pp. 190–1; the tears and exactions quotes are *Recueil*, I, no. 104, 1189 ordinance: 'ex pauperum et viduarum lacrimis'; Cartellieri, II, p. 84; the tortured quote is Gilles de Paris in *RHF*, XVII, p. 291. ll. 108–9.
20. A. Luchaire, *Social France*, pp. 9–10, 14, 18.

their turn these medieval vigilantes were attacked, hunted down and suppressed.

One can perhaps see the desire for more effective authority going hand in hand with the demand from towns and rural communities for more self-government, communal rights, and privileges. It was a movement which Philip recognized, following in his father's footsteps. A number of communities had their privileges confirmed by Philip in his early charters, at Chaumont, Pontoise, Poissy and Montreuil among others.[21] Towns in newly acquired demesne land might also be granted commune status, as at Amiens. These particular grants were made within the demesne, in areas where Philip needed to strengthen his hold against rivals, such as the Plantagenets. Such grants usually confirmed existing privileges, but others were in areas beyond the demesne, and here new grants as well as confirmations might be made.

Even within the demesne, Philip was often acting with the strategic defence of the whole kingdom in mind. Philip's first decade saw an extension of royal control through a restructuring of the system of officials; an extension of communal privileges through grants which recognized the aspirations of at least some communities; activity by the king to protect the weak and the Church. He was assuming the powers of a monarch with responsibilities for a kingdom, as well as those of ruler of only a demesne.

. . .

THE EXPULSION OF THE JEWS

Early in the reign Philip carried out an act which is repugnant to the modern world and difficult to explain. It must be seen in the context of the age, but still seems a cynical act aimed at political and financial gain. It was in line with the measures already discussed, showing Philip as his own man, prepared to break with previous policy. Louis VII had acted as the protector of the Jews. Monarchs often took this stance, since they profited from their financial dealings and usury, and in protecting the Jews were protecting their own

21. Baldwin, pp. 60–1; *Recueil*, I, confirmations nos 19, 35; grants: no. 59, p. 79 on Chaumont; no. 233, pp. 283–5 on Pontoise; no. 234, pp. 285–7 on Poissy; no. 236, pp. 289–90 on Montreuil.

interests. But anti-Semitism was rife and socially acceptable. The Jews were seen as the enemies of Christ; their usury was against the teaching of the Church. Almost every crusade was accompanied by pogroms and attacks on the Jews in the West.

Philip's motive may have been political. His father's protection of the Jews had gone beyond what many in the realm found acceptable. In 1179 Louis had recognized the legal existence of the Jews, and at Étampes a prévôt was permitted to arrest recalcitrant Christian debtors. When the Lateran Council ruled that Jews should not have Christian servants, Louis VII had protested to Alexander III, without effect. Another protector of Jews in France, the countess of Brienne, had caused public outrage by permitting Jews to practise usury and taking action to let them recover debts: said to include allowing a Christian peasant debtor to be stripped, have a crown of thorns placed upon his head, and be put on a cross and pierced with a lance. This story does not ring true, but it demonstrates the public attitude. Louis VII had gone further along the path of tolerance than the general populace or the Church was prepared to accept.

The conventional attitude is demonstrated by both the major chroniclers of the reign. Rigord calls the Jews the eternal enemy, while William the Breton sees them as hated by God, a plague, and guilty of criminal perfidy. Their existence in such numbers in Paris was to be abhorred. Rigord, exaggerating, says they held half the city. Philip's actions against them are praised for holy zeal and holy severity. The king consulted the hermit Bernard, in the wood of Vincennes, and followed his advice. In burning ninety-nine Jews for the act against a Christian debtor in Brie, Philip had 'avenged by fire the insult done to Christ'. The anti-Semitism was fired by invented atrocities, such as the story of Jews meeting secretly in caves beneath Paris, where they sacrificed Christians on Easter Day.[22]

22. Rigord, ed. Guizot, pp. 15, 17, 21, 22; William the Breton, *Philippide*, ed. Guizot, pp. 20, 21, 22; Rigord 'Vie' in *Oeuvres*, ed. Delaborde, pp. 24–31, p. 21: 'pietate commotus', p. 24: 'inimicos', p. 28: 'perfidi Judei'; William the Breton 'Philippide', ed. Delaborde, p. 22, l. 372: 'odio Deus', p. 23, l. 407: 'sanctoque rigore', p. 37, l. 763: 'zelo pia corde comestus'; William the Breton, 'Vie', in *Oeuvres*, ed. Delaborde, p. 181.

Philip issued an edict against the Jews in 1180, which led to many arrests. Their gold, silver and clothes were confiscated, and their persons ransomed. Only those who converted to Christianity were to be relieved of the additional taxes on them. In 1182 they were expelled from the royal demesne: a date in July was named for their departure with their families, though they were allowed to sell moveable property. Philip then 'ejected all the Jews from his own towns and castles'.[23]

The short-term gain for the crown was considerable. The property of the Jews was confiscated, and synagogues taken over and sometimes converted to churches. Philip was able to gain goodwill by enriching new Christian owners at the expense of the Jews. The ransom of Jews was said to have brought in 15,000 marks. The demolition of Jewish houses allowed the making of space for the building of the covered market at Les Halles in Paris, generally seen as one of Philip's great achievements. Out of the profits from this action, Philip made gifts to such as the furriers and the drapers in Paris. The latter received £100 from the value of eighty confiscated Jewish houses. Christian debts to Jews were cancelled, except that one-fifth of the value was to be paid to the crown: so the monarch gained the general gratitude of those who escaped much of what they owed, while at the same time making a quick profit for himself. Thus Abbot Hugh of Château-Landon was quit of his debts, but paid one-fifth or £45 to the crown, it was claimed for the protection of the realm. Whatever Philip gained from the Jews, he clearly 'received an immense amount of money from French Christians', says the chronicler Giselbert of Mons. Professor Baldwin sees this as an 'enormous windfall', but the term is somewhat misleading.[24] It was no windfall, no unexpected accident, but rather the result of determined policy. It was misguided policy from the point of view of finance, since the gains were short-term only, which in time the king realized so that he recalled the Jews. Politically it was playing to the baser if widespread attitudes of the age. It cannot but diminish our modern appreciation of Philip.

23. Giselbert of Mons, p. 131.
24. Giselbert of Mons, p. 131; Baldwin, p. 52.

. . .

PHILIP OF ALSACE AND THE HAINAULT MARRIAGE

The first five years of the reign of Philip Augustus were dominated by one of the major vassals: surprisingly, perhaps, not Henry II with his vast and menacing domains, but Philip of Alsace, the count of Flanders. The count had been given a guiding role by Philip's father, and had strengthened it by removing the young king from the influence of his maternal relatives. He arranged Philip's marriage to his own niece, Isabella of Hainault. The count of Flanders' influence need not have been harmful, indeed the separation from the powerful Champagne relatives was probably a blessing, and a priority for Philip, if he were to have any independence.

Louis VII had anticipated that Philip of Alsace's role would be benign. But although in the early stages this appeared to be the case, before long the count became a major threat to Philip, whom he believed he could manipulate. An account of the events of the early years can explain how this came about. It must, however, be said from the start that the young king's part in this development was never passive.

Philip of Alsace was arguably the greatest ever count of Flanders, rated highly by many of the county's modern historians, a remarkable man with a remarkable career.[25] The English chronicler, Walter Map, thought him 'of all the princes of these days, except our own king . . . the mightiest in arms and in the art of ruling'.[26] The count's long reign began, in practice, when his father went to the Holy Land, and ended in 1191 when he himself died on crusade. He did much to develop Flanders, encouraging the growth of towns and trade, draining the maritime plain, planning links between major towns and the sea, and founding the port of Damme in 1180.

25. On Philip of Alsace, see H. van Werveke, *Een Vlaamse Graaf van Europees formaat. Filips van de Elzas* (Haarlem, 1976), and 'La contribution de la Flandre et du Hainaut à la troisième croisade', *Moyen Age*, LXXVIII, 1972; among those who praise are G.G. Dept, *Les Influences Anglaise et Française dans le comté de Flandre au début du XIIIe siècle* (Ghent and Paris, 1928) p. 21, n. 26: reign 'one of the most important which Flanders knew'; D. Nicholas, *Medieval Flanders* (Harlow, 1992) p. 71: 'probably the most remarkable ruler of medieval Flanders'.
26. Walter Map, *De Nugis Curialium*, ed. M.R. James, C.N.L. Brooke and R.A. Mynors (Oxford, 1983) p. 279; Map, *De Nugis Curialium* ed. and trans. F. Tupper and M.B. Ogle (London, 1924), p. 178.

His marriage to Elizabeth of Vermandois in 1159 brought an addition to Flemish territories, a link made firmer by the marriage of Count Philip's brother, Matthew of Boulogne, to Elizabeth's sister, Eleanor. Elizabeth inherited Vermandois, along with the Amiénois and Valois, in 1164. The details of the affair are uncertain, but it seems likely that Philip of Alsace found her out in adultery in 1175. Diceto says that the count then had her lover, Walter de Fontaines, beaten to death and his corpse hung upside down in a privy.[27] As a penalty for her conduct the count demanded direct control of her lands, which he was already governing on her behalf. It was a transaction of doubtful legality, but was confirmed by Louis VII in 1179. Flemish control over these lands added a compact bloc between the Escaut and the Marne, and brought Flemish power to within 25 miles of Paris, making the county a more potent force in French politics.

Count Philip's sister Margaret had married in 1169 to Baldwin, who became count of Hainault in 1171. Their daughter Isabella became Philip Augustus's first queen. Powerful territorially, and now a close direct relative of the new king, Philip of Flanders was a force to be reckoned with in 1180. It is not surprising that the other great vassals began to see him as a threat. One English chronicler saw him as imposing his views on the young king, claiming that he 'advised tyranny on the French people' through his iniquitous machinations.[28]

In the later part of Louis VII's reign, Philip of Alsace had played an important part in opposing Henry Plantagenet. He had supported the position of Archbishop Thomas Becket, and had become embroiled in the 1173 rebellion by the sons against Henry. This had included involvement in invasions of both England and Normandy, though both failed, the first major checks to the ambitions of Philip of Alsace. The marriage of Philip Augustus to Philip of Alsace's niece, and the role of adviser which the Flemish count assumed, inevitably provoked hostility from the young king's mother and her Champagne relatives. In 1180 Philip of Alsace was

---

27. Ralph of Diceto, I, p. 402: 'sicut dicitur, in adulterio deprehensum'.
28. *Gesta Regis Henrici Secundi*, ed. W. Stubbs, 2 vols, RS no. 49 (London, 1867) I, p. 244: 'cujus consilio tyrannidem coepit exercere in populo Gallicano; contra iniques machinationes . . . machinabatur'.

the great man, but he was not without rivals and enemies. His position was less secure than he himself believed.

The marriage of Isabella of Hainault to Philip Augustus on 28 April 1180 was a political gain for the count of Flanders, but it offered equal prospects of advantage to Philip. His intended bride was described as beautiful, she was claimed to be descended from Charlemagne, while the marriage offered closer links with Flanders which loosened those with Champagne, and the dowry which she brought was the area later to be the county of Artois. An English chronicler forecast that if Philip of Flanders died without an heir, nearly all Flanders would fall to the French crown.[29]

Philip Augustus's political shrewdness was never more tested than in the early years of his reign. He needed to protect the monarchy from the various dangers posed by a group of powerful and at times threatening magnates. He must divide them against each other, must seek alliances, but without endangering his own independence. Philip dealt with his great vassals in an adroit manner for one so young. Later he would benefit from the political lessons learned.

When Henry II showed signs of friendship with Philip, the former rivals, Flanders and Champagne, were brought together against what they saw as a threat to their own interests. They were joined by the duke of Burgundy and the count of Hainault, and encouraged by Frederick Barbarossa. The coalition moved first against the king's friend, Ralph count of Clermont. However, Henry II again attempted mediation, and such was the influence of the experienced Plantagenet ruler that he was able to bring a temporary halt to hostilities.

In 1182 trouble between France and Flanders flared again, when the count's wife, Elizabeth of Vermandois, died. Her husband claimed her lands, pointing out that both Louis VII and Philip had recognized that they should be his. Those recognitions had ignored the rights of Elizabeth's sister, Eleanor, who now voiced her claims. Philip Augustus wriggled out of the royal support previously given to Flanders. He favoured Eleanor, and made claims for himself. The count of Flanders asked tartly if the previous royal promises meant

---

29. *Gesta Regis Henrici Secundi*, I, p. 245: 'fere totum comitatum suum de Vermedais usque ad Los'.

nothing. The king's equally abrupt reply was that Louis's grant had been for a limited period, and his own confirmation meaningless because made as a child. He concluded that the normal law of inheritance should prevail, there should be no special justice for the count. Philip had reversed his initial reliance on Philip of Alsace and now gave more priority to developing his own claims than to keeping on good terms with the count. But again a reluctant peace was achieved through the intervention of Henry II. By the treaty of La Grange in 1182, Philip of Alsace was permitted to retain Vermandois and Valois for life. The Amiénois was to go to Philip, and the count would pay reparations for damage inflicted during the war.

The Plantagenets' involvement in northern politics was restricted in this period by their own problems elsewhere. The family was divided against itself, as the sons fell out with the father and with each other. In addition they had to face baronial rebellion in Aquitaine. Even so, the fact that there was no opposition to Philip from the Plantagenets in the north was of significance, allowing him to be tougher with the count of Flanders than would otherwise have been the case.

A new cause of conflict emerged when Philip of Alsace announced plans to marry Matilda, the daughter of Alfonso I of Portugal. The marriage went ahead in 1183. The count of Flanders announced that his new wife was to have lands which he knew the king of France had claimed as his own. The count of Flanders sought to protect himself against Philip by seeking aid from Frederick Barbarossa. Again Henry II was instrumental in bringing the parties to a conference, where peace was made, though it did not long endure.

In 1184 Philip Augustus, provoked by the growing hostility towards him from Philip of Alsace, made a move which angered the latter: he sought divorce from Isabella, the count's niece. The decision to end his marriage was probably political rather than personal, aimed against the count of Flanders and to a lesser extent against the count of Hainault. It was also motivated by a desire to underline his independence of the count of Flanders, as earlier he had distanced himself from his Champagne relatives. It was a move which backfired, in that it failed to achieve a divorce, but which had something of the desired effect politically.

Queen Isabèlla was only fourteen, and the marriage may not yet have been consummated. Philip called a council at Senlis in March 1184, claiming that the marriage was invalid on grounds of consanguinity. One aim, some have suggested the main aim, was to detach Isabella's father from Philip of Flanders. The move also reinforced Philip's reconciliation with his Champagne relatives, who had always opposed the marriage.

Isabella, however, was no mere puppet. She felt no guilt over her marital conduct and made public demonstration of the fact. She took off her jewelled clothes and emerged from the palace clad only in a chemise, barefoot, and carrying a candle. She distributed alms to the poor, to beggars and lepers, entering churches in the city to pray. Those who had received her gifts gathered before the palace to demonstrate their support. Philip's counsellors advised him to restore the queen, pointing out that repudiation would lead to the loss of Artois. He had offered Isabella the chance to marry again, to choose a husband for herself, but she insisted on maintaining her position as queen of France, declaring: 'it does not please God that a mortal should enter the bed in which you slept'. The king backed down and Isabella was restored.[30]

Giselbert of Mons described a meeting between father and daughter at Pontoise, at which Isabella wept, saying she was wretched because her father and husband were in conflict, with her father supporting the count of Flanders against the king.[31] The divorce threat came as a shock to the count of Hainault. He was embroiled in local disputes, notably against his vassal Jacques d'Avesnes. The father's decision in 1184 to switch his allegiance from the count of Flanders to the king is a key moment in the struggle between France and Flanders during the 1180s.

The move brought advantage to the king, but it caused problems for the count of Hainault. He now found most of the northern princes allied against him: the count of Flanders, the dukes of Brabant and Louvain, the archbishop of

30. Giselbert of Mons, pp. 152–3; G. Bordonove, *Philippe Auguste, le Conquérant* (Paris, 1986) p. 65.
31. Giselbert of Mons, p. 154.

Cologne and Jacques d'Avesnes among them. Valenciennes and Mons came under attack. Hainault's only possible salvation was aid from France, so the count appealed to Philip, and at Christmas sought out his son-in-law at Loudun.

When the crunch came in 1185, Hainault sided with France against Flanders, a crucial element in the balance. The Plantagenets were engaged in their own internal squabbles, which Philip helped to stir. Affairs were building towards a showdown. The simmering warfare in the north which had bedevilled the early years of the new reign came to a head in 1185. The count of Flanders, frustrated by royal interventions in his affairs, was not prepared to accept the restrictions and losses imposed upon him.

The count's attacks against the king's allies, and into French territory, provoked Philip Augustus into greater military activity. When the count attacked Béthisy in Valois, the king ordered a gathering of forces at Compiègne. Some 2,000 knights and 140,000 men-at-arms assembled. In the meantime the king's ally, the count of Hainault, went on the offensive in Brabant against Jacques d'Avesnes. The count of Flanders was forced to retreat as the king advanced along the Somme. The climax came at Boves, a castle taken by the Flemish from the king's supporter Ralph de Clermont. It was an important stronghold, near Amiens, where the valleys of the Somme, Avre and Noye met.

The king besieged Boves, building various engines, including a 'cat' to shelter those engaged in undermining the wall. Philip broke down the gates, and in the smoke and dust which ensued, burst into the castle. The count of Flanders knew he was beaten. Neither Henry II nor Frederick Barbarossa offered to help him, and Jacques d'Avesnes made his peace with the count of Hainault. The count of Flanders had little choice but to come humbly before the king and prostrate himself, seeking pardon. The peace of Boves was made in 1185, confirmed at Aumale in November.

Gerald of Wales says that during the peace discussions, the king withdrew for a while, chewing thoughtfully upon a hazel twig. For a bet, one of his men approached and asked what he was thinking about. Philip replied that he was wondering if God would restore France to its former glory under himself. He could well contemplate that the agreement at

Boves was a step in the right direction, his 'first great accession of territory'.[32] The count of Flanders was forced to accept the carving up of the enlarged county he had put so much effort into constructing. The promise of reversions to the king, previously offered as bribes for his co-operation, were renewed.

The treaty of Boves showed the heart of the dispute to be the lands of Elizabeth of Vermandois, now divided in three. Elizabeth's sister Eleanor was to have Valois, though Philip Augustus retained rights there; the king of France was to have the lands we know as Artois; Vermandois itself was to be divided. The count of Flanders could remain count of Vermandois for life, but the king kept the Amiénois and the county of Montdidier, together with sixty-five castles, and on Philip of Alsace's death would gain the count's share of Vermandois.

Philip of Alsace remained a significant figure till his death on the Third Crusade, but his ambitious plans had been trimmed. He had set out to be greater than any previous count of Flanders. He had won the favour of Louis VII and began the new reign as the dominant figure in the land. He arranged the marriage of Philip to his niece and elbowed the powerful Champagne connection from court. He expected aid from Henry II and Frederick Barbarossa, both with reasons to oppose the king of France. But Henry II unexpectedly sought alliance with Philip, and Frederick made promises but did little. The count of Flanders' rise had provoked much enmity: he had alienated too many relatives and friends, his sister Margaret and her husband the count of Hainault among them. In the long run, the ambitions of Philip of Alsace did more damage than good to the prospects of his county. The treaty of Aumale was not only a bar to his plans but the beginning of the county's decline as an independent power.

. . .

PHILIP AUGUSTUS AND HENRY II

The initiative of the new concord between Philip and the Angevin ruler at the start of the reign is generally seen as

32. W.H. Hutton, *Philip Augustus* (London, 1896) p. 37.

having been Henry's, but it took both to achieve the agreement. It does seem that Henry II, in his later years, underwent a change of heart towards France after his hostility to Louis VII. Henry, described by one historian as 'the old beast', should have been the lurking menace for the new king; the Angevins overshadowed the young Capetian even at his own coronation.[33] But the perpetual enemy of Louis VII became the amicable protector of his son. Perhaps the death of Louis had purged the personal aspect of the hostility between the kingdoms, for a while. Perhaps by 1180 Henry felt content with his achievements and saw no immediate threat to the more stable 'empire' he had constructed. Possibly he was tiring of conflict and saw hope of peace with a young and more amenable king of France; possibly he relished playing the elder statesman. At any rate his desire for peace looks genuine, and if the new concord eventually broke down, the fault was more Philip's than Henry's.

The key moment was the conference in June 1180 held between Gisors and Trie. There were fears on both sides that war would be renewed. One of Henry's motives for seeking peace may have been the fear that, if antagonized, Philip would prove a more energetic and difficult opponent than Louis VII. Philip's inclinations, as a boy, had been aggressive. He once said he wished Gisors was stronger and richer, so that he would benefit when he regained it.[34] Most probably Henry saw an opportunity, with the change of succession, at last to escape from the hostility which had begun with the taking of Eleanor of Aquitaine as his wife.

Henry II, more than anyone, was responsible for the king becoming reconciled to his mother Adela and her brothers after the problems at the beginning of Philip's reign, which to an extent undermined the power of Flanders. But Henry tried equally hard to keep the peace between Philip Augustus and the count of Flanders. The peace made between Louis VII and Henry II in the treaty of Ivry in 1177 was renewed with Philip at Gisors in 1180. Henry recognized Philip's lordship and promised friendship. The mutual declaration at the

33. Bordonove, p. 81: 'le vieux fauve'; Baldwin, p. 7.
34. Bautier, 'Personalité', in Bautier, p. 37; Gerald of Wales, *Opera*, ed. J.S. Brewer, 8 vols, RS no. 21 (London, 1861–91) VIII, p. 289: 'vellem quod omnes lapides illi argentei vel aurei vel etiam gemmae pretiosissimae forent'.

end of the conference was to renew on oath 'alliance and friendship', with some more difficult issues left for arbitration.[35] As we have seen, Henry II surprised the West by treating the new king in a friendly, almost fatherly manner: renewing the peace of Ivry, acting as mediator between the king and Flanders. Henry tried to sustain this position, but the growing rift between Philip Augustus and the count of Flanders in the early 1180s tested it to breaking point.

Henry's troubles with his sons over the inheritance, together with their fraternal squabbles, distracted the Plantagenets from involvement in the fight between France and Flanders, which led to the defeat of Philip of Alsace in 1185. But it was difficult for Henry to ignore the king of France's insidious alliance with whichever son was in rebellion against himself: Young Henry in 1183, Geoffrey after his brother's death. Philip also encouraged the rebels in Aquitaine.

Henry's sons had charm and ability, but they were volatile and always squabbling. Henry the Young King had charisma and was popular, but some thought him treacherous, unpredictable, even unstable. Geoffrey was widely viewed as a troublemaker and unreliable. Richard was seen as warlike, and had already proved his military ability against rebels in Aquitaine. Young Henry, with support from his brothers Richard and Geoffrey, rebelled against his father, seeking more involvement in the government of the 'empire'. But he proved unable to get the better of his father, either in the great rebellion of 1173–74 or in 1183. The situation altered with the unexpected death of the Young King on 11 June 1183. He had been on the losing end in the war, and then contracted dysentery, became feverish, and died at Martel in Gascony.

His death solved one set of problems for Henry II but caused others. Henry now reorganized his plans, intending Richard to replace Young Henry as the heir in England, Anjou and Normandy, while Geoffrey would keep Britanny; the southern lands, previously Richard's, should now go to John. It was a sound enough plan, but it did not gain the acceptance of Richard, too closely attached to Aquitaine to relinquish his grip. The death also meant that Philip must

---

35. Roger of Wendover, *Flores Historiarum*, ed. H.G. Hewlett, 3 vols, RS no. 84 (London, 1886–89) I, p. 124: 'quod foedus et amicitiam'.

reshuffle his policy. He had encouraged Young Henry's rebellions and allied with him against Henry II. Now he sought to ally with Geoffrey.

Already, here, we find Philip Augustus pursuing a policy which gave him a chance against the otherwise powerful Angevins, the policy of seeking to divide the family against itself. Most modern historians accept at face value the accounts of Philip's friendly treatment of the Angevin sons, but the way this affection switched quickly from one to the other according to circumstance suggests that he was motivated by deliberate manipulative policy rather than personal affections. Thus he encouraged Young Henry against his father and against Richard, a move which undermined the friendly policy so far pursued by Henry II. Of course it is true that the Plantagenets stood to gain from being on good terms with him: for Henry II it allowed the consolidation of the great gains already made; for his sons in rebellion against their father, it provided the most powerful ally they could hope for. The alliances were therefore often insecure and short-lived, altering with circumstances, and as a result neither side obtained entirely what they sought. But Philip proved able to hold his own in a fluid and difficult diplomatic game.

Now, on Young Henry's death, Philip turned to the older surviving sons, Geoffrey and Richard, who became the object of his attentions as he sought to turn them against their father. After the deaths of Geoffrey and Henry II, he similarly befriended John in opposition to Richard; and later still Geoffrey's son Arthur of Brittany against John. To a degree, it worked: the internal hatreds of the Plantagenets, carefully orchestrated by Philip, often played into the French king's hands.

After Young Henry's death, Philip twisted the knife by demanding the return of Gisors and the Vexin, as the dowry lands of the widow, his sister Margaret. Henry claimed the lands were his, and an integral part of Normandy, and not liable to be given up. A temporary answer was found. Philip's other sister, Alice, already at the Plantagenet court and intended as Richard's wife since 1161, would receive the lands as dowry, which Henry would then retain, paying an indemnity of £2,700 (Angevin). Thus the problem was shelved but not solved; it would fester for another twenty years.

Philip's attempts to suborn Geoffrey had some success but came to a sudden end. In 1186 Geoffrey's mercurial life reached a suitable, if tragic conclusion. Philip Augustus had brought him to court, naming him seneschal of France. Geoffrey took part in a tournament in Paris on 9 June, was unhorsed, and trampled underfoot. He survived only briefly, in a fever. Much, perhaps superficial, grief was expressed at his death, and the French king arranged a splendid funeral with a lead coffin. Bertran de Born mourned: 'lovers have lost their leader'.[36] Philip himself somewhat dramatically expressed the will to jump in the grave with his recent friend, but forebore to do so.

Richard now became the heir apparent and Philip began to play on *his* frustrations and discontent against Henry, seeking to make him the new Angevin tool of France. Richard responded to Philip's blandishments, as had his two brothers before him, and of them all proved to be the most useful ally. Philip's aggressive intent seems clear. At every opportunity he made provocative demands on Henry: the recognition of Richard's rights, the return of Margaret's dowry, the wardship of Geoffrey's heir. In 1186 near Gisors he made one of many requests for the immediate marriage of Alice to Richard. It was a request which queried Henry's honour over his treatment of Alice at his court, where she spent twenty-five years, 'shamefully shut up in a tower'.[37] Many chroniclers repeat a rumour that Henry II had shamefully seduced the girl, who was under his protection. In the end it seems that Richard also came to believe the accusation, and when travelling on crusade claimed that Henry II had fathered a bastard on her.

A further act of provocation by Philip was the building, in 1186, of a castle threateningly near to the frontier stronghold of Gisors, which he clearly coveted. Henry de Vere, Henry's castellan at Gisors, rode out one day and saw building in progress at Vaux. On enquiring, he was told that Richard de Vaux was responsible under orders from Philip. The next day Henry de Vere returned with troops, intent on

---

36. Bertran de Born, p. 353, l. 52: 'Perdut an lor capdel li drut'.
37. William the Breton, *Philippide*, ed. Guizot, p. 90; 'Philippide', ed. Delaborde, p. 89, l. 632: 'quam turre reclusam/viliter'.

destroying the new castle. Workers on the rising walls saw him coming and gave warning, so that a French force emerged to block the approach, led by the two sons of Richard de Vaux. One of them, Ralph, was killed in the skirmish which ensued. Henry de Vere, fearing the consequences of his act, fled to Richard for protection.

Two conferences in the spring of 1187 kept the truce between Henry and Philip in being for a time; but Philip repeated his demands for the marriage of Richard and Alice to take place and demanded that Brittany come under his guardianship. In the summer Philip's patience evaporated and he invaded Berry, capturing Issoudun and Fréteval. He also besieged Châteauroux, but Henry was able to relieve the castle. Both sides prepared for battle in June 1187 but drew back from the brink when papal legates intervened, which William the Breton saw as 'victory without battle' for Philip.[38] A new truce was agreed for two years, but Philip was able to persuade Richard of his father's hostility. Richard returned to Paris with Philip, who treated him attentively: 'every day they ate at the same table and from the same dish, and at night had not separate chambers'.[39]

Philip's attempts to win over Richard had only intermittent success. Richard was more torn by loyalty to his father than Young Henry had been, and was intent on holding Aquitaine against all comers, suspicious of Philip as well as of his own family. In 1187 Philip made a second foray into Angevin territory, this time along the Loire, reaching Trou, but on Richard's approach, he returned to Paris, while Richard joined Henry.

A further conference near Gisors only served to create further hostility. Traditionally conferences between the kings of France and the dukes of Normandy occurred under an old elm, standing between Gisors and Trie at a place where many roads met; Diceto says its roots were inside French territory. Its trunk was so vast that four men with their arms

38. William the Breton, *Philippide*, ed. Guizot, p. 64; 'Philippide', ed. Delaborde, p. 64, l. 627: 'sine bello victor haberi'.
39. Roger of Howden, *Chronica*, ed. W. Stubbs, 4 vols, RS no. 51 (London, 1868–71) II, p. 318: 'in una mensa ad unum catinum manducabant, et in noctibus non separabat eos lectus . . . vehementem amorem qui inter illos esse'.

outstretched could scarcely encircle it.[40] At the conference in August 1188, Henry arrived first and took the best position in the shade, while the king of France spent the whole conference in the beating sun, interpreters moving back and forth between the kings.

Henry boasted that while the tree stood, so did he, and the French would not budge him: 'when I lose this tree, I shall accept the loss of all this land'. The young Philip was a less controlled person than he became in maturity, inclined to lose his temper. When the conference concluded, unsuccessfully, the frustrated and angry Philip returned to have the great elm chopped down and burned, vowing that 'there should be no more conferences here'.[41]

Henry II, provoked into a fatal move, attacked French territory, marching on Mantes. When Philip saw the flames of Henry's destruction, he rode furiously, outstripping his own men, and Mantes was saved. During the conference which followed at Bonsmoulins, in November 1188, Philip again drove a wedge between the Angevins. He offered to return his recent conquests if Henry would proceed with the marriage of Alice and recognize Richard as his heir. Henry procrastinated and Richard bluntly demanded his father's view on the inheritance; Henry's response was silence. Richard was furious: 'now I must believe what I had always thought impossible'. He turned to Philip, dropped to his knees, and offered allegiance and homage 'for all the possessions of his father beyond the sea', as though he were already king.[42] At last Philip's manoeuvring had produced a concrete result.

By 1189 Henry II was old and ill. Now Richard ignored all attempts at reconciliation. At La Ferté-Bernard the old demands were trotted out: Alice's marriage, Richard's recognition, and now, that if Richard went on crusade, John must go too. Henry refused, suggesting maliciously that Alice should marry John instead. A papal threat against Philip,

40. Ralph of Diceto, II, p. 55: 'intra fines Franciae radicatam'; William the Breton, *Philippide*, ed. Guizot, p. 69; 'Vie', ed. Delaborde, p. 189.
41. William the Breton, *Philippide*, ed. Guizot, p. 72; 'Philippide', ed. Delaborde, p. 71, l. 169: 'Hunce cum perdidero, simul hanc volo perdere terram'; Roger of Howden, II, p. 345: 'de caetero nunquam ibi colloquia haberentur'.
42. Roger of Howden, II, p. 355: 'de omnibus tenementis patris sui transmarinis'; Luchaire in Lavisse, p. 96.

unless he made peace, cut no ice. Philip pointed out that he
was dealing with a vassal, which was an internal matter, and
'it was not the duty of the Church of Rome to punish the
kingdom of France by its sentence, or in any other manner'.
He accused the cardinal of having 'smelled the sterling coins
of the king of England'.[43]

Richard and Philip resumed the war against Henry, taking
La Ferté-Bernard. By the time he reached Le Mans, Henry
was facing disaster. His men failed to hold the bridge over
the Huisne; and when he set fire to the suburbs, the flames,
'running along the walls', caught the town itself.[44] He had
vowed never to abandon Le Mans, the city he claimed to
love above all others, where he had been born and his father
buried. But Henry was a beaten man and had to retreat,
while Richard and Philip captured his baggage and ate his
dinner. Richard could have been captured by William the
Marshal, but the great knight allowed the prince to escape.
All the same it was a victory for the allies; Le Mans was taken,
and then Tours.

Henry rested his weary body at Chinon, his empire crum-
bling around him. He forced himself on to horseback to
confront his enemies at a conference at Ballon, but it was
bravado. There was a clear sky on a hot day, but as Henry
approached, thunder rolled and a thunderbolt fell between
them. As Henry advanced again, thunder rumbled once more
so that he nearly fell from his horse. Richard harshly declared
that his father was only shamming illness; Philip, more sym-
pathetically, offered a chair. Henry refused, but was forced
in the last hours of his life to accept the most humiliating
agreement of his career, the 'discreditable peace' known as
the capitulation of Azay.[45]

All Philip's old demands were finally accepted: Alice was
to be handed over, Richard to be recognized as heir. Philip
would keep his conquests in Berry and the Auvergne, and

---

43. Roger of Howden, II, p. 363: 'quod non pertinet ad ecclesiam
    Romanam in regnum Franciae per sententiam vel alio modo
    animadvertere ... sterlingos regis Angliae olfecerat'.
44. Roger of Howden, II, p. 363: 'muros transvolans civitatem accendit'.
45. Roger of Wendover, ed. Hewlett, I, p. 158: 'pacem ... turpissimam
    facere compulsus est'; Roger of Wendover, *Flowers of History*, ed. and
    trans. J.A. Giles, 2 vols (London, 1899) II, p. 75; Luchaire in Lavisse,
    p. 100.

Henry would pay 20,000 marks compensation. His own barons agreed that if Henry failed to abide by the treaty, they would join Philip. Henry spat defiance at his son: 'I hope God will not let me die before I have had my revenge on you as you deserve', at which Richard laughed.[46]

The old king was carried away to Chinon. When he demanded to see the list of those who had deserted, the first name was that of his favourite son, John. Henry's face changed colour, and though he uttered words, none could understand them. He had presumably suffered a stroke. Of his sons, only the illegitimate Geoffrey Plantagenet remained faithful and received his father's blessing. On 6 July 1189 Henry's bed was carried to the chapel and placed before the altar, where he suffered another stroke and died. He was deserted by practically everyone. His belongings were stolen by the servants, and the corpse was left only in shirt and breeches. Henry was buried at Fontevrault. When Richard came to view the body, blood ran from his father's nose, which was taken to signify that Richard was responsible for his death.[47]

Philip had won a victory over perhaps the most impressive of all the enemies he would face. Henry II had been defeated, humiliated, and forced to grant all that Philip demanded. It was the Capetians' 'first territorial acquisition at the expense of the house of Anjou'.[48] Those who see the Third Crusade as the great turning point in Philip's career must be reminded that in his first decade as king, Philip had defeated two of the most powerful princes in the West, Philip of Alsace count of Flanders and Henry II king of England; and he had made territorial gains at the expense of both.

. . .

PARIS

The first decade of the reign saw another significant development for France, in the emergence of Paris as a capital, partly through the efforts of Philip. Within this decade he

46. Luchaire in Lavisse, p. 99; Roger of Howden, II, p. 366.
47. *Gesta Regis Henrici Secundi*, II, p. 71: 'ac si indignaretur spiritus ejus de adventu illius'; Roger of Wendover, ed. Hewlett, I, p. 160: 'confestim manavit sanguis ex naribus regis defuncti'.
48. Fawtier, p. 144.

made all the main decisions required to attain this end: it was a remarkable achievement. His father had followed no major building programme, though the growth of Paris had begun with the building of the new Notre-Dame church through the efforts of Maurice, bishop of Paris. Even this work, however, was only completed during Philip's reign. The previous period also witnessed the rise of the Parisian schools; but again the major developments occurred under Philip, with the foundation of the first college and the making of statutes for the university.

Before Philip, Paris had been a relatively small town. Rouen was more of a capital for the Angevins than was Paris for the Capetians. The king had to share lordship with the bishop and with the count of Meulan. Twelfth-century Paris could still be enclosed by its old Roman wall, repaired by Louis VI.[49] The area within was a mere 25 acres. It would not be too rash to claim that Philip achieved a transformation of Paris; and it was the first decade of the reign which saw the major changes.

The first great college of the university, the Dix-Huit, was founded in 1180. On the left bank, from the schools already existing in the abbeys of Ste-Geneviève and St-Victor grew an organized institution, with associations of masters. In 1186 a confraternity was formed for the poor scholars. It was now that the main specialisms of Paris as a centre of learning emerged: in arts and theology, as well as in canon and civil law, and medicine. It attracted great figures in the world of learning; and Peter the Chanter assumed his office in 1183. Some of our information about the reign comes from those who had been students in Paris, including Gerald of Wales and Stephen Langton. The academic community formed about 10 per cent of the city's population, with clerics predominant. By 1215 the university had been granted statutes which governed it. Paris had become 'the capital of the intellectual world'.[50]

But Philip's main task was the rebuilding and modernizing of Paris, to make it a better commercial and residential

49. Bordonove, p. 292.
50. On Peter the Chanter see J.W. Baldwin's fascinating *Masters, Princes and Merchants, the Social Views of Peter the Chanter and His Circle*, 2 vols (Princeton, 1970); the quote is M. Druon, *The History of Paris, from Caesar to St Louis* (London, 1969) p. 75.

city. He renewed the privileges of various groups of traders in the city, from watermen to butchers, and made a great improvement in commercial facilities. The fair of St-Lazare in the confined Ile-de-la-Cité was moved to the Champeaux region on the right bank, where Philip had already established a grain market. The cemetery of the Innocents in this area languished under insanitary conditions, its graves desecrated. It was used as a dumping ground for rubbish, roamed over by pigs and other animals, and was used by prostitutes for their assignations. Now the cemetery was cleaned up and enclosed with a wall in 1187.

In 1182, as part of the persecution of the Jews, their houses were confiscated and demolished to increase the space for a market. In the following year two large buildings were constructed, known as Les Halles. They were used to store cloth, and later grain, for the Saturday market, and were enclosed by a wall with gates which could be locked at night. This provided new facilities for Parisian merchants and traders, the buildings being covered for protection against the weather.

Philip's other great addition to the city interior was a personal contribution, according to his closest chroniclers. Rigord has the story of Philip strolling through the hall of his palace to stand at the window, from where he often gazed upon the city and the ships passing along the Seine.[51] Now his eyes fell upon the street before the palace, a muddy track with numerous vehicles stirring up an unbearable stench from what were virtually open sewers. As a result of his observations, he summoned the prévôt of the city and other leading citizens, and ordered that the streets of Paris be newly paved in stone. This order was probably made in 1186, and was carried out on the major streets which quartered the city and on some of the major squares. Large three foot square blocks of sandstone were used and the work took ten years to complete.

Finally, the end of this decade saw work begin on a new enclosing wall for Paris. This appears to have been not so much a decision to protect a city which had grown vastly beyond its earlier wall, as an attempt to encourage future growth. The area enclosed was tremendously increased, from 25 acres to about 625 acres. In 1190 Philip also ordered the

51. Rigord, ed. Guizot, p. 47; Rigord, ed. Delaborde, pp. 53–4.

enclosing of the right bank by a wall studded with towers and gates. There were altogether over seventy towers, one of which still stands, in the rue Étienne Marcel. The wall enclosed the new market at the Champeaux and incorporated the new castle of the Louvre with the Tour Neuve at its heart. The order took ten years to fulfil, and then work began on the left bank, enclosing Ste-Geneviève. At least one academic complained about the excessive amount of building work and its luxurious nature, but his voice was drowned in the bang and clatter of the workers.[52]

Those citizens who relied on commerce could see that the changes brought them nothing but benefit. The policy of encouraging the city to expand was a success: Paris grew into its new walls and became the largest city north of the Alps. It became 'the capital of the realm' as well as its 'greatest fortified place', with its first Hotel de Ville, a royal treasury, and archives.[53] Paris as we know it had emerged: with its lordly buildings on the Ile, its two stone bridges leading to the conglomerations on either bank, and with housing for central governmental activities. Its growing population benefited from better streets, sanitation and water supply, a thriving commercial community with improved facilities, and a prestigious university, all protected within new, massive walls.

52. Druon, p. 92; Baldwin, *Masters*, p. 66: Peter the Chanter refers to a 'superfluity of building'.
53. Baldwin, *Government*, p. 346; William the Breton, *Philippide*, ed. Guizot, p. 9, refers to the capital; 'Philippide', ed. Delaborde, p. 11, l. 100: 'Que caput est regni'; Bautier, 'Philippe Auguste et Paris', pp. 323–40, in Bautier, p. 330, on fortification.

Chapter 3

PHILIP AUGUSTUS AND THE EAST

· · ·

FRANCE AND THE CRUSADES

In order to obtain an accurate and fair picture of Philip II's place in history, one must examine his role in the crusades. On the one hand it was more significant and more considerable than is sometimes realized; on the other hand it has been distorted by a false assessment of the relative roles of Philip and Richard the Lionheart. Philip went in person only on the Third Crusade (1189–92), and was only in the Holy Land for a matter of weeks; but he made an important contribution to this crusade, one might indeed argue *the* most important contribution. This is not often realized because the sources are weighted against a fair assessment of Philip's participation. The most detailed accounts are either Anglo-Norman in bias, including the linked versions in the *Itinerarium* and the work of Ambroise; or they are written in the Holy Land and more interested in local politics.

Because the Third Crusade was the only one which involved Richard the Lionheart, it is sometimes forgotten that although Philip did not go to the East again, he and his vassals played the major role in the Fourth Crusade (1202–4), which saw the conquest of Constantinople by the West. He was also involved in the Albigensian Crusade, which began in 1209, and which we shall deal with at more length in a later chapter. Philip Augustus was certainly more concerned with the crusades than any former king of France.

And France was the western nation most concerned with the early crusades. No kings had ventured on the successful First Crusade (1096–99), which had seen the capture of

Jerusalem and the establishing of the Latin Kingdom in the East. It was in the main an enterprise led by vassals of the French crown. The leaders included the bishop of Le Puy, Hugh of Vermandois, Robert of Normandy, the Norman Sicilian Bohemond, Robert of Flanders and Raymond of Toulouse. It was Godfrey of Bouillon who emerged as the ruler of the new kingdom, and his brother Baldwin who succeeded him; both came from Lower Lorraine.

The French role in the Second Crusade (1147–49) was again arguably the main one. This was the first crusade made by kings, Conrad III the Holy Roman Emperor and Louis VII of France. Both suffered initial reverses, Conrad more disastrous than Louis, and as a result the German contribution was much diminished. The failure at Damascus was shared by the two, but Louis stayed on longer in the East, and overall gave greater assistance to the defence of the Holy Land than his colleague.

The predominance of the French in the early western settlement of the Holy Land seems clear, and French kings were sought out when the settlers needed aid against the Saracens. Louis VII had corresponded with practically every important individual in the Latin Kingdom, including Amaury the king of Jerusalem, both of the two major ecclesiastical patriarchs, and the heads of the two great military orders. France, in its modern geographical sense, was the homeland of most of the medieval colonials in the Near East. There was still a link between the Norman Sicilians and France, which they also saw as their homeland. Roger II invited Louis VII to use the island of Sicily as a base for his journey to the East, though Louis in the end made other arrangements.

In short there was a strong connection between the realm of France, with its vassal principalities, and the crusading movement in its early days: providing the bulk of the leaders, the troops, the settlers, and the rulers in the Latin Kingdom. The king of France was the natural consultant for those from the kingdom of Jerusalem who sought aid from the West.

. . .

CAUSES OF THE THIRD CRUSADE

The First Crusade had defined what the movement was to be about. From ill-defined beginnings, concerned with pilgrimage and the defence of Christendom, it had become an expedition of conquest. The result had been the formation of four principalities centred in Antioch, Edessa, Tripoli and Jerusalem, which together made up the kingdom of Jerusalem. Here an amalgam of western Christians, mostly French, ruled a mixed population. The new state protected itself with formidable fortifications and a system of military obligations, but it was never powerful enough to rest easy.

The greatest threat to the Latin Kingdom's survival was a united and hostile Islam. Divisions within the Islamic powers of the region had allowed the successes of the First Crusade and offered hope throughout the new kingdom's history. But the twelfth century saw the emergence of a stronger Islamic power. Edessa fell, and by the mid-1180s Saladin had become ruler of an enlarged Islamic state which encompassed Egypt and Syria. His new Ayyubid Empire threatened to overwhelm the Christian kingdom. Saladin's successes were aided by the decline of the major Christian power in the Middle East, Byzantium. In the 1180s the Byzantine emperors were secure neither at home nor abroad. Isaac II Angelus (1185–95) made an attempt to revive relations with the West, but himself fell foul of domestic politics, being deposed and blinded.

The Latin Kingdom itself invited Saladin's attention. It staggered from crisis to crisis, lacking manpower and cohesion. Amaury I (1162–74), even in the eyes of his own chronicler, was an unimposing king with a speech impediment and an unimpressive appearance, fat and with breasts like a woman; but at least he provided some leadership.[1] After his death, the kingdom lacked any real head at all. The thirteen-year-old Baldwin IV (1174–85) was a leper, partly paralysed, and with halting speech. His nephew, the son of Sibyl and William of Montferrat, was crowned as Baldwin V (1185–86), another child king, only eight, who died within a year. Sibyl, against her brother's wishes, had married Guy of Lusignan, who became count of Jaffa and Ascalon. Through her, Guy (1186–92) became king. As has been said: 'such

1. William of Tyre, *A History of Deeds Done Beyond the Sea*, ed. E.A. Babcock and A.C. Krey, 2 vols (New York, 1943) II, pp. 297–300; William of Tyre, *Chronicon*, ed. R.B.C. Huygens, 2 vols (Brepols, 1986) II, pp. 867–8.

were the guardians of the holy city; a leper, a child, a woman, a coward and a traitor'.[2]

King Guy has been called 'a spineless, effeminate coward', 'a fool and a dawdler', and 'devoid of political or military competence'.[3] Certainly he was unable to restrain his most dissident and aggressive vassals. Rainald of Châtillon attacked Muslim caravans in 1180 and 1186, killing innocent pilgrims returning from Mecca, while Guy himself had attacked Arabs in Damascus, though they were under royal protection. The weakness of the Christian state inevitably attracted Islamic interest, while the lords of the kingdom of Jerusalem provided more than sufficient provocation for Saladin to declare a holy war against them.

Once committed to war, Saladin acted with shrewdness and determination; he sought complete victory. He provoked the Franks into a pitched battle by besieging Tiberias, the citadel on the shore. The battle of Hattin in 1187 was a great victory for Saladin and a dreadful disaster for the Franks and the Latin Kingdom.[4] Saladin's intention was to provoke battle, and to wage it on his own terms, denying the enemy water on a burning hot day. Guy ignored advice against attempting to save Tiberias.

Only Lake Tiberias offered hope of water for the thirsty Christian army. The only choices for Guy were retreat, death from thirst, or to try and fight through to the lake. Saladin had drawn him into a trap. The Christian army brought to the point, tried to break through, and fought bravely for the most part. Count Raymond, however, escaped, or possibly was allowed to go, while Guy and Rainald were among those captured.

The disgrace was compounded by the loss of the True Cross in its gold casing, encrusted with pearls and gems. It had been carried to inspire the army; its capture was demoralizing for the Christian kingdom. 'In one moment,' writes

2. E. Gibbon, *The History of the Decline and Fall of the Roman Empire*, ed. F. Fernández-Armesto, 8 vols (London, 1989) VII, p. 329.
3. R.L. Nicholson, *Joscelyn III and the Fall of the Crusader States, 1134–99* (Leiden, 1973), p. 140, as a fool; and A. Maalouf, *The Crusades Through Arab Eyes* (London, 1984), p. 185.
4. B.Z. Kedar,'The Battle of Hattin revisited', in B.Z. Kedar, ed., *The Horns of Hattin* (Jerusalem and London, 1992), pp. 190–207. The full Arabic punctuation is used there but not here.

a Latin chronicler, 'all the glory of the kingdom of Jerusalem passed from it.'[5] The loss of fighting men was disastrous. A year later the land was still 'covered with their bones, which could be seen even from a distance, lying in heaps or scattered around'. To mark his triumph at Hattin, Saladin erected a Dome of Victory on the site.[6]

Guy's kingdom was in dire straits. City after city fell or was surrendered to the Muslims, often with hardly a blow struck, as at Sidon, Beirut and the vital seaport of Acre. Now Saladin marched on Jerusalem and vengeance was taken for the Christian capture of that city a century before. Within the year the Latin Kingdom had been reduced to a sad shadow of itself, a handful of fearful strongholds perched on the Mediterranean coast. Tyre only survived because of the arrival of the crusader, Conrad of Montferrat, who inspired the citizens to resist.

The archbishop of Tyre, Joscius, set off for the West to seek aid. The defeat at Hattin and the rapid collapse of the kingdom of Jerusalem made dramatic news in the West and was the inspiration for the Third Crusade. To save the kingdom and counter this grim situation a new crusade was called. Pope Urban III (1185–87) had drafted an appeal for a crusade, but died before it could be issued, killed by the shock of the news of Hattin.

. . .

PREPARATIONS FOR THE THIRD CRUSADE

Philip declared 'we burn with desire to aid the land of Jerusalem', but the eagerness of the crusaders in the emergency was not very apparent in their preparations.[7] Frederick Barbarossa took the cross for the second time, and despite his age, set out well before the other two western monarchs, on 11 May 1189, but he never arrived in the Holy Land. The old

5. *Arab Historians of the Crusades*, ed. F. Gabrieli, trans. E.J. Costello (London, 1969) p. 135, Imad ad-Din on limbs; p. 125, Ibn al-Athir on bones. 'Itinerarium' in K. Fenwick, ed. and trans., *The Third Crusade* (London, 1958) p. 23, on glory.
6. Kedar, pp. 191, 207; and Z. Gal, 'Saladin's Dome of Victory at the Horns of Hattin', in Kedar, *Horns of Hattin*, pp. 213–15.
7. A. Luchaire in E. Lavisse, ed., *Histoire de France depuis les Origines jusqu'à la Révolution*, III, Pt I (Paris, 1911) p. 104.

emperor bathed in the River Göksu while journeying through Asia Minor, and drowned on 10 June 1190. He was buried at Antioch. Some of the German contingent continued their journey to the Holy Land, but without Barbarossa their numbers and their part in the crusade were diminished.

In 1185 Henry II of England and Philip Augustus declared a joint tax for the crusade. The bishop of Acre had come west in 1183; in 1185 the patriarch of Jerusalem, with the masters of the two military orders, also came seeking aid. Philip and Richard the Lionheart took the cross soon after the disaster of Hattin, Richard in November 1187, Philip in January 1188, but they did not reach Acre until the summer of 1191. Richard may have been the 'first to take up the cross', but he took even longer to arrive than Philip. The remarks of ecclesiastics and poets show that the delay caused criticism at home. Bertran de Born spoke to the Franks in the East of 'two kings who are slow to help you'; it was 'the voyage that they have forgotten'.[8]

Joscius, archbishop of Tyre, arrived at a conference between Philip and Henry II in January of 1188, at Gisors, 'in a fair meadow, broad and free'.[9] After he had preached a sermon, both kings agreed to go east, as did the count of Flanders. Their followers would wear distinguishing crosses: red for France, white for England, and green for Flanders.

There were reasons for delay, some quite genuine and unavoidable, such as the need to raise money, troops and provisions; the death in 1189 of William II of Sicily, who had intended to participate, and had offered a base for the pilgrims; and the death of Philip's first queen, Isabella, in 1190. Then the death of Henry II himself in 1189 required the reorganization of the Angevin Empire under its new master, Richard I (1189–99), and inevitably caused further delays

8. 'Itinerarium', ed. Fenwick, p. 29; 'Itinerarium', in W. Stubbs, ed., *Chronicles and Memorials of the Reign of Richard I*, 2 vols, RS no. 38 (London, 1864–65) I, p. 32. H.E. Butler, *The Autobiography of Giraldus Cambrensis* (London, 1937), p. 98; Bertran de Born, *The Poems of the Troubadour Bertran de Born*, ed. W.D. Paden Jr, T. Sankovitch and P.H. Stäblein (Berkeley, CA, 1986) p. 419, l. 25: 'del passatge qu'an si mes en obli'; cf. p. 417, ll. 6, 15–6.

9. Ambroise, *The Crusade of Richard the Lionheart*, ed. and trans. M.J. Hubert and J.L. La Monte (New York, 1976) p. 34; Ambroise, *L'Estoire de la Guerre Sainte*, ed. G. Paris (Paris, 1897) col. 3, ll. 113–14: 'Co fud entre Gisorz e Trie,/En la grant bele praeirie'.

for the crusaders. A faster and sharper response, however, would have brought more immediate and perhaps more dramatic effect. As it was, Saladin had four years after Hattin in which to consolidate his position. Only when the Latin forces arrived was there need for the Muslims to treat Frankish opposition seriously. Talk about Richard's ruthless and rapid money-raising must be put in this context.

After taking the cross, Henry II issued instructions for taxation in 1188, a tenth on income and moveable property, the revolutionary Saladin Tithe, revolutionary because it was a step in the direction of income tax. The Angevin system pushed through this measure, though not without complaint, but when Philip attempted a similar tax in France, the opposition was such that he abandoned it. This partly explains Richard's relatively greater wealth during the crusade, which he exploited to demonstrate his supposed pre-eminence over Philip as well as for use against the enemy.

The first cause of delay was nothing to do with Henry II's death, it came while he was still alive. Richard attacked the count of Toulouse. There was provocation for this act, but it showed a disregard of the crusading agreement. Raymond V then appealed to Philip for aid, and the renewed warfare postponed any prospect of crusade. It would appear that both the Plantagenets and Philip put their domestic quarrel before the needs of the Holy Land. Richard then abandoned Henry to ally with Philip, as we have seen, till Henry was hounded to his dismal death at Chinon in July 1189. In one sense Henry's death hastened rather than delayed the crusade, since peace was now re-established and both rulers set about serious preparations: raising money and making arrangements for government in their absence. At least Richard, far more clearly than Henry II, was enthusiastic to crusade.

Sixteen days after Henry's death, Richard made an agreement with Philip, which included the promise to marry Philip's sister Alice. If his later reasons for not marrying her were accurate, it is odd that he could make this promise as part of the peace on which the crusade was to be based; at the least it seems insincere. But the crusading plans were genuine; detailed arrangements were made, for example that no women should accompany the crusaders except laundresses of good reputation. Richard raised money, selling

rights and offices, pressing all and sundry. Those who were
burdened with money were relieved of their encumbrance.
Had a buyer been available, he would have sold London;
'he put up for sale everything he had'.[10] At first Richard made
his brother, John, and his half brother, Geoffrey, promise to
stay out of England for three years, but then relented in the
case of John.[11] John repaid him by fostering trouble in England. In Richard's absence there would be internal war and
disruption to government.

Compared to Richard, Philip's arrangements for his realm
were more detailed and more successful. Of course, his
earlier return put less strain upon the system than Richard's
empire was to suffer. The important document of June 1190
which shows us his measures is known as his Testament.[12] It
was a practical attempt to devise power, and to place checks
where needed. The main delegation of authority was to his
mother Adela and his uncle William archbishop of Reims.
They were to be more than figureheads, but were not allowed
full monarchical power. Perhaps the most interesting delegation of power was in allowing the citizens of Paris to take
part in the government of their city, evidence of great good
sense and a forward-looking mind. Arrangements for local
government were dealt with through baillis and prévôts,
and defence by provision for walls for Paris and other major
towns.

Although Richard is generally presented as the eager crusader, it was Philip who took the lead throughout in arrang-
ing meetings and pressing for movement. It was Philip, for
example, who sent Rotrou count of Perche to England in

10. Roger of Howden, *Chronica*, ed. W. Stubbs, 4 vols, RS no. 51 (Lon-
    don, 1869–71) III, p. 13; J.T. Appleby, *England Without Richard, 1188–
    99* (London, 1965) p. 13; Richard of Devizes, *The Chronicle of Richard of
    Devizes of the Time of Richard I*, ed. and trans. J.T. Appleby (Edinburgh,
    1963), p. 9: 'si inuenissiman emptorem, Londoniam uendissem'.
11. See Appleby.
12. A. Cartellieri, *Philipp II. August, König von Frankreich*, 4 vols (Leipzig,
    1899–1922) I, pp. 100–4; Rigord, *Vie de Philippe Auguste*, ed. M. Guizot
    (Paris, 1825) pp. 86–91; Rigord, 'Vie' in *Oeuvres de Rigord et de Guillaume
    le Breton*, ed. H-F. Delaborde (Paris, 1882–85) I, pp. 100–5; J.W.
    Baldwin, *The Government of Philip Augustus* (Berkeley, CA, 1986)
    pp. 73, 101–2, calls this the 'ordinary testament'; *Recueil des Actes de
    Philippe Auguste*, ed. H-F. Delaborde, 4 vols (Paris, 1916–79) I, no. 345,
    pp. 100–5.

November 1189 to arrange the assembly at Vézelay for 1 January 1190. Philip's letter to Richard asked if he were still planning to go to Jerusalem. The meeting was postponed to April and later to July. The eagerness of Richard to crusade has sometimes been exaggerated; it was important that he settle his lands satisfactorily before he could envisage leaving. As earlier, the French contribution was central to this crusade. Richard was but one, albeit the most powerful, of the vassals of the king of France. Indeed only one of the peers of France remained at home during the crusade, Raymond of Toulouse, the recent victim of Richard's aggression. The poet Conon thought that 'all good men will be on the pilgrimage'.[13] On 24 June 1190 Philip received his pilgrim staff and scrip, and the oriflamme, from William archbishop of Reims at St-Denis. It remained to finalize the arrangements for provisions and travel. Philip organized the taking of grain, vegetables, meat, biscuit, wine, horses, arms, silver and gold.

. . .

THE JOURNEY TO THE HOLY LAND

On 2 July 1190 the two kings finally met at Vézelay, in the hills, where vineyards flourished on the slopes.[14] Barbarossa had gone long before them and was already dead. The normal journey to the East by sea should have taken weeks or months, but again there were inordinate delays. Richard in particular made a very leisurely journey and was on occasions urged by Philip to speed up. As it happened, in the end, Acre was saved and with it the Latin Kingdom in reduced form, but the time lapse before the westerners' arrival could easily have resulted in all being lost. Only the arrival, well before the two kings, of Conrad of Montferrat and large parts of Philip's forces, saved the day.

Those who arrived before the kings were mainly contingents from the French realm, including the counts of Flanders, Bar, Dreux, Clermont, Blois, Champagne and Sancerre, together with Jacques d'Avesnes and the bishop of Beauvais.

---

13. J. Prawer, *The Latin Kingdom of Jerusalem* (London, 1972) p. 110.
14. Ambroise, ed. Hubert and La Monte, p. 43; Ambroise, ed. Paris, col. 10, l. 347: 'A Verzelay en la montaigne'.

Some of the Angevin forces also arrived early, but their main party journeyed with Richard himself. The French on the other hand mostly travelled in their own smaller groups, and Philip was accompanied only by a royal party.

From Vézelay the two kings set out on 4 July 1190, along opposite sides of the river. According to Ambroise, 'when roses were with fragrance filled, the time was ready', and off they set, to be met along the way by 'youths and maids and wives and vassals with water for the pilgrims'. The armies travelled separately, but kept contact. At Lyons, where 'the Rhône's water swelled and tossed', there was a crisis, when a wooden span of the bridge broke.[15] The kings had already crossed, but a hundred men fell in and two drowned.

Thereafter the kings parted again to make their own sea trips: Philip heading for Italy over the Alpine foothills, and Richard going to Marseilles. They planned to meet again in Sicily. Philip travelled to Genoa, where he paid for the passage of 650 knights and 1,300 squires, together with provision of food and fodder for eight months and wine for four months. He was joined again for a while by Richard, whose fleet had failed to turn up on time. Philip requested the loan of five galleys, Richard offered three, which the French king refused. It was the first sign of tension in their personal relations during the journey. His greater wealth and his possession of a fleet was flaunted by the Lionheart, and galling to Philip.

Throughout the journey, Philip made better time than Richard despite being ill on the way, arriving in Sicily on 16 September, with Richard making his appearance six days later. The Norman kingdom was in some turmoil in 1190. After the death of William II, his cousin Tancred count of Lecce had seized the throne. King Tancred (1189–94) faced internal rivals, a Muslim rebellion, and the threat of invasion by the new emperor, Henry VI (1190–97), who had married William II's sister Constance, hoping that this would bring him the succession to Sicily. Tancred, however, did

15. Ambroise, ed. Hubert and La Monte, pp. 41, 44, 45; Ambroise, ed. Paris, col. 8, ll. 277–9: 'Quant la rose suef oleit,/Li termes vint que Deus voleit/Que li pelerin s'esmeusent'; col. 11, ll. 387–90: 'Vallez e dames e puceles/Od biaus pichiers e od orceles/ . . . as pelerins'; col. 12, l. 413–14: 'Sor le Rogne/l'eve crestee'; and col. 13 for account of bridge.

have local support and had managed to repel Henry VI's invasion in 1191. William II had planned to participate in the crusade and had offered Sicily as a launching base. Dying, he had left a legacy to his father-in-law, Henry II of England. Tancred was less committed to the crusade than his predecessor, but was prepared to give some assistance. His own domestic security, however, was bound to take priority in his considerations.

Throughout the journey there is a stark contrast in the attitudes of Philip and Richard to their various hosts. Philip came quietly into Sicily in a single ship, prepared to accept the status quo, not keen to antagonize either Tancred or Henry VI the German emperor who was seeking control of Sicily. Philip faced a storm in the Straits of Messina, so that his food, wine and possessions had to be thrown overboard, but he arrived safely. The citizens rejoiced to see him and he was received with hospitality and housed in the palace.

Richard arrived with more pomp and show, and at once acted aggressively, demanding payment of his father's legacy and the return of his sister's dowry. He was placed in an official's house in the suburbs. The very nature of his arrival caused complaint from the Greeks and Lombards, who thought he acted as a conqueror rather than a visitor. The show of splendour was deliberate, and it provoked jealousy as well as fear. Richard was soon involved in local quarrels. Philip attempted mediation, but was accused of trying to use Tancred against Richard. The growing personal differences of the western kings turned what should have been a short and friendly stop into a prolonged conflict. Tancred went so far as to offer a marriage arrangement with Philip between their respective offspring, which Philip tactfully turned down.

Richard acted with his usual promptness and aggression. He was the master, and he would let all and sundry know it. He attacked those who offered any opposition or snub, capturing the Calabrian town of Bagnara, and seizing an island off Messina with its monastery in order to secure his stores. Monks who resisted were tortured to death. Near Messina he beat a man with the flat of a sword for trying to recover his own falcon from the king, till the sword broke. Outside Messina, 'a fine and fair town', he proceeded to build a siege tower, called Mategriffon, or 'Stop the Greeks', a clear sign of his attitude to the citizens, whom he referred to as 'vile and effeminate'. A gallows was erected and used for Messinese dissidents.

Angevin troops, taking their cue from Richard, showed contempt for the locals, and in turn received most of their abuse. Ambroise said they 'did heap upon our pilgrims scorn, fingers and eyes they mocked us with'.[16] The citizens taunted and attacked tailed Englishmen, some of whom they threw into privies. One English soldier quarrelled with a woman called Emma over the price of her loaves. When he struck her, the locals attacked and beat him, tearing his hair and trampling on him, leaving him for dead.

A conference was called between local officials and the kings on the next day, 4 October, but while it was taking place, there were disturbances involving the English. Despite Philip's expressed preference for caution, Richard at once took to arms and stormed Messina in which they were both guests. The citizens sought Philip's aid, and he did stop Richard's ships from landing. But though Philip disapproved of Richard's actions, he was not prepared to fight against his fellow crusader. Richard took Messina in less time than it took a priest to say matins, and sacked it. Women were seized and ill treated. Philip protested when Richard placed only his own standards on the walls. Richard backed down and they shared control of the town.

The tensions between the rulers in Sicily is of considerable interest for the fate of their crusade. Their personal relationship had clearly deteriorated, but not irretrievably. Richard was more aggressive to the locals, Philip more cautious; each distrusted the other's dealings with Tancred. But they both had enough sense to know that the crusade needed the efforts of both. They backed down from any final confrontation: Philip accepted Richard's acts, Richard yielded to Philip's demand for equal rewards for an action which had been his alone.

Tancred was forced to make an agreement, promising the payments Richard demanded, and incorporating a marriage

---

16. Ambroise, ed. Hubert and La Monte, pp. 48, 50; Ambroise, ed. Paris, col. 15, l. 513; col. 16, ll. 553–4: 'Lor deiz es oilz nos aportouent/E chiens pudneis nus apelouent'; P. Henderson, *Richard Coeur de Lion* (NY, 1958) p. 97.

for his daughter to Richard's nephew Arthur of Brittany, in which Richard recognized Arthur as his heir, disinheriting John. Philip demanded his share in Richard's gains. Richard and the English were annoyed because the French had stood aside in the fighting, and because Tancred claimed that Philip had been intriguing against Richard, apparently advising Tancred to stand up to Richard more. But a new settlement was made, and Richard gave Philip a third of his profit. Philip claimed that by prior agreement it ought to be half, but Richard reasonably argued that part was his sister's dowry. At any rate peace was restored, Philip declaring: 'let us end the business without quarrel'.[17] New regulations were issued for all the crusaders, concerning such matters as discipline and provisions, limiting prices, gambling and opportunities for quarrels.

Philip must have been exasperated when Richard caused yet another incident, this time with one of Philip's leading vassals, William des Barres. William was a courageous knight, 'strong as an iron bar', and seemingly a better horseman than Richard, which the king could not tolerate.[18] There was a previous history of hostility, since William had fought against Richard in the wars in southern France in 1188–89, and had once broken his parole, escaping on a page boy's runcey. But Richard's behaviour now was little short of childish.

The crusaders had been delayed in Sicily until better weather returned in the spring, and overcame their boredom by engaging in 'friendly' tournaments, using canes instead of lances. In one such conflict, William des Barres consistently bettered Richard, broke his opponent's cane and resisted the king's charges, until the infuriated Richard vowed eternal enmity, demanding that William give up the crusade: 'get thee hence and take care not to appear before me ever again'. Even when Philip intervened for William, Richard was

17. William the Breton, *Le Philippide, Poème,* ed. M. Guizot (Paris, 1825) p. 103; 'Philippide' in *Oeuvres,* ed. Delaborde, SHF, vols 210, 224 (Paris, 1882–85) I, p. 102, l. 144.
18. On Barres, *Gesta Regis Henrici Secundi,* ed. W. Stubbs, 2 vols, RS no. 49 (London, 1867) II, p. 46: 'super unum runcinum pueri sui evasit'; Roger of Howden, III, pp. 88, 93–4: 'Fuge hinc, et cave tibi ne amplius coram me compareas'; T.A. Archer, *The Crusade of Richard I, 1189–92* (London, 1888) p. 43; William the Breton, *Philippide,* ed. Guizot, p. 86.

adamant. William was sent away, though in the end he returned unobtrusively, and in the Holy Land earned Richard's forgiveness by his valour during the crusade. Richard had that determination always to be the victor which could not be controlled, even in such minor matters.

Richard's provocations were not over. He had saved till this moment to reveal his marriage plans. It has been argued that he was justified: that his father had abused his intended wife, Alice of France, Philip's sister; and that his new wife, Berengaria of Navarre, brought a valuable alliance which helped to protect his interests in southern France.[19] All very well, but why had he not resolved this before? It is probably correct that plans for the new marriage had been afoot for some time. Richard had deceived Philip into believing that he still intended to marry Alice. Now he denounced his father, Henry II: 'I am unwilling to make her my wife, because my father knew her, having a son by her', something he had presumably been aware of for some time, since his father had been dead for well over a year. Richard could hardly be surprised, when he so belatedly revealed his plans, if Philip was exasperated. If relations between the kings on the crusade were not at their best, Richard's conduct in Sicily must bear some of the blame.

Philip was annoyed, but was able to hide his feelings and seek a good deal.[20] There must have been a degree of relief that the long dilemma of Alice's marriage to Richard was finally finished. Philip swallowed his anger and pride and agreed, in return for Alice's dowry, to accept Richard's new marriage. Richard promised 10,000 marks, payable in Normandy, that is after the crusade. In later wrangling, Richard's envoys to the pope contradicted themselves over these events, suggesting a certain amount of embarrassment over their position.[21]

The personal hostility of the kings was growing. The author of the *Itinerarium* believes that at Messina Philip 'conceived

19. J. Gillingham, *Richard the Lionheart*, 2nd edn (London, 1989) pp. 163, 220.
20. Baldwin, p. 78; see Rigord, ed. Guizot, p. 94; Rigord, ed. Delaborde, pp. 107–8; William the Breton, 'Vie', in *Oeuvres*, ed. Delaborde, p. 191: 'Philippe mediante' between Richard and Tancred.
21. *Selected Letters of Pope Innocent III concerning England (1198–1216)*, ed. C.R. Cheney and W.H. Semple (Edinburgh, 1953) p. 7.

that hatred against King Richard which lasted during his life, and afterwards led him to the invasion of Normandy'.[22] But although Philip had reason to resent Richard's behaviour, he still showed some consideration for Richard, and insisted on waiting for him to arrive in the Holy Land before making the assault on Acre. Probably the hostility between the two kings took root in this period, but its full growth lay ahead. Again Philip was the first to move on. He left Sicily on 30 March 1191 heading directly for Acre. He had attempted to depart the previous autumn, but was driven back by the weather. Sailing during the winter was avoided because of the perils of bad conditions; suitable winds did not return until spring. Before going, Philip reminded Richard that he ought to keep his oath and sail with him as his liegeman.

Philip sailed past Paros, Crete and Cyprus to Acre. Richard welcomed Berengaria and Eleanor at Reggio in Calabria, and returned with them to Messina. When he sailed on 10 April, it was with Berengaria and his sister Joan. His journey still had the feel of a Mediterranean cruise, visiting Crete and Rhodes before going on to Cyprus. It was not all pleasant though, he spent ten days in Rhodes because of illness. Possibly this was the first sign of the illness which would lay him low at Acre, and explains at least a period of the delay before his arrival in the Holy Land. Philip arrived in Tyre, and was at Acre by 20 April, before Richard had even reached Rhodes.

Richard left Sicily on 10 April 1191. His attack on Cyprus is an important part of the crusade, but it seems to have come about by accident rather than design. The events in Cyprus were probably precipitated by the weather rather than by long-term planning. A storm drove part of Richard's fleet to Cyprus. The ship bearing his sister and Berengaria hove to off Cyprus and the ladies were in danger of capture. Richard followed them and harried the Byzantine pretender, Isaac Dukas Comnenus, who had declared himself emperor in the island in 1184. Richard demanded the release of the prisoners.

22. 'Itinerarium', ed. Fenwick, p. 36; 'Itinerarium', ed. Stubbs, p. 163: 'Rex Ricardus ... occupaverat Messanam, quam quilibet presbyter cantasset matutinas'.

In Cyprus Richard married Berengaria of Navarre, a girl 'more prudent than beautiful'.[23] Isaac did homage to Richard, but soon fled fearing how Richard would treat him. He eventually surrendered on condition that he would not be put in irons; Richard agreed and then fettered him in silver chains. Isaac was imprisoned, and died in 1195. The capture of Cyprus was one of the enduring achievements of the crusade. At long last Richard headed for Palestine.[24]

. . .

PHILIP IN THE HOLY LAND

Philip arrived in Acre on 20 April 1191 and was immediately recognized as the leading figure by the Christians there. Some have chosen to emphasize his quiet arrival and suggest he was therefore a lesser figure than Richard, but he had no need of pomp, and the reason he had only half a dozen ships was that most of his forces had arrived before him. The group with Philip was his demesne force. A French chronicler says he was 'lord of all the host', and Arab sources saw him as 'a great and honoured ruler, one of their mightiest princes, whom all the armies obeyed'; he 'assumed supreme command'. Again, however, Philip's position was put in the shade by Richard's more showy arrival. Some realized that Richard's 'kingdom and standing were inferior to those of the French king', but most were impressed by the confidence and wealth of the Angevin.[25]

Philip went first to Tyre and struck up a good relationship with Conrad of Montferrat. Conrad inherited the family principality of Montferrat in Italy in 1188. As a crusader, he arrived at Tyre when Saladin was mopping up the cities of the kingdom after his triumph at Hattin. Conrad's forceful

23. Richard of Devizes, p. 25: 'puella prudentiore quam pulcra'.
24. Ambroise, ed. Hubert and La Monte, p. 106: 'the king then had him held/In bonds of silver'; Ambroise, ed. Paris, col. 55, ll. 2044–6: 'Qu'en fers n'en liens nel meist:/Ne il nel fist, por cri de gent,/Ainz le mist en boies d'argent'. 'Itinerarium', ed. Fenwick, pp. 55–6; 'Itinerarium', ed. Stubbs, p. 203: 'non in ferrea, sed in vincula conjecit argentea'; in *Gesta Regis Henrici Secundi*, II, p. 167, the manacles are 'de auro et argento'; Rigord, ed. Guizot, p. 93; Rigord, ed. Delaborde, p. 108.
25. Philip Mouskes, *Chronique rimée*, ed. Baron de Reiffenberg, 2 vols (Brussels, 1836, 1838) p. 276: 'signior de toute l'ost'; Baha ad-Din in Gabrieli, pp. 212–13.

personality revived the resistance of Tyre and galvanized the kingdom into some sort of defence. Many now thought him the best hope to lead the kingdom. Conrad saw the need to take Acre and believed it was possible with western aid; he took Philip on with him to the siege.

Acre was an impressive and useful port, at the north end of a curving bay, possessing excellent fortification and a harbour chained against naval attack. The character of the long siege changed immediately. Guy's first attempts had seemed like a forlorn hope, his forces inadequate for the task; now there was hope of a conclusion. Philip and his men joined a camp which contained 'the flower of all the world'.[26]

Guy had besieged Acre with few men and apparently little hope of success, but his force clung on, gradually increasing in numbers, and became the rallying point for the ailing kingdom of Jerusalem. Conrad of Montferrat was becoming recognized as a natural leader, having married Guy's sister-in-law, Isabel, which gave him some claim to the kingdom. Guy's siege of Acre would have collapsed had not Conrad swallowed his pride and joined forces with him. Hope was fuelled by the gradual arrival of magnates and troops from the West; the remnants of Barbarossa's German force; some English and more French groups.

Philip's arrival marked the transition to expectation of Christian success. The king set about preparing for attack. He rode round the whole city of Acre 'to see from what part it might most easily be taken'.[27] He built throwing engines, hoardings and belfries, organized a mine, and completed the blockade. The new engines included 'The Evil Neighbour' and 'The Cat'; from common funds was built 'God's Own Sling', probably a trebuchet. The French filled the moat in preparation for an attempt at storming the stronghold.

At last the citizens within Acre began to realize their predicament. It was true that Saladin had countered the Frankish siege by bringing forces into the area; but he had been unable to remove Guy, and for all his efforts he had not been able to break the siege. Supplies which had been sent in while the blockade was incomplete now began to dwindle.

---

26. Ambroise, ed. Hubert and La Monte, p. 115; Ambroise, ed. Paris, col. 62, l. 2313: 'E la flur de la gent del monde'.
27. Eracles, in Archer, p. 55.

The besiegers themselves were suffering; the bishop of Salisbury flogged some for cannibalism, though lightly because hunger had driven them to it. If the Christian besiegers were dying from hunger, the Muslims inside were dying from thirst. They knew the rules of siege warfare; if they struggled on to the end and their city was taken by storm, their property and their lives were forfeit; surrender offered better chances.

Philip made ready for attack. Honourably he waited, as he had promised, for the arrival of Richard, so that they could lead the attack together. Whatever the tensions of the journey, as yet they could still work together for the great Christian aim of the crusade. As the weeks passed, while Richard delayed in Cyprus, Philip became increasingly impatient. He sent further messages rebuking Richard in words that Ambroise preferred not to record. The *Itinerarium* says that Philip accused Richard of 'neglecting necessary matters, and expending his endeavours on vain duties, and was presumptuously persecuting innocent Christians'. The chronicler thought Richard's response not suitable to repeat either.[28]

Richard was engaging in local political manoeuvres. Guy and his friends, worried about the rise of Conrad, had gone to Richard in Cyprus seeking 'advice and assistance', and helped Richard to subject the island.[29] Unwisely, the Lionheart gave his backing to Guy to rule the kingdom of Jerusalem. It could be argued that Richard, as an anointed king, was well advised to support a fellow monarch. But his decision fostered new divisions in the kingdom and delayed the unity which might have come under Conrad. It is clear that a majority of the local magnates preferred the solid virtues of Conrad to the chivalrous but weak Guy. Conrad was taken into Philip's circle as a *familiaris* and counsellor. Richard's support propped up Guy for longer than he would otherwise have survived. Guy's trip to Cyprus, incidentally, makes it quite clear that Philip rather than he was now in command of the siege of Acre. Philip settled down

28. Ambroise, ed. Hubert and La Monte, p. 100; Ambroise, ed. Paris, col. 51, l. 1893: 'E i ot tels paroles dites/Qui ne deivent pas estre escrites'. 'Itinerarium', ed. Fenwick, p. 53; 'Itinerarium', ed. Stubbs, p. 200.
29. 'Itinerarium', ed. Fenwick, p. 51: 'Itinerarium', ed. Stubbs, p. 195: 'petiturus consilium et auxilium'.

to the business in hand, but found leisure time for hawking. One day his large white falcon flew into the city; when Philip offered 1,000 dinars to ransom it, he was rather meanly refused.

In the view of one chronicler, Philip could 'have taken the city of Acre had he wished, but he waited for the coming of the king of England'. When Richard arrived the walls had already been broken in places: 'manfully through combat by King Philip and the French'.[30] Even after his arrival on 8 June, the English king seemed unwilling for a speedy attack. Philip also became suspicious over private negotiations between Richard and Saladin's brother, Safadin.

The provocative behaviour of Richard in Sicily was continued in the Holy Land. Philip had offered three gold pieces a month for men to serve him, which was considered a good payment. Richard immediately offered four, deliberately poaching men from Philip and again flaunting his greater wealth. He was intent on outshining Philip. Later both Philip and the pope accused him of seducing knights and kinsmen from the French king. And then Richard fell ill again.

Philip decided that the attack must go ahead now without further delay, and began the assault. A second attack followed three days later. Richard refused to participate. Acre came within an ace of falling on 3 July, without Richard's aid. The defenders made a racket to attract help from Saladin, while protecting themselves against Philip's engines by using Greek Fire, which destroyed them.

Then Philip yielded apparently to the same illness from which Richard was suffering. The French king recovered first and was able to rebuild his damaged engines. But probably, like Richard, he only appeared to recover for a time, before succumbing once more to the disease. Many others were also ill, and many died, including the count of Flanders. Philip had himself carried out under a shelter, to shoot against the Turks, discharging bolts from his crossbow, in advance of Richard doing the same.

The French miners succeeded in bringing down the wall and provided the opportunity for a storm attempt. The

---

30. Eracles in Archer, p. 55; William the Breton, *Philippide*, ed. Guizot, p. 206; William the Breton, 'Vie', ed. Delaborde, p. 192: 'muros civitatis jam fractos et viriliter a Philippo rege et Francis expugnato'.

heralds were told to announce an attack. The French gained
the walls but were repulsed. Their marshal, Aubrey Clément,
declared: 'This day I will perish, or if it please God, I will
enter the city of Acre.'[31] It did not please God; the ladder
he had climbed broke behind him from the weight of numbers and he was stranded on the wall, fighting bravely until
he was killed.

The city offered to surrender on terms the next day,
but Richard refused to allow it, as indeed did Saladin. The
rebuilt 'Evil Neighbour' broke part of the wall and shook to
its foundations the Accursed Tower, in which Judas was said
to have betrayed Christ for his pieces of silver. In a later
attack, after it had been mined by the French, the wall of the
tower collapsed with a roar. An English attack on 11 July also
came near to success before being held off. Some Saracens
in their distress threw themselves from the walls, and on 12
July the besieged finally surrendered on terms.

An agreement allowed the inhabitants of Acre their lives;
in return they promised to return the True Cross captured
at Hattin, to release the Frankish prisoners, and to pay a
ransom of 200,000 dinars within forty days. Unfortunately
for them the promise required Saladin's approval. The latter
had tried to stiffen resistance and had forbidden surrender,
but communication with the Muslims within the city proved
difficult, and Saladin had been unable to render sufficient
aid to save the city. When the message reached him: 'we can
do nothing but surrender', he sent a swimmer to forbid
it, but too late. The Frankish banners were already on the
walls.[32] In the end, reluctantly, Saladin resigned himself to
acceptance of the surrender, but still baulked at some of the
terms. Certainly he was slow to fulfil them.

The crusaders entered the city. Philip took over the palace, Richard the house of the Templars. It was Richard who
denounced Leopold of Austria for placing his own standard
on the walls. Richard was annoyed because Leopold received
better accommodation than himself.[33] He insulted Leopold
by having his standard thrown in the mud and trampled

---

31. 'Itinerarium', ed. Fenwick, p. 65; 'Itinerarium', ed. Stubbs, p. 223:
    'Aut hodie moriar, aut in Achon, Deo volente ingrediar'.
32. Baha ad-Din in Gabrieli, p. 217.
33. Mouskes, p. 282, l. 19717: 'le millor ostel'.

upon. Richard had made another enemy, one he would live
to regret.

On 28 July agreement was made over the division of Acre
and the kingdom. Prisoners and ransoms were to be shared
between the kings. Only Richard's support saved Guy from
oblivion: Philip and the kingdom's magnates all preferred
Conrad, 'the more capable and viable candidate'. Richard
and Philip had a fierce quarrel over their candidates. It has
been said with some justice that Philip 'showed greater political acumen in supporting the marquis than did Richard
in assisting Guy'.[34] Through Richard's insistence a compromise was reached: Guy was to have the kingdom of Jerusalem
for life, but on his death it would pass to Conrad. The rents
of the kingdom were to be shared between them. Guy was
to hold the south, with Jaffa, Caesarea and Ascalon; Conrad the north, including Tyre, Sidon and Beirut. There was
also the question of the fate of Cyprus. Philip claimed half
of it, according to their previous agreement over sharing
conquests. Richard, who had brought about that conquest
without any aid from Philip, refused, and responded by
demanding half of Flanders, whose count had recently died,
a claim which had even less justice. The personal hostility
between the kings, which had raised its head in Sicily, had
reappeared in the Holy Land.

. . .

PHILIP'S RETURN

With Acre taken, Philip turned his mind to home. He had
been very ill, and probably still was, though his illness had
not been allowed to hold up the siege. The two kings seemingly suffered from the same disease, referred to as leonardie
or arnoldia, thought to be trench-mouth, otherwise Vincent's
disease, or perhaps scurvy. Philip had a strong fever, which
caused him to tremble. The disease caused the hair and nails
to fall out, the body to swell, lips to become sore, and skin
to peel off in strips. Both kings insisted on fighting from
their sickbeds, shooting crossbows from under protective
cover. How far either had recovered by the end of July is

34. Baldwin, p. 79; Ambroise, ed. Hubert and La Monte, p. 26.

not certain. Richard had succumbed first, so it is probable that Philip's given reason for return, of continuing illness, was accurate, though Ambroise claimed: 'that malady is an excuse'. Philip's chronicler says that his illness was so violent that poison was suspected, and it seems probable that the French king was again genuinely and seriously ill.[35] Philip also had fears for the health of his only son, Louis. The latter had been ill in Paris, but recovered. Philip's fears, while he was himself ill, had been fostered by a report stemming from Richard that the boy was dead. Runciman sees this as possibly 'a piece of heavy buffoonery', but the *Estoire* thought it an attempt to kill Philip.[36] It is difficult to give much credence to the tale, but it says something of how Richard's character was viewed.

Philip had good cause to think he was needed in France. The prolonged absence of a monarch was always harmful to a state in this period. The king was the head of government, and for all the careful arrangements he had made, Philip knew there was no substitute for his own presence. If his only legitimate son should die, it would cause serious problems.

There was also the question of the future of Flanders. The careful claims Philip had previously made, and the agreements to end the conflict with the count, could now reach fruition after the death of Count Philip at Acre on 1 June 1191. Philip had vital interests in the succession to Flanders, which Cartellieri sees as his main motive for a speedy return.[37] In the end Philip gained Artois, the Amiénois, Vermandois and much of Beauvais; he could not have achieved this by remaining in the East and neglecting home affairs.

Arrangements needed to be made urgently for much of France, and the king needed to supervise them in person. Several other magnates had died during the crusade, including Theobald of Blois, Henry of Troyes, Stephen of Sancerre, and the counts of Vendôme, Clermont and Perche.

35. Ambroise, ed. Hubert and La Monte, p. 219; Ambroise, ed. Paris, col. 140, ll. 5259–61. 'Itinerarium', ed. Fenwick, p. 73 also has 'alleged sickness'; 'Itinerarium', ed. Stubbs, pp. 236–37; William the Breton, *Philippide*, ed. Guizot, p. 108; 'Philippide', ed. Delaborde, pp. 106–7, l. 269; William the Breton, 'Vie', ed. Delaborde, p. 193.
36. S. Runciman, *A History of the Crusades*, 3 vols (Cambridge, 1954) III, p. 52 and n. 1; Archer, p. 116; *Estoire*, II, pp. 179–81.
37. Cartellieri, II, pp. 240–4.

As Baldwin puts it: Philip 'had left the major barons of his father's generation buried in the Syrian sands'.[38] Others, including Henry of Champagne, stayed on in the East; as did Hugh of Burgundy, who would shortly be added to the list of those who died there.

If Philip was unwilling to continue the crusade, it is hardly surprising. Richard had been difficult to work with. One chronicler thought the two kings 'like their fathers, regarded each other with mistrust under the veil of friendship'.[39] After Philip's departure, Richard would quarrel with almost all the major figures to whom he was allied, including Hugh of Burgundy and Conrad of Montferrat. Richard had consistently sought to belittle Philip, provoking hostility over his marriage, over William des Barres, over the attack on Messina and aggression to the people of Sicily, over buying support from Philip's men at Acre. Richard, unlike Philip, had taken little note of the papal instructions for suitable conduct during the crusade, which included the wearing of only modest dress and not seeking after vainglory. Wendover suggests that Philip's departure followed 'a secret disagreement', apparently over Conrad.[40]

There were strong rumours that Richard intended Philip harm, and given the manner of Conrad's death it is not certain they were without foundation. Richard was again privately negotiating with the Saracens. Conrad was murdered by Assassins sent by the Old Man of the Mountain, the leader of the Shi'ite sect whose name came from their use of hashish and who believed in murder to accomplish their political and religious aims. It was said by many, including the bishop of Beauvais, that Richard had been responsible, and that is still accepted by some historians.[41] Philip received a letter to the effect that Richard was planning a similar fate for himself, and that four Assassins were pursuing him. The threat

38. Baldwin, p. 80.
39. 'Itinerarium', ed. Fenwick, p. 74; 'Itinerarium', ed. Stubbs, p. 238.
40. Roger of Wendover, *Flowers of History*, ed. and trans. J.A. Giles, 2 vols (London, 1899) II, p. 106; Roger of Wendover, *Chronicon sive Flores Historiarum*, ed. H.O. Coxe, EHS, 5 vols (1841–44) III, p. 43: 'occulta dissensio'.
41. A. Maalouf, p. 213; Ambroise, ed. Hubert and La Monte, p. 338: 'They said Richard had brought about/The murder of the marquis'; Ambroise, ed. Paris, col. 238, ll. 8885–92.

was taken seriously, and for a time Philip was guarded night and day, but after investigation he decided the information was false.

Philip had played a significant role in the crusade. Even an English chronicler believes 'he had worked well at the siege, spent money, and given good help, so that he was rightly deemed the most powerful of Christian kings'.[42] Under his command the city of Acre had been tightly blockaded and taken, the main achievement of the crusade. Some Anglo-Norman chroniclers reviled Philip for returning before completing the pilgrimage to Jerusalem. Perhaps the main aim of the crusade was the recapture of Jerusalem, but even after much further effort and loss, that was not to be achieved. Philip had played a major role in the main effort of the crusade, at Acre. French historians have seen this, and believe Philip 'fought valiantly in the East', but his part has been consistently undervalued by English historians, who attribute any success the crusade had to Richard. The recent and generally well received biography of Richard by Professor Gillingham considers that Philip 'made little impact on the state of the siege [of Acre]', and 'his crusading record remained a permanent slur upon his reputation'.[43] But Richard had been ill through almost the whole period between his arrival and the fall of the city, whereas Philip had played a longer and more active role in those events.

Philip left his share of Acre in the hands of Conrad, a wise move given Richard's subsequent actions. He also left the bulk of his forces to remain in the Holy Land under Hugh of Burgundy, who played a major, though often ignored, role in the rest of the crusade. Philip also left 100 knights and 500 sergeants for the use of Raymond of Antioch. He left to the duke of Burgundy gold and silver, 5,000 marks, and his rights in the prisoners. This share in the ransom money should have contributed sufficiently to the upkeep of the remaining French.

42. W.H. Hutton, *Philip Augustus* (London, 1896) p. 51.
43. Ambroise, ed. Hubert and La Monte, p. 219; Roger of Howden, p. 221, letter from Richard about Philip who 'abandoned the purpose of his pilgrimage, and broke his vow'. French historians, e.g. G. Duby, *France in the Middle Ages, 987–1460*, trans. J. Vale (Oxford, 1991) p. 212. English historians, e.g. Gillingham, p. 173: pp. 180–1.

Richard pressed Philip to swear to remain for three years, but Philip saw the damage such a prolonged stay might cause to his kingdom, and refused. Richard was worried about his own lands, especially if Philip returned before himself, despite the protection of crusade vows. He insisted that Philip swear not to take advantage, and to refrain from attack on Richard's lands until forty days after the English king had also returned. The duke of Burgundy and the duke of Champagne stood surety for Philip's word on all this.

Philip left Acre for Tyre on 31 July 1191, and three days later set sail. Off Pamphylia the ships were hit by a storm. The king asked what time it was, and was told midnight. He said: 'Fear not then, for at this hour the monks in our own land are awake and praying to God for us.'[44] He travelled via Tripoli, Antioch, Crete, Rhodes, Corfu and Otranto to Rome, where he was welcomed by Celestine III (1191–98). He received permission from Tancred of Sicily and the German emperor Henry VI to journey through their lands.

Philip reported to the pope on the satisfactory progress of the crusade, but also on the behaviour of Richard, whom he accused of treachery. The pope absolved Philip from the oath to go to Jerusalem. Continuing northwards, Philip met Henry VI at Milan, and the two shared their complaints against Richard. The French king crossed the Alps and was back in Paris by 27 December 1191. At St-Denis he prostrated himself before the relics in thanks for his safe return.

Like his father, Philip gained much in France from his crusading venture. Crusading glamorized the king; and the interest is demonstrated by the importation, in the wake of the crusade, of a variety of relics, from the stone used to kill St Stephen to the hair of St Peter, two teeth of the prophet Amos, the manger from Bethlehem, the incense from the three kings and John the Baptist's finger! Historians are divided between those who see the crusade as a turning point in Philip's rule, such as Baldwin; those who see it as doing 'much to open out his spirit'; or those who believe he was permanently damaged, returning bald, lame and neurotic.[45]

44. Hutton, p. 52.
45. On the turning point, Baldwin, p. 22; C. Petit-Dutaillis, *Feudal Monarchy in France and England from the Tenth to the Thirteenth Centuries*, trans. E.D. Hunt (London, 1936) p. 181.

It has been suggested that Philip benefited from a weakening of the magnates through the crusade, not only by premature deaths, but also by expenditure they could not afford, leading to 'a chronic lack of money among the nobles'.[46] Certainly he had returned with no great love for Richard in his heart, and with valuable experience of warfare and of the world beyond France. He would not crusade again in person, but he had not lost his interest in the movement or in the Christian cause.

. . .

RICHARD'S CRUSADE

The continuance of the crusade after Philip's departure is not our direct concern, but indirectly it has been used to denigrate Philip. It is therefore necessary briefly to assess Richard's achievements after July 1191. They have been exaggerated. The capture of Cyprus was useful, but the main achievement of the crusade was the recovery of Acre. The other successes simply followed from this. Richard made some further advances, but he also endangered the gains made by his subsequent aggressive behaviour. When Hubert Walter praised Richard to Saladin as having every quality, the latter politely agreed, but added that he lacked wisdom and moderation: 'I should prefer to have in me reason and measure and largesse than courage carried to excess.' Indeed his own chroniclers saw the same fault. William of Newburgh noted that he 'was wont to do many things without due deliberation and forethought'.[47]

Firstly he threw away much that had been gained by the victory at Acre by over-hasty treatment of the Muslim prisoners. Because, apparently, Saladin did not fulfil the terms of the treaty in time, the 2,700 prisoners, with but few exceptions, were cold-bloodedly killed. Given Saladin's sense of honour, it seems likely that, had he been allowed time, the terms would have been fulfilled. Richard himself had helped to cause the problem by not handing over his

---

46. H.E. Warlop, *The Flemish Nobility Before 1300*, Pt I Historical Study, I, Text (Kortrijk, 1975), p. 280.
47. Runciman, III, p. 73; Ambroise, ed. Hubert and La Monte, p. 442; Ambroise, ed. Paris, col. 326, ll. 12150–2: 'Je voldroie mielz que jo eusse/largesce e sens o tot mesure/Que hardement o desmesure'.

own prisoners punctually. By the executions he lost Muslim respect, and what would have been an enormous ransom. The Saracens believed Richard had 'acted perfidiously' and 'broken his promises'; it was a disgrace to the name of Coeur de Lion.[48] The ransom was vital: Philip had left a generous contribution to the continuing crusade, including his own rights to ransom. Without this expected payment, the remaining French troops were to find themselves in financial difficulty. For this Richard, not Philip, must take the blame.

Secondly, Richard muddied the political situation in the Latin Kingdom. His support for Guy against Conrad caused instability. In the end he agreed to let the magnates decide. They declared unanimously for Conrad who was 'much better able to defend the country', and against Richard's favourite. An Anglo-Norman chronicler agrees that Guy was 'simple-minded'.[49] At last, with Conrad as king, it seemed there might be some stability in the kingdom under a strong and respected ruler, a position which could have been reached much earlier but for Richard. Guy was compensated with the kingdom of Cyprus, paying back the Templars to whom he had given the island.

Within weeks, however, Conrad was dead. Two Assassins attacked him in Tyre. Some accused Richard of being involved in a conspiracy against Conrad, which seems improbable. It is, however, unlikely that Richard grieved much over the death of Conrad. Having abandoned the claims of Guy, he was now able to support a move for the succession of his nephew (and Philip's), Henry of Champagne, son of Henry the Liberal. He ruled the Latin Kingdom, but was never crowned. In 1197 he died when he stepped backwards from a window in Acre; the man who tried to save him also fell to his death.

The military continuation of the crusade was far from being entirely triumphant. Richard won the battle of Arsuf in 1191, engaged in several minor actions which demonstrated his bravery, and recovered a number of towns; but all this is much over-praised. Most of it was inevitable after the success at Acre. Richard's bravery was also frequently

48. Baha ad-Din in Archer, p. 129; Gabrieli, p. 208.
49. 'Itinerarium', ed. Fenwick, pp. 115, 122; 'Itinerarium', ed. Stubbs, pp. 335, 350: 'quod simplex erat et minus astutus'.

foolhardy, and he was lucky to escape with his freedom and his life on several occasions, as when keeping 'careless watch' during a reconnaissance.[50]

The role of the French in all this is also usually ignored. Burgundy was co-commander at Arsuf, riding up and down before the troops with Richard in advance of the battle; and such as the counts of Champagne and Dreux, and William des Barres played an important part in the victory. There were considerable periods when Richard himself was ill again, possibly with typhus, unable to command and dependent on his allies, yet he was constantly at odds with the French. According to one source, Burgundy composed a song against Richard with 'foul and gratuitous aspersions' (not detailed), which was performed in public by women and men; so Richard composed a song 'in revenge'.[51] When Richard lost any hope of keeping French support, 700 knights left the Holy Land, and he could not go on with the crusade.

Famously, despite two attempts, Richard never reached Jerusalem. The final decision to withdraw has been presented as sensible leadership, but then why had he undertaken two marches on the city? Jerusalem was almost certainly open to capture in the period immediately after Arsuf, but Richard was too cautious. Even the *Itinerarium* believed that 'if our men had known the true condition of the enemy, beyond a doubt Jerusalem might easily have been taken'.[52] There can be no doubt that he aimed at taking Jerusalem. It was his prime reason for staying on after Acre. In 1191 he had written in a letter: 'we hope to recover the Holy City within twenty days after Christmas'. Almost certainly he backed off because he feared for his communications, he feared defeat. Cautious and sensible perhaps, but a sad end to the enterprise. Most of the crusaders were bitterly disappointed at his caution, and he lost their backing. Richard himself yielded to despondency, pulling his surcoat over his eyes so as not to see the city he could not take, and weeping.

50. Ambroise, ed. Hubert and La Monte, pp. 189–90, 280.
51. 'Itinerarium', ed. Fenwick, p. 141; 'Itinerarium', ed. W. Stubbs, p. 395.
52. Gillingham, pp. 199, 211; 'Itinerarium', in Archer, pp. 204–5; K. Norgate, *Richard the Lionheart* (London, 1924) p. 192; J.B. Gillingham, 'Richard I and the science of war in the Middle Ages', in J.B. Gillingham and J.C. Holt, *War and Government in the Middle Ages* (Woodbridge, 1984).

The final agreement with Saladin in 1192 has been seen as a triumph, but it was a limited one. Saladin, generously, conceded access to Jerusalem; each side allowing the other free movement. The treaty meant the loss of some hard-won gains, including Ascalon, on which Richard had expended much effort, choosing to attack it rather than Jerusalem, and then putting money and effort into its rebuilding. Darum and Gaza were also dismantled, and control of Ramla divided. It had taken Richard two years to recover five cities of the whole kingdom, which Saladin had captured within a month. A reduced Christian state had been saved around Acre, but in truth the gains were limited and disappointing. The main achievement of the Third Crusade was the recovery of Acre, and it was Acre which ensured the survival of the kingdom, since it provided the necessary port for contact with the West.[53] Many westerners saw the treaty as a humiliation, and Richard may himself have been embarrassed by the agreement. When he received the peace document, he pleaded illness, saying he lacked the strength to read it. That the kingdom survived without further serious loss for some time was due to the death of Saladin in 1193 and the subsequent division of his territories. The truce lasted for four years.

When Richard finally left, it was a rash and costly return. Having remained so long, suddenly he would wait for nothing. He sailed dangerously late in the year, apparently without a planned route. Philip had secured his return by agreement with those through whose lands he must pass. Richard improvised, took chances, and paid the penalty. A storm pushed him to Corfu; he was wrecked near Aquileia. Richard chose to head through the lands of the duke of Austria, whom he had insulted in the Holy Land. He knew the choice was risky, and donned a disguise, a 'mean jacket' in order to help with the cooking; more likely to attract notice than to escape it, one might think.[54] He was recognized, Leopold captured him, and later handed him to Henry VI, also antagonized by Richard's actions during the crusade. Henry demanded an enormous ransom, well over the annual

53. J.H. Pryor, *Geography, Technology, and War: Studies in the Maritime History of the Mediterranean, 649–1571* (Cambridge, 1988) p. 130.
54. K. Norgate, *England Under the Angevin Kings*, 2 vols (London, 1887) II, p. 322; Henderson, p. 184.

revenue of England. Richard had put his power, his kingdom, even his life, at risk, and was fortunate ever to be released. Not surprisingly John and Philip did their best to prolong the imprisonment, making various offers to Henry VI, information concerning which Henry obligingly passed on to Richard. Richard was released on 4 February, having been imprisoned for over a year.

Richard's rash journey had put his lands at risk. He had feared that Philip would attack them and extracted an oath from him to prevent it. Strictly speaking Philip broke this oath, but the protection for the Angevin Empire could hardly be expected to extend indefinitely. It was intended to protect a crusader. While Richard was crusading, Philip had done no more than seek the lands that he thought were properly his, including Alice's dower lands. But once Richard was captured, he was no longer on crusade, and the odds were that he would never return. Philip began to deal with John as the head of the Angevin lands, and to take advantage of Richard's imprisonment.

During this period, Philip began mining the foundations of the Angevin Empire, resulting in its eventual collapse. It became clear that most of the continental Angevin lands were no longer firmly attached to Richard or John in the way they had been to Henry II. Defence against the French king was often half-hearted. Richard's capture and imprisonment was the period when the Angevin Empire began to crumble. Without this demonstration of the empire's weakness, Philip could not have been so confident of success later; precedents had been set for 1203. It is a mistake to see all this as the result of mere chance. Philip's decision to return early, Richard's decision to remain, and then to return at a time and in a manner which put himself at risk, were vital to the subsequent course of events.

. . .

THE FOURTH CRUSADE

Philip Augustus would not go east again, but he continued to be closely involved in crusading ventures from France. The Fourth Crusade was basically a French crusade. The 'unholy crusade' has been condemned for damaging the whole crusading movement.[55] Christians rather than Muslims or pagans were attacked at both Zara and Constantinople. In the latter case the crusade is accused of fatally weakening the Byzantine Empire. But it was also a sign of the growing power of western Christendom, and of France. The hand of Philip Augustus was never far from the helm of the Fourth Crusade; and when a new Latin Empire was established, it was French in leadership and structure. The main military force was French from the start, and resulted in a remarkable French colonization of the East.

Innocent III proclaimed the crusade in 1198, seeking a truce between Philip and Richard, which was agreed in January 1199. He could not interest the western kings in direct participation, and Richard's death created a new situation. Neither John nor Philip could think about leaving the West at this point, but they were prepared to co-operate in the venture. Many powerful magnates of France took the cross, including Louis of Blois, Baldwin IX of Flanders and his brother Henry, Geoffrey III of Perche, Simon IV de Montfort, and Theobald III of Champagne, who would have led the crusade but for his death on 24 May 1201. The crusade was proclaimed in France in 1198 by Peter of Capuano. The king's demesne and the territory of his Champagne relatives was the chief recruiting ground, and its leaders, as Innocent III acknowledged, were French. It was in the main 'an enterprise of the French nobility'.[56]

The leadership of the crusade depended mainly on the views of Philip Augustus. The king himself had refused the honour, but was instrumental in the choice first of Theobald and then, after Theobald's death, of Boniface of Montferrat, brother of Conrad. The close and supportive relationship with Conrad, which Philip had established during the Third Crusade, made a strong link to his brother Boniface and the Fourth Crusade. France had nothing to lose from a Byzantine Empire in the hands of French magnates, and Philip was likely to be less concerned by the choice of target than Innocent III.

---

55. J. Godfrey, *1204, The Unholy Crusade* (Oxford, 1980); J. Sayers, *Innocent III, Leader of Europe, 1198–1216* (Harlow, 1994) p. 172: 'an unqualified and dreadful disaster'.

56. *Letters of Innocent III*, p. 58 and n. 22.

It was in June 1201 at Soissons, in France, that a French assembly voted to nominate Boniface, and at Soissons again in August that Boniface agreed to lead the crusade after a meeting with Philip. When Boniface went to Rome for approval of his leadership, he took letters from Philip. He was elected to leadership by the crusaders, who were of course largely French. It was also Philip who encouraged Baldwin IX count of Flanders to crusade, through the treaty of Péronne.

After the crusade had captured Constantinople, a new election was arranged by the crusaders for the vacated imperial throne. Boniface clearly thought that as leader of the crusade he would be elected, but the twelve electors preferred Baldwin count of Flanders, though 'his title was to be grander than his actual power'. He was elected on 9 May and crowned on 16 May 1204 (1204–6).

Runciman thought the crusade's effects 'were wholly disastrous', but it rather depends on the point of view.[57] Byzantium became a Latin empire, indeed a French empire. The Burgundian Odo de La Roche became duke of Athens and Thebes, Louis of Blois took the duchy of Nicaea, Hugh de St-Pol had Demotika, and Guy de Nesle received Geraki. William de Champlitte ruled the Peloponnese, which later went to Geoffrey de Villehardouin who also conquered the Morea, as prince of Achaea. The southern mainland of Greece became virtually a French colony, with rulers in the Peloponnese, the Morea, Athens and Thebes. The walls of the castle in Thebes were covered with murals of the French conquest of the East. In the *Philippide*, the conquest is seen as making Greece French; while Pope Honorius III (1216–27) referred to Byzantium as 'a new France'.[58]

The Latin Emperor Baldwin's rule did not last long. He was captured by Ioannitsa in 1205 and died in captivity. His brother Henry of Flanders (1206–16) succeeded to the crown and proved the most able of the Latin rulers of the Eastern Empire. In turn the throne was filled by men who were vassals of Philip Augustus, including Peter of Courtenay (1216–21)

---

57. Runciman, III, p. 130.
58. *Crusaders as Conquerors: The Chronicle of the Morea*, ed. H.E. Lurier (New York, 1964) p. 298; William the Breton, *Philippide*, ed. Guizot, p. 153; Godfrey, p. 145: 'as it were a new France has been created'.

from the Gâtinais, related to Philip and given permission by him to take up the throne. The Christian state which survived in the Holy Land was also strongly influenced by the French; in 1210 John of Brienne was sent by Philip Augustus and the pope to become its king.[59]

At home the death and absence of nobles through the Fourth Crusade gave various opportunities to Philip Augustus. Those who died included Louis count of Blois, who left behind only a minor as heir, and Theobald III of Champagne, giving Philip a tighter hold over his county. Theobald's widow, Blanche, promised not to remarry without the king's consent. Foremost of the missing nobles was Baldwin IX count of Flanders, briefly Latin emperor until his capture in 1205 and his death in the following year. Philip had already imposed his authority over Flanders, and it may be that Baldwin's eagerness to go east was inspired by a desire to escape the tightening noose of the monarchy over Flanders. The death of Baldwin has been seen as 'a catastrophe from which Flanders never recovered'.[60] One might gloss that by adding that after the Fourth Crusade, French control of Flanders was greatly increased.

. . .

CONCLUSIONS ON CRUSADING

Philip himself did more than enough to continue the Capetians' reputation as supporters of crusading. He went on a crusade which was more successful than his father's venture, and played an important part in taking Acre, the main achievement of the Third Crusade. But Philip's interest was not confined to his own pilgrimage: he constantly sent contributions to the Holy Land, provided troops, left his main army to continue the crusade after his return to the West, and played a role in the choice of the kings of Jerusalem in the period. Philip also contributed significantly to the Fourth Crusade, having the dominant part in choosing its leader,

59. M.N. Hardwick, 'The crusader states, 1192–1243', in *A History of the Crusades*, ed. K.M. Setton, II, *The Later Crusades, 1189–1311*, ed. R.L. Wolff and H.W. Hazard (Philadelphia, 1962) pp. 522–54, p. 531; J. Richard, *The Latin Kingdom of Jerusalem*, 2 vols (Amsterdam, 1979) II, p. 349.

60. D. Nicholas, *Medieval Flanders* (Harlow, 1992) p. 75.

while encouraging his magnates and their forces to con-
stitute what proved to be largely a French army. In both
Byzantium and the Holy Land, Philip's reign saw the development of French-dominated states.

The news of his own journey, the success at Acre, the
surprising triumph at Constantinople, all fired the French
imagination. Crusading poems and songs soon proliferated.
That this interest was not confined to the reading classes is
clear from the tremendous response to the Children's Crusade, which arose spontaneously in Germany and France,
partly as a result of the preaching of the Albigensian Crusade.
But Jerusalem remained the prime target of crusading in
the popular mind.

Enthusiasm for crusading was further demonstrated in the
Albigensian crusade, albeit in various ways and for various
reasons. We shall examine this crusade when reviewing the
final years of the reign, but it must be included in an assessment of crusading under Philip. The crusade halted the
growth of a popular heresy and drove it underground. The
intervention of the monarchy in this crusade was a major
step in the eventual integration of southern France into the
Capetian realm.

All in all during the reign, crusading played a vital part.
Philip had directed crusading, at times to his own ends, but
also broadly in line with papal wishes. His crusading efforts
helped to reconcile him to the papacy after the difficulties
over his marriage. He built a bridge between the piety of
Louis VII, who went on the Second Crusade, and the saintliness of Louis IX, who would twice go on crusade. Of these
three monarchs, Philip was the only one to achieve any real
crusading success.

Chapter 4

THE CONFLICT WITH RICHARD I

. . .

RICHARD'S CAPTIVITY

In 1189 Richard the Lionheart was able to take over the Angevin Empire intact, despite Henry II's plans for division. This was partly because of the death of his brothers Henry and Geoffrey, and partly from being in alliance with his father's enemies just before Henry II's death. It meant that Henry's plans for John need not be applied. John's role, however, remained a problem, not solved by Richard's grant of six counties in England and of Mortain in Normandy. Another problem was of Richard's own making, his alliance with Philip Augustus. Philip expected reward from their combined success against Henry, in particular he desired control of the disputed area between their lands, the Vexin, around the valleys of the Epte and the Andelle.

Problems regarding the future of the Angevin Empire were shelved in order to undertake the crusade. Their mutual absence restored a degree of stability, reinforced by the usual papal guarantee to protect the lands of absent crusaders. Until Philip returned, the *status quo* was maintained. Philip's early return, at the end of 1191, brought an immediate change in the situation and a threat to the Angevin lands. Richard had anticipated this when he extracted promises from Philip before the latter's departure from the Holy Land. The threat to the Angevin position was increased by the death on crusade of Philip of Alsace, whose county of Flanders had been a major curb on Capetian ambitions, and the natural ally to the Plantagenets.

The Tours Chronicle presents a picture of Philip at this time as 'a fine man, well proportioned in stature, with a smiling countenance, bald, a ruddy complexion, inclined to eat and drink well, and sensual', wearing simple clothing, speaking few words, but feared. He was said to be rapid in judgement, but prepared to take advice. Gerald of Wales, looking back on this time, thought Philip had been eager to recover lost lands, and has him exclaim: 'will God never be willing to give to me, or another king of France, the glory of restoring to the kingdom of France its ancient estate, and the greatness which it had in the time of Charlemagne?'[1] This was a view enhanced by hindsight, but is a reminder that to some at the time Philip's ambitions seemed on a grand scale. There is no doubt from the historical interests of the age, that the achievements of Charlemagne were embroidered with tints of glorious rose, but they were framed in terms of a Frankish empire. And, for various reasons, Philip's men stressed his relationship with Charlemagne and sought parallels between the two rulers.

It is doubtful that Philip's targets were quite so broad, especially in 1189. It is more likely that he was aiming first to protect the area which his father had established as being under Capetian control. He was also fully aware of the claims to authority, ecclesiastical and lay, financial and judicial, which the French crown could make. There is no doubt that the monarchy's horizons were beginning to move, to expand. Even if in a vague manner, Philip was surely aware that it was possible to use these claims to impose his own authority over a wider geographical area than had been done by his predecessors.

In 1189 both defence and expansion meant keeping a close eye on his major rival, the ruler of the Angevin Empire. Anything Philip could do to lessen the power of the Angevins

---

1. R-H. Bautier, 'Philippe Auguste: la personnalité du roi', in R-H. Bautier, ed., *La France de Philippe Auguste, le Temps des Mutations* (Paris, 1982) pp. 33–57, p. 35; C. Petit-Dutaillis, *The Feudal Monarchy in France and England*, trans. E.D. Hunt (London, 1936) pp. 214, 215; 'Chronique du chanoine de Tours', in *Recueil des historiens des Gaules et de la France (RHF)*, ed. M. Bouquet and L. Delisle, 24 vols (Paris, 1869–1904) XVIII, p. 304. Gerald of Wales, *Opera*, ed. J.S. Brewer, J.F. Dimock and G.F. Warner, 8 vols, RS no. 21 (London, 1861–91) VIII, p. 294.

increased his own hopes of success. So he brought to bear all the force he could use, military and diplomatic, theoretical and practical, financial and judicial, ecclesiastical and social, in order to keep ahead of his rival. Complete defeat of the Angevin ruler, checkmate, would be the ideal outcome, but almost certainly Philip at first was far more concerned to react to any immediate threat or opportunity, to concentrate on the opening moves, to protect every pawn, to utilize his own strength by manoeuvring his pieces into as advantageous a position as possible.

The end of the game was barely in sight. Inevitably the conflict came to focus on certain areas where overlordship could in some way be disputed between the Plantagenet and the Capetian: the Vexin, areas along the Loire, Berry. It has been pointed out recently that the idea of clearly defined linear boundaries is inaccurate for much of the medieval period.[2] We should think more in terms of boundary zones and frontier areas, fringes where authority was uncertain. This view helps considerably in an understanding of the warfare of Philip's reign, particularly in the conflict with the Plantagenets. Much attention had to be given to individual fortresses and particular families, to establishing one's own jurisdiction against that of a rival, to having the decisive voice in the election of a cleric in the region. The reason was that like uncommitted voters in a modern election, the side these local frontier families chose to come down on was likely to be the winner. Most of the warfare and the disputes between the Capetians and the Plantagenets occurred in just such uncertainly committed regions. Both sides sought to ingratiate themselves in these areas with the local nobility, to push the advantages of their own rule, for example in providing justice, in taxation exemptions, in protection of the church, in protection against other secular lords. The chronicles of the day therefore often seem to concentrate on minor sieges and disputes. They took for granted that

2. D. Power, 'What did the frontier of Angevin Normandy comprise?', *ANS*, XVII, 1994, pp. 181–201; e.g. p. 184 on 'zones'; p. 188: 'a political border which was a far cry from a fixed line on a map'. See also J. Yver, 'Philippe Auguste et les châteaux normands: la frontière orientale du duché', *BSAN*, LIX, 1967–89, pp. 309–48; and J. Green, 'Lords of the Norman Vexin', in J. Gillingham and J.C. Holt, eds, *War and Government in the Middle Ages* (Woodbridge, 1984) pp. 47–63.

the reader would realize that behind these moves was a greater game.

Philip sought to gain advantage from his early return from the Holy Land. He has been accused of contemplating invasion of Richard's lands despite his oath, and only desisting because the French barons opposed it, but this seems to be a calumny. Philip's plans were more subtle and could be placed under a shield of legality. He properly claimed the lands promised by Richard at Messina, the return of his abandoned sister Alice at present locked in the Tower at Rouen, together with her dowry lands, including Gisors and the counties of Aumale and Eu.

Philip met the seneschal and nobles of Normandy and handed to the seneschal, William Fitz Ralph, the chirograph of their agreement made in Messina. The Lionheart's men refused to accept the legality of the document, questioning Philip's claim without Richard's authority. Richard had also sent back men to guard sensitive strongholds. Angevin chroniclers suggest that Philip presented a forged treaty of Messina in support of his claims, but he had no need to do so. Richard's rejection of Alice clearly meant she ought to be restored, together with her dowry lands. No crusading protection could apply to this; and there were no reasonable grounds for argument that she should be retained as a Plantagenet prisoner, though this is what Richard ordered. Gisors and territory in the Vexin were the lands in question. The French chronicler, Rigord, whose monastery regained estates taken by the Normans 'against all right', saw them as lands which Richard had usurped. In other words, Philip's aggression against this area was a legitimate target even while Richard was crusading. A recent work on John rightly sees the treaty of Messina as creating 'a wedge for future Capetian interventions in Angevin-held provinces'.[3]

Philip managed to use Alice, despite her imprisonment, by suggesting marriage instead to John, as he tried to win over the latter by promises. John was dissatisfied with his lot

3. Rigord, *Vie de Philippe Auguste*, ed. M. Guizot (Paris, 1825) p. 111; 'Vie' in *Oeuvres de Rigord et de Guillaume le Breton*, ed. H-F. Delaborde, 2 vols (Paris, 1882–85) I, p. 123: 'totum Vulcassinum Normannicum quod rex Anglie injuste possidebat'; 'quod rex Anglie Henricus injuste per violentiam longo tempore detinuerat, deinde Richardus filius ejus'; R.V. Turner, *King John* (Harlow, 1994) p. 49.

and lent a ready ear to Philip's suggestions. Only the advice of Richard's ministers and his mother Eleanor stopped him from going to Philip, for the time being. When Richard was captured in 1192, Philip's position improved considerably. It was doubtful if it could now be claimed that Richard was crusading and that the papal protection still applied. It is true that Richard had spelled out that Philip's oath was for a truce until after Richard had actually returned. But the position was certainly now muddied. No one had anticipated Richard's imprisonment, and no one could forecast how long he might remain in prison, or whether he would ever return. As William the Breton pointed out, Richard had 'offended many, so had much to fear'. His captor, Leopold duke of Austria, had been infuriated by Richard's actions at Acre; Henry VI, the German emperor to whom Richard was then handed, had been antagonized by Richard's activities in Sicily, and was quite prepared to ride out papal complaints. But others were shocked by the imprisonment of a respected crusader, and even the French chronicler Rigord thought the arrest was 'against all the custom of Christian states, which guaranteed free passage to all pilgrims'.[4] For Philip it was a dream situation. He was in no way to blame for Richard's predicament, and it offered him many opportunities.

Henry VI demanded an enormous ransom and there was doubt whether it would ever be paid. It was said that in a letter to John, Philip expressed the belief that the Lionheart would never escape.[5] The crusading truce could not last for ever. The French barons, who had been unwilling to act against the Angevin lands in 1191, seemed prepared to do so in 1192. Similarly, John, with prospects now of inheriting Richard's place, could no longer be restrained from meeting Philip and concluding a deal.

4. William the Breton, 'Vie' in *Vie de Philippe Auguste*, ed. Guizot, p. 209; William the Breton, 'Vie' in *Oeuvres*, ed. Delaborde, p. 195: 'quia multos offenderat, multos metuens'; Rigord, ed. Guizot, p. 110; Rigord, ed. Delaborde, p. 121: 'ipsum captivare contra morem omnium peregrinorum per quascumque terras christianorum secure transeuntium'.
5. Roger of Howden, *Chronica*, ed. W. Stubbs, 4 vols, RS no. 51 (London, 1868–71) III, p. 203: 'et quod ipse nunquam exiret de captione imperatoris Alemanniae'; Roger of Howden, *The Annals of Roger de Hoveden*, ed. and trans. H.T. Riley, 2 vols (London, 1853) II, p. 286.

Richard was imprisoned at Dürnstein, and later at Triffels, and was not finally released until February 1194. During this time the serious frailty of the Angevin Empire had been demonstrated. Government of England during Richard's absence proved far from satisfactory, despite recent efforts to argue its success.[6] The quarrels between the men Richard had chosen to govern in his absence were damaging, and stemmed especially from the arrogance, low birth and un-popularity of his favourite, William Longchamp, made bishop of Ely by Richard. Longchamp had differences with all the main figures who remained behind during the crusade: Hugh du Puiset, Richard's brother John, and Richard's half brother Geoffrey Plantagenet.

Richard had to send back a new representative, Walter of Coutances, to sort things out. Longchamp's enemies finally deposed him and forced him into exile. But government remained difficult, and this was made more acute by Richard's captivity. Longchamp was said to have 'oppressed the people with heavy exactions'.[7] The enormous demands made in order to satisfy the ransom did not help, though the return of Hubert Walter from the crusade did. He was elected archbishop of Canterbury in 1193. John's alliance with Philip led to the former's rebellion in England and civil war, with the justiciars acting on behalf of Richard besieging his own brother's castles.

Philip's attack was more successful than anyone imagined it could be. The legality of it was underwritten by an agreement with John. In 1193 John made an alliance with Philip, won over by recognition of himself as heir to the Angevin lands, for which he did homage in Paris. Richard's friends reported that his brother 'had made a league with death and a compact with hell'.[8] Richard showed little anxiety, believing

6. J. Gillingham, *Richard the Lionheart*, 2nd edn (London, 1989) p. 217, e.g. 'if Richard had returned in 1193 it would have been obvious to all, both contemporary writers and us, that the arrangements he had made for the government of his lands in his absence had worked extremely well'.

7. P. Henderson, *Richard Coeur de Lion* (New York, 1958) p. 151. Roger of Howden, ed. Stubbs, III, p. 72: 'plebem Anglie sibi commissam gravibus exactionibus premebat'.

8. Roger of Howden, ed. Riley, II, p. 281; Roger of Howden, ed. Stubbs, III, p. 198: 'foedus cum morte inierat, et pactum cum inferno'.

his brother would never persist when opposed. It was said that John even did homage for England, to which Philip could have no legitimate claim. More to the immediate point, Philip was promised possession of the disputed Vexin territories. The new allies planned a concerted effort: Philip against Normandy, John in England against his brother's men. This was backed by rebellion in Poitou by the count of Angoulême, and alliance with the count of Flanders. Philip's allies achieved little. Richard's representatives held their own in England, treating John as a rebel, restricting his authority and besieging his castles, while Count Adhemar was defeated and captured in Poitou.

But Philip's invasion of Normandy on 12 April, in conjunction with the count of Flanders, was a different matter. Lyons-la-Forêt and Neaufles were taken. Philip worked his way along the Epte, and Gisors, the key to the Vexin and hence to Normandy, was surrendered by Gilbert de Vascoeuil without a struggle. This was seen as treachery, since Richard had sent Gilbert back from Messina specifically to defend the place. He now did homage to his new lord, Philip, but was despised even by the French 'for the treason he had been guilty of to his master, the king of England'.[9] Gilbert held lands of Philip, and he was only castellan, not lord, of Gisors. Indeed many of the Norman lords who now went over to Philip, including those of Aumale and Eu, were vassals of Philip for lands elsewhere, as were the counts of Gournay, Meulan and Perche. Châteauneuf, Verneuil, Eu, Aumale and Le Vaudreuil were all taken. Philip overran the Vexin and reached Dieppe. Évreux was captured and handed over to John's keeping.

Philip's strategy had been to encircle Rouen, cutting supplies and putting pressure on the capital before he attacked it. Though it did not work at Rouen on this occasion, it is interesting to find Philip using propaganda to encourage surrender: he promised the citizens that if you 'allow me to enter peaceably, I shall prove a kind and just master'.[10]

9. Roger of Howden, ed. Riley, II, p. 289; Roger of Howden, ed. Stubbs, III, p. 206: 'propter proditionem quam fecerat domino suo regi Angliae'.
10. Roger of Howden, ed. Riley, II, p. 289; Roger of Howden, ed. Stubbs, III, p. 207: 'permittite me pacifice intrare, et ero vobis dominus mansuetus et justus'.

Rouen, however, resisted under the earl of Leicester, and though Philip brought up twenty-three engines, the French were forced to abandon their siege. Philip burned the engines and broke his wine casks, so as to deny their use to the enemy. He was still able to go on to take Pacy and Ivry, and now dominated north-eastern Normandy, the Vexin entry route, the Indre and the approaches to Touraine. According to a song, said to be written by Richard in captivity, the king complained, as well he might: 'my lord tramples down my land'.[11]

The subsequent peace made with Richard's representatives, Longchamp and William Brewer, at Mantes on 9 July, allowed Philip to keep these gains. Philip was also to have Loches, Châtillon-sur-Indre, Arques and Driencourt. He promised to halt the invasion, and Richard promised to do homage for his lands in France and pay 20,000 marks over two years before he would regain his territories, which were to be restored one at a time for each instalment of the debt that was paid. In 1193 there were serious plans for an invasion of England by the Flemish and French, nominally on John's behalf, including the gathering of a fleet at Wissant. But John's failures in England halted these plans.

Hostilities were resumed in 1194, and by the time agreement was reached with John, the latter was prepared to concede all Normandy east of the Seine except Rouen, all territory east of the River Itun south to Channebrun-sur-Avre including Verneuil and Évreux, together with key fortresses in the Loire valley, including Azay, Tours, Montbazon, Montrichard, Buzençais, Loches, Châtillon and Amboise. There were also gains for the counts of Blois and Perche. Philip proceeded to make good some of these promises, and captured Évreux and Le Vaudreuil. It is clear that on John's side this was done in desperation, after his failure in England, and Philip knew that should Richard return, he could not expect such an agreement to be accepted. Nevertheless, during Richard's absence, Philip 'had shaken the Angevin power in Aquitaine and in Touraine as well as in Normandy'.[12]

11. K. Norgate, *Richard the Lionheart* (London, 1924) p. 278.
12. F.M. Powicke, *The Loss of Normandy*, 2nd edn (Manchester, 1960, revised 1961) p. 98.

. . .

THE WAR BETWEEN PHILIP AND RICHARD

On 4 February 1194 Richard was released after a captivity of one year six weeks and three days. Prematurely anticipating the event, Philip had written to John that the devil was loosed. Western chroniclers accuse them of trying to persuade Henry VI to keep him in prison, making offers for either month by month payments, or virtually any deal Henry was prepared to accept. 'Behold how they loved him', commented Roger of Howden.[13]

At Mainz, on 2 February 1194, Henry VI is said to have shown Richard the letters he claimed that John and Philip had sent. This was such a frequent literary ploy in the period to indicate treachery that one must doubt its veracity. If true, it makes Henry VI no better than Philip or John, since not only had he imprisoned a returning crusader, but he had written to Philip with his 'kindly affection for us', encouraging support against 'the enemy of our empire and the disturber of your kingdom'.[14] The production of incriminating letters is always on the other side defended as being forgery.

Henry may, however, have been tempted by some such offer, and Richard's release was delayed. The pressures of conscience and honour, the attitude of Henry's own vassals, the reprimands of the Church, the pleas of Eleanor of Aquitaine the 'wretched mother . . . worn to a skeleton, a mere bag of skin and bone', finally brought Henry to the point. Richard, now become 'our dearly beloved friend', was released. The vast ransom had been paid, Richard demanding the names of all those who contributed, noting those who had not paid, in order that 'we may know to what extent we are bound to return thanks'! Henry VI had also extracted promises from Richard, which meant that the Lionheart would be more use to him as a king in the West than ever John would be.[15]

13. Roger of Howden, ed. Riley, II, p. 307; Roger of Howden, ed. Stubbs, III, p. 229: 'ecce quomodo amabant eum'.
14. Roger of Howden, ed. Riley, II, p. 278; Roger of Howden, ed. Stubbs, III, p. 195: 'inimicus imperii nostri, et turbator regni tui'.
15. Henderson, pp. 188, 198; D. Seward, *Eleanor of Aquitaine* (New York, 1978) p. 180; Roger of Howden, ed. Riley, II, p. 306; Roger of Howden, ed. Stubbs, III, p. 227: 'dilecto amico nostro Ricardo'; J.T. Appleby, *England Without Richard, 1189–1199* (London, 1965) p. 113.

Richard was given a safe-conduct to Antwerp and took his time going north, stopping for a time in Cologne. He had already, while imprisoned, managed to make contacts with vassals of Henry VI who might be useful against Philip, including the dukes of Swabia, Louvain and Limburg, and the counts of Holland and Montferrat. He made a leisurely journey along the Rhine, in the company of his mother, turning a number of contacts into positive alliances, lubricated by promises of cash. The attitude of some of these lords is shown at Cologne, where the archbishop preached a sermon, in the presence of Eleanor, on the text: 'The Lord hath sent his angel to snatch me from the hand of Herod'.[16] These contacts would turn into a bloc of allies in north-west Europe including some German bishops, several lords of the Rhineland, Brabant and Holland, later supplemented by the most important figure, the count of Flanders.

Richard arrived in England at Sandwich in the glow of a red sun on 13 March 1194, and was in London by 16 March. With Richard's presence, John's rebellion collapsed. After checking Richard's identity, to be sure he had returned, the castellans of both Tickhill and Nottingham surrendered. By 12 May Richard had already sailed for Barfleur to tackle Philip Augustus. John came to Richard at Lisieux and abased himself. Richard humiliated his brother, belittled him as a child led by evil counsellors, and then offered to pardon him, ordering a newly delivered salmon to be cooked for a reconciliation feast. All the same, it was some time before he restored John's lands.

John had to earn this restoration by fighting on Richard's behalf. He made a start by a double-dealing recovery of Évreux, which Philip had captured and handed over to John's safe-keeping. John now entered under the guise of still being Philip's man. Once inside he proclaimed himself for Richard and massacred the unfortunate garrison. According to the *Philippide*, he invited other French lords to Évreux, whose heads ended up on poles which were paraded around the city.[17] It was the sort of conduct which won battles but lost

16. A. Bridge, *Richard the Lionheart* (London, 1989) p. 213.
17. William the Breton, *La Philippide, Poème*, ed. and trans. M. Guizot (Paris, 1825) pp. 115–16; 'Philippide', in *Oeuvres*, ed. Delaborde, p. 115, ll. 458–60; William the Breton, 'Vie', in *Oeuvres*, ed. Delaborde, p. 196: 'decapitavit omnes, et capita palis affixit in circuitu civitatis'; Rigord, ed. Delaborde, p. 127: 'et plures quam turpiter decapitati'.

wars, and earned John a lasting resentment and distrust from the French. Richard may have been rash and aggressive, but he was widely respected; his brother came to be respected by none. The campaigns of 1194 were the beginning of a new war between Richard and Philip, with the Angevin Empire as the prize. According to Roger of Wendover: 'the kings played at castle-taking', but it was a serious game.[18] It was a war in which castles and mercenary forces played a dominant role, and was a more intense warfare than that between Philip and Henry II. Mercenary captains, such as Martin Algais, Mercadier and Cadoc, were given more authority, and as a result a more professional and ruthless element entered the campaigns. Such captains were well rewarded for their part. Mercadier, who claimed to 'have been placed at the head of [Richard's] army', received the lordship of Périgord; and for Philip, Cadoc received £1,000 a day, the lordship of Gaillon, and later the Norman fief of Tosny and Pont-Audemer.[19]

The war of 1194–99 is generally presented as one which Richard won. It is true that in this period Richard recovered most of the lands lost during his captivity, but it was not a convincing victory. In the first place it was a war of ups and downs, by no means always going Richard's way. In the second place the main success for Richard during 1198–99, when finally the recovery was achieved, was followed by his greatest disaster, his wounding and consequent death at Châlus-Chabrol.

In 1194 Richard set about raising money for the war. He was as ruthless about this as when raising funds for the crusade, and again there were political penalties. In a decade of considerable economic difficulty, Richard exacted enormous sums for the war, not least for a massive programme of castle-building. He sailed with a hundred ships 'laden with men, horses and arms', braving a storm rather than remain in England any longer, though he was forced back into port

18. Roger of Wendover, *Flowers of History*, ed. and trans. J.A. Giles, 2 vols (London, 1899) II, p. 145; Roger of Wendover, *Flores Historiarum*, ed. H.G. Hewlett, 3 vols, RS no. 84 (London, 1886–89) I, p. 243: 'et sic reges in castrorum captione luserunt'.
19. A. Luchaire, in E. Lavisse, *Histoire de France depuis les origines jusqu'à la Révolution*, III, Pt I (Paris, 1911) p. 114: 'eram dux exercitus ejus'.

for a while.[20] Only military success could compensate politically, and in the last analysis although Richard regained territories lost through his imprisonment, he made no new gains at Philip's expense.

William the Marshal exemplified the confidence recovered with Richard's return: 'the French will go away now'.[21] Philip had besieged Verneuil again on 10 May, but Richard made an immediate impact, his rapid march on Verneuil resulting in Philip's retreat. The citizens at Verneuil had the temerity to paint a cartoon of Philip on the gate, armed with a club, presumably to indicate his aggression. Philip must have found it particularly galling to have to retreat. Richard on entry insisted on kissing all the citizens; one hopes they appreciated their reward.

Richard then headed for Beaumont-le-Roger, which had rebelled against him, took it and destroyed the tower. The Lionheart's main objective, though, seems to have been not the repossession of Normandy, but recovery in the south. Aquitaine had always been his first love, and he quickly moved south, regaining several lost strongholds including Loches which he reached on 12 June. Philip's priority, in terms of offence, was the north and Normandy, whereas Richard's was Aquitaine and the south. But, of course, neither was prepared to yield in either region.

Philip went on to besiege Arques and defeat a small force, capturing twenty-five knights. He took Fontaines, a few miles from Rouen. The earl of Leicester set out from Rouen by night, intending to ambush Philip, but was himself trapped and captured. Philip was soon able to make a riposte to John's treachery: Évreux was retaken, sacked and burned. But then Philip was drawn southwards by Richard's successes there.

The engagement on 3 July 1194, at Fréteval in the eastern Vendômois, was a minor disaster for Philip, probably more damaging in the political than the military effects. Fréteval is presented by English chroniclers and historians as a major victory for Richard, but it does not deserve the label

20. Roger of Howden, ed. Stubbs, III, p. 251: 'cum centum magnis navibus onustis viris bellicosis, et equis et armis'.
21. Norgate, p. 294; P. Meyer, ed., L'Histoire de Guillaume le Maréchal, SHF, 3 vols, nos 255, 268, 304 (Paris, 1891–1901) II, p. 12, ll. 10431–52; l. 10452: 'Or s'en ira li reis de France'.

of a battle. It was one of many skirmishes in the war where each side sought to avoid the other, battle being only rarely sought by both combatants in this period. When skirmishes occurred, they were usually recorded by the side which emerged most successfully and ignored by the other. There is no reason why we should be so one-sided. In this case Philip himself avoided conflict, but the rear part of his force was engaged, and his baggage train captured together with the royal seal and archives, including signed documents, papers relating to deserters from the Plantagenets, financial accounts, and some silver. For a second time Philip eluded the pursuing Richard, this time accidentally by entering a church to worship while Richard rushed off on a wild goose chase. In the south Richard was then able to recover a number of strongholds, including Taillebourg, re-establishing his own seneschals in Anjou and Aquitaine.

In Normandy Philip still held the upper hand, and captured John's siege train in a skirmish at Le Vaudreuil. John had besieged Le Vaudreuil in July, but Philip made a rapid journey from Châteaudun in three days, which William the Breton says would normally have taken eight days.[22] He followed up with a dawn attack which caught John by surprise so that he had to flee, leaving behind his siege engines and provisions. A pattern emerged for the war, of fighting until the exhaustion of both sides led to a truce for the rest of the year. At the end of 1194, as usual, the truce of Tillières allowed each side to keep what it held at that moment.

The next year saw a lull in the war. At Le Vaudreuil in July a peace conference was held. Philip had besieged Le Vaudreuil, but saw that he would have to abandon it with Richard so close at hand. During the conference there was a great noise as the walls collapsed. Philip had continued the mining during the truce, so Le Vaudreuil would not be left intact in his enemy's hands. It was militarily valuable, but morally questionable, against the understood practices of war. Richard was infuriated and called off the conference.

Although the relative territorial strengths of the Plantagenets and the Capetians had altered little since Richard's release, Philip had made significant moves against the two

---

22. William the Breton, *Philippide*, ed. Guizot, p. 125; 'Philippide', ed. Delaborde, p. 125, l. 18.

most vulnerable areas of Angevin territory, the bordering lands of Normandy, and what Powicke calls 'the weakest spot' in the Angevin Empire, Berry.[23] A hold in this area would give Philip the possibility of attacking the Loire from the south and driving a wedge between Angevin lands in the north and the south. Here we see Philip's appreciation of the best strategical plan for the final defeat of the Angevins. So that although this war against Richard was inconclusive, and even in strictly territorial terms a setback for Philip, it was also a significant probe towards future success.

Richard finally released Philip's sister Alice in 1195, and in August Philip strengthened his hand in the north-east by marrying her to William count of Ponthieu, with Eu and Arques as her dowry. In November 1195 Philip followed this up by a move against north-eastern Normandy. Richard had besieged Arques, but was forced to abandon it. Philip now sacked Dieppe, which was set ablaze with Greek Fire, together with the ships in the harbour. When Philip retreated from Dieppe, Richard tried a surprise attack, issuing from the woods, but again only managed to strike the rear, and with less success than on the previous occasion.

In the south, Richard's captain Mercadier had taken Issoudun, which Philip sought to recover. Richard's approach ended the attempt, and the truce made on 5 December 1195, converted in January 1196 into the treaty of Louviers, shows the gradual progress that Richard had made in the war. Philip would return Berry, Issoudun and Graçay, but keep the Norman Vexin, Neufmarché, Gaillon, Nonancourt, Vernon, Ivry and Pacy. Philip still had the upper hand, keeping the vital Vexin, and having made war and done damage in Richard's territories north and south.

It was a good year for Philip in 1196. Part of Richard's problem was a potential new area for conflict in Brittany. Philip was happy to encourage dissension anywhere within the Angevin territories. Since John had deserted him after Richard's return, it was only natural that Arthur of Brittany should attract interest as a potential ally within the Plantagenet ranks. Arthur's claim to be Richard's heir was possibly better than John's, and recognized by Richard himself in Sicily. Arthur's mother, Constance, was discontented with

23. Powicke, p. 106.

her position. She was the widow of Richard's full brother Geoffrey and had been given Ranulf earl of Chester as a second husband, a match she found unacceptable. They had ceased to live as man and wife. Now, when she was invited to Normandy by Richard, her husband made her his prisoner. Constance's Breton subjects appealed to Philip for aid and rebelled against Richard. Richard then had to pacify Brittany where, as Professor Gillingham suggests, he won the war but lost the dispute.[24] Arthur's guardians evaded Richard and took the young man to Philip's court, where he became a useful pawn in the war.

Rigord says that Richard again broke the truce, taking Vierzon by a ruse, breaking an oath to its lord.[25] Richard regained Nonancourt without a fight, using treachery and silver. Its castellan, Nicholas d'Orphin, joined the Templars and went off to the Holy Land to contemplate his disgrace. In July Philip set up his engines for a seven-week siege of Aumale, which Richard came to relieve. On this occasion it was Richard who hesitated to fight and was beaten in a skirmish, making a 'shameful flight'.[26] William des Barres abandoned three captives and their ransoms in order to have a go at his old enemy, but to no avail. It was Alan of Dinan who unhorsed the king, though Richard remounted and retreated. Aumale surrendered on 20 August and was demolished. Richard had to pay 3,000 marks to ransom the garrison.

A further setback occurred for Richard at Gaillon over the Seine, which he besieged, possibly to cover building operations at Les Andelys.[27] As on other occasions, careless of his safety during a reconnaissance, he was wounded in the knee by a crossbow bolt shot by its castellan, the mercenary captain Cadoc. His horse was also wounded, fell, and rolled on to Richard, who had to be carried to safety. The injuries took a month to heal, and explain the further lull in the war. Philip went on to recapture Nonancourt with its fifteen knights.

24. Gillingham, p. 260.
25. Rigord, ed. Guizot, p. 131; Rigord, ed. Delaborde, p. 135; Rigord, ed. Guizot, p. 122 makes the same accusation against Richard on an earlier occasion.
26. William the Breton, *Philippide*, ed. Guizot, p. 135; 'Philippide', ed. Delaborde, p. 134, l. 255: 'fuga . . . turpi'.
27. Powicke, p. 112 and n. 108.

In 1196 Richard began work on new fortifications at Les Andelys on the Seine, erecting the magnificent castle of Château-Gaillard, towering on the limestone cliff over the river. Richard's enthusiasm for the project is underlined by his readiness to offend Walter of Coutances archbishop of Rouen so that he could take over this church land for his castle. The fortification of Les Andelys is nowadays usually viewed as an aggressive move, producing a stronghold well placed for a future invasion of France. William Marshal saw it as the beginning of 'the great war', presumably meaning the war that led to the loss of Normandy; and William the Breton believed he built it 'because he thought he would in some way recover his lands from there'.[28]

In the context of 1196, however, Richard's thoughts were more likely to be defensive after the loss of Gisors, and certainly there was never any major invasion of France by either Richard or John while they held Château-Gaillard. According to Diceto: 'our enemies used to enter Normandy by that route', and Richard told the pope that his motive was defence.[29] It was a very costly construction; the record from the Norman exchequer reveals an expenditure of some £11,500 (Angevin) over only two years, an amount which far exceeded any other castle spending of the period. It was an imposing and elaborate project, involving the diversion of streams to enclose the town, the making of a pool between the old and the new towns, and a stockade over the river on the south side. The castle was the most advanced of its day, towering on the rock, with three enclosures and a keep. Richard himself directed operations on his *bellum castrum*, and it became his favourite residence, but at first Les Andelys brought more trouble than gain, Archbishop Walter's protest over the way the site was taken leading to an interdict on Normandy so that unburied corpses littered the streets.[30]

28. *Guillaume le Maréchal*, II, p. 16, l. 10564: 'lores comença la grant guerre'; William the Breton, 'Vie', ed. Guizot, pp. 221–2; William the Breton, 'Vie', ed. Delaborde, p. 208: 'inde ut terram suam quocumque modo recuperaret'; cf. William the Breton, 'Philippide', ed. Delaborde, p. 193.
29. Ralph of Diceto, *Opera Historica*, ed. W. Stubbs, 2 vols, RS no. 68 (London, 1876) II, p. 155.
30. Powicke, p. 204, note A, pp. 204–8, gives details from the Norman Exchequer Roll concerning the building.

Richard's only main gain in 1196 was the development of his coalition against Philip, the great catch of the year being Raymond VI count of Toulouse. By an agreement, Richard now ended the Forty Years' War begun by his father, and made a peace cemented by marriage between Raymond and Richard's widowed sister, Joan. Richard had to renounce those rights to Toulouse which had spurred Henry II to war in the first place.

On 15 April 1197 Richard made a raid against St-Valery, part of Alice's dowry, in the territory of the count of Ponthieu. Relics were seized, five ships burned in the harbour, and the sailors hanged. Wendover suggests these were English ships treacherously supplying the enemy.[31] In May Richard raided the Beauvaisis, thus taking a more offensive stance, while Milly-sur-Thérain was captured by Mercadier. Here William the Marshal knocked down the constable, William de Monceaux, and as exhausted as his captive, sat on him for a rest and 'to guard him'. More important perhaps, John and Mercadier managed to trap Philip of Dreux, the bishop of Beauvais, a militant ecclesiastic who had offended Richard on crusade by supporting Conrad, and since then by leading an embassy to Germany against his release. The bishop was imprisoned at Rouen, not as a bishop claimed Richard, but as a knight who had fought 'fully armed, helm laced'.[32]

The bishop of Beauvais complained to Pope Celestine III (1191–98) for taking no action to release him; but the latter made only a half-hearted protest, telling him he had got what he deserved for his militant life-style: 'into the pit you have made, you have deservedly fallen', 'you have worn the

31. Roger of Wendover, ed. Giles, II, p. 167; Roger of Wendover, ed. Hewlett, I, p. 269: 'naves ex Anglia . . . ad deferendum victualia regi Francorum et aliis inimicis suis'.
32. *Guillaume le Maréchal*, ll. 11196, 11221, ll. 11105–11264; III, pp. 149, 155; II, p. 40, l. 11231: 'S'asist desus por lui tenir'; II, pp. 52–3, ll. 11593–5: 'Ne fu pas comme avesque pris/Mes comme chevalier de pris,/Toz armez, le hielme lacié'; D. Crouch, *William Marshal* (Harlow, 1990) pp. 75–6; S. Painter, *William Marshal* (Baltimore, 1933) pp. 110–11. J. Gillingham, 'Richard I, galley-warfare and Portsmouth: the beginnings of a royal navy', *13th Century England*, VI, 1997, pp. 1–15, suggests a deliberate naval policy by Richard in these years.

hauberk and the alb, the helmet and the mitre'.[33] At one point the bishop escaped and clung to a church knocker, expecting sanctuary, but he was unceremoniously dragged away and sent to Chinon under even harsher conditions. Richard turned down a ransom offer of a thousand marks, and when a papal legate demanded the bishop's release in 1198, Richard again angrily refused, offering to castrate the legate for his troubles! The bishop would not be released until after Richard's death.

In July 1197 Richard's coalition was greatly strengthened by a settlement with the count of Flanders. This resulted from coercion rather than friendship, Richard having placed an embargo on English trade with Flanders, showing that economic sanctions sometimes work. The embargo was lifted, and back payment of the suspended pension to Count Baldwin was to be made up. As a result Baldwin attacked Philip's lands, taking Douai, Bapaume, Péronne and Roye, and besieging Arras. Philip moved on the threatened area, first recapturing the recently surrendered Dangu, which guarded a ford over the Epte.

The count abandoned Arras and was defeated, but Philip overreached himself, marching northwards into Flanders. The count broke the bridges behind the king, until his supplies were cut off and Philip was trapped. He was able to escape by making an agreement with the count in September. On his return to France and safety, Philip claimed that the agreement had been made under duress and 'a rebel vassal has no right to impose conditions'.[34] For Philip there was no permanent loss from the episode, apart from the opportunity it gave Richard to make headway in Berry, where he captured ten castles including Vierzon.

Baldwin of Flanders renewed the war in September 1198, attacking Artois and taking Aire, which surrendered without a fight. He besieged St-Omer, which appealed to Philip for aid. Aid was promised, but did not arrive in time. Philip had focused attention again on the Vexin. His destructive raid

33. J.T. Appleby, *John, King of England* (London, 1958) p. 75; Roger of Howden, ed. Riley, II, p. 402; Roger of Howden, ed. Stubbs, IV, p. 23: 'in foveam quam fecisti, merito incidisti', 'loricam pro alba, galeam pro mitra'.
34. Luchaire in Lavisse, p. 117.

saw the burning of eighteen places. He was beaten back to Vernon, though William the Breton says he won a victory before the retreat in which twenty knights were captured.[35] Philip escaped with little harm done, though the Angevin chroniclers relished the opportunity to ridicule Philip, largely on the grounds that he rode off on an elderly horse called Morelle.

Richard raided into the French Vexin, and Philip attempted to save Courcelles, whose surrender on 27 September he did not know about. Here occurred the second of the skirmishes in which Philip was worsted in this year. The retreat to Gisors was crowed over by Angevin chroniclers – Howden repeats it three times – but it was not a serious defeat.[36] Richard had expected the French to cross the Epte at Dangu, but Philip surprised him by heading directly for Gisors. Mercadier and a local knight, Hugh de Corny, had seen the French and reported to Richard, who insisted on making an immediate attack: 'like a hungry lion upon its prey'.[37] The French force of only 200 knights retired.

Philip had escaped from a trap, but suffered an accident when heading into the safety of Gisors. The weight of the retreating French broke the bridge over the Epte, and many fell in the water. Eighteen knights were drowned and Philip was among those who fell in. He 'rolled over and over in the mud' wrote one; and 'drank the water' added another.[38] But Philip was dragged out safely and got into Gisors, then headed back to Les Andelys. Perhaps a hundred knights were captured outside Gisors, but the limitations of the victory are shown by the fact that Richard could not press on to take Gisors itself. Indeed Philip was immediately ready for another attack, raiding into Normandy south of the Seine, which Richard had to counter with a raid into the Vexin. Peace negotiations failed because Philip was not prepared

35. William the Breton, *Philippide*, ed. Guizot, p. 141.
36. Roger of Howden, ed. Riley, II, pp. 428, 430, 431; Roger of Howden, ed. Stubbs, IV, pp. 55–6, 58, 59–60.
37. *Guillaume le Maréchal*, III, p. 145; II, p. 31, ll. 10993–5: 'Comme li lïuns femeillos/Qui de mangier est angoissos/Cort a sa poreie s'i(l) la trove'.
38. Roger of Wendover, ed. Giles, II, p. 175; Roger of Wendover, ed. Hewlett, I, pp. 278–9: 'in coeno jacens'; Roger of Howden, ed. Riley, II, p. 428; Roger of Howden, ed. Stubbs, IV, p. 56: 'et bibit ex ea'.

to include Flanders as Richard demanded, and the conflict again ended with a truce until the new year.

By 1199 Richard had regained most of the lost territory, but the war was not quite over. Although Philip was prepared to surrender his losses to date, no agreement was reached, despite papal pressure for a peace. In his usual reticent manner, Richard damned the legate and told him: 'flee from here traitor, liar, trickster and simoniac'.[39] For the proposed marriage between Prince Louis and Richard's niece, Blanche of Castile, Gisors was to be the agreed dower, ensuring its passing to the French monarchy. The two kings met on 13 January 1199, or at least approached each other, Philip on horseback on the bank, Richard in a boat on the river. But there was no final peace, Richard still refusing to release the bishop of Beauvais, and only a truce was agreed for five years. Philip did make peace with the count of Flanders in the treaty of Péronne, by which he made some restorations, but he retained Arras, Lens, Bapaume and Hesdin.

A chronicler claims Richard had 'recovered with sword and spear his alienated rights'. But somehow in English accounts the episode at Châlus, despite Gillingham's persuasive arguments about the nature of the siege, is not seen as part of the war.[40] It has generally been thought that Richard went in search of treasure, said to have been found and kept by the local lords. According to William the Breton, it had been found by a peasant under the command of Achard, lord of Châlus, while Rigord describes it as consisting of an object in gold with an inscription, portraying an emperor and his family at a gold table. So many chroniclers, both French and Angevin, mention the treasure in one way or another that it is difficult to dismiss the story altogether. It sounds possible that some Roman hoard was discovered. In any case, Gillingham is surely right that Richard's major

39. P.N. Lewis, 'The wars of Richard I in the West', M.Phil. thesis (London, 1977) p. 207; *Guillaume le Maréchal*, III, p. 155, II, p. 53, ll. 11618–20: 'Fuiez de ci, dant traïtor,/Mentieres, trichieres e fals/E d'iglises simonials!'
40. 'Itinerarium', in K. Fenwick, ed. and trans., *The Third Crusade* (London, 1958) p. 164; 'Itinerarium', in W. Stubbs, ed., *Chronicles and Memorials of the Reign of Richard I*, 2 vols, RS no. 38 (London, 1864–65) I, p. 446: 'alienatum jus suum cum augmento quoque potenter in hasta recuperavit et gladio'; Gillingham, ch. 2, pp. 9–23.

motive was to deal with a rebellion fostered by the encouragement of Philip.[41] The southern lords were not difficult to stir up; like Bertran de Born, they were 'pleased when the truce between pounds sterling and pounds of Tours was broken'.[42]

Richard had probably broken the truce by sending Mercadier southwards, which ended in a beating for the latter when ambushed by French counts. There were accusations against Philip for breaking the truce by building a castle near Les Andelys, which, however, under pressure he agreed to demolish. As Richard's alliance with the count of Flanders had borne fruit in 1197, so now Philip's encouragement of the count of Angoulême had even more significant consequences. English historians like to see Gisors as 'the fit ending of Richard's war with Philip Augustus', but it was not the final event. As William the Breton expressed it, now 'God visited France'.[43]

In March Richard came to besiege the castle of Châlus, which belonged to the viscount of Limoges, one of the leading rebels. It was on the lower of two hills over the Tadoire. On the evening of 26 March Richard made a reconnaissance of the castle, 'examining in which spot it would be most admirable to make the attack'.[44] As on previous occasions, he did not take the precaution of protecting himself adequately. This time the result was fatal. After supper Richard went to see how things were going, shooting the odd crossbow bolt himself. A crossbowman on the walls, who had been batting away Angevin bolts all day with a frying pan, and whose father and two brothers had been killed by Richard, aimed a hopeful shot at the king and hit him in the angle between shoulder and neck. The wound did not

41. William the Breton, *Philippide*, ed. Guizot, p. 144; 'Philippide', ed. Delaborde, p. 144, ll. 496–7; Rigord, ed. Guizot, p. 145; Rigord, ed. Delaborde, p. 144; cf. William the Breton, 'Vie', ed. Delaborde, p. 204; Gillingham, p. 22.
42. Bertran de Born, *The Poems of the Troubadour Bertran de Born*, ed. W.D. Paden Jr, T. Sankovitch and P.H. Stäblein (Berkeley, CA, 1986) pp. 460–1, ll. 14–16: 'per qe.m plai gerra ben facha/e.m plai qan la treg'es fracha/dels esterlis e dels tornes'.
43. Powicke, p. 122; William the Breton, 'Vie', ed. Guizot, p. 219; 'Vie', ed. Delaborde, p. 204: 'visitavit Deus regum Francorum'.
44. Roger of Howden, ed. Riley, II, p. 452; Rogor of Howden, ed. Stubbs, IV, p. 82: 'explorantes in quo loco esset commodius insultum facere'.

appear to be fatal and Richard was able to mount and ride
back to camp, but he was said to be so fat that the bolt was
difficult to extract, and Mercadier's surgeon like a 'butcher'
mangled the king's shoulder. The queen mother, Eleanor,
was called to the side of her ailing son, and within the week,
on 6 April 1199, he died in her arms. 'As the day ended, so
ended his life.' She mourned: 'I have lost the staff of my
age, the light of my eyes.'[45] The last blow in this war had
recovered all the advantages for Philip. As in the war with
Henry II, the last and the triumphant word was with Philip.
He immediately confirmed his advantage by going on to
Évreux, which he retook.

. . .

CONCLUSIONS ON THE WAR BETWEEN PHILIP AND RICHARD

Before Richard's return from captivity, Philip had advanced
across the Norman border and won something like thirty
fortresses. He had pushed forward the French border to
an additional ring of territory around Rouen. This advance
included a whole string of castles along the border with Normandy, including Gournay, Neufmarché, Nonancourt and
Tillières. He had also taken strongholds in a pincer from
the east of Normandy and on its coast, including Eu, Arques
and Dieppe. And among the acquisitions, in a pincer from
the west, were fortresses which were uncomfortably close
to Rouen from the Plantagenet point of view, including Le
Vaudreuil and Pont de l'Arche. In general Philip had gained
by Richard's absence and imprisonment, but had been
unable to retain most of these gains once Richard had
returned. This was partly due to Richard's military abilities,
and partly from a tendency by all concerned to return to
things as they had been, once Richard was back. Already by
the end of 1195 two-thirds of the captured places had been
retaken by Richard, and Philip for the most part retained

45. Roger of Howden, ed. Riley, II, p. 453; Roger of Howden, ed. Stubbs,
IV, p. 83: 'carnifex'; Seward, p. 83; Henderson, p. 243; K. Norgate,
England under the Angevin Kings, 2 vols (London, 1887) II, p. 386;
Ralph of Coggeshall, *Chronicon Anglicanum*, ed. J. Stevenson, RS
no. 66 (London, 1875) p. 96: 'cum jam dies clauderetur, diem clausit
extremum'.

only the gains along the frontier. There can, nevertheless, be little question of the significant losses sustained by the Plantagenets during the captivity, when Richard's rivals 'made cruel assaults upon his castles, without cause'.[46]

The war was not one-way traffic, and Richard also had setbacks in the war which followed his return. Philip attacked twenty-five places during the war and took twenty-one of them. The Angevins in the same period failed seven times, twice under Richard in person. Philip's defeats at Vernon and Gisors are well known, but he also had victories in similar skirmishes at Le Vaudreuil, Arques and Aumale. There was no real pitched battle during this stage of the war, and none of the sieges were truly decisive; there is no saying how things might have gone had Richard survived.[47]

The death of Richard brought the war to a conclusion in Philip's favour: he could now expect some advance in Normandy and Berry. John was in a relatively weak position; even his succession was not secure against the claims of his nephew Arthur of Brittany. The Angevin Empire was staggering under the demands of the recent war and in particular of Richard's expenditure on troops, fortification and allies. Regular scutages had been demanded for the war, three years in succession from 1194. Norgate saw Richard as 'at his wits' end', and quotes Richard's own poem: 'there is not a penny at Chinon'.[48]

The demands of war left other marks, not least a growing reluctance in England to becoming involved in continental affairs, particularly in southern France, where few English barons had any personal attachment. The first signs of a problem in receiving military service appeared in 1196, when the saintly Hugh bishop of Lincoln claimed that he did not owe knights for overseas service: 'I am well aware that the Church of Lincoln is bound to do the king military service, but only in this country; outside the boundaries of England no such thing is owed.'[49] He was supported by the bishop of

46. 'Itinerarium', ed. Fenwick, p. 164; 'Itinerarium', ed. Stubbs, p. 443: 'castra ejus in Normannia, crudeliter grassantibus aemuli ejus sine causa'.
47. J. Gillingham, 'Richard I and the science of war in the Middle Ages', in Gillingham and Holt, pp. 78–91.
48. Norgate, *Richard*, p. 321.
49. Norgate, *Angevins*, II, p. 349; D.L. Douie and Dom H. Farmer, eds, *The Life of Saint Hugh of Lincoln*, 2 vols (Edinburgh, 1962) II, p. 99:

Salisbury. Dissatisfaction in England was made more acute by famine and plague through the 1190s, and was demonstrated by a rebellion of the lesser citizens in London.

There were marks left in Normandy too, not least from the ravages of war. 'Nothing is safe, neither the city to dwell in, nor the highway for travel,' reckoned the clergy of Hereford and Lincoln when coming to Normandy.[50] Part of Philip's success was to demonstrate how damaging opposition to himself could be, and Normandy had borne the brunt of the war. Richard and the Angevins had frequently done homage to the kings of France, and aggression against one's lord was not approved. As one writer put it: 'the king of England did not deign to be obedient to his lord'.[51] It had been difficult for Richard to find a justifiable stance. The ambivalent attitude of the Norman castellans is demonstrated by the number of those who would hand castles to Philip with no more than token resistance.

In the view of Bertran de Born, who would not see the final outcome, this was a war without a winner, a battle between a falcon and an eagle, in which neither could gain the decisive victory.[52] Philip's father had once brought his troops to Rouen, during the great rebellion of 1173–74. Even more threateningly, Philip's own advance, during Richard's captivity, had seen him rapidly overrun Normandy to the walls of Rouen; it was a precedent he would not forget. Such demonstrations of Norman vulnerability encouraged hopes of even greater success.

'scio equidem ad militare officium domino regi, set in hac terra solummodo exhibendum, Lincolniensem ecclesiam teneri; extra metas uero Anglie nil tale ab ea deberi'.

50. Powicke, p. 129; St Hugh, II, p. 132: 'Nichil iam tutum, non ciuitas ad inhabitandum, non ager publicus ad uiandum'.
51. Powicke, p. 112 and n. 105; the Anonymous of Béthune, in *RHF*, XXIV, Pt II, p. 758.
52. Bertran de Born, pp. 378–79.

Chapter 5

THE DEFEAT OF THE ANGEVIN EMPIRE

.   .   .

JOHN'S ACCESSION

The year 1199 offered much to Philip Augustus. Richard the Lionheart had been a doughty opponent. Every succession was a period of some vulnerability for a medieval monarchy, and the succession to the Plantagenet lands in 1199 was particularly so. John's succession in 1199 was less certain than Richard's had been ten years before, and more difficult. William the Breton thought he succeeded 'under the most inauspicious circumstances'.[1]

John had rebelled against Richard during the latter's crusade and captivity, and had never received a major command or province to rule. As a result, in 1199, he had no experience of government and no solid power base. His only independent experience had been the unfortunate expedition to Ireland under his father. And a good deal was already known to the detriment of John's personality. It would not take a genius to believe in 1199 that the Plantagenets would not be as well led under John as they had been under Richard.

In Sicily, not long before the marriage to Berengaria, when his expectation was no doubt to be succeeded by his own offspring, Richard had named his nephew Arthur of Brittany as his heir. He is, however, likely to have favoured John's

---

1. William the Breton, *La Philippide, Poème*, ed. and trans. M. Guizot (Paris, 1825) p. 152; 'Philippide' in *Oeuvres de Rigord et de Guillaume le Breton*, ed. H-F. Delaborde, SHF, vols 210, 224 (Paris, 1882–85) I, p. 151, ll. 14–15; cf. p. 149, l. 623.

succession at the last, when Arthur was in Philip's hands. But given Richard's remarks about his younger brother, and the experience of his dubious loyalty, one cannot believe that Richard had any great enthusiasm for his brother's succession to his position. Arguably Arthur had the better case for inheritance than John; his father, Geoffrey, had been an older brother of John, so Arthur came by a prior line of descent. Richard's recognition of Arthur as his heir while he was in Sicily suggests that the rules were not hard and fast. William Longchamp, with his legal training, expressed the view that Arthur had the prior claim. It was a situation ripe for Philip Augustus to take advantage, and he was only too happy to play on Angevin uncertainties over the succession. John became king of England, but Philip accepted Arthur's homage for most of the continental lands of the Plantagenets.[2]

In the event, in 1199, some areas of the continental Angevin Empire declared for John, but Maine, Anjou and Touraine initially favoured Arthur, and there remained a question mark over John's right, which Philip Augustus was able to exploit. To most of the French counties which had been part of the Angevin Empire, John was a more distant and remote prince than either his father or his brother had been. At least in the south, where Capetian influence was also relatively slight, Eleanor was still a force, and she held firm for her youngest son: she ceded Poitou to John and received it back from him for life. While she lived, John's rights there were protected, but he would need to exert himself if he were to become powerful there in his own person.

John was able to claim the treasury at Chinon in Anjou, but Plantagenet authority in its own ancient demesne, with the frequent absences enforced by ruling the Angevin Empire, had seriously declined. Outside the old patrimony of Greater Anjou, the position of the Plantagenets had perforce to depend on the strength and efforts of the individual prince, whether Henry II or Richard I.

Even in Normandy, Angevin rule was, in the view of Lewis Warren, 'already a guttering candle when John came to the

2. See R.V. Turner, *King John* (Harlow, 1994) pp. 48–52; and J.C. Holt, 'The *Casus Regis*: the law and politics of succession in the Plantagenet domains 1185–1247', in E.B. King and S.J. Ridyard, eds, *Law in Medieval Life and Thought* (Sewanee, TN, 1990).

throne'.[3] This probably exaggerates the position, though guttering candles do sometimes recover their flame. The revenue of Normandy was still reasonably sound, but the death of Richard had opened new questions over the future of the duchy. Nevertheless John was invested as duke of Normandy at Rouen on 25 April, and crowned king of England in London on 27 May.[4] After the death of Henry II, his sons had no easy recognition throughout the lands he had ruled: Richard was established in Aquitaine, but only after long years of fighting, and his hold elsewhere was more tenuous. John had no continental power base at all.

There were a number of weaknesses in John's position. Richard's marriage to Berengaria had given the Lionheart the useful Navarre alliance, which had proved beneficial at several points during the conflict with Philip in the south. John could not expect the same close co-operation. Richard had spent much time in the south and associated himself closely with the politics of the region, where John to date had played no important part. In Poitou John could only call on the support of five castellans, as against fourteen for Richard.[5] He also lacked the prestige of his brother, with his crusading and military leadership; indeed John was nicknamed 'softsword' in 1200, a reputation which he never altogether overcame.[6]

In 1199 John was not without hope; but progress must depend on strenuous activity. Arthur was only twelve, and enthusiasm for his rule was not strong outside Brittany. There were also those princes and lords who looked to maintain the Angevin alliance as a bulwark against Philip and his ambitions for expansion, and both Baldwin of Flanders at Rouen, and Renaud of Boulogne at Les Andelys, did homage to John.

3. W.L. Warren, *King John*, 2nd edn (London, 1978) p. 90.
4. See D. Crouch, *The Image of Aristocracy in Britain, 1000–1300* (London, 1992) pp. 14–15, 53; and G. Garnett, ' "Ducal" succession in early Normandy', in G. Garnett and J. Hudson, eds, *Law and Government in Medieval England and Normandy* (Cambridge, 1994) pp. 80–110. On finance, see J. Gillingham, *The Angevin Empire* (London, 1984) p. 72; D. Bates, 'The rise and fall of Normandy, c.911–1204', in *England and Normandy in the Middle Ages*, p. 34.
5. Turner, p. 83.
6. Gervase of Canterbury, *The Historical Works*, ed. W. Stubbs, 2 vols, RS no. 73 (London, 1879–80) II, pp. 92–3; p. 93: ' "Johannem mollegladium" eum malivoli detractores et invidi derisores vocabant'.

Philip decided to test out John's strength. After seizing Évreux and Conches, he devastated Normandy to its border. The Évrécin was an area at the heart of Philip's plans for attack: near the south-eastern border of Normandy, and close to the most obvious approach route into the duchy, the Seine.

In the same year Philip attempted to link his effort more closely to that of the supporters of young Arthur. Maine had never rested easy under Norman, or for that matter Angevin, domination. Philip thought he could use Maine as a route from his own territories, along the southern border of Normandy and so towards Brittany. However, when he moved into Maine, where he took and destroyed Ballon ostensibly on Arthur's behalf, Philip antagonized William des Roches, a key magnate whom Luchaire has called 'a sort of governor general in the Loire region'.[7] William des Roches complained that Ballon was under his jurisdiction and that the king was treating Maine as conquered territory. Philip declared he could do what he liked with whatever he took from John, but in the end was forced to abandon the invasion of Maine. William des Roches deserted Philip and was recognized as seneschal by John, who appointed him castellan of Chinon. While such major lords were prepared to support John, Philip would have difficulty in taking over any large section of the Angevin Empire. The signs were that John would take up the mantle cast down by his brother; Philip could hardly have expected any rapid change of fortunes, and had to anticipate a continuation of the long war of attrition.

Philip's capture of the bishop-elect of Cambrai, and his exchange for the captive bishop of Beauvais, whom John finally released, closed one long-running cause of hostility. Philip and John met on 15 January 1200 and agreement was finally reached on 22 May. Philip seems to have resigned himself to John succeeding to Richard's position, but he was still capable of some hard bargaining before acknowledging him as heir to Richard's territories on the continent.

The treaty of Le Goulet, made at the conference place near Les Andelys, was a recognition of Philip's strength.[8] John

7. A. Luchaire in E. Lavisse, *Histoire de France depuis les Origines jusqu'à la Révolution*, III, Pt I (Paris, 1911) p. 124.
8. *Recueil des Actes de Philippe Auguste*, ed. H-F. Delaborde, 4 vols (Paris, 1916–79) II, no. 633, pp. 178–85.

had to do homage and pay a heavy relief of 20,000 marks sterling. Philip asserted his claims to eastern Normandy, receiving the Évrécin and the Vexin except for Les Andelys. Philip's son Louis was to marry John's niece, Blanche of Castile; Philip was to keep her at court and look after her dowry lands in the Vexin, together with Issoudun, Graçay and the fief of Andrew de Chauvigny, all of which John handed to Philip.

Despite their tender ages, the marriage of Louis and Blanche was carried out next day by the archbishop of Bordeaux. Arthur of Brittany would be John's man, but could not forfeit his lands without Philip's assent, while the counts of Flanders and Boulogne promised to return to the French king's allegiance. It has recently been suggested that, by Le Goulet, John went further than previous Angevin rulers in acknowledging Philip's rights over the Plantagenets, which he confirmed by the payment of an enormous relief.[9] By the treaty John would receive back Angoulême and Limoges. He also promised not to give further aid to Otto in the Holy Roman Empire.

In 1200 John had little choice but to agree; his position in 1199 had looked so precarious that the treaty of Le Goulet could almost be seen as a victory, but one hesitates to go so far as claiming 'a triumph of John's diplomacy'; and with hindsight the 'victory' looks somewhat pyrrhic. One has more sympathy with the view that it was 'a great success for Philip Augustus'. As Professor Turner has pointed out, the treaty allowed Philip 'to assert his court's authority', which he would shortly utilize. John was allowed to take up his position as Richard's successor, but Philip had forced him into some damaging concessions.[10] Philip's gains in the Vexin and in

9. E.M. Hallam, *Capetian France, 987–1328* (Harlow, 1980) p. 183: 'To secure his lands against the claims of Arthur of Britanny, John made enormous allowances to Philip in the Treaty of Le Goulet in 1200, which neither Richard nor Henry II would ever have considered. He rendered homage to the French king, he paid him an enormous relief, thus acknowledging Philip's right to decide the succession . . .'

10. Gillingham, p. 67; J. Boussard, 'Philippe Auguste et les Plantagenêts', in R-H. Bautier, ed., *La France de Philippe Auguste, le Temps des Mutations*, Actes du Colloque International organisé par le Centre National de la Recherche Scientifique, 1980 (Paris, 1982) pp. 263–89, p. 279; Turner, p. 117.

Berry provided the entry points for his coming invasion of Plantagenet territories.

For the time being the English king, now 'our dearly beloved and faithful John', was able to tour the old Angevin lands which had been returned to his lordship.[11] Afterwards in Paris he was welcomed by Philip and given presents. So far as one can see at this point, Philip was prepared to accept that the Angevin Empire would remain a powerful entity, and that John would be its ruler.[12] He must, however, have harboured memories of the sudden collapses in that empire during the great rebellion against Henry II and during Richard's imprisonment. Philip would look to exploit any weakness that might offer opportunities, and might anticipate that John would prove a less durable enemy than Richard. From previous experience, it is also likely that Philip would watch especially for opportunities against Normandy, and in the troubled southern areas near the Loire.

July of 1200 found Philip again, despite the apparent peace, probing at the region of the Seine which seemed his best route for entry into the duchy, returning to both Évreux and Vernon. The frequency of Philip's appearances in this region speak surely not of fears for defence, but about an intention of aggression.[13] In 1200 he travelled occasionally to Paris and through the demesne, but spent a good deal of his time in that sensitive borderland.

Now John made a prime error, a disastrous mistake, though several recent historians have seen it as 'a good stroke of business', or even a 'wise move'. He separated from his first wife, Isabella of Gloucester, in order to marry Isabella of Angoulême, the count's daughter, whom he had met during his summer tour. She was about twelve and he was thirty-five. It has been argued that this brought John a useful

---

11. Roger of Howden, *The Annals of Roger de Hoveden*, ed. and trans. H.T. Riley, 2 vols (London, 1853) II, p. 508; Roger of Howden, *Chronica*, ed. W. Stubbs, 4 vols, RS no. 51 (London, 1868–71) IV, p. 148: 'dilectum nostrum et fidelem Johannem'.
12. *Recueil*, II, no. 633, p. 180: by Le Goulet, John was to hold from Philip 'pacem quam frater suus rex Ricardus fecit nobis'.
13. The travels of Philip noted in this chapter are based upon evidence from his acts, this evidence being preferred above other sources or assumptions. At Vernon and Évreux in 1200: *Recueil*, II, nos 635, p. 186; 646, pp. 205–6; 647, pp. 206–8.

alliance with the important county of Angoulême, which is true; but he lost more than he gained by making the match.[14] The marriage to Isabella of Angoulême, on 24 August 1200, antagonized the powerful family of Lusignan. Hugh the Brown of Lusignan had been betrothed to Isabella.[15] The Lusignans had been allies of Richard, their lands in Poitou holding a vital bridge between Plantagenet territories to the north and the south. Now they complained to Philip as their overlord at John's treatment of them. John not only failed to compensate the family, but turned on them and seized their properties. He drove them into Philip's welcoming arms.

The episode provided Philip with a suitable pretext for a new invasion of Angevin territory. Roger of Howden even suggests that John's marriage was made 'by the advice of his lord, Philip, king of France'. Though Philip was to gain much from it, the accusation seems improbable. More likely to be the case is Howden's other explanation, that 'John, king of England, had a fancy for her'.[16] But the English king's prime intention may have been to break Lusignan power in the area, possibly fuelled by resentment of his brother who had been the ally of the Lusignans, and who had arranged the match between Hugh and Isabella in the first place. John did at least succeed in one way where his brother failed: his own new marriage was reasonably successful, and it did produce a male heir.

14. G. Duby, *France in the Middle Ages, 987–1460*, trans. J. Vale (Oxford, 1991) p. 218; Hallam, pp. 183, 130: 'a prudent move'; C. Petit-Dutaillis, *The Feudal Monarchy in France and England from the Tenth to the Thirteenth Centuries*, trans. E.D. Hunt (London, 1936) p. 217; Gillingham, p. 67: 'much to be said in favour of this marriage'.
15. William the Breton, *Philippide*, ed. Guizot, p. 155; Roger of Wendover, *Flowers of History*, ed. and trans. J.A. Giles, 2 vols (London, 1899) II, p. 188; Roger of Wendover, *Flores Historiarum*, ed. H.G. Hewlett, 3 vols, RS no. 84 (London, 1886–89) I, p. 295; *The Life of Saint Hugh of Lincoln*, ed. and trans. D.L. Douie and H. Farmer, 2 vols (Edinburgh, 1962) II, p. 184: 'the adulteress who forsook her lawful husband shamelessly for his rival'.
16. Roger of Howden, ed. Riley, p. 183; Roger of Howden, ed. Stubbs, IV, p. 119: 'in consilio domini sui Philippi regis Franciae'; Roger of Wendover, ed. Hewlett, I, p. 295 simply repeats Howden: 'consilio regis Francorum'.

. . .

PHILIP'S POSITION AFTER 1199

John's accession gave Philip an opportunity to take stock and re-assess his position. Any king in the period was forced to defend his own, and it was natural policy to compete with one's neighbours for control of the frontier regions between their respective territories. That Philip came into conflict with the Plantagenets seems almost inevitable. In the twelfth century that struggle had not seemed to reach a do-or-die position; it had rarely been more than a struggle for disputed border areas. There had been two occasions when the French monarchy had threatened a more severe outcome: during the rebellion against Henry II by his sons in 1173–74, and during the imprisonment of Richard the Lionheart in 1194. But even had the French king been victorious on those occasions, the most likely consequence would have been a re-ordering of Plantagenet lands in the hands of Plantagenet claimants. In the event neither effort had been entirely successful, but the proximity to collapse, especially on the second occasion, gave Philip cause to consider what other outcome there might be.

Philip began to play an old game, giving support against the head of the family to a Plantagenet claimant, this time Arthur of Brittany against John. But this was the point when Philip also began to think in terms of direct gains for the French crown, especially in Normandy and those areas bordering immediately on Capetian demesne lands along the Loire. His readiness to consider an invasion of England also demonstrates that his ambitions were expanding beyond stirring up the Plantagenets against each other, and beyond conflicts over border territories only. He never achieved this wider aim entirely, but he began to think in terms of the destruction or diminution rather than simply the containment of the Plantagenets.

Otherwise Philip continued to follow the usual course of pursuing any opportunity for expansion. There was no reason why proven tactics should not still be employed in a broader strategic plan. Thus he always sought to divide the Plantagenets against each other, and now it was Arthur who gained his aid against John. He continued to issue propaganda

137

concerning the benefits to the Church from Capetian rather than Plantagenet rule, in order to win ecclesiastical support for his actions. He continued to cajole secular lords into preferring his lordship and justice to that of the Angevins, seeking to win over men to his allegiance, particularly if they were powerful in disputed regions. He also made efforts to keep them within his allegiance, with a tight system of pledges which operated throughout his territories, from the the borders of Flanders to the Touraine and Berry. Thus he extracted promises of allegiance, with guarantees from neighbours, which would result in financial penalties if broken.[17]

Medieval government was always largely geared to war, but in the early thirteenth century Philip's government took on a very clear focus in that respect. Much was poured into improving the defence of towns and castles. As a paymaster of mercenaries Philip now edged into first place, thereby attracting numbers and quality of troops. These payments were now on a scale which suggests ambitions beyond simply defence: border castles, garrisons and large numbers of mercenaries would be necessary in a war of expansion.

If life seemed to have returned to normal with John's recognition as overlord of most of the former Angevin territories, and if the balance between France and the Plantagenet Empire seemed to have been re-established, then time would show this appearance to be misleading. Philip had made significant gains in his position by the treaty of Le Goulet. John had to recognize Philip's agreement with Flanders at Péronne, and accepted the count of Flanders' subordination to the French king. Similarly John had to abandon his alliance with the Holy Roman Emperor, Otto. John's opponents, the count of Angoulême and the vicomte of Limoges, were restored. Most importantly, the disputed Norman border territories of the Évrécin and the Vexin, except for Château-Gaillard, were accepted as Philip's, together with Issoudun and Graçay in Berry. Over the next two years obstacles were removed to allow a new bite at the inviting cherry of the Angevin Empire.

The focus of Philip's intentions was also made clear by the settlement of problems elsewhere. Of course it was

17. J.W. Baldwin, *The Government of Philip Augustus* (Berkeley, CA, 1986) pp. 267–8.

impossible to clear the decks entirely, but in the early years of the thirteenth century Philip arranged matters so that he could direct almost all his military effort against the main enemy, the Plantagenet King John. In 1201 the agreement with the papacy, pressed for by Philip in letters, patched over the worst of the troubles resulting from Philip's marriage.[18] In 1200 Baldwin of Flanders was enticed to abandon John, and made terms with Philip in the treaty of Péronne. At this point Philip thought it worth his while to concede St-Omer and Aire to the count, in return for detaching him from John.

In 1201 Renaud of Boulogne also made his peace with Philip, and Philip's son by Agnes de Méran, Philip Hurepel (aged one), was to marry Renaud's daughter Matilda. At the same time Renaud's brother married the daughter of Philip's ally, the count of Ponthieu. Among Philip's grants to Renaud was Mortain, formerly John's own county. Philip's largely unforced concessions, and his willingness to forget past differences, suggest that his reasons lay elsewhere: that he was preparing the way for a new attack on John. In the following year the count of Flanders and several other potentially difficult French nobles left on the Fourth Crusade, encouraged on their way by the king.[19]

Philip did not exploit the situation to any great degree immediately, but waited for opportunities to arise. Nevertheless, in the year following the treaty of Le Goulet, as in the previous summer, Philip maintained his personal presence in the Seine border territory. During 1201 he moved from Senlis to Vernon in March, appearing there again in May, and possibly also later in the year, as well as going to Gisors, Mantes and Pontoise.[20] He was maintaining his presence in the border territory, but there was no serious threat from John at this time, and we might therefore surmise that Philip's purpose was more of a reconnaissance for future attack.

One relevant event was the death of Constance of Brittany in August; her son Arthur was now of an age to take centre

---

18. *Recueil*, II, no. 676, pp. 232–4: in which Philip explained the reasons for his recent activities, and demanded the legitimization of his children by Agnes; no. 685, pp. 245–6, is more threatening.
19. *Recueil*, II, no. 680, pp. 239–41, encourages his vassals to crusade.
20. *Recueil*, II, nos 674, pp. 230–1; 675, pp. 231–2; 677, p. 234; 686, p. 247; 693, pp. 255–6; 695, pp. 258–9; 696, pp. 259–60.

stage. Philip knighted him in 1202 and encouraged him in aggression against John in Aquitaine. Arthur did homage for most of the Plantagenet continental lands, though not for Normandy. In an act of 1202, Philip made known that he had received Arthur's homage for Brittany, Anjou, Maine and the Touraine: 'when, God willing, one of us shall acquire them'; but as regards Normandy: 'if we should acquire it and God should grant it to us to acquire, we shall retain it for our demesne, as much of it as pleases us, and to our men who have sustained losses on our behalf, we shall give to them what pleases us of the land of Normandy'.[21] This reservation over Normandy must have been Philip's decision, and indicates that the French king was viewing the duchy differently from the other Angevin lands, perhaps because of its wealth. It certainly suggests that he was already developing ideas about a possible future for the duchy within his own direct grasp. Given the later integration of Normandy into the royal demesne, this action in 1202 is an important hint at Philip's thinking. There were also plans for Arthur to marry Philip's daughter Marie when she came of age.[22] Had Arthur succeeded, with Philip's aid, he would no doubt have held Brittany, but it is unlikely he would have also received Normandy.

The Lusignans, having waited to see what John might offer in the way of compensation for taking as his wife the girl promised to Hugh, and having received nothing, made formal appeal to Philip. A challenge against John was now possible, but Philip made no hasty moves. John was summoned, and homage demanded. He was to default several times before Philip took punitive action. As so often, Philip made sure that he had acted correctly within the law, giving John every possible chance to respond and fulfil his duties, so that whatever action the French king took could be demonstrated as just and legal. John then raised a force against Philip and entered Poitou, invading La Marche

21. *Recueil*, II, no. 723, pp. 292–3: p. 293: 'quando, Deo volente, vel nos vel ipse ea acquisierimus'; 'De Normannia sic erit quod nos id quod acquisivimus et de eo quod Deus nobis concedet acquirere ad opus nostrum retinebimus quantum nobis placuerit, et hominibus nostris qui pro nobis terras suas amiserunt dabimus id quod nobis placuerit de terra Normannie'.
22. *Recueil*, II, no. 709, pp. 278–9.

which he took. He granted it to Isabel's father, the count of Angoulême, a clear statement of his intentions in the area. He also attacked Eu, in Normandy, because it was held by Ralph de Lusignan. The Lusignans now had added reason for encouraging Philip to intervene.

As with Philip's intentions for Normandy, so for his general intentions of how to achieve his long-term aims, there are hints in the period before he attempted full-scale invasion. French kings had often in the past been forced to rely on their claimed rights, as one of the few ways to establish any authority over recalcitrant vassals. Legal rights had always played a major part. Now that the king of France was becoming genuinely powerful, these claims could be put to even greater effect. So Philip sought to gain a hold over all his vassals by claiming the right of jurisdiction over them in the royal court. Philip used the decisions of his court to demonstrate that legally he was in the right. It became a regular part of his method of expansion of royal power.

John refused the summons to Philip's court on the grounds that dukes of Normandy only met the king on the border of their duchy. Philip responded that in this case John was summoned as count of Poitou. In any case John's claim was no longer true, the Plantagenets themselves had broken the old tradition. Geoffrey of Anjou, John's grandfather, had been the first Norman duke to go to Paris. There was probably a formal judgement made against John in Philip's court, and in 1202 that court declared Aquitaine and Poitou to be forfeit. It has been suggested with some reason that this measure was 'quite revolutionary', as the principle had not previously been applied to magnate principalities.[23] It is a measure of the extending power of the monarchy under Philip Augustus.

What looks like a reconnaissance period in 1201, when, as we have seen, Philip hovered around the Norman border in the region where the Seine ran from French territory into the duchy, was repeated in the following year. In 1202, after some time in that same area, the king suddenly pushed further west, heading for Gournay and then Arques.[24] Until

23. Duby, p. 218; Petit-Dutaillis, p. 219.
24. *Recueil*, II, nos 719, pp. 287–9; 720, pp. 289–90; 721, pp. 290–1; 723, pp. 292–3; 724, pp. 293–4; 725, p. 294.

that point he had contented himself with following up the promises of the treaty of Le Goulet, and had set about establishing his authority over a number of places which John had failed to hand over, including Boutavent, which Philip captured. He also took Eu, Aumale, Driencourt, Lyons-la-Forêt, Longchamps, Orgueil and Mortemer. Philip besieged Gournay, moving into a much more threatening district of Normandy. Whereas in 1201 Philip had concentrated on the border area south of the Seine, he was now strengthening his position in the border area to the north of the river, and increasingly westwards. The attack on Gournay was the first serious sign of a more aggressive intent.

The castle of Hugh de Gournay was defended by a stone wall and a deep moat filled with water from the River Epte. Near the wall had formed a great lake, like a stagnant sea enclosed by an embankment. Philip, using a kind of engine to cut into and perforate the rampart, pierced the surrounding dyke so that the water rushed out, 'as turbulently as where the Rhône joins the Saône'.[25] The landscape became a seascape, water covering fields, houses and vineyards, uprooting trees in the flood. People fled for the higher ground. The waters smacked into the rampart and destroyed the castle in moments, so that Philip was easily able to take it. He later rebuilt Gournay and restored the area now under his own authority.

His actions up to the taking of Gournay might have been anticipated as no more than filling in the details of the treaty made two years previously. But then John must have been surprised by Philip's move against Arques in 1202. This effort only makes sense if Philip's previous activity was already building towards a more aggressive stance. Through the year he had been moving gradually further into Normandy, northwards around Rouen. In July 1202 he suddenly leaped forward against the stronghold of Arques, a key position well to the north of Rouen, and not so far from the coast. It looks very much like the first move, since John's succession, to begin a new attempt at the conquest of the duchy.

By 1202 John seemed to have survived his accession crisis; it looked on the face of it like business as usual in the

25. William the Breton, 'Vie', in *Oeuvres*, ed. Delaborde, p. 208: 'quodam artificio ingenio usus, aggerem incidi et perforari fecit'.

Angevin Empire. Other than in Brittany itself, the Angevin lands showed little enthusiasm for Philip's protégé, the young Arthur. In England and elsewhere, John was accepted as ruler. When Philip attempted further disruption, he had no great success. But now began the first phase of his serious aggression against John, showing that he had merely been biding his time. In 1202 Philip invaded Normandy, giving support to the Lusignans and to Arthur. The French king took Conches and Le Vaudreuil; he came to the relief of Moret from which John fled, leaving his tents, engines and utensils behind. Philip prepared to besiege Arques, but then came a severe setback. The move into Normandy proved to be premature thanks to events at Mirebeau, and Philip had to withdraw for the time being, but his intentions were surely now clear.

The reason for Philip's retreat was the one occasion when militarily John out-trumped him. The English king had heard that his mother, Eleanor of Aquitaine, was trapped at Mirebeau. Arthur by now had many reasons for hostility to John, including the fact that John held his sister a prisoner. He declared 'I know how much my uncle hates me ... I demand my rights.' While Philip aimed against Normandy, Arthur of Brittany, with men and money provided by the French king, progressed eastwards along the Loire, then attacked and took the town of Mirebeau in Poitou. There the elderly queen mother, Eleanor of Aquitaine, was besieged and trapped in the keep which still held out. John rushed to her aid, with the speed which had succeeded on other occasions for Richard and for Philip, covering 80 miles in two days, 'quicker than is to be believed'.[26]

John stormed the place at dawn, taking his enemy by surprise; Geoffrey de Lusignan was still eating pigeon for his breakfast. Not only was Eleanor saved, but Arthur of Brittany was captured along with Geoffrey de Lusignan, Hugh the Brown, Andrew de Chauvigny, Savaric de Mauléon and 200 knights. It was the high point of John's continental career. Arthur was taken to Falaise in a vehicle which was

26. William the Breton, *Philippide*, ed. Guizot, p. 164; 'Philippide', ed. Delaborde, p. 164, l. 326: 'Novi me quantum patrus meus oderit'; Roger of Wendover, ed. Giles, II, p. 204; Roger of Wendover, ed. Hewlett, I, p. 314: 'citius quam credi fas est ad Mirebellum castrum pervenit'.

'a new and unusual mode of conveyance'.[27] Philip had to abandon the siege of Arques to deal with the consequences of John's victory.

The fate of Arthur, who had 'disappeared', is not known for certain, but suspicions have always been voiced against John. The evidence, such as it is, points to the English king's guilt.[28] Belief that John was responsible for Arthur's death undermined the king's reputation, and hence his position. Imprisonment might have seemed acceptable, but murder was less easily condoned. The coup at Mirebeau, which had seemed such a blow to Philip, turned to his favour through the widespread conviction that John had killed young Arthur. John's harsh treatment of his nephew seems also to have been the main reason for William des Roches' return to Philip's allegiance in 1203. Others took a similar path, including Aimery de Thouars and several barons from Anjou and Poitou. This disaffection seems to have been the beginning of the end for John in the old heartlands of Plantagenet territory. In addition, John's success had sparked the resentment of the Breton lords, and they too joined Philip. Arthur's killing was also a cause of trouble with some of John's leading English barons, not least William de Braose.

Mirebeau was a setback for Philip, but in general his prospects looked promising. The widespread belief that John had murdered his captive nephew was significant in turning men towards Philip in the war of allegiances, which he was in any case on the way to winning. By 1202 John had failed to keep most of Richard's hard-won alliances: the counts of Flanders, Blois, Perche, Boulogne and Toulouse were among those who moved into Philip's camp. Some nobles had deserted John, some had taken the option to go on the Fourth Crusade, itself in some cases an excuse to escape from Philip's anticipated revenge. Theobald of Champagne's death in 1201, whose only son was born posthumously, further strengthened Philip's position of domination over his

---

27. Roger of Wendover, ed. Giles, II, p. 204; Roger of Wendover, ed. Hewlett, I, p. 315: 'vehiculis . . . novo genere equitandi et inusitato'.
28. Roger of Wendover, ed. Giles, II, pp. 204–6; Roger of Wendover, ed. Hewlett, I, p. 316; Warren, pp. 81–4; Margam Annal in *Annales Monastici*, ed. H.R. Luard, 5 vols, RS no. 36 (London, 1864–69) I, pp. 3–40; Ralph of Coggeshall, *Chronicon Anglicanum*, ed. J. Stevenson, RS no. 66 (London, 1875) p. 145.

nobility. Philip's acts show him intervening to manage the affairs of the Countess Blanche in Champagne in this period, when he also took her son into his own hands and under his protection.[29]

. . .

PHILIP THE CONQUEROR

Militarily the key to the loss of the Angevin Empire was Philip's invasion of Normandy in 1203, and particularly the siege of Château-Gaillard, Richard's 'beautiful daughter' which guarded the Seine.[30] John's problems and his personal inadequacies offered an opportunity better than any in the past. Philip had always wanted glory for the Capetian monarchy, and had long sought to diminish the power of the Plantagenets. His ambitions against them had for some time focused on Normandy and the Loire. Ever since the duchy of Normandy had linked with the kingdom of England, it had been a thorn in the side of the Capetians. Its proximity to the heart of the Capetian demesne, and its wealth, made Normandy Philip's first target.

The attempts against Normandy in 1173–74, and during Richard's captivity in 1192–94, show that this was no new ambition. But Philip by the early thirteenth century was a more powerful and confident monarch than in the days of Henry II and the Lionheart. Philip now had the experience of tough wars against Henry II and Richard, he had been on crusade and taken part in the siege and capture of Acre. There had also been sufficient time to assess John's abilities, and Philip knew him as an unreliable ally, a poor leader of men, and one who had already given cause for those who followed him to doubt his honour.

Philip had tested John in the difficult period after his accession. John's new marriage, and his treatment of Arthur of Brittany, were doing Philip's work for him. By 1203 the French king was ready to move again. During the previous period he had clearly been building his strength in preparation for a major attempt against the Plantagenets. He

29. *Recueil*, II, nos 678, pp. 235–8; 759, 776, pp. 349–50.
30. K. Norgate, *England under the Angevin Kings*, 2 vols (London, 1887) II, p. 380 and n. 1.

had strengthened his hold on vital fortresses along his best entry points into Normandy, especially those along the upper reaches of the Seine. His attack on Gournay and his expedition to Arques in 1202 pointed the way to full invasion. Then he had been delayed by Arthur's capture at Mirebeau, now he was ready for another and even greater attempt.

In the first half of 1203, Philip was once more hovering around the borderlands of Normandy. He may have been at Mantes in April and Évreux in June, and he was certainly at Le Mans in April.[31] He had in the previous years followed the route of the Seine into Normandy first along the south bank, then along the north. He had advanced at one point as far as Arques and, given the history of previous Capetian attempts at the invasion of the duchy, there can be no doubt that his ultimate target was Rouen, also of course on the Seine. What all these preliminary moves demonstrated to Philip was the significance of the powerful fortified complex at Les Andelys, lowering over the river, and close to his most obvious points of advance. He must therefore, in order to control the Seine route and win Rouen, first take Les Andelys and its castle.

Philip commenced the siege of Château-Gaillard in August 1203. To improve his position he followed the initial moves of his 1202 campaign, first attacking and taking Conches. When Philip advanced to besiege Le Vaudreuil in June its commanders, Saher de Quincy and Robert Fitz Walter, simply surrendered to him, despite the fact that the place was well fortified and provisioned. John, for reasons known only to himself, claimed that this key fortress in the Seine valley had surrendered at his orders, probably rather than admit he had not been able to send aid.

Philip also took Montfort-sur-Risle and Beaumont-le-Roger, which were handed over when Hugh de Gournay and Peter de Meulan surrendered. The lack of heart among John's vassals facilitated the conquest. Radepont was besieged in August and soon fell. Le Vaudreuil and Radepont are the keys to Philip's campaign to this point, standing close respectively to the south and north bank of the Seine, almost opposite each other. With those two fortresses in his hand, it would be

31. *Recueil*, II, nos 750, pp. 324–5; 753, pp. 327–8; 754, pp. 328–9; 755, pp. 329–30; 756, pp. 330–1; 757, p. 331.

difficult for John to send supplies or aid through to Château-Gaillard from Rouen. Philip was isolating Les Andelys and preparing for the next stage forward to Rouen itself.

The castle of Château-Gaillard was part of the costly fortifications erected by Richard the Lionheart at Les Andelys. On the island was a dwelling worthy of the greatest princes.[32] Bridges joined it to the land on either side. A dyke had been built to block access from the river, using rocks and oak. The French broke through this and were able to supply their own camp. Philip built his own bridge of boats to replace that destroyed by the garrison, and had towers constructed on boats, which both defended his bridge and were used to attack the castle.

The castle covered the heights of a great rock standing sheer over the river, too high to see the top from the French side, and 'rising to the stars'.[33] It could only be approached from the land direction, where the entrance was elaborately and brilliantly protected. There was a triangular outer bailey, which would have to be crossed before reaching a heavily fortified middle bailey, which itself still guarded the inner sanctum: an internal enclosure containing the keep. The whole outer landward side was further protected by a ditch and the outer bailey was separated from the middle bailey by a great gully. The final enclosure was guarded by another ditch and was constructed unusually of semicircular linked towers. Within the enclosure was the massive donjon. Richard had boasted that he could hold such a site even if it were made of butter.

John's garrison was commanded by the determined Roger de Lacy who, unlike most of the king's castellans in Normandy, was ready to make a fight of it. John made one major attempt to relieve Château-Gaillard, sending a concerted attack by river and by land. At least it was intended to be concerted, but the wrong intelligence had been gathered about the tides which made that part of the river navigable, and John's ships were late arriving.

There is no further evidence on this river attack but, knowing the situation, it seems worth pausing to consider what

32. William the Breton, *Philippide*, ed. Guizot, p. 178; 'Philippide', ed. Delaborde, p. 178, ll. 41–2: 'dignos/Principibus summis'.
33. William the Breton, *Philippide*, ed. Guizot, p. 178; 'Philippide', ed. Delaborde, p. 178, l. 53: 'tanquam velit astra subire'.

had happened. We have seen that Philip now commanded castles close to the river on either bank between Rouen and Les Andelys. How had the English fleet evaded this danger point? It would seem to explain the decision to come through the night, a dangerous business. John's fleet did not have freedom to come as and when it chose, and this may have contributed to the disastrous delay in its arrival. This allowed the French to hold off the unsupported night attack by the land force under William Marshal and Lupescar. The land force, which was the main threat, was massacred 'like sheep by a wolf'.[34] Then, when the river force finally arrived, it could be dealt with separately.

The French bridge was broken but repaired by torchlight before the river force came. The land force had been seen off already when the fleet belatedly arrived with the dawn, and the alarm sounded again. The French could now concentrate on the new threat, and defended themselves from their bridge and towers, and from the river bank. Archers shot from the heights and heavy weights were dropped on to the English. One large beam, heaved from above, sank two ships, and finally the attackers retreated. The Le Noir brothers captured two boats and made a pursuit. The French attacked the stockade. A swimmer called Galbert climbed the wooden palisade round the island bearing vases apparently filled with Greek Fire tied to his body, and then set off an explosion 'like Mount Etna'.[35] The palisade and the houses within it caught fire, and the island was captured.

The Plantagenet relief attempt for Château-Gaillard had failed and, as a result, support for John in Normandy crumbled away. Philip was able to ring Les Andelys until the stronghold was quite isolated. He improved his own camp defences, building a new wooden tower and a double ditch around the enemy complete with a palisade and its own wooden towers. Hills were flattened to make platforms for his throwing engines, and a covered way was constructed to protect the movement of his men. The besiegers were given improved accommodation, with cabins built of branches and straw.

34. William the Breton, *Philippide*, ed. Guizot, p. 185; 'Philippide', ed. Delaborde, p. 184, l. 189.
35. William the Breton, *Philippide*, ed. Guizot, p. 191; 'Philippide', ed. Delaborde, p. 191, l. 359: 'Evomit ignitos ambustaque saxa per Etnam'.

Roger de Lacy held on, but without help from John the position was impossible. It was only a question of time before the blockade would force the garrison to surrender. Roger sent out hundreds of people, including women and children, so that there would be fewer mouths to feed. At first some of those expelled were let through the French lines, but then several hundred were refused, and had to try and survive in caves for months, trapped between the two forces, living on scraps and grass. One was a pregnant woman who gave birth in this no-man's land. When a chicken was dropped by accident from the castle walls, the poor outcasts fell on it and devoured it completely, feathers and all. Philip from the bridge later heard the cries of these abandoned unfortunates, and was moved to sympathy on learning of their plight. He gave orders that they should be fed and allowed to go through the lines. One man emerged clutching the skin of a dog, which he refused to give up because it was the only thing which had kept him alive. He relinquished it finally with reluctance in return for bread, which he stuffed greedily into his mouth, but was scarcely able to swallow.[36]

William the Breton derides the English king for leaving the fighting to others, making John say: 'I will stay in a safe place with my dog.'[37] In fact in September John did raid into Brittany, presumably trying to divert Philip's efforts from Les Andelys, but though he sacked Dol and burned its cathedral, he failed to entice the French king from his objective. John found that he could no longer travel by direct routes from one place to another in the old Plantagenet lands because so much was now in French hands. He was 'like a rabbit trapped in a patch of corn which the mower is steadily reducing'.[38] On 5 December John sailed from Barfleur; he never returned to Normandy.

Philip brought up provisions for the winter to Les Andelys and dug additional protecting trenches. Belfries were constructed, some of green oak roughly hewed. In February 1204 the outer bailey of the castle of Château-Gaillard fell, after

36. William the Breton, *Philippide*, ed. Guizot, pp. 199–201; 'Philippide', ed. Delaborde, p. 198, ll. 545, 549, p. 199.
37. William the Breton, 'Philippide', ed. Delaborde, pp. 181, 184, l. 192: 'ego cum cane tuta tuebor'.
38. Warren, pp. 92–3.

being mined and having faced an onslaught from hurling engines.[39] The king himself, sensibly clad in helmet and armour, encouraged his men to attack. They broke through the outer defence by climbing a tower. Their ladders were not long enough for the task, so they hewed out footholds in the stone using daggers and swords.

Then Philip broke into the castle's middle bailey. His men found an unpleasant but effective way in, by climbing up a garderobe chute to enter a house built by John in 1202 on the south-east side of the rock, the upper part dedicated as a chapel. Peter Bogis climbed on a friend's shoulder and entered the cellar, letting down a rope for his comrades. He was later rewarded for his initiative with the grant of a knight's fee. Once in, they used fire to bring down the door, which awoke the defenders to the danger, but the fire was spreading. In the confusion the intruders were able to open the gate and release the drawbridge to let in their fellows. The buildings in the middle bailey were reduced to ashes.

During slack periods in the siege, Philip found time to tour recently acquired regions, appearing twice at Vernon.[40] At Château-Gaillard, there still remained the final enclosure and the keep, to which the defenders now retired. Philip and his men spotted the only design fault in the great castle. The bridge into the inner bailey was solid rock, it could not be moved or easily destroyed by the defenders, and it gave perfect cover for his own men to mine the wall. The castle was finally taken on 6 March 1204, when twenty knights and 120 men-at-arms surrendered.

John had left Normandy in December 1203, and never returned. The king's conduct remains puzzling, and was at the least inconsistent and irresolute. John's countrymen thought him shamed by his lack of action: Philip 'is taking your castles, he is binding your castellans to their horses' tails and dragging them shamefully to prison'.[41] John did

39. William the Breton, *Philippide*, ed. Guizot, p. 204; 'Philippide', ed. Delaborde, pp. 202–4: 'grossos petraria ... mangonellusque minores/ Et Pugillares ... Nec balista vacat ... nec funda ... nec arcus'.
40. *Recueil*, II, nos 777, pp. 350–1; 781, pp. 353–4.
41. Roger of Wendover, ed. Giles, II, pp. 214, 207, 208; Roger of Wendover, ed. Hewlett, II, p. 8: 'omnimodis cum regina sua videbat deliciis'; and I, p. 316: 'cum regina epulabatur quotidie splendide,

make some attempts to stem the tide: first setting a new line of defence at the River Touques, then trying to improve the defences of Rouen, and finally seeking to negotiate a saving peace, but it was a case of too little and too late.

The year 1204 cannot quite claim to be the *annus mirabilis* of Philip Augustus – that must be reserved for his triumphs of 1214 – but the year in which Normandy collapsed must run it close. With the fall of Château-Gaillard, Plantagenet Normandy fell apart. Town after town, castle after castle surrendered. As with Les Andelys, so with Rouen, Philip worked his way around the target, gradually isolating it. The capital had always been his eventual target in the duchy. He first aimed against southern Normandy, moving along the River Risle. He thus foiled John's attempt to defend the River Touques, and then moved on to the valley of the Orne, making what has been called 'a brilliant left-hook'.[42]

In three weeks during May Philip took Argentan and Falaise, and reached the Normandy coast near St-Pierre-sur-Dives.[43] Lupescar, who commanded the supposedly impregnable Falaise, surrendered within a week, and went over to Philip. Like Geoffrey of Anjou before him, Philip captured the central bloc of the duchy before closing in for the kill at Rouen. Domfront, Caen, Bayeux and Lisieux fell into his hands as western Normandy collapsed. Caen, standing amidst fertile fields and meadows, offered no resistance at all.[44] It did not possess enough in the treasury to pay for its own defence, and the Plantagenet archives for the duchy were smuggled away to England. In the far west of Normandy, Philip's Breton allies under Guy de Thouars took both Mont-Saint-Michel and Avranches, then joined the French king at Caen.

---

somnos que matutinales usque ad prandendi horam protraxit'; p. 317: 'cepit jam illa et illa castella, et castellanos vestros caudis equorum turpiter alligatos abducit'; Petit-Dutaillis, p. 215; F.M. Powicke, *The Loss of Normandy*, 2nd edn (Manchester, 1960, revised 1961) pp. 162–3; K. Norgate, *John Lackland* (London, 1902) p. 93; Turner, *King John*, comments on John's character and mental state, e.g. pp. 20, 124–6, 261–5.

42. Warren, p. 97.
43. *Recueil*, II, nos 788, pp. 361–2; 789, pp. 362–7; 790, pp. 368–9; 791, p. 370; 792, pp. 370–1; 793, pp. 371–2; 794, p. 372; 795, p. 373.
44. William the Breton, *Philippide*, ed. Guizot, p. 213; 'Philippide', ed. Delaborde, p. 211, ll. 22–8, l. 25: 'pratis et agrorum fertilitate'.

Now only Arques and Rouen in the east offered resistance in Normandy. Rouen, the major objective, was protected by double walls and triple ditches, but by now morale was low and isolation increasing. Having gained control of most of the surrounding area, the French closed in. Philip captured the barbican at the head of the bridge, and the citizens of Rouen themselves destroyed four arches of the bridge in a vain effort to prevent the French from crossing.

Philip had arrived at Rouen in May of 1204. On 1 June the Norman capital, under John's 'trusty and well-beloved' Peter des Préaux, agreed to yield to Philip if no aid was received within thirty days. The city was given no hope from John and surrendered on 24 June, even before the time of the agreement was up. Normandy's fate was settled, the whole duchy was in the hands of the Capetian king, which in the words of William the Breton, 'was something one had never thought possible in any circumstances'.[45]

How far John was responsible for the loss of Normandy and much of the continental Plantagenet Empire has been a matter of some debate. Warren has defended John, while Gillingham has blamed him, suggesting that so long as the Lionheart was alive the Angevin Empire was in good health. Obviously there were various factors at play in the fall of the duchy, and there is no single explanation, which means that all the blame cannot be placed upon John. Professor Bates has seen the 'fall' of Normandy, from an independent principality, as a more gradual process. He has suggested, at least by implication, that the duchy only 'rose' and was powerful when the French monarchy was weak.[46] The practice of Norman magnates in going over to the enemies of the dukes was not a new phenomenon and cannot alone be the explanation of John's failure; problems for the dukes from families based in the border areas had never been absent. Yet the suspicion remains that things were badly managed by John and made worse than they otherwise would have been.

The Angevin Empire had never broken out of the framework of being, with regard to its continent possessions, always

45. Norgate, *John*, p. 99; William the Breton, *Philippide*, ed. Guizot, p. 219; 'Philippide', ed. Delaborde, p. 217, ll. 176–7: 'Sic fuit ex toto Normannia subdita Franco,/Quod nullo casu contingere posse putavit'.
46. Bates, 'The rise and fall of Normandy'.

in some way under the lordship of the kings of France. The absorption of Normandy into a larger political entity in both the 'Norman Empire' of the Conqueror and his immediate successors, and into the Angevin Empire of Henry II and his sons, meant that the duke was no longer able to concentrate solely on ruling Normandy. His presence was less, his interests often elsewhere. Through most of the twelfth century the duke was in no sense even a Norman. It is not surprising if loyalty to an increasingly remote ruler had waned through that period.

King John's aged mother, Eleanor of Aquitaine, who had done what she could to prop up his position, died on 1 April 1204. This seriously weakened his hold on the duchy of Aquitaine. Men from the south, who had come to respect the often-present Richard, and who had remained loyal while Eleanor was still alive, were without the same sense of duty to her younger son, and now rushed to do homage to Philip. The collapse of the southern Angevin Empire in 1204 was as much a voluntary surrender as a conquest.

Philip, as well as his campaigns in Normandy, had begun operations to the south. These were stepped up in 1203–4. He moved along the Loire and took Saumur. The losses to Philip in Normandy had their effect upon those watching from the south. The county of Anjou collapsed in the face of the efforts of William des Roches and the mercenary captain, Cadoc. The men of Maine, Touraine and Poitou, the latter considered of 'vacillating faith', were ready to leave John's allegiance for Philip's.[47]

Within weeks of the fall of Rouen, Philip was on the move, rapidly mopping up Angevin strongholds in the Loire region through August and September.[48] In August he was at Châtellerault, and then moved on to take Poitiers, Loudun, Montreuil and Parthenay. He had to besiege both Chinon and Loches: the former was taken in September, when Hubert de Burgh was captured; at the latter a similar fate awaited its commander, Gerard d'Athée. John was losing his best commanders as well as his strongholds. Before news of

47. William the Breton, *Philippide*, ed. Guizot, p. 223; 'Philippide', ed. Delaborde, p. 227, l. 449: 'Quo solitum variare fidem cor novit eorum'.
48. *Recueil*, II, nos 826, pp. 403–4; 827, pp. 404–5; 828, pp. 405–7; 829, pp. 407–9; 830, pp. 409–11; 839, pp. 418–19; 841, pp. 420–1.

one disaster could reach him, another had occurred. A great swathe of Angevin territory south of the Loire fell to Philip, including Niort, Tours and Amboise. Although John's partial recovery is sometimes treated as close to a triumph, it truly was partial, and not much of a defeat for Philip.

One must question how far Philip ever expected to take over the whole of the Plantagenet territories. It seems clear that Normandy had always been his major target and the area he was most concerned to retain. In the south it is unlikely that his ambitions stretched beyond taking over Greater Anjou at best. His success in so doing seems to have satisfied him. At several points one can see that his interest in Aquitaine was of limited extent: it had proved beyond the capacity of his father to move that far afield, its history left it rather apart from the other Plantagenet territories, and it had remained more the land of Eleanor of Aquitaine than of her husband. This attachment had passed to her son Richard, but to no one else in the family.

Philip appreciated the need for caution, and had no wish to over-extend his efforts unprofitably in the south, at the possible cost of damage to his gains in the north. In 1205, when very much in the ascendant in his struggle with John, Philip moved about in his new conquests in Normandy, from Les Andelys to Le Vaudreuil, and within the more northerly area of Greater Anjou, from Chinon to Tours.[49] He kept to the region where his interests were greatest. Later, even when it was made clear that he would receive papal approval for expansion into that region during the course of the Albigensian Crusade, Philip was reluctant to venture so far south militarily.

When Henry II had married his daughter Eleanor to Alfonso VIII of Castile, Gascony had been the dowry, which would pass to her on the death of her mother, Eleanor of Aquitaine. After the latter's death, Alfonso sought to make good that agreement for his own benefit, entering Angevin territory. The birds of prey around the Angevin lands were closing in for the pickings, and Philip saw no immediate reason to block their path or hinder their additional help

---

49. *Recueil*, II, nos 871, pp. 460–1; 872, p. 462; 881, pp. 470–1; 882, pp. 471–2; 883, p. 472; 887, p. 475; 895, pp. 483–5; 903, p. 493; 904, p. 494; 905, pp. 494–6; 905, pp. 496–7; 906, p. 497; 908, p. 499; 909, pp. 499–500; 910, p. 500; 911, p. 501; 912, pp. 501–2; 913, pp. 502–3.

against John. Philip was happy to command his northern gains and leave the south to his allies, at least for the time being.

Meanwhile Prince Louis and William des Roches led an expedition to Brittany. In 1206 Philip himself followed into Brittany, entering Nantes and Rennes.[50] Nantes had surrendered, and by a 1206 charter Philip was recognized as having 'all of Brittany in his hands'.[51] Anjou, Brittany and Maine were lost to John, and Philip's thoughts moved as far as completing his efforts in Poitou, and even to an invasion of England. The best that can be said for John is that he salvaged something from this calamitous wreck.

John's attempts to bring forces from England to the defence of his continental lands were foiled by lack of co-operation from his barons. Two expeditions were planned in 1205, for Normandy and Poitou, but the Portsmouth effort had to be abandoned, and in the end only a skeleton force went to Poitou under the earl of Salisbury. The Gascon towns, without help from John, held out against Alfonso, and Gascony was cleared of its invaders. Niort and Poitou moved from Philip back to John in 1205. John's seneschal in Poitou, Savaric de Mauléon, played an important role in this rearguard action. It was a desperate position for the Plantagenets, but the rolling triumph of the Capetian had been stemmed, at least for the time being, and Philip was ready to call a halt and concentrate on keeping what had been won. He never seriously attempted the complete conquest of Aquitaine.

John returned to France in 1206 in an effort to recover lost lands, reaching La Rochelle on 7 June. Niort was relieved, Montauban taken, and Saintonge recovered. Angoulême, his wife's county, was a rare exception which had stayed loyal. Some of the nobles began to doubt the wisdom of leaving the mainly absentee Plantagenet overlord for the more powerful French monarch. The viscount of Thouars returned to John's allegiance, bringing most of northern Poitou with him.

But when John reached Anjou, Philip acted, and the belated Angevin recovery ground to a halt. Again Philip seemed

50. *Recueil*, II, nos 946, pp. 537–9; 947, p. 539; 948, p. 540; 949, pp. 541–2; 950, p. 542.
51. Luchaire in Lavisse, p. 140.

to be stating that his interest was in keeping Normandy and Greater Anjou, rather than further expansion. John retired rapidly to La Rochelle and thence to England. When a two-year truce was agreed between Philip and John, on 26 October 1206, the Plantagenet was allowed to keep Gascony and part of Poitou, but the rest of the continental Angevin Empire was lost. Philip seemed to be sated, and gave priority to stabilizing and consolidating the vast areas he had won and retained.

. . .

CONCLUSIONS ON THE WAR BETWEEN PHILIP AND JOHN

Philip's best hopes for victory over the Plantagenets had come to fruition. Time after time, against Henry, Richard and John, he had sought to divide the Angevins against themselves, and to foment trouble within Angevin territories. He had persistently raided Angevin lands in order to show up the failings of their protective authority. He had used propaganda to encourage surrenders. Wendover says he went around Normandy 'explaining to the citizens and castellans that they were deserted by their lord', and that his authority was superior to that of his rivals.[52] Such reminders were at times accompanied by crude threats: for example, that if men opposed him they would be hanged or flayed alive. He offered both the carrot and the stick: preferential treatment from a more powerful lord on the one hand; penalties for opposing him on the other. Philip's own lands had suffered little in comparison to those of the enemy during the war against the Plantagenets, itself a reminder of the benefits of peace and protection to be had from *his* lordship. It is also a demonstration of the generally aggressive nature of his efforts: fighting an offensive not a defensive war, forever foraying into enemy territory.

The Angevin Empire had serious internal defects. It had been assembled haphazardly, virtually the one-man empire of Henry II. It had not had the time to develop as a unity, and in some ways never became one. Jean Dunbabin and

---

52. Roger of Wendover, ed. Giles, II, p. 208; Roger of Wendover, ed. Hewlett, I, p. 319: 'ostendens civibus et castellani se a domino suo fore derelictos'.

John Gillingham have in different ways seen signs of attempts to bring unity to the Angevin Empire, but in all honesty little was achieved in this direction beyond a beginning which was never fulfilled.[53]

Within such a collection of authorities and allegiances, rebellion and conflict were always near the surface. The very vastness of the Angevin Empire made its government difficult, the seas between Ireland and England, England and the continent, increasing the problems. Its peoples were diverse and often had traditions of hostility to each other. In some parts Angevin control was recent and the Plantagenets were bound to be seen as alien conquerors. To a king of Philip's capacities the opportunities for stirring trouble and creating divisions were myriad.

John could not retain the allegiance of key men in his lands: stronghold after stronghold which had the capacity to resist, capitulated. William des Roches, Aimery de Thouars, Robert d'Alençon, Hugh de Gournay, Peter de Meulan, William de Hommet, Lupescar: the list of deserters is almost endless. The poet who thought 'a man's heart is worth all the gold of the realm' had in mind John's inability to win those hearts, as well as his oppressive taxation. Ralph of Coggeshall said John could not go to aid Château-Gaillard 'through fear of the treason of his men'. Or, as William the Marshal had put it to John: 'you have not enough friends if you provoke your enemies to fight'; treachery he thought had become 'a kind of epidemic'. It was John's unanswerable dilemma.[54]

William the Marshal himself drifted over to Philip, doing liege homage to the French king. He subsequently refused to fight for John against Philip on the continent because of this homage. As John put it, observing that even the Marshal had gone to Philip: 'by God's teeth, I see that none of my barons are for me'.[55] The Marshal was one of many barons

---

53. J. Dunbabin, *France in the Making, 843–1180* (Oxford, 1985) pp. 346–50; Gillingham, pp. 59, 63–4.

54. Petit-Dutaillis, p. 221; Warren, pp. 88, 92; Norgate, *John*, p. 99; Ralph of Coggeshall, p. 144: 'eo quod suorum proditionem semper timeret'; *L'Histoire de Guillaume le Maréchal*, ed. P. Meyer, 3 vols, SHF nos 255, 268, 304 (Paris, 1891–1901) III, pp. 93–4.

55. Norgate, *John*, p. 109; *Guillaume le Maréchal*, III, p. 181; II, p. 110, ll. 13184–5: 'Par les dentz Dieu! bien vei que nus/De mes barons n'i est o mei'.

PHILIP AUGUSTUS

with lands on the continent who turned from John to Philip, won over by the success of the latter and the knowledge that in France having Philip as a master was more likely to preserve a hold on your lands than serving John. But Philip's strategy was fundamentally a military one. The well-known words of Jordan Fantosme on the best military strategy of the age are well demonstrated by Philip. Jordan, through the mouth of Philip count of Flanders, recommended the policy of first destroying the enemy's lands, wasting them, and then besieging his strongholds. Demoralization of the populace of Normandy, and of the men of the English king, was the inevitable and intended consequence of such activity. This had been precisely Philip's method.[56]

Normandy in particular suffered from the wars, both from Philip's raids and from the depredations of John's mercenaries. William the Marshal thought that, on John's behalf, Lupescar pillaged as though he were in enemy country and 'making war'.[57] Gerald of Wales was inconvenienced by the disruption of 1202–3, having to delay his journey, getting robbed, and on his return being arrested, for all of which he blamed 'the war between the kings'. He considered that the war had rendered Normandy 'most insecure and perilous'. The gloomy prognostication of St Hugh of Lincoln on the Plantagenets seemed to have come true: 'as the ox eats down the grass to the roots, so shall Philip of France entirely destroy this race'.[58]

Professor Baldwin believes that Philip won little by war in the period after his return from crusade, gaining more from negotiation and deaths. This is perhaps true of the war

56. Jordan Fantosme, *Chronicle*, ed. and trans. R.C. Johnston (Oxford, 1981) pp. 32–3, no. 41, ll. 439–48; p. 34, no. 42, ll. 449–50; especially l. 450: 'Primes guaster la terre (space) e puis ses enemis'.
57. *Guillaume le Maréchal*, III, p. 171; II, p. 89, ll. 12598–606: 'Por quei?- Par fei, quer Lovrekaire/Le(s) menot de si mal randon/Que il perneit tot a bandon/Quant que il trouvont en la terre/Ausse com s'ele fust de guerre'; Gillingham, p. 76.
58. H.E. Butler, *The Autobiography of Giraldus Cambrensis* (London, 1937) pp. 263, 318; Seward, *Eleanor of Aquitaine*, (Newton Abbot, 1978) p. 251; Hugh of Lincoln, II, p. 185: 'Quamobrem Gallicus iste Philippus regiam Anglorum ita delebit stirpem quemadmodum bos herbam solet usque ad radices carpere'.

158

against Richard, which was in Baldwin's mind, but it under-values the French king's military achievement in general.[59] Of course, there were negotiations and agreements through-out these wars, and Philip showed himself adept in these moves, but in the end the Angevin Empire was destroyed by war. Nor was this only war against John. Philip's earlier successes against the Plantagenets had worked like a drip-ping tap, wearing away their hold on the continental lands. The dying Henry II had been brought to final humiliation; Richard had to spend his last five years trying, and not quite succeeding, to win back what had been lost to Philip during his captivity. As for John, he was quite simply defeated in war in the campaigns of 1203–6.

There were many contributory factors to Philip's eventual victory over the Plantagenets. The defeat and elimination of other powerful princes in France, which left him more able to concentrate his energies against the Angevins, was one such factor. Baldwin of Flanders left on crusade in 1202 and was replaced by a weak regency government; while the count of Champagne had died the previous year, again leaving a weaker regime behind with his widow trying to protect the son born after his father's death. Philip had helped to engineer this situation, but he also had fortune on his side. The result was that he needed to spend little time worrying about other magnates and could put all his energy into the war against John.

Another important factor was finance; the ability to pay for necessary resources was essential for successful war. There will probably always be argument over the relative wealth of the Plantagenets and the Capetians through this period, the records simply do not allow a conclusive view. Philip was improving his resources before this triumph, introducing new systems by 1202. The *prisée des sergents* was in effect a tax to pay for the army. Records of its collection survive from 1194 and 1202, and show that by the later date the system had been revised and improved, and could safely meet the needs of the moment. Philip was thus able to add some £27,000 to an existing sound balance of over £60,000, to finance his attack on the Plantagenet lands.

59. Baldwin, p. 99.

The surviving accounts of 1202–3 themselves reveal how Philip had tightened up his financial organization.[60] His healthy position at this time contrasts with the increasing problems of financing Angevin activities. Powicke suggests that Norman revenues brought in enough to finance thirty garrisons, but the Angevin ruler was in fact having to support forty-five. John's was forced into levying additional taxation, and this together with the expensive employment of mercenaries caused further resentment in Normandy. John even had to extract an oath from the Normans to protect his own mercenary captain Lupescar; and the wide rancour against mercenaries in general was to be manifested in Magna Carta.[61] A recent analysis of John's income shows that his revenues from England were low in the period up to 1202 and only recovered thereafter through swingeing taxation, the major rise coming after 1208.[62] This is taken to show that John's losses abroad were not due to finance. But in fact figures from the continental lands are not used in this analysis because they are not available. Common sense suggests that the warfare from 1202, and the losses sustained from then onwards, must have seriously diminished his continental income. The fact that he had to make supreme efforts to increase his English income argues that in order to maintain his presence on the continent he was having to rely on the only source available to him. It was a desperate throw. Had his attempts at recovery abroad succeeded it might have had a good outcome for him. When those attempts failed, the enormous taxation demands in England, which had led to growing resentment and opposition, boiled over into the Magna Carta rebellion.

If Philip were to succeed in the conquest of lands from a fellow Christian, it was important that he had, if not the approval, then at least the acquiescence of the papacy and the Church in France. Philip had some problems with the papacy, which by and large he overcame; and on the whole his relations with the Gallic Church were good. His attitude was more flexible to Church reforms and privileges than that of the Plantagenets, notably with regard to the freedom

60. Baldwin, pp. 173–5; Bates, 'The rise and fall of Normandy', p. 34.
61. Powicke, pp. 234, 238.
62. N. Barratt, 'The revenue of King John', *EHR*, CXI, 1996, pp. 835–55.

of church elections. This undoubtedly helped him to gain support in the Angevin areas which he was seeking to take over, and produced a greater willingness by the Church outside those areas to accept his actions.

Philip also made efforts to prepare local populations to accept a change to his lordship. The growing power and wealth of towns was vital in this respect. Philip's readiness to recognize communes, at least outside his own demesne, and especially in areas he was seeking to win over, encouraged ambitious towns to accept his authority rather than that of the less generous Plantagenets. This attitude continued to be apparent in the period immediately following his conquests, when towns such as Rouen benefited from his support.

Philip was responsible for a good deal of military construction, in both castles and urban defences, and it is notable that most of the castle-building itself occurred within towns, where one might view the castle as a citadel. For example, he built new towers at Rouen, Chinon, Bourges, Orléans and Péronne, and the Louvre itself in Paris. Although privileges were granted to towns both within the old demesne and within the newly conquered areas, a royal presence was also to be felt. Philip matched the increased privileges given to towns with an increased ability to keep an eye on their activities.

A similar flexibility in attitude to that offered to the Church may by noted in his castle policy, so that men holding castles might feel reasonably secure in their own position. His treatment of such men was less ruthless than that of the Plantagenets, accepting legal recognition of his overlordship without pressing for the same personal domination that his enemies preferred.[63] This did not mean that he was not aware of the need to keep command, which was often underlined by making agreements to render the castle to the king when necessary, but it was clearly on the understanding that the castle would then be restored to its holder. Nor was Philip careless about obtaining control of key castles; it was rather that he approached this in a legal manner, acquiring the necessary lands by legal means, as through exchanges. Thus,

63. L. Carolus-Barré, 'Philippe Auguste et les communes', in Bautier, pp. 677–88, p. 682; C. Coulson, 'Fortress-policy in Capetian tradition and Angevin practice: aspects of the conquest of Normandy by Philip II', *ANS*, VI, 1983, pp. 13–38.

for example, he embodied into acts the means whereby he obtained such fortresses as Falaise or Mortemer.[64] In this way he both supported his own offensive campaigns and kept control of conquered areas afterwards.

Those previously Angevin castles which came into his control were chiefly either those of prime central importance, as say at Caen, Falaise, Poitiers or Chinon, or else of significance for maintaining his links from the ancient demesne lands into these newly won territories, in particular along the rivers, and especially the Seine for Normandy as at Château-Gaillard, and the Loire as at Saumur for the more southerly acquisitions. The list compiled for the royal archives in or before 1210 included 113 royal castles and fortresses.

In many ways the defeat of the Plantagenets was the key achievement of Philip's rule. It lacked the dramatic triumph of Bouvines, which was the climax to the reign, but many of his other successes followed from, or benefited from, the winning of such vast areas from the Angevins. He became a more respected ruler, as well as a wealthier and more powerful one. All men had to revise their assessment of him and his kingdom; he had become one of the great rulers of his day. There seems no reason to discard the title granted to him in the fifteenth century, though not much used since, of 'Philip the Conqueror'.[65] This success had not been gained accidentally. It had required diplomacy and propaganda, as well as enormous administrative effort, but it was primarily a military success. Philip had shown his ability at gathering provisions, raising adequate forces, conducting countless and often difficult sieges, while combating probably the best commanders of his day.

It is not always clear who was responsible for novel developments in warfare, but Philip was often in the van. He used mercenaries as effectively, if not more so, than the Plantagenets, and paid them more consistently. He made use of horse sergeants using crossbows, probably before Richard the Lionheart, providing a force which gave greater mobility in the field and added strength to garrisons. He probably used Greek Fire and possibly trebuchets. The evidence for

64. Baldwin, p. 296 and n. 189.
65. P. Contamine, 'L'Armée de Philippe Auguste', in Bautier, pp. 577–94, p. 577.

neither of these is firm, but there are hints in both cases. We know that Richard used Greek Fire, as had his grandfather Geoffrey of Anjou, and Philip like Richard must have encountered its use in the East.[66] William the Breton's descriptions are not clear enough to be certain, but the employment of sudden fire, and the use of heavy stones for throwing engines, indicates a strong probability that these two new weapons were in Philip's armoury. He also employed *magistri* as military engineers, often in pairs, as shown in Register A. Here the evidence is incontrovertible, and shows that Philip gave proper prominence to technical improvements in warfare, and was prepared to employ and pay the best men. The use of *magistri* is a further indication that he would also have available the latest throwing engines, since such men were responsible for work on these, as well as in building fortifications.

As for Philip's castle-building, it was more extensive than Richard's, and of the greatest influence in castle architecture. No one contributed more to the introduction of round towers in castle design, found in at least twenty of his castles, including the Tour du Roi at Laon, the Tour du Coudray at Chinon and the Tour Talbot at Falaise.[67] Round towers, which were better designed to prevent damage from throwing engines or mining than rectangular towers, were the design of the future for castle architecture. The origin of their development at this time is not clear. They were after all not novel, and date back to ancient times, indeed the twelfth-century cultural renaissance has been suggested as the possible inspiration for the revival of this idea. The influence of the crusades in making contact in the East with Byzantine and Islamic architecture is another possibility. What can be said is that Philip clearly saw the value of round towers, and was the first in the medieval west to use the design with frequency. His wealth, and the widespread fortifications undertaken during his reign, ensured that round towers would became a key factor in both urban and castle architecture. All the demesne towns, and many others, were fortified under him.

Under Philip Augustus too, the Capetians began to develop an interest in the sea and their own naval power. Philip had

66. J. Bradbury, 'Greek Fire in the West', *History Today*, XXIX, 1979, pp. 326–31.
67. Baldwin, p. 299.

experienced humiliation during the Third Crusade from the lack of a French fleet. But it was not so much the Mediterranean as the Channel which inspired this new thrust in royal military activity. Philip was led less by defensive thoughts than by the idea of a naval invasion of England. He had seaborne allies, but he also put money into building ships for himself. It cannot be said that these efforts were notably successful, but that is often the case with first steps. Philip's conquest of the Plantagenet lands in France itself gave a considerable impetus to royal interest in the western seaboard. It might also be noted that Eustace the Monk, who is said to have revolutionized the design of English warships, had previously been employed by Philip. [68]

Throughout his wars Philip showed a clear grasp of strategy. His campaigns were not blind and pointless castle games, as they are sometimes presented. The campaigns of Richard the Lionheart have been shown to demonstrate his ability as a strategist, an intelligent general. We no longer need to be defensive about recognizing such abilities in medieval commanders. From the very first Philip had recognized the significance of the Vexin as the best entry point into Normandy; and similarly he noted Berry as the key to the southern Plantagenet lands. His conquests against John show a logical and intelligent progression: strengthening his base, preparing the way by raids and by taking over key strategic points, and then attacking in force along lines where his communications were protected, lines which were most commonly along the route of rivers. He then chose the right targets for eventual and enduring success.

In the Vexin Philip had exploited every possible advantage; including the fact that the frontier line was not clear historically, and that the archbishopric of Rouen incorporated the whole Vexin. It was frontier country, with several lords having lands held from both lords, and therefore often giving a dual and divided allegiance.[69] The French crown, with Louis VI, had claimed the old county of the Vexin as its

68. Contamine in Bautier, pp. 580, 583; A. Erlande-Brandenberg: 'L'architecture militaire au temps de Philippe Auguste: une nouvelle conception de la défense', in Bautier, pp. 595–603, pp. 596–8.

69. J.A. Green, 'Lords of the Norman Vexin', in J. Gillingham and J.C. Holt, eds, *War and Government in the Middle Ages, Essays in Honour of J.O. Prestwich* (Cambridge, 1984) pp. 47–61.

own, and in consequence was presented with the oriflamme by St-Denis, whose fief it was. Geoffrey of Anjou had ceded the Norman Vexin to Louis VII, though Henry II had reclaimed it in 1160. On the whole the Capetian grasp of the French Vexin was safer than the ducal grasp of the Norman Vexin. In any dispute between the two masters, the local lords were placed in a dilemma, and increasingly they sought their solution by allegiance to France rather than to the duke-king. Philip hammered away without stop until these areas were his. But it was also in the delicate manipulation of his rights and advantages that Philip showed his mastery.

Philip's military caution and common sense also meant that no defeat was decisive. His minor campaigns always had a clear target; and his major campaigns were models of planning. The administrative documents show the care and caution in his planning: the gathering of the necessary provisions and weapons, the payment of troops and garrisons. He also prepared his way with political propaganda: offering freedoms to the Church, benefits to secular lords, and encouraging the resort to his own justice which he sought to show as superior, besides providing himself with a legal justification for any act he took.

The campaigns themselves, particularly from 1203, show how much Philip had learned from the hard struggles against Henry II and Richard the Lionheart. The way in which Philip isolated and then captured Château-Gaillard, isolated and then took Rouen, are perfect demonstrations of the military logic of an excellent commander of his time. The success in Normandy, along with Philip's continued military pressure and his superior management of the local nobility, was the catalyst which rapidly transformed Maine, Anjou and Brittany into Capetian rather than Plantagenet regions. The effects of his success on the wealth and prestige of the monarchy make it one of the high points of medieval French history.

Chapter 6

PHILIP AUGUSTUS AND
THE PAPACY

. . .

PHILIP'S PERSONAL PIETY

Philip Augustus, by the end of the first decade of the thirteenth century, had established a power and authority greater than that of any previous Capetian king. He was at the height of his capacities, though his achievements were yet to reach their peak. He had got the better of his main secular opponents: the count of Flanders and the rulers of the Angevin Empire. Those powers still represented a considerable threat, but that would not climax again until 1214. In the first decade of the thirteenth century, the papacy was probably the main political threat to Philip. He is generally viewed as cold and calculating, but in his relations with the Church we find quite a different sort of person, at times governed by passion, and also at times moved by what we have no right to see as other than genuine personal piety.

Philip was involved in the encouragement of Church reform and often co-operated with the papacy, though he was inclined to follow in the steps of reform rather than initiate it, which he did not see as his province. It is no doubt true that much of the important development in the Church in this period went ahead without much aid or influence from Philip. It was an age which saw developments in, for example, Church architecture, sculpture, manuscript illumination, enamel work and religious music. Philip was no great patron of the arts, but he was involved to some extent in new church building, both as a patron and through those he encouraged. The new movements in monasticism and reform also received at least his protection and occasional

166

support. One could well argue that the political and economic stability which Philip's reign brought to France were themselves of great benefit to the Church.

The Christian elements in Philip's position were strong: French kingship was traditionally seen as sacred, the king naturally as a 'protector of the Church'. As we have seen, it had been a major factor in the survival and development of the Capetian monarchy. Philip strengthened this position by regular worship and emphasis on his faith. At vital moments in his career he publicly asked aid from God, and gave thanks to God afterwards for his successes. Before the Third Crusade, he wept emotional tears outside St-Denis. His action of praying in church before arming for the battle of Bouvines is well known. Nor should we see his conduct as merely a mask.

His court was notably more severe and proper than that of the Plantagenets. Philip forbade swearing; those who failed to respect this were either fined twenty sous, to be paid to the poor of Christ, or ducked in the river.[1] Philip himself, on at least one occasion, ordered the latter punishment to be executed. To a degree, the strictly moral court of St Louis was modelled upon that of his grandfather. In one *exemplum* Philip intervened when a knight was punished, in Paris, for harming a young citizen on one of the bridges over the Seine. The young man had been swearing, and the knight felt he needed punishment which he meted out in person; Philip in his turn had the knight freed and the youth punished again.[2] The story shows that Philip had a lasting reputation for being opposed to swearing. Gerald of Wales favourably contrasted Philip's personal language with the ripe oaths favoured by the Plantagenets. Philip's cleaning up of Paris also contained a puritanical element; the re-development around the Cemetery of the Innocents was partly inspired by a wish to clear away from a sanctified site the merchants and prostitutes who frequented it.

1. William the Breton, *La Philippide, Poéme*, ed. and trans. M. Guizot (Paris, 1825) p. 21; 'Philippide' in *Oeuvres de Rigord et de Guillaume le Breton*, ed. H-F. Delaborde, SHF, vols 210, 224 (Paris, 1882–85) I, p. 23, ll. 395–400.
2. J. Le Goff, 'Philippe Auguste dans les exempla', pp. 145–55 in R-H. Bautier, ed., *La France de Philippe Auguste, le Temps des Mutations* (Paris, 1982) p. 149.

Philip's treatment of the Jews was seen by his own supporters as favoured by the Church and by Paris, as the result of 'a holy severity', and was part of a then approved Christian attitude.[3] The Church opposed usury, which Jews engaged in, and which was condemned for example by the council of Paris in 1213. Concerning his expulsion of the Jews, Philip sought and followed advice from the respected hermit of Grandmontain de Vincennes, Bernard de Boschiac.[4] We may view his actions against the Jews with dismay, but to the vast majority of his contemporaries it was an act to be praised.

Philip also supported the Church in its attempt to stop tournaments, in this case both a view which we tend not to share and one at odds with the average lay attitude of his day. Philip advised his son not to get involved in this activity; at the prince's knighting he was made to swear that he would not attend tournaments, even as a spectator. Philip risked scorn from the secular world in seeking to support what was in essence a Church reform of lay Christian conduct.

The king is often condemned, usually by the poets and those who quote them, for his lack of court patronage to the arts. This may not be seen as a commendable attitude nowadays and tends to be criticized by modern historians, but Philip was again following the Church line of his day, which forbade payments to actors and entertainers. Rigord notes that Philip presented cast-off clothes not to actors as others did, but to the poor.[5]

Philip is sometimes criticized for his less than generous gifts to the great churches and abbeys. But there are some interesting trends in Philip's almsgiving which suggest that to him this was more than an impersonal duty. For example, one notes the frequency with which he made grants to aid lepers and smaller, frailer new religious orders, as well as alms to the genuine poor. Many of his charters benefited lepers, such as concessions about using dead wood in the forest of Iveline to the lepers of Linas, and in the wood of Halath to the lepers of Senlis. An example of his interest in the poor

3. William the Breton, *Philippide*, ed. Guizot, p. 21; 'Philippide', ed. Delaborde, p. 23, l. 407: 'Pulsis Judeis, sanctoque rigore fugatis'.
4. R. Foreville, 'L'image de Philippe Auguste dans les sources contemporaines', pp. 115–32 in Bautier, p. 124.
5. J.W. Baldwin, *Masters, Princes and Merchants: The Social Views of Peter the Chanter and his Circle*, 2 vols (Princeton, 1970) I, p. 202.

is found in the charter giving royal protection to a house of charity for thirteen poor people at Orléans.[6] His will specifically left money to the poor, for the correction of abuses, for aid to orphans and lepers, as well as for the promotion of crusading, including grants to the Hospitallers and the Templars.

Philip was also prepared to protect Church rights and to support Church reform, even against the interests of the magnates. The chronicler Joinville records that Philip told one of his counsellors that he would rather forfeit his own rights than quarrel with one of God's priests. According to William the Breton, Philip accepted a division of authority between Church and state, saying: 'the government of the realm is enough for me. I leave it to the men of God to deal with the service of God.'[7] The slightly later *exempla* often show Philip as a protector of the Church, putting a special emphasis on justice. Of course he could fight like a tiger to define and defend what he believed were his own rights, for example over the division of authority in the courts, but he did see and accept a genuine and strong role for the Church.

Philip made grants to new and reforming monastic orders. Among the beneficiaries were the Cistercians. In 1221 Philip offered royal protection to all the houses of this new, growing and vigorous order. Philip was not the most open-handed of monarchs to great and established churches, and was specific about favoured groups. He preferred to make confirmations of other people's grants and to recognize rights, rather than to give land or cash. As a result he has been called 'parsimonious', though this is harsh; careful is perhaps more accurate.[8] His generosity waned as the reign progressed and his security increased.

Philip was conventionally protective of the ancient abbeys, giving them numerous confirmations of their privileges as

6. *Recueil des Actes de Philippe Auguste*, ed. H-F. Delaborde, 4 vols (Paris, 1916–79) I, p. 153, no. 124; p. 183, no. 152; p. 263, no. 218.
7. R. Fawtier, *The Capetian Kings of France*, trans. L. Butler and R.J. Adam (London, 1964) p. 25; Joinville, *Histoire de Saint Louis*, ed. N. de Wailly (Paris, 1868) pp. 237–8, 265; A. Luchaire in E. Lavisse, *Histoire de France depuis les Origines jusqu'à la Révolution*, III, Pt I (Paris, 1911) p. 214.
8. B. Guillemain, 'Philippe Auguste et l'Episcopat', pp. 365–84, in Bautier, p. 365.

well as new grants. But he made no new Benedictine foundations, simply giving moderate support to existing houses.
Many of his gifts did not even come from his own pocket,
for example he redistributed the wealth which streamed into
France in the form of relics and valuable objects after the
looting of Byzantium in the wake of the Fourth Crusade.
Philip favoured the Benedictine houses, but he did not dig
deeply into royal resources in order to do so.

Philip's almsgiving and financial aid to the Church was
moderate. He was more lavish with military aid to Churches
which needed assistance, and in grants of privileges and
moral support, than with cash. But he was noticeably more
generous to the less well-to-do, those perhaps in greater need
than the established houses: for example to small houses
and new orders. This mirrored the attitude of his age. His
only major foundation was Notre-Dame de la Victoire in
1215 for the Victorine canons of Paris, who represented one
of the newer elements in the religious orders, but it was as
much a political act to commemorate his triumph at Bouvines
as a sign of generosity to the Church. Nevertheless, that the
relatively humble Victorines should be the beneficiaries of
this most notable example of his building patronage has
significance. Even in this case, though, the new house near
Senlis depended partly for its finance on the bishop of Senlis.
In his will of 1222 Philip did leave £240 per annum to La
Victoire and £2,000 for building expenses.

Philip also left large sums to the Templars and Hospitallers,
relatively new orders which benefited from his gifts and
encouragement, reflecting his interest in the crusades and
the Holy Land, and also the usefulness to the crown of the
Templars who looked after the royal treasure. Philip, as we
have seen, also gave help to the expanding new order of
the Cistercians, including special privileges to the whole
order, as well as to individual houses. He took interest too
in other new monastic groups: the Carthusians, the orders
of Fontevrault and Grandmont, and in hermit groups. A
number of these were, for example, given exemption from
paying the Saladin Tithe.

Even so, much of the major Church reform work of the
period passed with little royal notice. There were some interesting elements of social reform in what was occurring: the
lay participation in orders such as Cîteaux; the role of women

in such orders as Fontevrault; the care for the disadvantaged, as in the new abbey of St-Antoine in Paris for former prostitutes. But one could not fairly credit the king with these developments, except to note that he did not oppose them.[9]

There were many advantages to Philip in having the co-operation of the Church. At key points in the reign, in justification of his actions, he underlined that either he was working on behalf of the Church, or that the Church had given his project its backing. At the age of eleven, it was said that at mass the Lord appeared to Philip, with the result that he put his face to the earth, wept, and vowed to devote his life to good works. On campaign in the south in 1188, at Leuroux, it was claimed that Philip was fighting justly against Richard the Lionheart, with God on his side. The land was parched, but a sudden shower of rain fell and, though the hot weather had dried up all the rivers, a stream suddenly flowed clear and deep from which the whole army, together with its horses and beasts of burden, was able to drink its fill. The stream ran in a torrent as never before in summer, but dried up again once Philip passed on. This was of course interpreted by Philip's chroniclers as showing the favour of heaven, but they knew they were propagating a view which Philip wanted publicized.[10] Philip himself sought to emphasize divine support for his actions when about to fight the greatest battle of his career at Bouvines. He attended mass, prayed, and then had the oriflamme carried before him like an ecclesiastical banner, proclaiming: 'God will lead us into battle and we shall be his ministers. The Church assists us with its prayers ... we fight on the Church's behalf.' Afterwards victory was celebrated with the singing of hymns and the placing of captured weapons in churches.[11]

When preparing to invade England, at the papacy's behest, Philip was not surprisingly angry when the pope made an agreement with John, and then forbade the invasion. Nevertheless Philip governed his anger and, in obedience to the

9. Rigord, *Vie de Philippe Auguste*, ed. and trans. M. Guizot (Paris, 1825) p. 139; Rigord, 'Vie', in *Oeuvres*, ed. Delaborde, p. 140.
10. William the Breton, *Philippide*, ed. Guizot, p. 67; 'Philippide', ed. Delaborde, p. 67, ll. 45–55.
11. William the Breton, *Philippide*, ed. Guizot, pp. 316–19; 'Philippide', ed. Delaborde, pp. 313–14; William the Breton, 'Vie', in *Vie de Philippe Auguste*, ed. Guizot, p. 301.

papacy, abandoned his expensively prepared expedition. This shows that Philip was willing to accept papal rulings even when he disagreed with them strongly.

It seems likely that Philip genuinely believed in divine intervention. In 1196, after a period of dreadful storms, he personally walked in a procession bearing Church banners, to entreat the intervention of God. For two years running there had been heavy rains followed by severe flooding. Philip gave alms to those who suffered and encouraged the Church to provide aid. Rigord says the abbey of St-Denis gave the poor all the money it had.[12] In the second year's flooding, whole villages were submerged and the Seine bridges broke. Then came the procession with the relics of St-Denis carried at the fore, and the waters were blessed by the clerics. Rigord says God was asked to lower the waters and he did. However, in the procession of 1206, when relics were taken over the Petit Pont at night because of the storms, the bridge collapsed; the chronicler does not claim divine intervention on this occasion.

Just as divine favour was always claimed for Philip, so it was always held that his foes were the enemies of God. In other words, Philip was presented as fighting on the side of God and the Church, and always in a just cause. For example, Renaud de Dammartin count of Boulogne was accused by William the Breton of oppressing churches, pillaging the poor, orphans and widows, parading his concubines in public, and being excommunicate. No wonder he got his comeuppance through Philip acting on God's behalf. Otto IV (1209–14), Philip's opponent at Bouvines, was accused of being 'a destroyer of Church property', a persecutor of the Holy Church, an excommunicate, who 'causes the tears of the poor, and the pillager of churches and clergy'.[13]

There was even a move at the king's death to make Philip a saint, which William the Breton thought his just deserts. A number of miracles were attributed to him, albeit rather unspectacular ones. It is difficult today to view Philip as having this degree of sanctity, but it reminds us that he was a devoted son of the Church. He was seen as 'most pious', the most Christian monarch, the defender of the faith, the

12. Rigord, ed. Guizot, p. 123; Rigord ed. Delaborde, p. 132.
13. William the Breton, 'Vie', ed. Guizot, pp. 252–3.

protector of the Church, the champion of the Church. This was the Capetian tradition, and, as William the Breton realized (and no doubt the king himself), it was useful that Philip be viewed in this manner. Philip's actual piety is impossible to gauge, but his public persona was that of a pious king.[14]

As good a summary as any of Philip's reputation and conduct is found in another *exemplum* recorded by Stephen de Bourbon. In these stories, used for sermons, Philip was the first French king to figure. In a vision, a cardinal witnessed St Denis presenting Philip's soul to demons in order to send it to hell; but they decided to send it to purgatory instead, because after debating his qualities, they found that he had at least honoured the saints, respected Church feasts, and defended churches, priests and religion.[15]

. . .

INGEBORG OF DENMARK

Most medieval biographies of kings are forced to be more a history of the reign than a biography in the modern sense. This need not be disturbing, so long as the reader understands the constraints placed upon the historian. In Philip's case we do have detailed works by two people who knew him well, the prose works by Rigord and by his own chaplain, William the Breton, as well as the latter's poem. We also have a wealth of administrative records from a period when many such records were instructions issuing directly from the monarch, some in letter form. They sometimes betray his views, and his feelings about the work he was initiating, and about his life in a broader sense.

Very few medieval biographers are blessed with any records which are more personal, and which would allow a truly interior view of their subject. Even works such as that on William the Marshal are suspect from this angle because they are works of literature, not written by the subject himself; and if not quite fiction, then not quite fact either. There

14. William the Breton, *Philippide*, ed. Guizot, pp. 16, 24, 333, 375, 380–1; 'Philippide', ed. Delaborde, p. 306, ll. 597–8, pp. 16, 24, 333, 375, 380–1; p. 15, l. 201: 'rex sacratus', p. 25, l. 445: 'divini zelo'; Philip Mouskes, *Chronique Rimée*, ed. Baron de Reiffenberg, 2 vols (Brussels, 1836–38) II, p. 422.
15. Le Goff in Bautier, p. 150.

are some exceptions, for instance the autobiographical writing of Guibert de Nogent, but such works are few and far between.

With Philip we do not have the good fortune to possess close personal documents. Therefore, when we come to the vital matter of his marriages, although we have a good deal of external information, it is impossible to know the feelings of the central characters. Inevitably our conclusions will seem unsatisfactory; we can but present the material and hazard some suggestions, in the end we cannot know the whole truth. The marriages are central to the life, and each was in some way remarkable and unusual. Like Philip, we shall consider that he had three marriages, rather than only the two which the papacy accepted. Indeed, by all accounts, he was fondest of his third wife, Agnes de Méran, whom the papacy refused to recognize as his proper wife. It was his insistence on maintaining the liaison with Agnes which brought on Philip's head the condemnation of Rome. The marriage caused the greatest difficulty Philip would experience in relations with the Church throughout the reign.

In general, medieval society was prepared to overlook the peccadilloes of kings. Women were often seen as encouraging sin and blamed as seducers. A thirteenth-century writer asked what is woman? and answered himself: 'the confusion of man, an insatiable beast, a continual anxiety, a never-ceasing strife, the shipwreck of an unchaste man, a human slave'. But oddly, there was a wide condemnation of Philip's treatment of both Isabella and Ingeborg, and an even more vehement attack on his relationship with Agnes.[16] Innocent III's defence of women may have been something more genuine than mere policy, it may reflect change in the Church's attitude to women, and a greater desire to protect their position. In any case, Philip seems to have received a more thorough drubbing from the Church than might have been expected from action in previous cases of a similar kind.

16. Roger of Howden, *The Annals of Roger de Hoveden*, ed. and trans. H.T. Riley, 2 vols (London, 1853) II, p. 515; Roger of Wendover, *Chronicon sive Flores Historiarum*, ed. H.O. Coxe, EHS, 5 vols (1841–44) IV, p. 154: ' "quid est mulier?". "Hominis confusio, insaturabilis bestia, continua sollicitudo, indesinens pugna, viri incontinentis naufragium, humanum mancipium" ', this is an insertion half a century later, taken from the *Speculum Historiale* by Vincent of Beauvais.

Philip's first marriage had been made for political reasons. It went through one very serious crisis, but could by and large be thought a successful marriage and produced Philip's legitimate heir, Louis, in 1187. The marriage was suggested by Philip of Alsace count of Flanders, seeking to cement his position at court in the new reign. The wife he found for Philip was his niece, Isabella of Hainault, daughter of his sister Margaret and her husband, Baldwin count of Flanders.

The count of Hainault had at first opposed the match, because he had been happy with an existing agreement to marry his daughter to the count of Champagne. But consideration of the new suggestion showed possible gains for both parties. For Philip there were potential gains in the dower lands, and the promises of what might come to the crown in certain circumstances. Philip of Flanders at the time had no heir. We have already followed the process whereby the lands, which have been called Philip of Alsace's 'Picard hegemony', later known as Artois, together with the Amiénois, Vermandois and Valois, did indeed eventually fall to the French monarchy.[17]

Isabella and her family were also descended from the Carolingians through Charles of Lorraine, and we have seen the value to the monarchy in this period of being able to claim Carolingian ancestry. Then too, Philip could hope to gain greater influence over the count of Hainault by a marriage to his daughter, and was eventually successful in detaching him from his allegiance to Flanders. Before this time, as Giselbert of Mons makes clear, the count of Hainault 'was not obliged at all to the king of France, since he neither did homage nor had any agreement or household obligation to the king'. In the long run, it was Philip rather than the count of Flanders who benefited most from the match.[18]

Philip and Isabella had married at Bapaume on 28 April 1180, and after a dispute the new queen was crowned at St-Denis. It was on this occasion that the pushing of a knight who was among the throng led to an overhead lamp shedding oil over those present. One optimistic source claimed that it was 'like a sign of the abundance of the gifts of the

17. J. Dunbabin, *France in the Making, 843–1180* (Oxford, 1985) p. 354.
18. Giselbert of Mons, *La Chronique de Gislebert de Mons*, ed. L. Vanderkindere (Brussels, 1904) p. 127.

holy spirit poured on them from on high'.[19] One hopes the
happy couple appreciated their blessing. The marriage was
not at first consummated because, while Philip was fifteen,
Isabella was only ten. One cannot but wonder if the relatively common experience in that period of marriage to a
pre-pubescent girl, and the inevitably delayed sexual element
in the union, did not in Philip's case make some contribution to his desire for divorce in 1184, and his conduct at the
start of his second marriage.

In 1184 the match seemed to be in trouble. Philip sought
a divorce on the grounds of consanguinity. A contemporary expressed a lay view: that marriage to someone related
in the third degree was perfectly acceptable, but 'if I find I
do not like her any more, because of that affinity, I could
be granted a divorce'.[20] At this time Isabella, still only fourteen, had not become pregnant, and this may have been an
additional factor for divorce. At Senlis Philip declared that
the marriage was over, which caused an immediate hostile
reaction.

Isabella made a dramatic appeal against her husband's
announcement: dressed in a shift she appeared barefoot in
public, touring the churches of the town, and winning the
sympathy of the citizens, who gathered to demonstrate their
support for her before the palace. Giselbert of Mons reflected their views, accusing Philip of treating her 'unjustly'.
Philip heard the racket outside and sought advice from his
counsellors, including the bishop of Beauvais. He was advised to withdraw from evil and restore her as his wife. Philip
tried to persuade Isabella to accept divorce and promised to
console her with a decent marriage to one of his barons,
but she refused: 'it does not please God that a mortal should
enter the bed in which you slept'. Giselbert paints a touching picture of both daughter and father weeping at their
predicament. In the end Philip took back Isabella, and the
count of Hainault promised to aid the king, even against
the count of Flanders if necessary. Some historians have
claimed Philip was simply manoeuvring to detach Hainault

19. J-P. Poly and E. Bournazel, 'Couronne et mouvance: institutions et
    représentations mentales', pp. 217–36 in Bautier, p. 233.
20. G. Duby, *The Knight, the Lady and the Priest*, trans. B. Bray (London,
    1983) p. 209; Baldwin, *Masters*, p. 335.

from the Flemish alliance, but although this was the consequence of the episode, it was surely not the cause.[21] Isabella produced two stillborn children, followed by a son Louis on 5 September 1187, and died bearing stillborn twins on 15 March 1190. There were to be no more unquestionably legitimate sons for Philip. Nevertheless he now had a son and heir, albeit one who seemed weak in health. The fears for the young Louis's health meant there was a perceived need to insure the succession with further offspring. The question of a second wife was shelved for the duration of the crusade, apart from a few tentative moves without conclusion, but it would not be put off for ever.

Philip's choice then lighted upon Ingeborg, a Danish princess. Her father was the late King Waldemar I of Denmark (1157–82), and now her brother held the throne as Cnut VI (1182–1202). When Cnut died in 1202, his brother Waldemar II (1202–41) would succeed. Again the motives for Philip's choice seem primarily political. Denmark could prove a useful counter against the Empire from whose clutches it was trying to escape and, with its naval strength, could assist in Philip's planned invasion of England. Denmark was a larger country, by some 60 per cent, than it is now, and dominated the southern Baltic.[22] Philip by the match gained the Danish reversion of a claim to the English throne from Cnut the Great (king of England 1016–35); and having as yet no navy, obtained a promise of aid from the Danish fleet for a seaborne invasion of England, together with supporting forces. There was also to be a considerable dowry of some 10,000 marks.

Arrangements were made and Ingeborg, accompanied by the bishop of Röskilde, came to Philip. She was eighteen, Philip nearly ten years older, and one might have anticipated a happier beginning to the new marriage than to his first. They first met at Amiens on 14 August 1193 and were married on that very day. The events of the following twenty-four hours are impossible to unravel in terms of motive,

21. Giselbert of Mons, pp. 152–4; R-H. Bautier, 'Philippe Auguste: la personalité du roi', pp. 33–57 in Bautier, p. 41.
22. T. Riis, 'Autour du mariage de 1193: l'épouse, son pays et les relations françoises-danoises', pp. 341–61 in Bautier, p. 343. See J. Gillingham, 'Richard I, galley-warfare and Portsmouth: the beginnings of a royal navy', *13th Century England*, VI, 1997, p. 10.

though we know what happened in public. The young couple were crowned by Philip's uncle, the archbishop of Reims. During the ceremony Philip suddenly went deathly pale and began to tremble.[23] After the wedding he sent his new wife away. She was never to be his wife in more than name.

The explanation of this dramatic event is impossible to determine, but it is so important that some conjecture is admissible. Philip sought a divorce on the grounds of consanguinity, which fifteen witnesses swore to be true. Philip and Ingeborg were fourth cousins, but the papacy still gave its considered opinion that the marriage was valid, and in any case it is hardly a satisfactory reason for Philip acting as he did. He would overlook the same scruples on a later occasion with Agnes de Méran.

In truth, there were more problems with the Church over the relationship with Agnes, which Philip soon entered into, than there were over Ingeborg. By making this new, illicit, and widely criticized liaison, Philip turned the majority of Church opinion against himself. The relationship with his new female partner, Agnes de Méran, was said to be bigamous, adulterous and incestuous. Innocent III suggests another possible cause for the king's change of heart, claiming that Philip's advisers were to blame, giving him 'evil counsel' and sowing 'the seeds of hatred and discord'. It is true that the initial political causes for the marriage to Ingeborg quickly lost their value, but again there is little to support the suggestion that political advice was really at the root of his sudden revulsion.[24]

The only explanation offered by the sources closest to Philip is that Agnes had bewitched him, and 'because she was a sorceress, he could not face this long-desired wife [Ingeborg] without horror'. The effect on Philip had been 'undoubtedly at the instigation of the devil'. William the

23. W.H. Hutton, *Philip Augustus* (London, 1896) p. 161; C. Petit-Dutaillis, *The Feudal Monarchy in France and England from the Tenth to the Thirteenth Centuries*, trans. E.D. Hunt (London, 1936) p. 181; A. Cartellieri, *Phillip II. August, König von Frankreich*, 4 vols (Leipzig, 1899–1922) III, pp. 10, 19–20, 64, 78.

24. G. Duby, *France in the Middle Ages, 987–1460*, trans. J. Vale (Oxford, 1991) pp. 209–10; Duby, *Knight*, p. 205; Roger of Wendover, *Flowers of History*, ed. and trans. J.A. Giles, 2 vols (London, 1899) II, p. 142; Roger of Wendover, ed. Coxe, III, p. 91: 'quam a se consilio iniquio amoverat ... odium et discordiam seminare'.

Breton reinforces this with talk of curses and spells which resulted in the king loving her less, so that he 'deprived her of his person'.[25] The way these comments are phrased suggests that Philip's relationship with Agnes predated the marriage to Ingeborg, though otherwise we do not know this. It would be a possible cause for some readiness to reject Ingeborg; yet it is not sufficient in itself, for Philip had neverthesless allowed the marriage arrangements to reach fruition.

The sorcery charge seems unlikely from what we otherwise know about Ingeborg, who is praised on all sides for her virtue, and this particular explanation is generally dismissed nowadays as ridiculous. It does, however, give one important clue to the puzzle: the charge of sorcery was sometimes offered as a reason for a husband's impotence. It is possible that Philip had been unable to perform on the marriage night, though we know that on other occasions he could be sexually successful with other partners. Blaming the wife's magical practices might have been a face-saving cover for his own inadequacy. Sorcery itself was accepted by the Church as grounds for divorce. Professor Baldwin suggests that the reason for the break, whatever it was, 'must have been personal and sexual', and we concur.[26]

We cannot, however, know the reason for Philip's sudden distaste, if that is what it was; there are simply no clues. Ingeborg is described as 'beautiful in face, more beautiful in her soul', tall and blonde. Wendover called her 'a lady of remarkable beauty'; Stephen de Tournai thought her 'more gracious than Rachel, and not inferior to Helen'; while to Rigord she was the most beautiful of the sisters of Cnut VI, who had long been 'the object of [Philip's] desires'.

In Cartellieri's view the marriage was 'a means to an end, not a political end in itself'.[27] The evidence suggests that

25. Rigord, ed. Guizot, p. 112; Rigord, ed. Delaborde, p. 124: 'instigante diabolo ... ut dicitur, maleficiis per sorciarias impeditus, uxorem tam longo tempore cupitam, exosam habere cepit'; William the Breton, *Philippide*, ed. Guizot, p. 210; William the Breton, 'Vie', ed. Delaborde, p. 195.
26. J.W. Baldwin, *The Government of Philip Augustus* (Berkeley, CA, 1986) p. 83.
27. Hutton, p. 160; Roger of Wendover, ed. Giles, II, p. 133; Roger of Wendover, ed. Coxe, III, p. 79: 'puellam mirabili decore praeditam'; Riis in Bautier, p. 342; Rigord, ed. Guizot, p. 112; Rigord, ed. Delaborde, p. 124: 'sororem suam pulcherrimam'; Cartellieri, III, p. 79.

political causes for the marriage were less important than in some cases, and that Philip had demonstrated personal desire for the match. There could have been an element of over-expectation in Philip's attitude, and so an increased sense of disappointment when in some way she failed to please him. Or if our guess at his own temporary impotence is correct, a consequent attachment of blame to his partner might have resulted. No one, apart from the king, found fault in her person. Her only known failing is that she was unable to speak French, though she was educated enough to know Latin.

Philip did on one occasion mention the need to take care in marriage, when he later warned his son Louis against being as quick-tempered as himself, suggesting perhaps a confession that when marrying Ingeborg and then dismissing her, he had acted too abruptly. One wonders if perhaps she was just too virtuous and chaste; Innocent called her 'not only pure, but even a saint', a view reinforced by Rigord who considered her a saintly girl, an ornament of all the virtues, a model of innocence. Perhaps Philip, with his enhanced views on religion, needed a more earthy partner to arouse him. Perhaps, as has been claimed of Ann of Cleves in a later period, Ingeborg simply had bad breath or some similar fault which was sufficient to alienate her husband. We can only conjecture.[28]

At any rate Philip's repugnance was immediate and en-during. All the efforts of his own Church, and the Church in Rome, failed to move him. There would be one or two moments of compromise, but he could never bring himself to live with Ingeborg as a normal husband and wife. There were political grounds for ending the marriage, which some historians have emphasized. The position with regard to England changed, the Danish alliance therefore offered less; but this was at best a subordinate reason for rejecting her. The likelihood of reconciliation was not aided by Ingeborg's brother making an alliance with the emperor Otto IV, but this too was clearly not a fundamental explanation of their estrangement.

28. Duby, *France*, p. 226; Hutton, p. 171; Rigord, ed. Guizot, pp. 112, 147; Rigord, ed. Delaborde, p. 124: 'puellam sanctam et bonis moribus ornatam'.

Yet for all the mystery, in some ways an understanding of Philip's action is hardly easier than comprehension of Ingeborg's reaction. He felt revulsion and did all he could to break the marriage. She on the other hand persisted in her attempts to remain queen against all his continued and determined efforts to remove her. He left her no illusions about his wishes. Philip wanted to send her home; she refused to go. He sought divorce on the grounds of consanguinity; she refused. The Gallican Church at the council at Compiègne, headed by Philip's uncle the archbishop of Reims, accepted Philip's case; but the papacy was less tolerant. Philip was granted his divorce by the French clergy, but the evidence was not watertight, and the papacy reversed the French decision. Later the archbishop changed his mind, advising Philip to obey the papal demand and restore Ingeborg; at which Philip chided him as a fool and a half-wit for giving the divorce judgement in the first place.

Even in France there was divided opinion over this matter. Philip's biographer, Rigord, disapproved of the divorce, calling the clergy who accepted it: 'mute as dogs who did not know how to bark'. Though the bishops mainly supported Philip through the crisis, there were doubts in the ranks of the clergy about the propriety of Philip's position. Peter the Chanter, a papal judge delegate for the divorce in 1196, wanted Philip to take back Ingeborg, and Gilles de Paris expressed the same opinion, criticizing the bishops for allowing the king to marry Agnes.[29]

Had Ingeborg been prepared to accept an end to the marriage, the matter could have been settled. The papacy had granted divorce in comparable cases. It has been suggested that 'nowhere was canon law so open to confusion as in marriage'. King John had rid himself of his unwanted wife Isabella of Gloucester; Matthew count of Boulogne twice shed his marital partners; Mary the daughter of Eudoxia, with the acceptance of the Church, was twice repudiated, by Bernard IV de Comminges an elderly libertine, and by Pedro II king of Aragon. Philip's father, who retained a pious reputation, had been able to end his union to Eleanor of

29. Rigord, ed. Guizot, p. 113; Rigord, ed. Delaborde, p. 125: 'facti sunt canes muti non valentes latrare, timentes etiam pelli sue'; Baldwin, *Masters*, pp. 8, 41.

Aquitaine; Frederick Barbarossa had similarly been allowed to break his marriage to Adela von Vohburg.

But the papal and reforming viewpoint was hardening on this question, and one might see Philip's marriage as a test case. It certainly spurred discussion in Paris, the centre of innovative and reforming ideas. Peter the Chanter argued for reforms in the system, to make the claims for divorce more restrictive, a position later accepted by Innocent III.[30] Philip thought, with some reason, that he was being treated more harshly than other monarchs.[31] Given the circumstances, Philip's claim that the marriage had never been consummated may well be true, and could certainly have been accepted, had not Ingeborg denied this too, claiming that they had engaged in sexual intercourse. When she heard of his intention to divorce, she denounced the evil of France, and appealed to Rome, crying 'Mala Francia, mala Francia; Roma, Roma'.[32]

Given Philip's behaviour, Ingeborg's claim that the marriage had been consummated seems puzzling, and one would have thought the assertion unlikely, but how is it possible to disprove her statement? It much diminished the likelihood of a condoned divorce. The papacy was presented with a wife who claimed to be properly married, as she had been in the eyes of the Church, who with justification denied the grounds of consanguinity, who without possibility of contradiction except by Philip claimed that the marriage had been consummated, and whose ill-treatment won sympathy from all and sundry. Not surprisingly, the papacy sided with her, and tried to persuade Philip to take her back. Innocent III, recently elected pope, sent Philip a letter to this effect in May 1198, and an interdict on France followed later in the year, after the king had failed to take the advised action.

Ingeborg was to spend some twenty years virtually imprisoned in various places by her husband: in castle prisons, hunting lodges, and convents. Philip tried to arrange for her to take the veil, without success. Her brother appealed on her behalf for her freedom, but Philip imprisoned the

30. Baldwin, *Masters*, pp. 333, 335; A. Luchaire, *Social France at the Time of Philip Augustus*, trans. E.B. Krehbiel (New York, 1912) p. 363.
31. Luchaire, *Social France*, pp. 368–9; Baldwin, *Masters*, p. 335.
32. Luchaire in Lavisse, p. 145.

Danish ambassadors who brought the request. She was treated harshly by the unsympathetic Philip, having to sell her clothes and jewels in order to live. In 1203 she wrote to the pope complaining that 'he fails to treat me as a wife', and 'no one dares to visit me, no priest is allowed to comfort my soul. I am deprived of the medical aid necessary for my health. I no longer have enough clothes, and those I have are not worthy of a queen ... I am shut in a house and forbidden to go out.'[33]

That Philip's distaste for Ingeborg was on personal grounds, and not because he was homosexual, was soon made clear. He sought and found another wife. It was this action which thoroughly soured relations with the papacy. Agnes was the daughter of Berthold IV count of Méran in the Rhineland. Like Ingeborg, she offered an alliance with an imperial connection. Her father was a Hohenstaufen supporter, a relation and ally of Philip of Swabia. Philip continued to act as if his French divorce was final, and married Agnes in June 1196. So far as one can see, apart from the tension caused by political problems and religious censures, it was a successful union. They were joined in a marriage ceremony, and Agnes acted at court as the queen. She provided Philip with two children, Marie and Philip nicknamed Hurepel or shockheaded; the son's hair is said to have emulated his father's unruly mop.

By the marriage to Agnes Philip virtually removed the hope of a compromise with the papacy. Innocent III proclaimed it his task to defend 'persecuted women' such as Ingeborg. In the pope's view Philip should, at the very least, have waited until the second marriage was properly ended by the Church before engaging on a third liaison. Popes Celestine III (1191–98) and Innocent III in turn condemned his action, and the papacy never recognized the third marriage. Angevin chroniclers revelled in the scandal, Howden considering that Philip had 'unjustly repudiated his wife', referring to Agnes as the 'adulteress'. Even loyal chroniclers criticized the match: Rigord saw it as 'against the law and the will of God', and William the Breton refers to her as a 'concubine'. Because of the hopelessness of his 'forbidden love', one modern historian, with a certain exaggeration, has

33. Luchaire in Lavisse, p. 148.

compared their love to that of Tristan and Iseult. In understanding Philip, we must always take into account these acts
of personal revulsion and insistence on remarriage against
all advice. The normally shrewd and controlled king had
human weaknesses in his make-up, and they caused him
much trouble.[34]

When Philip failed to respond to papal demands for the
restoration of his second wife, Innocent threatened and then
issued an interdict on France. Many of the French clergy
ignored it and remained loyal to the king on the issue. The
interdict was carried out only in Paris, Senlis, Soissons,
Amiens and Arras, and Philip, 'violently angered', hounded
the clergy who obeyed the papacy, charging them with having no care for the poor.[35]

Eventually the pressure did prove sufficient to force Philip
into making a move. He began negotiations with the papacy
and promised a reconciliation with Ingeborg, agreement
being reached at St-Léger-en-Yvelines. As a result, the interdict was raised in September 1200. But Philip's promise seems
to have been simply a diplomatic tactic; Ingeborg was not
restored and Agnes was not removed. Ingeborg remained a
prisoner, now at Étampes, while Agnes stayed with the king.
The Church called a new council, at Soissons, to deal with
the matter in 1201, under two cardinals as judges. When it
looked as if the outcome might be embarrassing for Philip,
after an impassioned plea by a priest on Ingeborg's behalf,
the king suddenly turned up and seized Ingeborg. To the
astonishment of the cardinals, Philip rode off with her, thus
preventing any judgement. He proclaimed that he and
Ingeborg would be reunited and not separated again, but
soon reneged on his promise and refused to remove Agnes
from court, this time on the pretext that she was pregnant.

The situation was only resolved by the death of Agnes at
Poissy in 1201; she was buried at Mantes with royal honour.
It is clear that as long as she lived, Philip was not prepared to

34. G. Bordonove, *Philippe Auguste, le Conquérant* (Paris, 1986) p. 134;
    Roger of Howden, ed. Riley, II, p. 455; Roger of Howden, ed. Stubbs,
    IV, pp. 147–8: 'quod eam de jure non deberet cognoscere'; IV, p. 113:
    'adulteram suam' and p. 138; Rigord, ed. Guizot, p. 155; Rigord, ed.
    Delaborde, pp. 150–1: 'contra legem et Dei decretum'; William the
    Breton, 'Vie', ed. Guizot, p. 220.
35. Bautier, 'Personnalité', in Bautier, p. 40.

throw her over, however great the pressure from the Church. His fondness for her is demonstrated by his favour for her children, considered by the Church to be illegitimate. The son, Philip Hurepel, received vast estates in five counties, and was betrothed to the daughter of the count of Boulogne, whose lands he later took over, creating a model for the later *apanage* settlements on royal sons. The daughter, Marie, was first married to the marquis of Namur and when widowed, after being offered as a partner to the king of Aragon, was remarried to the duke of Brabant.

When Agnes de Méran died, a compromise with the Church was possible at last. Philip promised to restore Ingeborg, and a relieved Innocent III, much in need of French aid, agreed to legitimize the two children of the union with Agnes, Philip Hurepel and Marie, in November 1201. Ingeborg was now treated somewhat better, but never truly as a wife. Philip found his sexual outlets elsewhere, and produced an illegitimate son, Peter Charlot, by a 'damoisele' of Arras.[36] He also considered other possible candidates for a new marriage, for example the daughter of Herman the landgrave of Thuringia in 1210, but never pursued this to a conclusion.

In 1213, when Philip again desired the aid of Denmark for a projected invasion of England, Ingeborg was finally restored at court 'as queen if not as wife'. By this time, the king's worries about the succession had been lessened, since his son Louis now himself had a son and heir. In effect Philip had defied the papacy over his third marriage for twenty years. He does not appear to have ever truly repented his actions, only to have regretted the consequences from time to time. He once wrote to Innocent III about 'the wrong you have done me, me personally', and that seems to have been his real feeling about the matter.[37] After Philip's death, Ingeborg entered a convent at Corbeil, at her own wish, where she spent time praying for Philip's soul, no doubt with some fervour. He had left her 5,000 marks in his will, and she quietly lived a further fifteen years, recognized as queen by Louis VIII (1223–26) and Louis IX (1226–70).

36. A.W. Lewis, *Royal Succession in Capetian France: Studies in Familial Order and the State* (Cambridge, MA, 1981) p. 164; Philip Mouskes, p. 318, l. 20724.
37. Luchaire in Lavisse, pp. 150, 153.

PHILIP AUGUSTUS AND INNOCENT III

The dominant pope during Philip's long reign was the great
Innocent III (1198–1216). It is doubtful if Philip's relations
with the papacy would have been so problematic with any
other pontiff. Innocent was a relatively young and vigorous
occupant of the papal throne, born in about 1160, and
elected in 1198 at the age of thirty-seven. He was a stronger
pope in vigour and physical health than was usual at the time.
He had a sharp mind and good legal knowledge. Relations
with Philip were by no means normally bad. The very first
letter Innocent despatched as pope was to Philip in 1198:
'to a very special son of the Roman Church . . . we send our
first letter'.[38]

Innocent himself had a liking for France and had been a
student in Paris, which helps to explain his interest in its
king and in its developing university at Paris. There are two
good portraits of the pope: with large ears, close eyes, long
thin nose, tight mouth. He remains a solid physical presence, hovering over almost every political crisis of the day.
He was a busy and conscientious man, and his wit and power
impress in the many surviving letters. He has been praised
as 'the greatest canonist and statesman who sat on Peter's
throne for a thousand years'. His achievements ranged
widely, from reorganization of the curia to support of the
Franciscans.[39]

But Innocent III was not without faults, and not without
failures. He was one of the most political of popes, claiming
'for reason of sin' to be able to intervene in almost any secular dispute. Many then and since have felt that this was not
the best way for the Church to proceed, leading as it did to
a great deal of involvement, and even partisanship, in secular political affairs.

Philip was perhaps Innocent III's most astute opponent
in this matter, allowing the Church its proper place, but no
more. Several times Philip reproved the papacy for intervening in secular matters. On one occasion, when dealing with

38. M. Maccarrone, 'La papauté et Philippe Auguste: la décrétale Novit
ille', pp. 385–409 in Bautier, p. 385.
39. C.H.C. Pirie-Gordon, *Innocent the Great* (London, 1907) p. 187.

Henry II, Philip declared: 'it is not in the power of Rome to pass judgment on the king or kingdom of France for taking arms to punish rebellious subjects'. The papal legate was also accused by the French of being bribed by Henry to take his side. A letter of Innocent's in 1203 recognizes Philip's point and treads warily: 'we do not intend to judge concerning the fee ... but to decide concerning the sin'. There were limits to the situations in which Innocent could justify the Church's interventions.[40]

Many historians have seen Innocent III as a great political pope who established his authority over the secular rulers within western Christendom. He humbled John, who resigned his throne to the pope and received it back as a fief; he supported Otto of Brunswick in his success against Philip of Swabia for the Empire, and then aided the young Frederick II to regain it for the Hohenstaufen. Historians generally list Philip as one of those kings he humbled, largely with reference to his second marriage to Ingeborg of Denmark; but this is a claim which can be challenged. The papacy's need of French support, a traditional alliance, was too common and too pressing to wish for any great breach in their relationship.

Philip had certain advantages over other monarchs of his day in his dealings with the Church. His family had developed a tradition of working with the Church, including the defence of the Church within their own realm. Philip's treatment of heresy is another example of action within France which was in line with general Church policy, and therefore helped to keep Philip in the good books of the papacy. It is true there were times when his response to requests for aid was more dilatory than the Church would have liked, but he consistently acted against heresy, and had no quarrel with the Church's view on it.[41] Philip gave more aid to the Church against heresy than the other monarchs of his day.

Philip had inherited a Capetian tradition of loyalty to the Church and co-operation with the papacy. He had been

40. Roger of Wendover, ed. Giles, II, p. 72; Roger of Wendover, ed. Coxe, II, p. 438: 'ad ecclesiam Romanam non pertinere in regem vel regnum Francorum per sententiam animadvertere, si rex Francorum in homines suos demeritos et regno suo rebelles injurias suas ulciscendi causa insurgit ... sterlingos regis Angliae'; Maccarrone in Bautier, p. 398.
41. R.I. Moore, *The Origins of European Dissent* (London, 1977) p. 9.

brought up to believe that a king should be pious, a spiritual
father to his people, a protector of the Church and the poor.
The monarch's task was to act on God's behalf in these
causes. Philip made efforts to emulate his father's Christian
conduct, and was at least conventionally pious. He made
gifts to the Church, supported a number of the new religious orders of his day, went on crusade, opposed heresy,
and encouraged Church reform. At times there was clearly
a warm regard for the Church's welfare, even a passion,
stemming from his religion; for the crusade, he proclaimed
that he 'burned with desire' to fulfil his pilgrimage.[42]

Philip seems to have had a genuine admiration for poor
but devout priests as against hypocrites or lax prelates. He
once, at an episcopal election, gave his staff of favour to a
poor cleric, warning him that in office he might soon become
as fat as his fellows. On the whole Philip allowed more freedom in Church elections than other monarchs of his day, in
line with papal policy. Philip also gave considerable support
to the newly developing university in Paris, favoured by the
papacy, where theology was the main study. It was through
his judgement that the students came to be treated as hon-
orary clerics, with the legal privileges which that entailed. In
general the papacy had little to complain about over Philip's
attitude. He compared well with other monarchs of his day:
Henry II, held responsible for Becket's death; Otto IV, who
showed little gratitude to the papacy for the aid he received.
The papacy addressed Philip as a loyal son, at times even
with deference.

We should regard Philip as a king who preferred diplomacy to war, again the path favoured by the Church. So far
as we can see he was an active, genuine believer. At critical
moments of his life, as before the battle of Bouvines, he
was guided by his religion. The failure of his second marriage was the main obstacle to an excellent relationship with
the papacy, but even that thorny dispute did not in the end
destroy the good relationship beyond repair. The popes
found that their need of the French monarch's support was
too great to allow a permanent breach. The popes of his
day recognized that it would be unwise to antagonize him if
it could be avoided. Although he did not always respond

42. Bordonove, p. 98.

positively, Philip could be approached with some hope on most matters where the Church needed state co-operation, from crusades to reform. Philip himself had good reason to want a smoothly running relationship. The Capetian monarchy had consistently increased its authority by working with the Church. Philip himself would feel benefit at many points in his reign, as when the Church made little attempt to interfere in his expansionist policies, since by and large he allowed more privileges than his rivals had done.

The details of Philip's place in the history of crusading are dealt with in other chapters, but it would be wrong to omit in this section all mention of the movement. It played an important part in his relationship with the papacy. His western wars brought papal censure because they prevented crusades; his participation in the Third Crusade, and his encouragement of other crusades, helped to counter this and improve relations with Rome. His enthusiasm for crusading, despite only a brief stay in the Holy Land, was consistently expressed, and almost certainly genuine. His chaplain, William the Breton, says that before the Third Crusade he was keen to deal with Saladin, 'the tyrant of Egypt and Syria ... greatly moved to see the Holy Places ill treated', and desirous of visiting the Christian sites. It was an age of enthusiasm for crusading, from the knights who hoped to gain from the Fourth Crusade to the young people who streamed southwards on the Children's Crusade. In his will Philip left money for his son to crusade to the East, God permitting.[43] Whenever French and papal interests coincided, there was co-operation.

Philip gained much in France from the crusades. Although some criticized his early departure from the Third Crusade, the papacy received him well on his return, and his reputation in France stood high. If the Fourth Crusade was a disaster for the papacy, it brought benefits to France in wealth, in power in the East, and in the redirection of princely and magnate activity. If the Albigensian Crusade was an unfortunate attack on Christians which helped to debase the crusading ideal, it nevertheless had papal backing. It also brought

---

43. William the Breton, *Philippide*, ed. Guizot, p. 65; 'Philippide', ed. Delaborde, II, p. 65, l. 8: 'Egypti Syrieque tyrannus', and p. 66, ll. 15–16; Bautier, 'Personnalité', in Bautier, p. 49.

benefit to the Capetian monarchs, being the catalyst whereby, from their northern base, they came to rule the south and hence the whole of France.[44]

The invasion of England was undertaken by Philip, even if not technically as a crusade, nonetheless clearly at the pope's instigation. When the papacy withdrew that permission because of John's submission, Philip was angry but still abandoned his personal participation.[45] As with the Albigensian Crusade, Philip was prepared to take action only when the Church had given the go-ahead, on the grounds that he would be fighting a just war, but was unwilling to commit himself if there were legal doubts or papal opposition.

There were other affairs where co-operation was more difficult, and policies less easily merged. Thus the papacy and Philip had their own particular axes to grind in the Holy Roman Empire. Philip's main concerns were fear for Capetian interests in the border areas with the Empire, for countering German aid to Philip's political enemies outside the Empire, and to oppose the growth of rival Plantagenet interests there. The papacy, on the other hand, sought to have an emperor who would favour ecclesiastical reform, and who would not threaten papal interests in Italy.

The pope was forever encouraging Philip to support his chosen imperial favourite of the moment, but co-operation was inevitably going to suffer if that favourite did not fulfil Philip's own requirements. Thus Innocent III supported Otto of Brunswick against Philip's preferred competitor, Philip of Swabia. Otto was the nephew of Richard and John, the son of a marriage intended to make a link for the Plantagenets within the Empire. Otto had also been favoured by Richard, and made count of Poitou by him. Innocent was aware that his choice was equivalent to a pat on the back for the Plantagenets, but warned Philip not to cause trouble, advising him not 'to try and tame tigers'. However, just as

44. W. Ullmann, *A Short History of the Papacy in the Middle Ages* (London, 1972) p. 225; J. Sayers, *Innocent III, Leader of Europe, 1198–1216* (Harlow, 1994) p. 172.
45. Baldwin, *Government*, p. 208, accepts that it was a crusade: 1213 'Innocent threatened John with deposition and called upon the French king to lead a crusade against this opponent . . .'; though n. 73 reminds of the dispute over this point, noting comments from C.R. Cheney, S. Painter and A. Cartellieri.

Philip was obedient to Church policy whenever he felt it possible, so he was always prepared to oppose that policy if it was against the interests of France, or if it were diminishing his royal rights.[46]

On the early death of Henry VI in 1197, the candidates for the imperial throne were Frederick of Hohenstaufen, who was only three and therefore dropped from the reckoning; Philip of Swabia, the old emperor's brother; and Otto of Brunswick, son of Henry the Lion and nephew of Richard the Lionheart. On the whole Philip of Swabia, the French king's choice, seemed the strongest candidate, but he died in 1208. Otto was then crowned in Rome the following year, but was soon out of favour as an ungrateful beneficiary of papal aid; by 1211 Otto was himself excommunicated.

Innocent realized that in Otto he had mistaken his man, and wrote to Philip, admitting it: 'If only, dearest son, I had known the character of Otto, who now calls himself emperor, as well as you did . . . It is with shame that I come to write this to you, who so well prophesied what has indeed come to pass . . . we shall never abandon France.' He now had to hope that France would not abandon him.[47]

There were, however, many times when papal and French interests coincided; and the battle of Bouvines, which led to the downfall of Otto IV and the triumph of Frederick II (1215–50), was such an occasion. The triumph of Frederick is often seen as relying upon papal support, but in many ways it depended more on Philip's victory in 1214. One also wonders how much of a success for the papacy Frederick's success was in the longer term, when Germany and southern Italy were united in the hands of the new Hohenstaufen emperor, with the papal lands perilously placed between the two.

Much the same was true of Philip's triangular relations with the papacy and the Plantagenets. In this case, Philip required papal support for his territorial expansion and during the various conflicts. He did not always obtain it, but in the end the Angevin Empire collapsed, and the papacy accepted the outcome. The Church knew that it often stood to gain from the fact that Philip allowed more scope for

46. Luchaire in Lavisse, p. 153.
47. Luchaire in Lavisse, p. 155; Sayers, p. 92.

191

reform than did the Plantagenets. Also, for some years, the papacy wanted to bring the recalcitrant John to heel, and during that period Philip was the chosen instrument.

England was placed under interdict in 1208, and John excommunicated in 1209. Philip was promised by the pope that 'he and his successors should hold possession of the kingdom of England for ever'. In 1212 Philip, with regard to England, promised 'to avenge the insult which had been cast on the Universal Church', and John's deposition by the pope was read out to the council of Soissons. But then came John's submission to the papacy in 1213, a blow to Philip, halting his own aggressive plans against England and diminishing the hopes of his son Louis's actual invasion.[48] The papacy, having accepted John's abasement, made threatening noises against France to stop the invasion, and when Louis still went ahead, papal opposition to the project reduced his hopes of success.

It will never be entirely clear how far Philip countenanced his son's invasion of England, which will be discussed in more detail in the final chapter. It seems probable that Philip's attitude was one of half-hearted support, because he favoured his son more than he sympathized with John, but at the same time allied to a feeling that his son's move was unwise and better avoided. Philip was clearly angry that the pope had set up the invasion, let him make all the expensive preparations, and then at the vital moment stepped in to prevent it, but Philip would almost certainly have let the matter drop had it not been for Louis's enthusiasm.

The invasion of England threatened the good relationship between France and the papacy, since John had become a papal vassal at the time of submitting to Innocent III. When Louis, intent on going ahead with the invasion, sent a deputation to Rome, it was told: 'your lord is not worthy of our greeting'.[49] The opposition of the Church played an

48. Roger of Wendover, ed. Giles, II, pp. 259, 260; Roger of Wendover, ed. Coxe, III, pp. 241–2, p. 242: 'ipse et successores sui regnum Angliae jure perpetuo possiderent'; Luchaire in Lavisse, p. 162; J.T. Appleby, *John, King of England* (London, 1958) p. 190; R.V. Turner, *King John* (Harlow, 1994) pp. 167–8 disputes the deposition, though he accepts that chroniclers record it.
49. Roger of Wendover, ed. Giles, II, p. 367; Roger of Wendover, ed. Coxe, III, p. 372: 'quod dominus vester non sit dignus salutatione nostra'.

important part in the defeat of Louis's invasion. In the end
the invasion was abandoned, and relations between Philip
and the new pope then improved. Louis's next military venture, against the Albigensian heretics, was much more to the
liking of the Church, and further helped to heal relations.

Another factor which modified the papal attitude to Philip
was the consistently loyal attitude of the Gallican Church
itself. In 1216 the synod at Meaux actually ignored the pope's
letter excommunicating Philip. The papacy found it could
go so far, but then had to compromise with the local Church.
The papacy condemned war in the West and tried to prevent war between Christians, often using the crusade as a
reason for not wasting military effort in the West. The popes
assiduously sought to keep the peace, and diplomacy between
warring nations was almost invariably in the hands of clerics,
often of papal legates.

In the wars between Philip and the Angevins, the papacy made efforts to bring about peace, for instance in 1198,
1199, 1203–4, 1206 and 1214. Innocent III chose men to
represent him who could be seen as neutral in the western
conflicts, often Italians. Philip in his turn was always careful
to appoint suitable French clerics to represent his interests
at the papal court. There was a telling moment, after his
conquest of Normandy, with the papacy making efforts to
cushion John's losses, when the English king, in contrast to
the watchful Philip, failed to send an embassy to represent
him or to counter the men active on Philip's behalf.[50]

The papacy also knew that it owed a debt to Philip in his
treatment of his subjects. Not every king would have been
so successful in curbing the anti-clerical attitudes of some or
the warlike behaviour of others. Philip undertook numerous
expeditions on behalf of the Church against local magnates,
and was almost invariably successful. Philip's encouragement
of reform, of new monastic movements, his hostility to tournaments and bad language, was by no means a common
secular outlook. Philip had to keep in subjection such men
as Bertran de Born, who wrote: 'to war I am attuned, for I
do not keep or hold any other law . . . I keep myself amused

50. B. Bolton, 'Philip Augustus and John: two sons in Innocent III's vine-
    yard', *The Church and Sovereignty, c.590–1918: Essays in Honour of Michael
    Wilks*, ed. D. Wood (Oxford, 1991) pp. 113–34, especially pp. 118,
    123.

with war and tournament . . . everyone is impatient to fight.'
He despised the pacific attitude of Philip, but the king proved
to be a tougher contender than Bertran anticipated.[51]
Innocent's efforts and interventions were not always successful. The crusade with which Innocent III was most intimately connected, the Fourth, was from the papal point of
view an absolute disaster. And a number of the political
successes claimed for Innocent were fortuitous: the death
of Philip of Swabia allowing Otto to succeed; the victory of
Philip at Bouvines making possible the accession to power
of Frederick II; while John's fear of Philip's intention to
invade was the main cause of his submission to Innocent,
after five years of resisting papal claims with impunity. There
can be no doubt that Innocent III was a great pope, but his
political achievements have been exaggerated, and in Philip
Augustus of France he met his match.

51. Bertran de Born, *The Poems of The Troubadour Bertran de Born*, ed.
    W.D. Paden Jr, T. Sankovitch and P.H. Stäblein (Berkeley, CA, 1986)
    pp. 251–3, p. 251, ll. 22–4: 'Ab gerra m'acort,/q'ieu non teing ni
    crei/negun'autra lei'; p. 253, ll. 37–9: 'C'ab aisso.m conort/e.m teing
    a deport-/gerra e tornie,/donar e dompnei'; p. 365, l. 14: 'a cada un
    sera tart que gerrei'.

Chapter 7

PHILIP AND THE CHURCH
IN FRANCE

. . .

THE GALLICAN CHURCH AND THE CAPETIANS

There is clearly an overlap between Philip's relations with
the Church in France and his relationship with the papacy. In
France, for example, he encouraged Church reform, encouraged new monasticism and suppressed heresy. All these royal
endeavours improved his relations with the papacy. In this
chapter we shall examine developments in the Church in
France and incidents that affected the links between Church
and crown occurring within his realm, particularly with a view
to seeing how such matters affected the connection between
Philip and his own Gallican clergy, not least because as with
his relations with the papacy, such things influenced political as well as religious affairs.

Of course many of those aspects we have already covered
with regard to the papacy affected relations with the Gallican
Church, such as Philip's personal beliefs and attitudes to
religion and reform, his interest in crusading, his marriages,
as well as the views, requests and orders issuing from Innocent III. It is unnecessary to repeat the details of those considerations. We simply need to note firstly that all examples
of good co-operation with the papacy resulted in better
relations with his own Church, and secondly that those questions where there was dispute with the papacy, although causing problems for him in France, never seem to have entirely
soured his working relationship with the French clergy as
a whole.

In many ways Philip reflected those traditional Capetian
qualities of a Christian monarch which made for harmony

with the Gallican Church. His public piety, his encouragement of monasticism, his flexible attitude to ecclesiastical
elections, were examples of why Philip was generally viewed
in a friendly manner by his own clergy.

A monarch was also expected to make gifts to the Church.
Philip followed in this tradition but, it is claimed, without
any great generosity. One historian sees him as 'the most
material' of monarchs.[1] He preferred to make gifts which did
not impoverish the crown. It is a matter of opinion whether,
all things considered, this is to be praised or condemned.
An *exemplum* shows Philip's reputation for the kind of caution over money for which the English often condemn the
Scots (surely without foundation). One must be reminded
that these tales about Philip are unlikely to be literally true,
but what they reflect is the way in which the king was
seen. We have already encountered the tale in which Philip
gave only a small coin to a beggar who asked for alms in the
name of the king's ancestors on the side of Adam, on the
grounds that if he gave a coin for all his relatives in that
particular line, there would be nothing left for the realm.
Philip's grants to the Church were modest, but not unim-
portant, and they were targeted. As we have seen, he tended
to favour the poor and weak, the new and less established
monastic orders, and churches with a close connection to the
monarchy. But his gifts were broadly spread, and few elements in the French Church had serious cause to complain.

Philip also protected the Church in a thousand small ways.
The surviving charters are only a proportion of those issued,
but they are littered with confirmations of Church rights: over
property, over exemptions, over various claims. For example,
an early act took the monastery of Charlieu under his protection, at the request of the abbot of Cluny; another took
into protection the church of Sarlat in Périgord; or again
the king confirmed to the monastery at Villarceaux the right
to a proportion of the value of the salt on every boat passing
under the bridge at Mantes. Royal protection of such rights
was invaluable for the smaller abbeys and churches.[2]

1. E.M. Hallam, *Capetian France, 987–1328* (Harlow, 1980) pp. 198–9; C.
   Petit-Dutaillis, *The Feudal Monarchy in France and England from the Tenth
   to the Thirteenth Century*, trans. E.D. Hunt (London, 1936) p. 259.
2. *Recueil des Actes de Philippe Auguste*, ed. H-F. Delaborde, 4 vols (Paris,
   1916–79) II, nos 20, p. 28; 22, pp. 32–3; 160, p. 194.

Philip was also a conscientious protector of the Church against secular harassment. This may be viewed as pure self-interest, and was certainly a means for increasing royal power, especially outside the demesne, but there is no doubt that his energy in this respect was appreciated by the clergy. Such activity was not new, but the growing power and authority of the French crown meant that Philip's efforts to protect the Church were both more successful and more widespread. He made numerous expeditions in response to ecclesiastical appeals against overbearing local secular magnates; and he was energetic beyond the call of mere duty in response to such appeals. Even on his deathbed he exhorted his son and heir Louis: 'My son, I beg you to honour God and Holy Church . . . as I have done.'[3]

The Capetian kings had long claimed rights over the Church which set them apart from other princes in France. In early days it was one of their few opportunities to rise above other princes, who were often more wealthy and more powerful than themselves. The basis of this was their position with regard to the Church within their own demesne, but it was the ability to extend their influence beyond the demesne and into the territories of other great lords in France which set the Capetians apart. As we have seen, Philip's father had employed this tactic with some success, and Philip would continue it. For example, he took homage from a number of bishops in areas of territorial dispute, including Cahors, Limoges and Clermont.[4] The benefits of such a policy were cumulative. It is noticeable that during the Albigensian Crusade, the local bishops frequently sided with the monarchy against both the local magnates and the pope.

Philip developed further the royal link with the abbey of St-Denis both as a place which had become 'a family necropolis' and as an extension of the idea that Denis was the royal patron saint. This was a case of Philip patronizing a truly great and wealthy abbey. St-Denis received many favours from the monarch, including various grants, but it was rather his interest in its affairs, his regular physical presence there,

3. Petit-Dutaillis, p. 259; A. Cartellieri, *Philipp II. August, König von Frankreich*, 4 vols (Leipzig, 1899–1922) IV, Pt II, p. 569.
4. Petit-Dutaillis, p. 263.

and his association of the abbey with his family which counted for most. It was also in line with the additional emphasis given to Paris as a capital. The crown and sceptre used at Philip's coronation were sent to St-Denis. The king continued granting favours to the abbey and, when going to war, made much of the use of the oriflamme which was kept there – largely in order to promulgate the idea of divine backing for his expeditions. On return to Paris from his crusade, it was to St-Denis that he first went to give thanks to God for his return.[5]

Philip also pursued a claim to be the defender of the whole Church in France, a monarch to whom the papacy and the regional Churches might turn for aid. Of course he used this position to further his own ends, and to deal with recalcitrant lords, but he also responded positively to appeals for aid, and many Churches recognized how much they needed this royal counter to magnate power. Posing as the protector of the Church was also a useful propaganda tactic and often gave Philip the chance to proclaim that he had the right to intervene in a region where he was seeking new authority, and to assert that his intervention was just. It was an important part of his effort to extend royal authority over his enemies and especially the Plantagenets, notably in Normandy and the Vexin, and especially in advance of his conquests. At Noyon he gave support to the canons of Notre-Dame against the mayor, who as a result was forced to release a servant of the canons whom he had arrested, and even to pay them an indemnity.[6] It was also a means of helping to establish his authority in a region after conquest.

A number of Philip's early military exploits were in defence of the Church; the first example being against the lord of Charentan in Berry, in order to protect the Burgundian Church. Thus he also opposed the duke of Burgundy, the count of Chalon and the lord of Bourbon on behalf of the Church, and provided secular support for such prelates as the bishop of Clermont against the count of Auvergne, or the bishop of Beauvais.

5. A.W. Lewis, *Royal Succession in Capetian France* (Cambridge, MA, 1981) p. 49.
6. A. Luchaire in E. Lavisse, ed., *Histoire de France depuis les Origines jusqu'à la Révolution*, III, Pt I (Paris, 1911) p. 212.

Philip, however, expected his pound of flesh: he would defend the Church, but at a price. When making land grants, he normally reserved the royal right to military service and to *gîtes*, or hospitality, including demands for wagons and pack horses, though he sometimes substituted a rent in place of the performance of a duty. When the see of Reims failed to send its expected military quota to his aid, he did not quickly forget. In 1201 the clergy of Reims appealed for assistance, but he reminded them of the time when he had required troops and they had given him only prayers. Now when they were asking for help against the count of Rethel and others, Philip responded: 'you have aided me only with your prayers; now you are under attack, I shall aid you in the same way'. He offered them his prayers rather than the military aid they expected.[7] As a result Reims promised in future to send its quota when demanded by the king, and Philip then gave the requested aid.

There was a similar conflict in 1210, when the bishops of Orléans and Auxerre refused to provide their due military service, and Philip simply confiscated their estates. Nor was the king prepared to yield up what he saw as established secular rights of justice; the Church courts had their place, but he resisted their encroachment upon his own jurisdiction. On one occasion he directly instructed his agents to make sure that the citizens of St-Quentin were *not* sent before a Church court in a matter that he considered within the secular province.

Nevertheless the loyalty to Philip from the Gallican Church was consistent and important. The most telling moments were those when the papacy had reason to combat Philip's policies or conduct. The most critical episode was the long-standing difference with the papacy over his second marriage and his liaison with Agnes de Méran. French bishops granted Philip a divorce from his second wife Ingeborg of Denmark which, as we have seen, the papacy later repudiated. The papacy time and again pressured the French bishops to oppose Philip, and with some success, but he never lost

---

7. Luchaire in Lavisse, p. 212; William the Breton, *La Philippide, Poème*, ed. and trans. M. Guizot (Paris, 1825) p. 36; 'Philippide' in *Oeuvres de Rigord et de Guillaume le Breton*, ed. H-F. Delaborde, SHF, vols 210, 224 (Paris, 1882–85) I, pp. 37–8, p. 38, ll. 786–7: 'Vos prece me sola nuper juvistis, eadem/Lege relativa vice prelia vestra juvabo'.

at least a modicum of support even during the period when the papacy placed an interdict on his lands. Most French bishops, including the archbishop of Reims and the bishops of Chartres, Orléans and Beauvais, refused to observe the interdict.

As with military service, so on this occasion, Philip expected loyalty, and was prepared to punish disloyalty. When the bishops of Paris and Senlis observed the interdict, Philip ravaged their lands in punishment. Paris was undoubtedly a special case with regard to Church–state relations. Historically the bishops of Paris had power within the city, which to a degree Philip recognized, being often generous to the Parisian Church; but he was not prepared to be other than first within his own capital, and this led to clashes with both of the bishops during his reign, Odo and William. But, again, while pressing for his own rights, he was prepared to acknowledge the proper claims of the bishop of Paris too. In 1222 Philip made an acceptable settlement with Bishop William over their respective rights within the city.

. . .

CLERICS IN ROYAL GOVERNMENT AND ADMINISTRATION

Perhaps the most important, and certainly the most obvious, area in which there was co-operation between king and Church, was in the government and administration of the realm. The clergy were the king's educated, literate and numerate subjects. Very few laymen could compete in this field; and those that could were mainly of the high nobility, and not available for any but the highest services to Philip. A Christian king had need of his own clerics for acts of worship, for the conduct of the Church in France, and for dealing with the papacy. But beyond that, the whole operation of government, including diplomatic embassies, the preparation of documents, and administration in general, revolved around those royal servants who had sufficient education, and this necessarily required Church participation. And, if many of his administrators were lesser men, most of them were also ecclesiastics.

Philip depended increasingly on men of lesser social rank in his administration, though one or two prelates figure prominently, in particular his own uncle, William the archbishop of Reims. This was another example of close co-operation between crown and Church within France. Archbishop William was a major adviser in the early reign, the monarch's 'right hand man', his 'vigilant eye', a 'second king', who was trusted sufficiently to act as one of the two regents during Philip's absence on crusade.[8] Another prelate and relative who played a significant, if not very spiritual part in the reign was his cousin Philip of Dreux, the bishop of Beauvais, who, for example, negotiated with the Holy Roman Emperor on the king's behalf during the Lionheart's imprisonment.

There were also the counsellors of the king, most of whom were churchmen. These were men who in general stayed close to the king at court, and whose advice was sought on a regular basis. They were men involved in the day-to-day running of the realm. Some were rewarded with bishoprics, including the sons of Walter the Chamberlain, who became bishops of Noyon, Paris and Meaux. William the Breton speaks of the 'wisdom and incomparable value in advising' of Brother Guérin, one of the king's closest counsellors, an educated man and also seen as 'second after the king'.[9] Guérin was a Hospitaller who became bishop of Senlis, and was at the battle of Bouvines, scouting for the king and giving good military advice, dressed in his Hospitaller habit – which perhaps at least gave him an excuse for participating so actively in military matters. Another adviser, Haymard, was also a member of the military orders, in his case of the Templars. It may be that a clerical education combined with the warlike activities of the Military Orders made such men especially useful to the king.

There was also the whole corps of clerks who served the royal government in chancery and elsewhere, writing the letters and documents, authenticating them, keeping

8. J.W. Baldwin, *Masters, Princes and Merchants: The Social Views of Peter the Chanter and his Circle*, 2 vols (Princeton, 1970) I, p. 32; Luchaire in Lavisse, p. 235; *Recueil*, I, no. 109, p. 137: 1184: 'in consiliis nostris oculus vigilans, in negociis dextra manus'.

9. Rigord, *Vie de Philippe Auguste*, ed. and trans. M. Guizot (Paris, 1825) p. 267; Rigord, 'Vie' in *Oeuvres*, ed. Delaborde, I, p. 256: 'regis Philippi magnanimi specialis consiliarius effectus, in aula regia propter prudentiam et incomparabilem consilii virtutem ... quod quasi secundus a rege negotia regni inculpate tractabat et ecclesiarum necessitudines ... in litteratus'.

accounts, making judicial records, preserving the archives. Among the less elevated clergy who worked for Philip were his chaplain, William the Breton, who wrote the two great works on the reign, one in prose the other in verse, as well as Andrew the Chaplain with his literary achievement, and Adam the Clerk who was the first known keeper of the royal accounts.

Duby suggests that many such clerks were not numerate, but this is surely wrong; his evidence is not convincing, and there is much to the contrary.[10] These curiales were not always admired by their fellows in other branches of the Church. It was not always agreed that close service of a secular ruler and attendance at court were suitable activities for soldiers of Christ. John of Salisbury was one who thought their energies could have been better employed elsewhere.

Clerics also worked in many areas for the king, centrally and locally, dispensing royal justice, undertaking missions on the king's behalf, acting as diplomats and messengers. Philip appointed Peter the Chanter, who had been a papal judge delegate, to act as a royal judge. This again was a task which some in the Church frowned upon because there was a problem over the imposition of blood penalties, which were not considered to be within the proper jurisdiction of a cleric. But Peter was himself sensitive to the reform movement and an able man, so there was little opposition to such an appointment. Philip's ability to select the right men was part of his achievement.

As with his bishops, so with his administrators, Philip won from them loyalty and long service. With very few exceptions, his clerical administrators sided with their king even against papal remonstrations. Sometimes they were rewarded with great offices, and sometimes they received valuable gifts, but mostly the rewards were moderate, and it is clear that great worldly gain was not the spur which drove them. Whatever he seems like to us, to his close clerical servants such as William the Breton, Philip was a good master, a worthy king whom it was their duty to serve. Overarching the occasional conflict between papacy and monarch was the enduring cooperation of king and clergy in governing the kingdom.

10. G. Duby, *France in the Middle Ages, 987–1460*, trans. J. Vale (Oxford, 1991) pp. 174–7.

. . .

EPISCOPAL ELECTIONS

One area in which co-operation was vital if major conflict was to be avoided was in the choice of major prelates, and especially bishops. In this period a bishop necessarily was a man of political importance with landed wealth, as well as a representative of the Church with spiritual duties. One major concern of Church reform during this period was to gain freedom of elections for ecclesiastical office from intervention by secular powers, in particular elections to bishoprics and abbacies. In his own lands, Philip rarely interfered in elections, provided the normal courtesies were observed. As a result, there were few election disputes in the royal demesne. Philip once wrote in a letter that 'the canons of the Churches of France have liberty to elect their bishop'; and it was generally true.

At the same time, royal bishoprics nearly always went to the king's men, and the regalian bishops were consistently loyal to the king. It was not that Philip lacked an interest in elections: when about to leave on crusade, he expressed the view that the men elected should be 'pleasing to God and useful to the realm'. He was certainly happy to see royal relatives or royal clerks preferred, but he was prepared to use his own powers with restraint, and to allow the Church the privileges it had already gained. He was content not to interfere unreasonably in elections, but equally glad to see men pleasing to himself elected. His restraint did not prevent this from occurring.[11]

Philip could be sharp with clerics on the subject of royal rights, though, if he thought they were overstepping the recognized boundaries, and always guarded his position carefully. Stephen de Gallardon recorded a conversation between Philip and Peter the Chanter, the Parisian master. They discussed the election of bishops, and Peter was taking a high Church line. Philip sought to bring him down a peg by asking why it was in ancient times that so many bishops were saints, whereas now none were. Peter replied 'because foolishness always arrives unbidden'. Philip then asked: 'by

11. B. Guillemain, 'Philippe Auguste et l'épiscopat', pp. 365–84, in R-H. Bautier, ed., *La France de Philippe Auguste, le Temps des Mutations* (Paris, 1982) pp. 379–80.

the lance of St James what does that have to do with my question?'[12] Peter answered tactfully that in present times kings influenced elections, and therefore got the sort of bishops they deserved. He was no doubt thinking of such men as the warlike bishop of Beauvais, Philip of Dreux. It was a rather oblique criticism of the king, but it also suggests that at the time people realized that for all that he was better than most monarchs with regard to allowing freedom of elections, he nevertheless exerted enough influence to point elections in the direction he desired.

Rigord describes an actual election at his own abbey of St-Denis.[13] Philip was passing by, apparently by chance, but came into the church 'as if entering his own chamber'. The monks assembled to ask the king for the right to elect their own abbot. Philip graciously agreed, and then they returned to their own chapter. It is a nice example of the king using his own powers in the accepted way, but acting courteously and not interfering with the proper role of the monks. Hugh the prior was elected, a candidate acceptable to all concerned, and Philip confirmed the election.

In the newly acquired Angevin lands, Philip's hand was noticeably lighter than that of his predecessors. Even before the conquest of Normandy, his attitude won him support from the Church. In Normandy he promised freedom of elections, guaranteed the rights of the bishops, and kept his promises. Often in consequence of his tolerance, candidates favourable to himself were elected; in other words he gained the desirable end, but without the undesirable means. There is a clear contrast with Plantagenet practice. In 1172, with regard to the Winchester election, Henry II had bluntly declared: 'we order you to hold a free election, but we forbid you to elect anyone except Richard my clerk'.[14]

Philip also took under his own more direct protection the bishoprics and abbeys of the royal demesne, where the crown had regalian rights. Philip extended the number of Churches which came under his direct influence, and yet at the same time relaxed the royal demands upon them. From Normandy and the Loire Valley ten new bishoprics were brought under

12. Baldwin, *Masters*, p. 171.
13. Rigord, ed. Guizot, p. 57; Rigord, ed. Delaborde, pp. 65–6; quote on p. 65: 'sicut in propriam cameram suam'.
14. W.L. Warren, *King John*, 2nd edn (London, 1978) pp. 159–60.

his sway. In Register A, up to 1212, there were nineteen regalian abbeys listed; by the time of Register C, up to 1229, there were twenty-nine named, and it is known that the list was not complete.[15]

Though intent on keeping his influence over regional Churches as wide as possible, Philip was prepared to give up in return some of his own rights, even regalian rights, especially in areas where he was trying to establish his authority for the first time, as for example at Langres and Arras on the border with the Empire in 1203–4, or in Normandy where he abandoned some of the rights previously enforced by the Plantagenets. William the Breton thought that the Plantagenets had 'usurped' these rights from the Church, and that Philip restored them.[16] There were some instances of royal agents pillaging bishoprics during a vacancy, for example on the death of Maurice bishop of Paris, or at Auxerre in 1206, and sometimes vacancies extended to a year and more; but by and large Philip did not prolong vacancies and tried to be fair about regalian rights, at times restoring what had been taken from the Church.

. . .

THE UNIVERSITY OF PARIS

The king's encouragement of the development of Paris was also appreciated by the papacy through its interest in the new university, which indeed became a university proper only under Philip. Its new regulations, its concentration on theology, its judicial privileges, were all pressed for by the Church and allowed by Philip.

There was a riot in 1200 in which a number of students were killed. A German student at Paris had been elected to the bishopric of Liège and was waiting to take up his post. His servant was buying wine in a tavern when he was beaten up by some locals. Then a number of enraged German students came to the tavern and a brawl erupted. This resulted in violence spreading to the streets around, and to a full-blown riot, an outlet for the constant bad feeling between

15. J.W. Baldwin, *The Government of Philip Augustus* (Berkeley, CA, 1986) pp. 181, 305–6, 308, 314.
16. Luchaire in Lavisse, p. 214; William the Breton, *Philippide*, ed. Guizot, p. 222; 'Philippide', ed. Delaborde, pp. 219–20.

citizens and students. The locals assembled under the prévôt to attack the German student quarter, as a result of which the bishop-elect and a number of other students were killed. The university masters then appealed to Philip to intervene. The king braved the hostility of the citizens of Paris by taking the side of the students, imprisoning the prévôt of the city, and declaring that from henceforth students should be given privileges at law equivalent to those of clerks: 'the juridical status of clerics'.[17] The unfortunate prévôt was later to die when trying to escape by climbing over a wall, falling fatally.

Philip's intervention here, though pleasing to Rome, was brave, especially given his normal wish to ingratiate himself with the Parisians. He had helped the fledgling university at the risk of antagonizing the citizens of his favoured capital. Under his protection, a college organization began to emerge between the last two decades of the twelfth century and the first decade of the thirteenth century. In 1210 Innocent III issued a bull recognizing the university as a legal corporation. This was followed in 1215 by the papal legate, Robert de Courson, promulgating rules to govern the length of study at the new university, and the role to be played by the masters: 'every student must have a master to whom he attaches himself'.

One student writing home claimed 'we live in a good stylish house', but may have simply been trying to keep his parents happy, since, according to Stephen Langton, himself a student, the left bank lodgings were fairly basic, with the bed being no more than a heap of straw.[18] Masters were generally not wealthy, and they also often had dwellings in the poorer districts, on occasions with a prostitute having the lower part of the house. Evidence for university faculties appeared first in 1213, and for the organization of students by nations in 1222 – though the earlier incident with the German students suggests that something of the kind was already in existence.

17. Roger of Howden, *Chronica*, ed. W. Stubbs, 4 vols, RS no. 51 (London, 1868–71) IV, pp. 120–1; Roger of Howden, *The Annals of Roger de Hoveden*, ed. H.T. Riley, 2 vols (London, 1853) II, pp. 484–5; J. Verger, 'Des écoles à l'université: la mutation institutionelle', pp. 817–46 in Bautier, p. 824.
18. A. Luchaire, *Social France at the Time of Philip Augustus*, trans. E.B. Krehbiel (New York, 1912) p. 94; Baldwin, *Masters*, p. 130.

The university also produced a number of men who became significant in the Church in France and beyond, and a number of leading figures with influential ideas in the movement for Church reform. It was one of the most productive examples of co-operation between monarchy and papacy, with the result that Paris came to be referred to as the 'new Athens'. Perhaps Philip had foreseen, more than the citizens, that in the long term a prestigious university would bring great benefits to the city itself.[19]

A second French university appeared during Philip's reign at Montpellier, concentrating on medicine. It received a charter from the local lord in 1181, and statutes in 1210. About 150 medics have been identified in France in the period, including three women, though one of these was apparently bearded.[20] The Church to some extent was anxious about some of the newer studies at the emerging universities, including the growing interest in pagan Greek works. There was fear that this would lead to a questioning of orthodox belief, and hence the papal interest in stressing and guiding the theological studies at Paris. Nevertheless the Church was affected by such intellectual investigation, mostly undertaken by men of the Church, and itself underwent change through the influence of university masters and former university students; Church reform, Church reorganization, a doctrinal defence of orthodoxy against heresy, and perhaps even 'the regeneration of Christian society' resulted from the work of Parisian students and masters.[21] The university had become an entity in its own right, contributing to the cultural renaissance of the day.

. . .

HERESY

Philip's treatment of heresy is another example of action within France which also coincided with general Church policy, and therefore helped to keep Philip in the good books

19. Verger in Bautier, pp. 830, 839.
20. G. Beaujouan, 'Une leute préparation au "décollage" des sciences (quadrivium et médecine) dans la France de Philippe Auguste', pp. 847–61 in Bautier, p. 850.
21. J. Châtillon, 'Le mouvement théologique dans la France de Philippe Auguste', pp. 881–904 in Bautier, p. 890.

of the papacy. It was an age when religious ideas were bub-
bling and threw up unorthodox beliefs as well as new monastic orders. The papacy attempted to clarify definitions of
orthodoxy and did its best to suppress alternative views.

It is true there were times when Philip's response to
requests for aid against heretics was more dilatory than the
Church would have liked, but he consistently acted against
heresy and had no quarrel with the Church's view on it; he
was content that if a heresy was condemned by the Church
it should be suppressed with aid from the state. Philip was
not noticeably fanatical in his repression of heretics, but in
any case he could rightly claim that even in his harsher
efforts against heretics he was following the Church's wishes.
It was a decree of Innocent III in 1199 which brought heretics under the law for treason, and led to the more vicious
treatment of them by secular states.[22]

Philip was prepared to take punitive action against heresy
in his realm on behalf of the Church, for example against
heretics in northern France. A number of the *publicani*
heretics were burned at Arras in 1182. Again the king followed the Church ruling of 1184, which required secular
punishment for declared heretics; and did so once more in
1210, when the heretical followers of the Parisian master
Amaury de Bène were condemned by the councils of Sens
and Paris. Their enemies accused this group of debauchery
and making promises to women with whom they had sinned;
they were handed over for punishment and ten were burned.
The remains of their dead leader, Amaury, were dug up
from the grave and scattered to the winds.

Philip, in tackling the problem of the *cottereaux* in Berry,
was again following the Church's line in treating them as
heretics.[23] It was a common concept that these hired soldiers were outside the normal rules of society. To equate
them with heretics, as the Church did, may sometimes have
been correct, but probably more often was not. They were
nevertheless seen as a cause of disturbance, an obstacle to
peace, and were often the common enemies of both the
secular forces of law and order and the ecclesiastical forces

22. R.I. Moore, *The Origins of European Dissent* (London, 1977) p. 9.
23. See, for example, J.F. Verbruggen, *The Art of Warfare in Western Europe
during the Middle Ages*, trans. S. Willard and S.C.M. Southern (Oxford,
1977) pp. 120–4, where they are called *coterelli*.

for peace. In Berry they were accused of stamping on holy objects, vomiting, blaspheming and throwing stones at holy images – from one of which, in a miracle, blood was said to have run.[24]

Innocent III's initial handling of the Albigensian problem was cautious; he began with attempts at persuasion for a return to orthodox belief, using the Cistercians and the newly developing mendicant orders as his agents. Philip never went ahead of the Church in his actions against heresy and was similarly careful, declaring 'that the cart should not go before the oxen', meaning that it was up to the Church to act first and condemn the heretics before he could take action which would be properly legal.

When Philip was made an offer for his intervention against the Albigensians by the papacy in 1204, which included the right to confiscate Cathar lands, he was not tempted, declaring that the land was not the Church's to give. He refused to act against Raymond count of Toulouse, when first requested to do so, on the grounds that the Church had not yet condemned the count as a heretic: 'you have no right to take such measures, since you have not condemned the count as a heretic'. This is often seen as a purely evasive manoeuvre, but it reflects exactly the normal Church attitude, and as always Philip did not act until he could legally and morally justify his use of force: 'condemn him first as a heretic, then you can invite me to confiscate the demesne of my vassal, legally'. He was concerned, as at other times, to resist the papacy's involvement in a matter which he saw as being between king and vassal: the land 'is held from us alone'.[25]

During Philip's reign Catharism in southern France was the greatest problem of heresy facing the Church. It sprang partly from weak Church rule in the region and partly from the failings of the appointed clerics. Abuses recognized by the reforming Church were rife in the area.[26] Disrespect

24. William the Breton, 'Vie' in *Vie de Philippe Auguste*, ed. Guizot, p. 245; William the Breton, 'Vie', in *Oeuvres*, ed. Delaborde, I, pp. 230–2; Rigord, ed. Guizot, pp. 31–3; Rigord, ed. Delaborde, I, pp. 36–7.
25. Petit-Dutaillis, p. 278; R-H. Bautier, 'Philippe Auguste: la personnalité du roi', pp. 33–57, in Bautier, p. 47; Duby *France*, p. 241.
26. Luchaire, *Social France*, p. 51; R. Manselli, 'Spiritualité et hététerodoxie en France au temps de Philippe Auguste', pp. 905–26 in Bautier, pp. 919–22.

for the local Church was shared by the secular lords of the region, and a number of atrocities were committed against the Church by local magnates and their men, often with impunity. For example, the men of Raymond-Roger count of Foix killed a canon of the abbey of St-Antonin and blinded a monk. The complaisance of the local nobility was the biggest problem for the Church in dealing with the Cathars, and the reason why Philip's aid was so keenly sought.

Catharism is seen as a dualist heresy which had spread from Bulgaria and the Byzantine Empire to the West. Its chief figures were called bishops, and there was a priesthood of *perfecti*, the perfect or pure ones, who dressed in black. The 1163 council of Tours referred to 'a new heresy which has recently appeared in the region of Toulouse, spreading like a cancer'. Raymond V count of Toulouse had earlier written to the abbot of Cîteaux concerning the heresy: 'it has penetrated everywhere ... The most important people in the land are corrupted. The crowd has followed their example and abandoned the faith, so that I neither dare nor can halt this evil.'[27] The contrast was stark between the lax and wealthy orthodox clergy and the Cathar leaders, who lived in poverty and travelled about barefoot, preaching and ministering. Such a simple and godly life attracted people to the heresy, and may be compared in this respect with hermit movements and some of the new monastic groups. But Catharism also possessed its own beliefs and questioned those of the Church. William the Breton said the heretics seduced simple folk with their false dogma, denied marriage and thought eating meat was a crime.[28] They rejected most of the sacraments of the Church: they denied the real presence and the power of priests, opposed child baptism, scorned the use of the cross as a symbol, and had their own rituals.

In January 1208 the papal legate, Peter de Castelnau, was killed at St-Gilles near Arles, and Count Raymond, who was seen as sympathetic to the heretics if not himself one of their number, was suspected of ordering the murder. The count's

27. Moore, p. 198; J. Dunbabin, *France in the Making, 843–1180* (Oxford, 1985) p. 303; J. Sumption, *The Albigensian Crusade* (London, 1978) pp. 23–4.
28. Philip Mouskes, *Chronique rimée*, ed. Baron de Reiffenberg, 2 vols (Brussels, 1836–38) II, p. 382; William the Breton, *Philippide*, ed. Guizot, p. 21; 'Philippide', ed. Delaborde, II, pp. 23–4, ll. 407–13.

lands were placed under interdict and he was excommunicated again. The papacy sought Philip's aid. But although he was prepared to let those who wished undertake the crusade, he was as yet unwilling to take any active role. Nevertheless, under the Church's proclamation to destroy the heretics, the crusade assembled in 1209, with Simon de Montfort as one of its leaders.

Raymond VI did submit to the papacy and humbled himself in public. He took an oath to expel heretics from his lands, and on 18 June 1209 acted out his penitence in public, naked to the waist, pulled along by the neck, and flogged with a birch. He was given absolution, and even joined the crusade, but he could not halt it. The Albigensian Crusade became an invasion of southern France by the Capetian north, though the king was not initially involved in person. It was a half-hearted invasion, since most of those who engaged to participate did so only for a limited period and soon returned to the north. But among the few who went were some fanatical individuals, not least Simon de Montfort, and they achieved more than might have been expected.

It was Simon de Montfort's military ability and persistence which brought about the crusade's successes, often with very small armies, which could be maintained in any strength only during the campaigning season. The great military triumph of the crusade was the battle of Muret in 1213. The southern aristocracy had been propped up by the support of Pedro II king of Aragon. The intervention of the king of Aragon aroused Capetian interest, since he was a rival for overlordship of the southern magnates; this was a challenge which could not be ignored. Philip was an orthodox Christian ruler, prepared in general to fall in with the will of the Church against heretics; but in this case he seems to have been moved to action more by fears of the increasing Aragonese interest in southern France than by hostility to the heretics or even by the promise of lands.

At Muret, against the odds, Simon de Montfort won a great victory, and the king of Aragon was killed. In the aftermath of the battle, the papacy became lukewarm in support of the crusade, beginning to siphon off troops for efforts elsewhere. The pope had been eager for northern French assistance, but was not eager for Capetian domination in the south. Rome sought to hold up the rights of the comital house of Toulouse in the person of Raymond's son, who became Raymond VII. But the crusade had slipped out of papal control. The Capetian monarchy had become more directly involved once Prince Louis took the cross in 1213; homage was accepted by Philip from Simon de Montfort, now count of Toulouse, at Melun in 1216.

The death of Simon de Montfort in 1218 offered the opportunity of direct royal action. Philip allowed his son Louis to go south in 1219 with a battery of bishops, though seemingly the king himself still had no great enthusiasm for the venture. Even in 1221, when Pope Honorius III (1216–27) offered a Church tax for the purpose and indulgences, as well as the lands of Amaury de Montfort, Philip was not keen to participate, though he allowed his son to go. Probably, as before, he was concerned that Capetian power in the south should be seen to depend on rights of overlordship and not on grants from the papacy. His ambitions had apparently been satisfied with the defeat of Aragon, and did not stretch to making energetic efforts for territorial expansion on his own behalf. As always he was concerned not to overstretch his resources and risk losing the gains already made in north and central France.

Amaury de Montfort, unable to maintain the support his father had won, finally resigned his position in favour of the Capetians. Some southern nobles had been replaced, but there was no widespread settlement by northerners. Royal power in the south stood higher than it had ever been, and would never be relinquished. It was an important moment in the political unification of France. But it was a development which seems on the whole to have been against Philip's personal inclinations. Such Capetian enthusiasm as we find came rather from his son Louis. Nevertheless Philip's role in combating heresy, in an age when it posed a considerable threat to the Church, had been valuable. At this time heresy was never allowed by the monarchy to flourish in the north, and was significantly attacked in the south. During the reign there had been no great gap between the ambitions of the king and the Church over how to deal with heresy, and Philip had probably given more aid to the Church against heresy than the other monarchs of his day. Again co-operation was the keynote of Philip's policy, always with the major proviso that there was no clash with royal interests.

There were major gains for the monarchy from the clash with the Albigensian heretics, but they appear to have come almost by accident rather than by Philip's design. As with the Plantagenets, so in the far south, Philip seems to have feared employing his resources too far and threatening his real achievements in the north. His very restraint probably did as much as anything to ensure the eventual victory of the monarchy in the southern region.

Chapter 8

THE TRANSFORMATION OF FRENCH KINGSHIP

Professor John W. Baldwin, whose work on Philip Augustus is the most important by any modern historian, has called the reign 'a quantum leap in the development of the Capetian monarchy'.[1] This chapter and the following one are dependent on the work of Baldwin whose chief study of the reign, *The Government of Philip Augustus,* is a more massive work than this present volume, and based on much original research. Even so, we need not agree with all of Baldwin's conclusions. We do not intend to make a detailed examination of the workings of Philip's government, though we shall survey what is known. This chapter attempts to focus primarily on Philip's personal part in government, on the changes introduced during his rule, and the effects which these changes had on the French monarchy.

As with Philip and the Church, this is an area of the reign which merits its own study, though for different reasons. In this case, modern historians have given the weight of their attention to the subject. The authors of the major studies of the reign, Alexander Cartellieri and Achille Luchaire, paid much attention to chronicle accounts, the former producing an enormously detailed narrative account of the reign. Because of its depth, Luchaire shied away from another history of the reign, though he wrote several works on Philip, which also had a chronicle rather than documentary basis. It is true that Léopold Delisle based his work on charters and administrative records, but he never completed his promised history of the reign.

1. J.W. Baldwin, *The Government of Philip Augustus* (Berkeley, CA, 1986) p. xvii.

The modern trend to concentrate on government records has inevitably led to more emphasis on those aspects which they illuminate more fully. But equally, the recent work, with its focus on governmental institutions, can unbalance our view of the reign as a whole, in its twelfth- and thirteenth-century context. Baldwin expressed himself content to rely on Cartellieri's use of chronicles for his own narrative passages.[2] It seems important to marry the two approaches, and even in our study of government to take note of what contemporaries thought about it, and how it slotted into the context of the period.

Our main difference with Professor Baldwin is over the pace of change. Baldwin argues for a first decade that was mainly reliant upon tradition and an almost revolutionary change after the crusade.[3] This has been a common view of Philip's reign, and is one reason we have given weight to the period before the crusade and to the crusade itself. It has become clear that many significant changes had already been introduced by 1190, and many were incorporated into the Testament, which arranged for the government of the realm during the Third Crusade. The winning of additional areas for the demesne, and the development of greater royal authority throughout the realm, may be seen not as the main cause of novelty in government, but as provoking a need for pragmatic solutions, based on a methodology already largely worked out during the earlier years. It meant an expansion of the system, rather than a radical change to it.

2. Baldwin, *Government*, p. xix, explains that each narrative section 'unabashedly relies on Cartellieri's work'. See A. Cartellieri, *Phillip II. August, König von Frankreich*, 4 vols (Leipzig, 1899–1922); A. Luchaire in E. Lavisse, ed., *Histoire de France depuis les Origines jusqu'à la Révolution* (Paris, 1911) III, Pt I; and A. Luchaire, *Social History at the time of Philip Augustus*, trans. E.B. Krehbiel (New York, 1912); L. Delisle, ed., *Catalogue des actes de Philippe Auguste* (Paris, 1856); D. Bates, 'Léopold Delisle, (1826–1910)', in H. Damico and B. Zavadil, eds, *Medieval Scholarship: Biographical Studies on the Formation of a Discipline*, I: History (New York and London, 1995) pp. 101–13.

3. Baldwin, *Government*, calls 1190–1203 'The Decisive Decade', seeing the period to 1190 as one dominated by 'The Capetian Legacy'; and p. 101: 'the third crusade ... constituted a great divide between the government bequeathed by the early Capetians and that crafted for the future by Philip Augustus'.

Thus, for example, the most significant officials of Philip's later government, the baillis and prévôts, had been used before the crusade; indeed prévôts were of eleventh-century origin. Nor was there great change in the method of central decision-making; Philip was already employing a small circle of central advisers, and was turning away from the great officers as ever-present counsellors. The Testament makes clear that the royal treasury was already based in the Temple in Paris before the crusade, and shows the new importance given to leading citizens in Paris in government by that time.

In the areas newly won by Philip, the king generally allowed existing procedure to continue, and only slowly introduced his more advanced demesne methods, often not overthrowing what was there. Of course the newly acquired areas brought added wealth and power, and required reaction by central government, but this was not the main spur to innovation. Philip's government saw many gradual and important changes, but they were not for the most part either sudden or revolutionary.

We can give a reasonable outline of the structure of Philip's government, of the role of his entourage, and the operations of such departments as the chancery. It is obvious that Philip's personality was stamped upon this stucture, for example in his running down of the great magnate offices, and in the employment of lesser men who were more personally tied to him. The tenor of his government owed much to his own attitude, for instance his carefulness with finance, his restrained generosity, and the objects of his gifts and privileges. Joinville tells a story of Philip advising the young St Louis, his grandson, that: 'one should reward the household, to one more to the other less, according to how they served you', and that no man could become a good ruler who was incapable of being as firm in refusing as he was generous in giving. This reported attitude certainly fits with what we know of Philip's mode of rule.[4]

4. R. Fawtier, *The Capetian Kings of France*, trans. L. Butler and R.J. Adam (London, 1964) p. 25; Joinville, *Histoire de Saint Louis*, ed. N. de Wailly (Paris, 1868) pp. 237–8: 'Car li roys Phelippes mes aious me dist que l'on devait guerredonner à so mesnie, à l'un plus, à l'autre moins, selonc ce que il servent'.

. . .

THE POWER OF THE MONARCHY

The Capetian monarchy was an institution, with traditions and restrictions. But the personal element in the medieval period always remained a significant factor. To what extent the government of any individual king was personal is not easy to determine. In general it is true that counsellors could advise, but could not normally decide policy. Others were there to obey the will of the monarch, perhaps to help form it, but not to take over from it. Philip's views were shaped by many influences: by observing his father's work, by his father's advice, by his own education, by the advice he received from counsellors, by the experience of governing, by the views of churchmen, theologians, popes and fellow rulers, but in the end they were *his* views and could be imposed to the extent of the power of the monarchy at the time. Philip's court and government reflected his own personality. Gerald of Wales pointed out its contrasts with the Plantagenet court, the French king's being more sober as we have seen, more quiet in tone, more proper, with swearing forbidden. Philip brought about significant changes: less reliance on the magnates, a lesser role for his family; a greater place for the selected close counsellors and for relatively humble knights.[5]

It has been suggested that Philip's intellectual gifts were 'modest', which, although direct evidence is not easily available, seems to conflict with what we know about the king's abilities.[6] He was able to deal with the bright men around him, such as Peter the Chanter. He was able to supervise governmental development and the administration, which needed a considerable grasp of accounting as well as a degree of literacy. His ability to deal with the papacy reveals a clear understanding of legal argument and his rights, and a firm determination to protect them. He was rarely outmanoeuvred by even the cleverest of his opponents.

Philip went to war as any leader of his period would, but he was more prepared than most to seek and make peace.

5. J.W. Baldwin, 'L'entourage de Philippe Auguste et la famille royale', pp. 59–75 in R-H. Bautier, ed., *La France de Philippe Auguste, le Temps des Mutations* (Paris, 1982) pp. 59–60.
6. Fawtier, p. 25.

Rigord said that Philip's aim was 'to deliver the weak from the tyranny of the strong', and that 'his first triumph is to see peace re-established'. His tolerance and mild temper puzzled the aggressive Bertran de Born, who thought the French needed a leader and had not found one in Philip, who did not become angry. Bertran preferred the attitude of Richard the Lionheart, for whom 'peace and truce have never been noble'. For Bertran it was a sneer to suggest that Philip liked peace even more than the noted diplomat Archbishop Peter of Tarentais. Bertran had cause to regret his underestimation of Philip, when the king later used his authority to replace Bertran as lord of Hautefort. No doubt that act was executed on the advice of counsellors, and Bertran could further nurse his belief that Philip was 'badly advised and worse guided'.[7]

Philip did in fact at times lose his temper, but usually with some point, as when he chopped down the elm on the Norman border, declaring by actions rather than words that he no longer accepted the Plantagenet stance on their rights to bring the king to the edge of their territories before they would hold discussions. Nor were his diplomatic activities always appreciated by his enemies. He could manoeuvre and manipulate with the best of them; he was the 'sower of discord' according to one English chronicler. To take just one example of his methods: in the conquest of Normandy he knew that Rouen was the key, which afterwards he would need to govern. Therefore he did not simply crush Rouen, and chose to discuss with the leading citizens what they would gain from surrender. If allowed in, he promised: 'I will prove a kind and just master to you.' In modern times he has been called 'a statesman of the first water', 'the first royal statesman in French history'; it is a reputation which in this country we have somehow failed to recognize.[8]

7. Rigord, *Vie de Philippe Auguste*, ed. and trans. M. Guizot (Paris, 1825) pp. 42, 81; Bertran de Born, *The Poems of Bertran de Born*, ed. W.D. Paden Jr, T. Sankovitch and P.H. Stäblein (Berkeley, CA, 1986) p. 361, l. 46: 'c'anc patz ni fis no.il fon genta'; and ll. 50–1: 'Lo reis Felips ama la pais/plus que.l bons om de Tarantais'.

8. Roger of Wendover, *Flowers of History*, ed. J.A. Giles, 2 vols (London, 1899) II, p. 142; Roger of Wendover, *Chronica*, ed. H.O. Coxe, EHS, 5 vols (London, 1841–44); Roger of Howden, *The Annals of Roger de Hoveden*, ed. and trans. H.T. Riley, 2 vols (London, 1853) pp. 451, 289;

With taxation Philip was moderate, with justice he showed mercy, he was 'the clement king'.[9] He was careful in taking hostages and imposing fines and sureties, rarely demanding more than was just. Sureties or cautions were used to help keep the peace; those who think the Tudors innovated in using bonds and recognizances to keep the peace ought to look at the way Philip used sureties. Thus after Bouvines many large sureties were placed on individuals on pain of their keeping the peace; for example, it would have cost Eustace de Ren £3,000 if 'the said Eustace went against the king, or the Lord Louis, or against the land of the king'. Similarly Robert de Courtenay must 'serve the lord king faithfully or risk all his worldly goods'.[10]

The new edition of the registers contains a long list of 'securities' or 'cautions', which underlines the significance of this method of keeping tabs on various of his subjects. Jews on the demesne had to swear under penalty not to leave the demesne. The constable of Normandy furnished various guarantees for fidelity to the king, with pledges from such as the bishop of Lisieux. The count of Eu and his brothers gave guarantees that they would faithfully serve the king. The viscount of Brosse himself, and five others on his behalf, pledged their lands to guarantee his fidelity to the king. What all these cautions demonstrate is how the king imposed promises backed by threats on all manner of subjects whose fidelity was in doubt in any way.[11]

Roger of Howden, *Chronica*, ed. W. Stubbs, 4 vols, RS no. 51 (London, 1868–71) IV, p. 81: 'seminator discordiae', III, p. 207: 'ero vobis dominus mansuetus et justus'. C. Petit-Dutaillis, *The Feudal Monarchy in France and England*, trans. E.D. Hunt (London, 1936) p. 179; R-H. Bautier, 'Philippe Auguste: la personnalité du roi', pp. 33–57 in Bautier, p. 36.

9. William the Breton, 'Philippide', in *Oeuvres de Rigord et de Guillaume le Breton*, ed. H-F. Delaborde, SHF, vols 210, 224 (Paris, 1882–85), II, p. 35, l. 711; William the Breton, *La Philippide, Poème*, ed. and trans. M. Guizot (Paris, 1825) p. 33.

10. *Registres de Philippe Auguste, Les*, ed. J.W. Baldwin, with F. Gasparri, M. Nortier and E. Lalou, *RHF*, Documents financiers et administratifs, VII, Texte (Paris, 1992), no. 54, pp. 415–16; nos 59, 66, 74, 80, pp. 418, 423–4, 429–30, 435.

11. *Recueil des Actes de Philippe Auguste*, ed. H-F. Delaborde, 4 vols (Paris, 1916–79) I, pp. 385, 386, 387, 389.

Philip was generally modest and unassuming, as we have seen in contrast to Richard the Lionheart both in Sicily and in the Holy Land. Bertran de Born thought the French king presented his deeds in tin-plate rather than in gilt. But Philip was aware of the need to present a regal figure, dignified if not flamboyant: a public face of modesty but a recognition of his own powers. The scene painted by Mouskes of Philip entering a church and praying: 'I am but a man, as you are, but I am king of France', has a deep truth to it. There is also a story of Peter the Chanter telling Philip what were the attributes of an ideal sovereign; Philip replied that he should be contented with the king that he had.[12]

The efforts to show his connection back to Charlemagne demonstrate Philip's effort to bolster the Capetian position. His mother, Adela, and his first wife, Isabella of Hainault, both claimed descent from Charlemagne. His natural son was named Peter Charlot, after the great emperor. And the Carolingian claim seems to have become generally accepted. Innocent III declared: 'it is common knowledge that the king of France is descended from the lineage of Charlemagne'.[13] No doubt there was some weakness in the argument, but William the Breton refers to him as 'the descendant of Charlemagne', and the Welshman Gerald believed that Philip aimed to restore the monarchy to 'the greatness which it had in the time of Charlemagne'.[14]

Philip wished to present an imperial image of French monarchy, hence the use of an eagle on his seal, the label 'Augustus' applied by Rigord, his sister's marriage to two Byzantine emperors, and the raising to the Latin imperial throne of two of his brothers-in-law. The same point was being emphasized when the sword of Charlemagne had been brandished at Philip's coronation ceremony.[15] As one of the

12. Bertran de Born, p. 211, ll. 51–2: 'quar vey que sos fagz estanha/que li valrion mais daurat'; W.H. Hutton, *Philip Augustus* (London, 1896) p. 101; Philip Mouskes, *Chronique Rimée*, ed. Baron de Reiffenberg, 2 vols (Brussels, 1836–38) II, p. 359; A. Vernet, 'La litterature latine au temps de Philippe Auguste', pp. 793–813 in Bautier, p. 795.
13. G. Duby, *France in the Middle Ages*, trans. J. Vale (Oxford, 1991) p. 226.
14. Gerald of Wales, *Opera*, ed. J.S. Brewer, J.F. Dimock and G.F. Warner, RS no. 26 (London, 1861–91) VIII, p. 294: 'celsitudinem et amplitudinem quam tempore Karoli quondam habuerat reformare queat'.
15. Giselbert of Mons, *La Chronique de Gislebert de Mons*, ed. L. Vanderkindere (Brussels, 1904) pp. 127, 130.

Parisian masters wrote in 1210: 'the king is emperor in his realm'.[16] The royal family was being distanced from other families, however noble; royal power was being set above noble power. It was not just a question of wealth and lands, but of the nature of monarchy, its prestige, its religious and mystical significance. The claimed association with Charlemagne, by the twelfth century a powerful figure in legend as well as a great historical emperor, was an important part of this process.

Philip was a tough-minded individual, he would not otherwise have been such a great king. Those who had experience of dealings with Louis VII found Philip a much harder opponent with more steel in his character. He had tremendous determination, and strong views on basic policies. Before his father's death, while still a teenager, Philip was prepared to rule, issuing charters without his father's consent, reacting against some of his father's policies. Before long he threw off the shackles of his mother and her powerful family, and soon afterwards of the count of Flanders. The English chronicler Howden thought he did it because he 'despised and hated all whom he knew to be familiar friends of his father', which seems a distortion, but at least underlines the point that Philip was of independent mind from the first.[17]

Philip preferred his close counsellors to be lesser men who accepted their subordinate role without question. We may be clear that his policy expressed his own views. There was an encounter at one of the conferences between Philip and King John which occurred between Boutavent and Gaillon, when the two kings were 'face to face for an hour, no one except themselves being within hearing', a brief comment but one which allows a sudden and vivid insight into the personal nature of thirteenth-century diplomacy.[18]

16. P. Ourliac, 'Législation, coutumes et coutumiers au temps de Philippe Auguste', pp. 471–88 in Bautier, p. 476.
17. Roger of Howden, ed. Riley, p. 519; Roger of Howden, ed. Stubbs, II, p. 196: 'et omnes quos noverat patri suo fuisse familiares, sprevit et odio habuit'.
18. Roger of Wendover, ed. Giles, II, p. 182; Roger of Wendover, ed. Coxe, III, p. 141: 'segregatis omnibus utriusque regni magnatibus, collocuti sunt ore ad os quasi unius horae spatio, nemine praeter ipsos duos eorum colloquium audiente'; cf. Roger of Howden, ed. Stubbs, IV, p. 94: 'ore ad os'.

Of course Philip took counsel, and made a point of doing so, but he was too independent a man to be dominated by another. And though inclined to prefer diplomatic solutions, he was a good enough warrior to win respect; as William the Breton said 'his arm was powerful in the use of weapons'.[19] Bouvines was the most important battle of the age, and Philip was the victor. Where the loss of documentary evidence from the earlier period often makes it impossible to be certain that Philip was the innovator or the initiator, a knowledge of his character, his able leadership and his drive, make him far and away the likeliest candidate. One of Philip's major achievements was to shift the balances of an intricate system of government in France in favour of the Capetian monarchy, so that its views were more often heeded, and came to be heeded in areas where that had not previously been the case.

In the demesne, Philip's predecessors had won the battle for control, but Philip improved the royal position, especially through the use of baillis. These had been introduced in the first decade of the reign, before the Third Crusade. The Testament, which arranged for government during his absence on the crusade, allowed for the baillis to report to the regents on the prévôts, officials with a long history. Baillis were less tied to particular territories than prévôts, at least in their early days. By 1203 there were twelve baillis, who worked from established centres rather than within defined districts. They often operated in pairs, for example in Paris, and may have owed something in origin to the itinerant justices of the Plantagenets. Like the latter, they possessed judicial functions, but only as a part of their work. Another suggestion is that they derived from the ancient Carolingian *missi dominici*. Probably they were introduced to fulfil a need, in order to place a check upon the prévôts, without regard to either Carolingian or Plantagenet methods.

Most baillis held their positions for long periods, William Menin for thirty-two years. The prévôts dealt with regular and fixed incomes, while baillis' commissions were more flexible and less tied, dealing with a 'pot pourris of many accounts', including occasional and irregular income. Part

19. William the Breton, 'Philippide', ed. Delaborde, I, p. 6, l. 2; *Philippide*, ed. Guizot, p. 5.

of their task was to hold monthly assizes and deal with complaints.[20] Three times a year they made reports to central government in Paris. An unexpected appointment as bailli in Normandy was the mercenary captain, Cadoc, though he was later imprisoned for profiteering. It suggests that Philip realized that the task of the bailli in newly won Normandy was not going to be easy and required a man with military capacities. It also reminds us of the non-specialist nature of these officials in their early days.

The geographical extension of monarchical influence went hand in hand with an increase in royal power. The territorial acquisition was considerable under Philip: including Artois, Vermandois, Normandy and much of the Loire Valley. One result was an increase in royal bureaucratic activity, and in the number of royal agents to cope with this. In 1190 there were fifty-two prévôtés; by 1203 there were sixty-two. The wider area brought in larger taxes, and hence added strength to the monarchy. It has been said that Philip 'dismantled the political structure of France', but if that is so, and it sounds more extreme than was really the case, it was in order to reassemble it in a more coherent fashion through his administration.[21]

Closer supervision by Philip of his local government had beneficial results for the monarchy, not least an increase in revenue. From the ancient demesne, and from ancient rights, Philip brought in more money than his predecessors. The additional territory, which at least doubled, and by some calculations quadrupled the demesne, together with increased efficiency in its running, saw an almost revolutionary increment in royal power. Wrote one chronicler: 'he increased and wondrously multiplied the kingdom of France'.

The levying of taxes in the new areas was achieved without arousing great resentment. Philip's caution in not making excessive demands was a significant part of his success. In areas which had not been governed directly, he often demanded less not more than his predecessors, as for example

20. R-H. Bautier, 'La place du règne de Philippe Auguste dans l'histoire de la France médiévale', pp. 11–27 in Bautier, p. 19; Baldwin, *Government*, pp. 134, 146.
21. Baldwin, *Government*, p. 196.

in Hesdin and Auchy, where he reduced rents 'for the good will of his new subjects'.[22]

At the monarch's personal discretion was the disposal of his family in marriage. This remained an important means of both making and cementing alliances. The marriages arranged by Philip therefore provide information on his policies. His major enemy was clearly the Plantagenet dynasty, but marriage-making between the rivals formed a major part in peace efforts. Thus Philip's sister Margaret married Young Henry; his sister Alice was betrothed to Richard and, when that failed, was offered to John. In the end these sisters were passed to other husbands: Margaret to King Bela of Hungary, and Alice to the count of Ponthieu. The former showed Philip's eastward-moving interests, the latter created another counter to the Plantagenets. Attempts at the use of marriage to make peace with the Plantagenets did not end there; Philip's own son, Louis, was married to Blanche of Castile, a niece of King John, and Philip's children by Agnes de Méran were also used: Philip Hurepel married the heiress of the county of Boulogne; Marie was betrothed to Arthur of Brittany, and then married in turn to Philip of Namur and Henry of Brabant, significant figures in the Flemish political arena. Philip's third sister, Marie, was married to the count of Champagne, helping to remake an old alliance within the realm.

The weight of the monarchy's power did not press evenly throughout the realm. Within the demesne, there was direct rule, which had been fought for by the Capetians over generations. Here the monarchy's power was experienced at its fullest extent. Indeed monarchical power elsewhere rested upon royal security within the demesne. This central significance was recognized for instance in the structuring of the registers. Philip improved the monarchy's position in the demesne from a good starting point. He also extended the area of the demesne, and the ability to enforce royal rights throughout France, for example with regard to the Church. The very word 'France' was coming to mean the whole realm as well as the lands directly ruled by the king.[23]

22. Duby, *France*, p. 227, from the *Grandes Chroniques de France*; Baldwin, *Government*, p. 157.
23. J.W. Baldwin, *Masters, Princes and Merchants: The Social Views of Peter the Chanter and his Circle*, 2 vols (Princeton, 1970) I, p. 161.

The increase in Capetian royal power had much to do with the definition, enforcement and enlargement of amorphous rights, both religious and legal, throughout the realm. Hence the significance of emphasizing the mythical background of the dynasty: the co-operation with the abbey of St-Denis and its dynastic saint, the stress upon Charlemagne as an ancestor, and the encouragement of belief in the power of the royal touch. This theorizing presented the image of an ideal monarchy, with much emphasis on the defence of Christianity. In contemporary terms: 'to serve God is to reign'.[24]

Rights over all subjects were stressed, allowing interference with noble successions and marriages, and participation in urban government, giving a reason to transfer judicial process from other authority and placing it under royal supervision, and claiming the right to enforce taxation where it had not existed in practice before. Philip has with some justification been called 'a king of the people'.[25] Towns and merchants benefited from his grants of privileges.

Stress upon the supremacy of the royal court allowed Philip to justify attacks upon magnates who failed to accept royal superiority, and especially on King John who was also duke of Normandy and count of Anjou. The vital judgement on John in 1202 was given against him as the recalcitrant duke of Aquitaine, thus overcoming any claim John made about the rights of the duke of Normandy to meet the king only on the border between their lands.

One of the tasks of monarchy was to keep the peace, both in terms of law and order within France, and in the responsibility for defence of the realm. Keeping law and order was no easy matter in the land of Bertran de Born and his like, who could claim: 'to war I am attuned, for I do not keep or hold any other law'. Bertran opposed the truce of God, which Philip supported.

Royal responsibilities gave the king the right to call on military service, to hold courts of justice and to enforce their decisions. Philip proved to be not only an excellent diplomatic peace-maker, but also a very successful peace-keeper.

24. J-P. Poly and E. Bournazel, *The Feudal Transformation, 900–1200*, trans. C. Higgitt (New York, 1991) pp. 186, 195, 332, 338.
25. Hutton, p. 152.

He made efforts to restrict private war. With his victory at Bouvines, Philip brought a more secure peace to the realm than had been known in living memory: 'the whole land was at peace for a long while', wrote one grateful subject.[26]

. . .

PHILIP AND THE NOBILITY

The monarchy had some controls over the nobility. Philip sought to use such rights as he had with regard, for example, to wardship or widows, and was always careful to extract what he could by agreement with any magnate family which needed his help, as when a minor succeeded as head of the family. At times Philip influenced the succession of the nobility, notably of Ferrand of Portugal to the county of Flanders. One of the shifts in the balance of power in the period was between the monarchy and the rulers of the great principalities of France. Most of the greater duchies and counties came under closer royal supervision with Philip Augustus, including Flanders, Champagne and Burgundy, as well as Normandy and the other Angevin lands in which he recovered authority.

Philip, often acting as protector of the Church, became the enforcer of peace in areas well outside the old demesne, and he maintained peace by seeking the personal submission to himself of recalcitrant nobles. Thus the lord of Rozoy, brought to heel by Philip in 1201, was forced to swear: 'I put myself at the disposition of my lord Philip', as well as having to make reparations for the damage he had done to the Church. The promise to render castles on demand was part of this process, as imposed on the count of Perche in 1211 or the lord of Montmorency in 1218. Robert of Dreux admitted: 'I do not have the right to install a castellan in my castle unless he has taken an oath to the king. The men of my county of Dreux will swear never to betray the king, and to serve him as necessary.'[27]

As in the principalities, so in central government, the power of the magnates was diminished at this time. The great

---

26. Bertran de Born, p. 250, ll. 22–4: 'Ab gerra m'acort,/q'ieu non teing ni crei/negun'autra lei'; Duby, *France*, p. 226, from the Béthune Chronicle.
27. Luchaire in Lavisse, pp. 206–7.

offices of state held by magnates were reduced in significance, and sometimes not filled at all. In the principalities socially humbler agents of the king increasingly became governors. The independent seneschal virtually vanished, except in newly acquired territories, where the older system was allowed to survive, and where a magnate might be encouraged to transfer his allegiance to Philip, as did Aimery de Thouars or William des Roches. Such acquired servants aided Philip in the process of conquest. But in Normandy, which came under direct royal rule, no seneschal was appointed; here Philip brought in his baillis. The comparison with his own lands is significant: one of the tasks of the seneschal was to oversee local government. When the use of seneschals was dropped in France in 1191, baillis were needed to take over that role; and when the seneschal was removed in Normandy, baillis were again introduced.

Feudalism has for long seemed to be a construct of modern historians, placed rather uneasily over an actual medieval society which it did not quite fit. There was an actuality of relationships between lords and lesser men, and between kings and their magnates; there were understandings over conditions on which lands were granted by greater men to lesser; there were obligations to overlords, especially to the king, in respect of several matters, not least over a debt of military service. But there was no neat pyramid of relationships, and no 'system' with set rules for all.

Susan Reynolds has demonstrated how the term 'feudalism' has become a construct, throwing into question much of what had previously come to be accepted, not least over what we mean by 'fief' and 'vassal'. Of particular importance to us, she has opened a new debate on just when 'classical feudalism' came into anything like actual being. She brings together some of the previously expressed doubts over this: as Elizabeth Brown's question of whether feudalism existed at all; or Poly and Bournazel's conclusion that the fief was 'a political and legal idea', modelled on the ideas of the royal entourage of Philip. But Reynolds accepts that after 1300 the definitions made in the previous century *had* brought about a recognition of the fief in a feudal sense.[28]

28. S. Reynolds, *Fiefs and Vassals* (Oxford, 1994) especially ch. 7, pp. 258–322.

The most common meaning of the term fief in our period seems to be not so much a unit which owed obligations, but rather a conglomeration of lands belonging to the superior lord, as in the king's fief. When the word fief was used to denote a territory owing obligations, it therefore proved an acceptable term in that it did not offend the subordinate by emphasizing his submission, but rather flattered his pretensions by making comparison of his holding with those of his social betters.

The king declared he could owe homage to no one. An abbey might like to claim that lords who held lands from it should do homage *si rex non esset*, but when it was the king he did no homage. This point was repeated to the Church at Amiens, where the ecclesiastics had to agree that the king 'cannot and ought not to do homage to anyone'.[29] An example which demonstrates the point occurred in 1192 when Philip took over part of the demesne of the count of Clermont, who had previously done homage to the bishop of Paris for it; Philip refused to do so. The king was emphasizing the monarchy's place outside the rules that applied to the nobility.

One of Susan Reynolds's most interesting arguments is that feudalism was essentially a legal definition of what already existed, fitting it into patterns convenient to lords and lawyers. She clearly shows that land in the period was held much more firmly than we have been inclined to think; and that what we see as 'freehold' is not so very different from how most medieval landholders viewed their own rights. She is surely right that what often mattered most was not some legal nicety, but an acknowledgement by a lesser man of the power and authority over him of a greater; the obligations were only a sign of what mattered most, recognition of the power of the lord, and not the be-all and end-all of the arrangements.

Somewhere around the fringes of her argument is the feeling that at about the time of Philip Augustus something akin to feudalism was becoming visible. What is probably the case is that Philip and his government contributed significantly to this development. The legal training behind the

29. J-P. Poly and E. Bournazel, 'Couronne et mouvance: institutions et représentations mentales', pp. 217–36 in Bautier, pp. 221–2.

development may have been more Italian than French, but it was in France that it was most clearly applied. The composition of Philip's entourage, particularly his employment of lawyers, together with his encouragement of learning at Paris, his extension of power within the existing demesne and in a wider territory, and especially his desire for a legal justification and framework for this extension, aided enormously in the making of agreements which we might properly call feudal. It was Philip who probably set in motion the methods whereby homage and fief came to be associated with 'political subjection'.[30]

On one level this relates to Philip's relationship with the greatest princes and lords in his realm: the dukes and counts, the great lords. Philip was intent on showing his superiority over all lay lords in his kingdom: enforcing his claims upon them, insisting on attendance at his courts, arbitrating between them, above all making himself militarily superior. In the end his control rested primarily on his military power and on his royal agents rather than on any obligations and duties owed to him. The much vaunted claim that 'the king cannot and ought not to do homage to anyone' was little more than a statement of the king's special position. It was presented as the statement of a traditional right not a new demand. In 1203 with regard to Vermandois Philip insisted: 'our predecessors the kings of France were not wont to do homage to anyone'.[31] In other words, although the king could receive lands which had once belonged to another, his power would always be greater than theirs, and no permanent obligation to that person or institution could be entered into.

One cannot call the 'feudalism' of Philip's time classic; there is probably no period when it was. There were always practices which seem at best 'semi-feudal'. One of the most interesting examples of the age is the *fief-rente*, the payment of money rather than the granting of land in return for a regular obligation, usually military. The Capetians had employed this method of obtaining military service since at least 1155, and regularly under Philip. Register A records ninety-three such arrangements, and there were more later.

30. Reynolds, pp. 272, 277, 321.
31. Baldwin, *Government*, p. 261.

But our very description of the agreement seems an attempt to fit what was essentially a money payment into what some would prefer it to be, a feudal one.[32]

Arrangements whereby land was given, and in return military service was promised, were more a sign of the times than of what had been normal in the past. Lords would always get what they could out of any settlement. There need not be a 'feudal' agreement for the king to obtain troops. Thus when Philip, after his marriage to Isabella of Hainault, asked for armed men from the count, the latter's chronicler Giselbert points out that the count owed nothing to the king, but he sent 3,000 foot voluntarily out of goodwill.[33] Military aid was an act of loyalty and a recognition of lordship as much as an admission of legal or feudal debt.

Homage from the princes was the acknowledgement of Philip's power in their territory. Philip would naturally prefer to aid the prince who acknowledged him than one who did not. This sort of mutual gain is clear in the homage that Arthur of Brittany performed for what at the time were largely Angevin territories in Poitou, Anjou, Maine and Touraine as well as Brittany. The Plantagenet kings did homage to Philip for their continental lands: Henry II in 1183, Richard the Lionheart in 1188 and 1189, and John in 1200. Even Henry II in 1180, when not under pressure, had been prepared to call Philip 'my lord', and to have Philip treat him 'as my man and my *fidelis*'.[34]

In the same way Philip proclaimed the competence of his own court to deal with these greater lords. The conquest of Normandy was preceded by the summons of John to the king's court in Paris, and by the making of legal judgements against him when he failed to attend. Renaud de Dammartin was also brought to book through the king's court; Philip would only promise restoration if Renaud agreed to abide

32. *Recueil*, I, p. 169, no. 139, Compiègne 1185, about Amiens; p. 185, no. 155, Compiègne 1185–86; III, no. 1309; Baldwin, *Government*, p. 273. NB the Plantagenets had employed *fiefs-rentes* from a much earlier date.
33. Giselbert of Mons, p. 127: 'qui in nullo regi Francorum obligatus erat', he adds that the count neither did homage nor had any agreement with the king.
34. E.M. Hallam, *Capetian France, 987–1328* (Harlow, 1980) p. 172; *Recueil*, p. 9, no. 7, 1180: 'dominum meum', 'sicut hominem et fidelium meum'.

by 'the judgement of the royal court and the barons of the realm'.[35]

The recognition of the king's power was the point of many of Philip's charters. Authority over the princes was reinforced by the acknowledgement of royal dominance by men directly under the power of those princes: the power of the king to call directly upon them, the necessity for the king as well as their own lord to confirm their dealings. One notes, for example, how Philip accepted homage from William the Marshal after the conquest of Normandy, though William had clearly been the man of King John, and maintained that he still was.

In lands which had been beyond Capetian control, those in the north-east under imperial influence, those in the far south, Philip often took homages from the minor nobility, for example from Bertran de la Tour, Pons de Montlaur and Hélias de Périgord. Many lesser lords sought agreements with the king for their own protection. Hugh de Bergé placed his castle under the king's control and promised that it would never be detached from the crown of France. Other lesser nobles simply changed their allegiance to support the king; thus Gossuin de Warin abandoned Philip of Alsace count of Flanders for King Philip, having killed one of the count's sergeants. And such transfers could also form part of an imposed peace. When Philip of Flanders submitted to the king at Boves, his former man, Robert de Boves, became a king's man. Robert then addressed the count of Flanders: 'lord count, I was your man, but now, God willing, because of your deeds . . . I have to swear in the court of the lord king'.[36]

In effect treaties were agreed which acknowledged the king's power. Early in the reign, when Philip intervened on behalf of the Church, he was demonstrating a new direct authority of the crown in areas beyond the demesne; for example after his expedition to Burgundy in 1186, when that duchy was brought to heel. Again, in defeating Philip

35. William the Breton, 'Vie', in *Oeuvres*, ed. Delaborde, I, p. 245: 'si vellet stare judicio regalis aule et baronum regni'; 'Vie' in *Vie de Philippe Auguste*, ed. Guizot, p. 253; cf. 'Philippide', ed. Delaborde, II, pp. 252–3, ll. 118–19.
36. Luchaire in Lavisse, p. 210; *Recueil*, II, pp. 2–3, no. 479, 1194–95; Giselbert of Mons, p. 185.

count of Flanders, the king forced an agreement upon him, taking back lands once confirmed to the count by Louis VII and by Philip himself. The count complained about the reversal: 'it would not be good if the king's promise is worth nothing'. Philip ignored this and kept the lands; he claimed that his father's concession had been for a fixed period only, and that his own had been made as a child and was therefore without force: 'do you want one justice for others and another for yourself? No. You must keep the law. Force and right give supremacy to the lord who demands just things.'[37] The king, when it suited him, could ignore what later historians saw as feudal laws.

Although Philip was related to the comital house through his mother Adela, he still made efforts to increase royal authority in Champagne, and insisted on homage from Count Theobald III (1197–1201) in 1198. Whenever a principality was in a position of weakness, Philip intervened, demonstrated his right to regulate affairs, and made an agreement which recognized this. When Theobald III died in 1201, he left only a daughter and a pregnant widow, Blanche. Philip imposed a treaty on Blanche whereby she could not remarry without his consent, and her children would be brought up under royal supervision in royal castles. The second child proved to be a boy, and in time became Count Theobald IV (1201–53, king of Navarre from 1234), who in 1214 did homage to Philip. He did not reach his majority until 1222, by which time Philip had managed to tie Champagne more tightly into the realm.

Similarly, when Odo III duke of Burgundy had died in 1218, he left a widow, Alice, and a minor heir in Hugh IV. Alice promised not to remarry without royal consent. Or again, on the death of Geoffrey of Brittany in 1186, Philip had demanded wardship of his daughter, and then of his posthumous son Arthur. Philip guaranteed Brittany to Arthur so long as he remained loyal, but otherwise the fate of his lands would be 'upon the lawful judgement of his court'.[38] Thus, too, on the death of Philip of Alsace count of Flanders

37. William the Breton, 'Philippide', ed. Delaborde, II, p. 42, ll. 43–4; l. 43: 'Non decet ut tanti sit frivola pactio regis, /Non decet ut regis fiat revocabile verbum'; p. 43, l. 78: 'Vis aliis aliud, aliud tibi dicere juris?'; *Philippide*, ed. Guizot, p. 41.
38. Roger of Howden, ed. Riley, II, p. 511.

in 1191, Philip made an agreement with his widow, Elizabeth, whereby she renounced rights over certain lands, and agreed that other territories would go to Philip on her death.

And when King John was recognized by Philip at Le Goulet in 1200, having formerly looked very weak in trying to impose his claims on the Plantagenet lands, Philip extracted a large payment of 20,000 marks in relief, which amounted to an admission of the French king's rights over the territories concerned. These relief payments, equivalent to a succession tax, and not normally paid in the past, were carefully demanded and collected by Philip: 5,000 marks from Baldwin VIII for Flanders in 1191, £4,000 from the count of Blois in 1212. Philip even claimed the right to approve succession to the great principalities. When John succeeded to Normandy, Philip was asked why he proved so hostile to the new English king 'who had never done him any injury'; he replied that it was because he had taken over Normandy 'without his permission', and that he should have done homage.[39]

In 1196 Baldwin IX count of Flanders (1195–1206; Latin emperor, 1204–6) promised to submit all disputes with the king to the royal court, thus acknowledging its supremacy. Doing homage, he announced: 'I Baldwin, count of Flanders and Hainault, make known to all men present and to come that I have agreed and sworn to my liege lord Philip . . . to give him aid, openly and in good faith . . . and to be judged by those who ought to be my judges in the court of the king of France.'[40] When his uncle, Stephen of Sancerre, had been defeated, he prostrated himself at the king's feet and was forced to recognize that Sancerre came under the king's law. Philip kept control of the heiresses to Flanders and regulated their marriages; he was instrumental in the choice of Ferrand of Portugal to succeed in Flanders (1212–14, released 1226, d.1233), and took homage from him. When Simon de

39. Hallam, pp. 130, 169; Roger of Wendover, ed. Giles, II, p. 183; Roger of Wendover, ed. Coxe, III, pp. 141–2.
40. Fawtier, pp. 62–3; *Recueil des historiens des Gaulles et de la France*, ed. M. Bouquet and L. Delisle, 24 vols (Paris, 1737–1904) XIX, p. 352, letter of Innocent III to Philip: 'Ego Balduinus, Comes Flandrensis et Hainensis, notum facio universis praesentibus pariter et futuris, quod ego concessi et juravi domino meo ligio Philippo . . . bona fide et sine fictione ipsum juvabo contra omnes homines . . . et me facere judicare per eos qui me judicare debent in curia Regis Franciae'.

Montfort became count of Toulouse (1215–18) through the Albigensian Crusade, he did homage to Philip as duke of Narbonne, count of Toulouse and viscount of Béziers and Carcassonne. Thus the king had his lordship over the Midi recognized more clearly than had previously been the case.

Philip's age was one in which it became more common to make written records, hence the proliferation of charters. Many existing rights and customs were now first recorded, and the recording at the same time underlined and demonstrated the king's position. For example, now the customs of Hainault were recorded, and now the lists of those obliged in one way or another to the king were drawn up in registers. The authority of the king over all noble holdings was claimed in writing; this was no hierarchy of fiefs, only a royal predominance over everyone.

The king's authority over the nobility in our period was not primarily 'feudal'. When one examines the feudal obligations, one finds that commonly the nobility expected to be, and was, exempt from paying them. The payment of taxes and of feudal aids fell most heavily not on the nobility but on lesser men. What nobles more often owed was the obligation to attend court. Philip was attentive to his nobles, but he reduced their role in central government, enforced their recognition of his own authority over them, especially through judgements of the royal court, and brought most of the great principalities from a position of near independence to one of subordination to the monarchy. He also went some way towards breaking the allegiance of the lesser nobility to their own regional prince rather than to himself.

. . .

GOVERNMENT AND THE TOWNS

It would be pressing matters too far to suggest that Philip had a clear urban or economic policy, yet many aspects of his government involved relations with towns both in the demesne and outside. In general he encouraged the communal ambitions of greater cities, especially outside the demesne, and particularly in sensitive areas such as Normandy or Picardy, on 'the frontiers of the demesne'.[41] He was also aware of the

41. Fawtier, p. 207.

aspirations of merchants, notably in Paris, granting and confirming privileges, encouraging the university, improving the paving and fortifications, building a covered market for the merchants at Les Halles, giving Paris advantages over other trading cities, allowing its citizens a part not only in their own government but even in national government under the Testament. Customs were confirmed to the butchers of Paris, to buy or sell their beasts alive and dead freely; no one could become a butcher of Paris unless the butchers themselves had sworn him in.

Philip was aware of the profitability of trade and fairs, and of the potential benefit to the crown of that profitability; he gave protection to fairs and those travelling to them, for example in 1185 to merchants from Flanders, Ponthieu and Vermandois travelling to the Compiègne fair, or in 1209 for those going to the Champagne fairs. There was profit in all this, including that from merchants using the protected royal routes with marked stages; the stage at Bapaume for example made some £1,400 a year.

It is clear from the lists in the registers that the towns were a significant part of Philip's resources, and recognized as such, not least as a source for taxation and for military forces. Demesne rights are noted for thirty-two towns in Register A.[42] It was important for developing towns to have an expanding population, often drawing in serfs from neighbouring districts. Philip's royal towns were especially successful in obtaining new citizens, and as a result there were complaints from the lords who lost their labour.

The growth of communes during the reign is extremely important. The communal movement was not new, and the crown had given a grudging acknowledgement beforehand. A commune was an association recognized by the crown, consisting of free laymen, making an oath for a peaceful union, for mutual benefit and defence.[43] The commune would deal with its own administration, justice and tax collection, with certain reservations. It would train and raise its own militia. By and large citizens sought communal status for their town,

42. *Recueil*, I, no. 135, p. 164, 1185; Luchaire in Lavisse, p. 225; Bautier, 'Place' in Bautier, p. 21; Hallam, p. 158.
43. L. Carolus-Barré, 'Philippe Auguste et les communes', pp. 677–88 in Bautier, p. 678.

and monarchs were wary of the degree of independence which commune status allowed.

From early in the reign Philip made frequent recognitions of commune status, for example at Chaumont in 1182, Amiens in 1185, Pontoise in 1188. His was not an inflexible policy, and some communes were abolished, some not recognized. Usually the reasons for his decisions were political. Philip was cautious of allowing too great an independence for towns within the demesne, though he often granted other privileges. Sometimes he chose to acknowledge and back the opposition to commune status from other interested parties, notably the Church, as at Laon. Sometimes it especially suited his purpose to grant commune status to towns in areas he sought to conquer or had just won over, and new communes were founded, for example, in Normandy at Les Andelys and Nonancourt.[44]

Philip knew that in recognizing a commune, he was binding the citizens of that town to him. A delicate balance had to be struck. Would the crown gain more in loyalty from a grant, or would it be able to gain the same without loss to itself? The fact that Philip decided well is demonstrated by the general loyalty he received from towns and from citizens. The charters granting commune status were proudly retained, in Beauvais it was forbidden to remove the document: 'in no event will it be taken outside the city'.

At critical moments in the reign the communes, having made an oath of fidelity to the king, proved staunch military supporters. Those around Paris have been seen as forming 'a veritable shield' for the capital. From the point of view of the communes, or for cities with aspirations in that direction, the king was their natural ally, a counter to the main opponents of their independence, the Church or the magnates. At Poix, even though the lord, Walter Tirel, was ready to confirm the commune status granted by his father, the citizens still sent a delegation to Paris to seek the king's confirmation. Walter and the citizens were admitted to the palace, and asked Philip to take the commune under his protection, which he did, granting them a sealed charter to that effect. Royal guarantee was obviously valued above any other.[45]

44. Hallam, p. 162.
45. Carolus-Barré in Bautier, pp. 685, 682; Luchaire in Lavisse, p. 232.

The income from the towns was considerable. The demesne towns might well be seen as the solid foundation of Capetian finance. The *tailles* collected by the king's baillis from the major demesne towns were large: £2,995 from Paris, £1,500 from both Étampes and Orléans, nearly £7,000 in total.[46] It has been claimed that 15 per cent of royal income came from Paris alone.

It is noticeable that the towns in newly acquired regions were often not pressed as hard as the old demesne towns, almost certainly for political reasons, since the king was seeking to win their loyalty. The movement of Capetian power into Flemish territory brought a closer contact with the most highly developed towns in western Europe, with their expanding cloth industry, long-distance trade, and widespread communal style of government. Arras and St-Omer would come directly under French control, and most of the other towns moved towards closer co-operation. The peak of Flemish prosperity came after Philip's triumph against the counts, not before.

The ways in which Philip recognized the importance of trade and of a burgeoning economy are manifold. His charters are full of grants and recognitions of privileges, concerning both status and particular rights and exemptions. Philip's more outgoing policy to the towns also coincided with a leap forward in their prosperity. The economic boom was visible. There existed that elusive feel-good factor, as expressed by William the Breton, who saw the fields of his native Brittany now on all sides filled with vines, fertile soil, with salmon and eels widely available from fishing, together with the flourishing of trade.[47]

There were some problems related to the economic boom. It is possible that the quality of goods did not always keep step with the growing quantity and profit. There is a story told by Jacques de Vitry about the standard of meat sold in Paris. One customer tried to get a reduction in his payments on the grounds that he had been a regular customer for seven years; 'seven years?' replied the butcher in surprise, 'and you're still alive?' There was also an ambivalent view

46. Baldwin, *Government*, p. 158.
47. William the Breton, *Philippide*, ed. Guizot, pp. 287–8; 'Philippide', ed. Delaborde, II, pp. 284–5.

on usury. The attack on the Jews was justified on the grounds of their making profits denied to Christians; but the new expansion of trade and finance required more sophisticated banking. In one way or another, usually through exchange mechanisms, credit and usury were necessarily creeping into use. One notes that Philip quietly let the Jews back in to Paris after all the fuss about expelling them. But, as is usually the case, people will accept some difficulties if they believe the overall trend to be satisfactory.

. . .

GOVERNMENT AND DEFENCE

One of Philip's considerations was for defence, against actual and potential enemies. Clearly he had not seen the towns as hostile to himself, since he encouraged a large-scale building programme of walls and urban castles, not least in Paris itself, which was given walls 4 metres thick, a series of wall towers, the great castle of the Louvre, a large moat, and a host of other defensive improvements.

Philip's first register records work on the walls of Laon, Compiègne, St-Mard and Melun, among others, with ditches being dug up to 11 metres deep and 19 metres wide. There were specifications for the height of curtain walls, for gates and towers. In several cases major new towers were built to improve the defences, as at Bourges by 1190.[48] The registers record instructions sent to builders of the new fortifications, such as Garnier the mason or Gilbert the ditch-maker. These men were referred to as masters and were clearly not lowly labourers. By the end of the reign every single town of importance within the demesne was walled and incorporated a fortress. Some 113 fortresses were listed in the register by 1210, and Registers A and C together mention nineteen individual builders.[49]

Architecturally there was much of interest in Philip's programme of fortification. The predominance of round towers in the new structures is notable: some eighteen new cylindrical keeps were built, often of three storeys, at a total

48. P. Contamine, *War in the Middle Ages*, trans. M. Jones (Oxford, 1984) p. 107; Baldwin, *Government*, pp. 296–7.
49. Baldwin, *Government*, pp. 299, 552 n. 212, 296: Garnier 'cementarius', Gilbert 'fossator'.

cost of about £27,000. Later there was a tendency to prefer quadrilateral enclosures, often incorporating round towers. One of his greatest structures, the Louvre castle in Paris built in about 1200, had round towers incorporated in an overall quadrangular plan. Its western walls were 4 metres thick and it had flanking towers of more than 8 metres in diameter. The central keep was cylindrical and 31 metres high. The castle included residential accommodation for the royal family and others. There was a drawbridge in the eastern gate, and a wet moat surrounded the whole castle. It has recently been called 'a defence of the first rank'.[50]

The instructions for Dun-le-Roi, in Berry, were to follow the plan of the Louvre, which clearly became a model for later fortification. Philip's tower at Issoudun was cylindrical in essence but with a strengthening spur on the side most likely to be attacked. It was an early example of this type, known as *en bec*. Castles which incorporated round towers included Villeneuve-sur-Yonne, Orléans, Laon and Péronne. Philip was probably also responsible for the addition of round towers to the Plantagenet fortifications at Gisors, Falaise, Rouen, Vernon, Verneuil, Lillebonne and Chinon; and to other castles at Beauvais, Bourges, Cappy, Compiègne, Corbeil, Montargis and Montdidier. All his round towers possessed at least two floors. Unusually Philip's towers were all constructed from uniformly sized blocks of matching stone. His addition to Falaise, later named the Talbot Tower, was pierced by a shell during the Second World War, but still survives. Philip built about twenty great round towers altogether, apart from numerous rounded towers in wall defences.

A number of his structures had the *en bec* strengthening at the base, particularly on the vulnerable side. The towers built at captured Loches are examples of this. His last major castle, at Dourdan, has a very interesting plan, with a massive round keep in the north corner of the curtain. This inevitably reminds one of the later tendency in castle construction to concentrate defence on the walls rather than the interior, with wall towers replacing central keeps as the

50. A. Erlande-Brandenburg, 'L'architecture militaire au temps de Philippe Auguste: une nouvelle conception de la défense', in Bautier pp. 595–603, p. 601; J. Bousssard, 'Philippe Auguste et Paris', in Bautier, pp. 323–40, p. 329.

main residential accommodation. Again Philip's planning seems to be pointing the way to the future.[51]

Philip took a personal interest in the building work, for example in the choice of sites. Sometimes the records show his own orders being sent, for example concerning the building of the wall turrets at Melun. In three cases he is said to have assisted in 'devising', or perhaps setting out, the foundations. The gateways were sometimes double and sometimes had drawbridges. At Compiègne, for example, Gautier de Mullent was instructed to 'plaster and repoint the wall with limestone inside and out, and make four simple gates with double turrets and ditches fifty feet wide and thirty feet deep'.[52]

As we have suggested above, we see the purpose of the registers, one of the mainsprings of Philip's government, as being geared to the raising of military forces. It was essential to record where and when military service was owed, and in what form. Effort was also expended on fortification for Paris and all the main towns, including the improvement and construction of numerous castles. In the registers, Philip spent over £33,000 on the fortification of cities, and the total expended was almost certainly greater still. In the view of a leading military historian, Philip's force was 'made of stones more than of men'.[53]

Philip's castle-building was focused in the royal demesne, where it has been seen as a systematic building campaign.[54] Sometimes, as at St-Medard, the king was concerned to maintain royal control over the castle, independent even of its own commune of Soissons. Elsewhere he sought to maintain castles in territories he was seeking to acquire. Castles for Philip were used for offensive campaigns as well as for defence. Sometimes he built anew, otherwise his castles received improvements and repairs. After the conquest of Normandy, Philip possessed a hundred castles on the demesne, with forty-five of them in Normandy.

---

51. Baldwin, *Government*, pp. 294–302, and plates 8–14.
52. Erlande-Brandenberg in Bautier, pp. 596, 602; Contamine, *War*, p. 107 and n. 105.
53. P. Contamine, 'L'armée de Philippe Auguste', pp. 577–94 in Bautier, pp. 593–4; Baldwin, *Government*, p. 297.
54. Baldwin, *Government*, pp. 296, 299.

Philip's castle-building efforts have been compared in their intensity with those of Edward I. The records show that his buildings were often massive. The tower at Villeneuve-sur-Yonne was over 27 metres high, with walls almost 5 metres thick; its surrounding ditch was over 13 metres wide; it possessed two drawbridges, and hoarding to cap the walls made of wood and reinforced with iron.

Philip was also interested in the defence of the realm in more general terms. Outside the demesne he built new structures and repaired existing ones, while encouraging others to do the same, sometimes loaning money for the purpose. He granted out castles to men he could trust in delicate regions. He even built castles to pass on to such men, as for example Sully-sur-Loire to the bishop of Orléans. When castles were granted, he was adamant about his right to take them over when necessary, usually engaging others on oath to see that this would be done.[55]

As in Philip's treatment of the Church, where he allowed freedom of election to major offices more readily than did the Plantagenets, so he pursued a similar policy with regard to those who held castles from him. The way such policies match up does more than anything to suggest that they were deliberate and stemmed from a personal attitude to government. Philip sought recognition of his overlordship and insisted on rights to be handed castles at need, but he also recognized the claims of their lords and did not disturb those rights unduly. As has been said: 'the fortress-policy of Philip II until after Bouvines was moderate and only mildly interventionist, whereas John's was ruthlessly *dirigiste* and opportunistic from first to last'.[56]

Evidence for Philip's activities is to be found in charters which were kept in the Louvre, many of which were non-royal, including 105 charters which have some reference to fortress-policy. Many of them deal with the mechanics of handing over a castle or other stronghold when Philip should require its use, or 'rendability' as it has been termed. Part of the point of rendability was that it could be seen as a

55. Contamine, *War*, pp. 111, 114; Baldwin, *Government*, pp. 294–8, 301.
56. C. Coulson, 'Fortress-policy in Capetian tradition and Angevin practice', *ANS*, VI, 1983, pp. 13–38, p. 15.

temporary arrangement during a crisis. The term of royal control might be indefinite, but the arrangement did not remove the castellan's claim to continue holding the castle once the crisis had passed, and this was implicit in the agreements. Indeed this was also put into practice, as in the case of William the Marshal, whose castles were taken over and then restored in 1205.[57]

Philip may have been moderate, but he was also careful, and the arrangements for handing over castles were precisely detailed, with oaths, specified fines or punishments, and named guarantors. As always Philip sought to provide a legal basis for his activities. The provisions nevertheless show clearly that Philip bestowed a degree of trust on his lords to safeguard castles for him, quite unlike the distrust demonstrated by King John.[58]

Philip was the first Capetian king to give any serious thought to the raising of naval forces. He began the reign with no navy and had to rely on others for any sea-going operation, including his passage for the Third Crusade. For both commercial and political reasons it became increasingly necessary to give thought to the provision of ships. He gained an outlet to the western sea via Ponthieu, and then the acquisition of the Plantagenet lands vastly increased his seaboard. The reliance on allies such as the Danes or the Flemings was not always satisfactory. As Philip turned to ideas for the invasion of England, so he began to raise ships for his own use, as in 1213, including the building of new vessels. Some 1,500 ships were mentioned in this year; and in 1215 Philip's fleet had the capacity to carry 7,000 men. At least some of these ships were of a considerable size: there is mention of three ships of about 30 tons each in 1213, and of ten large ships in 1217. On his own ship the commander Eustace the Monk built a wooden castle 'so large that all regarded it as a marvel'. Some vessels also carried stone-throwing engines.

The formation of fleets in 1213 and 1217 was the origin of a French royal navy, which Philip IV (1285–1314) would later develop.[59] In the initial plans for the invasion of Eng-

57. Coulson, p. 38.
58. Coulson, pp. 15, 23.
59. M. Mollat du Jourdin, 'Philippe Auguste et la mer', in Bautier, pp. 605–23; quote from p. 618.

land, Philip had been forced to seek help from Denmark. But in 1213, although the fleet was to have little success, Philip built and assembled 'his own ships, and as many others as he could collect', and arranged for provision of corn, wine and meat. On that occasion the invasion was called off, and instead the fleet was directed in a raid against Flanders which led to the disaster at Damme, when 400 of the 1,500 ships were captured and Philip had to order the burning of the rest to prevent them falling into enemy hands. These early French naval efforts had little success, so that an English chronicler thought Philip's subjects 'not well skilled in naval warfare'; and even William the Breton admitted that: 'the French do not know the ways of the ocean'.

Failure in this new venture by the inexperienced French was hardly surprising, but the attempt was still significant. A new fleet was assembled in 1217, when Louis's invasion of England was enabled to take place, though the fleet in the end suffered another defeat. Eustace, 'knight of the sea as well as the land', was beaten by the English fleet, which was said to be twice the size of his own force. But Philip had seen the need for a navy, taken a bold step, with the result that the history and achievement of a sea-going French nation had begun. The later success of a nation with both a navy and an army was the direction in which Philip was taking France: it is the eventual effect not the initial failure which is most worthy of note.[60]

Executive decisions for military action were made by the king, with advice from his most intimate counsellors. The close and personal nature of decision-making is demonstrated in a revealing description of Philip's sudden determination to invade Normandy in 1203. He made the decision personally in the middle of the night, and then called to him just four men, including Guérin de Glapion, Bartholomew de Roye and one of the Clément brothers, to announce his decision and to seek their advice on it.

Philip's household was the basis of his command, with himself at the head, his constables and marshals having spe-

60. Roger of Wendover, ed. Giles, pp. 261, 400; Roger of Wendover, ed. Coxe, III, p. 243 and IV, p. 29; William the Breton, *Philippide*, ed. Guizot, p. 276; William the Breton, 'Vie', ed. Delaborde, I, p. 314: 'miles tam mari quam terra probatissimus'; Mollat du Jourdin, pp. 618, 623.

cific military duties, and about half of the household made up of knights who could be used, if required, for military purposes. Certain figures there were especially significant in this respect, including members of the Clément family and William des Barres, men who would act as commanders and close military companions of the monarch. Mercenary captains also moved in Philip's immediate circle, in particular the greatest of them, Cadoc. In peacetime such men might fulfil administrative duties, including the keeping of law and order, serving as baillis and other officials; in war they were the vital command centre of the army.

There was need for a certain amount of expense on appearance, for colourful arms, new armour and impressive trappings. The king was still in this period the war leader, and it was important that his banner and his person should be noticed, should stand out from others. Hence all the ceremonial around the oriflamme from St-Denis, half military banner, half religious symbol; hence too the use of the royal banner with the distinctive fleur-de-lys. Mouskes admired this 'cloth of blue silk with the golden flowers of the arms of the king of France, the whole unit wearing the same'.[61]

The tax system was geared, if necessary, towards war. The registers are full of lists of service owed and of military resources available. There are also the *prisées des sergents*, recording the quotas of military service from the demesne towns and abbeys, which show the war levy in 1202–3, for example, raising £26,453. Register A recorded what was owed from places in the demesne, and what had to be paid in lieu of personal service. The record of what service was owed by churches and of the king's regalian rights, like so much else in the administration, revolved around the contribution to war from the Church. Military service was owed by all the bishops within the royal demesne, and by twenty-five bishops altogether in Register A.

Finance was of course intimately associated with war. As Bertran de Born admitted: 'I cannot make distant war without wealth.' The records show Philip raising money in the crisis years and spending it on fortifications, raising troops

---

61. J.F. Verbruggen, *The Art of Warfare in Western Europe during the Middle Ages*, trans. S. Willard and S.C.M. Southern (Amsterdam, 1977) p. 74; Philip Mouskes, II, ll. 17406–9.

and fighting wars, including the provision of supplies and of equipment for sieges, and also in compensation to the Church for property damaged in the fighting. Knights, crossbowmen, sergeants both mounted and on foot, and garrisons, all required payment. The fact that Philip paid his troops about 30 per cent higher wages than King John paid to his men is surely significant.[62] Commonly a captain received the money for his men as well as for himself; thus Cadoc was given lump sums with which to reward his mercenaries. Sworn mercenary bands led by captains such as Cadoc, taking a mutual oath not unlike that sworn by the urban communes, were becoming an essential part of warfare. Mercenaries must be hired, and increasingly they must also be controlled.

There was a procedure for times of emergency, when cash passed directly through the chamber, allowing the king personal management of war finance. But of course, as we have seen, finance and administration in general were much concerned with warfare. The organization of war was a major administrative act. Provisions must be collected and transported, men must be protected in the 'tents and pavilions' which Bertran de Born loved to see rising in the meadows. In Register A are listed the obligations of thirty monasteries to provide pack horses, and for eight of them to send wagons.[63] It gives some idea of numbers to see that about 2,000 knights were raised by the king in 1185 for his war against Philip count of Flanders.

It is also interesting that the main source of Philip's forces was the royal demesne, reflected in the focus on the demesne in the contents of the registers. Register A has lists of knights in groups of five under bannerets, from the demesne. Register E has 1,299 knights, to which may be added the 452 from 1207. The same register records the method of providing garrisons for castle-guard from districts around castles, for example at Pacy twenty-two knights were to do forty days service. A muster list for 1214 shows forces assembled with three bishops and eleven magnates, these levies too being chiefly from the demesne. Baldwin has gone

62. Baldwin, *Government*, pp. 172, 283, 169; Bertran de Born, p. 373, l. 14: 'q'ieu puosca loing osteiar ses aver'.
63. Verbruggen, p. 39; Baldwin, *Government*, p. 283; Bertran de Born, p. 339, ll. 6–7: 'e plai me qand vei per los pratz/tendas e pavaillons fermatz'.

so far as to say that 'Philip's army was purely a domanial affair'.[64] This is not strictly the case, since forces came from the nobility throughout the realm, from the communes, and as mercenaries for hire both from France and elsewhere. In the end too, the army depended on finance and support from the realm as a whole. Obligatory service fell largely not on the nobility, but on ordinary peasants and citizens.

Under Philip Augustus the nation-wide responsibility of the monarchy for defence became more apparent and more real. Philip made the demesne secure. He extended royal control over national defence. He developed a system of fortification for the realm. The army became larger and extremely effective, resulting in major conquests. Philip's attempt, for the first time, to turn France into a naval power, may have lacked success, but the failures in this respect are not representative of the effects of Philip's efforts at transforming the monarchy as a whole. It was *because* Philip had set about reforming and streamlining royal administration, and therefore royal wealth and resources, that all his successes had come about. The proper emphasis is that success in war depended upon administrative development, rather than that administration developed as a result of successful expansion. Because Philip had transformed the nature of the monarchy, he was also able to transform the balance of power within the boundaries of France.

64. Baldwin, *Government,* pp. 295, 280–1.

Chapter 9

THE FOUNDATIONS OF PHILIP'S GOVERNMENT

The previous chapter reflects mainly the public face of Philip's government, this chapter looks more at, if not quite a private face, then a less public one. The transformation of the Capetian monarchy was only possible because it was founded upon a secure base. We now need to examine that foundation more fully in order to understand the process. Because of the number of surviving records from this period, it is possible to examine more closely the day-to-day working of royal administration, and this we shall now attempt.

Much of this chapter depends upon the records of routine government operations. But although there are sufficient records to answer our purpose in general, there is a major problem. In 1194, at Fréteval, Richard captured the records which travelled with the king. William the Breton gives some indication of what these records were, but beyond that it is impossible to know exactly what was lost, or how complete was the loss. The chronicler says there were signed documents and books of financial accounts, tax registers and the records of the royal fisc, 'the registers by which one knew in advance what was owed at the treasury, what and how much should be the subsidies, what each was supposed to pay, the heading of the *cens*, of *taille* or for feudal dues, who was exempt and who was condemned to *corvée* service, who were the serfs of the glebe and the household serfs, and finally by what services a freedman was still tied to his lord'. Howden adds the information that also captured were papers from 'all the subjects of the King of England who had deserted him'.[1]

1. William the Breton, 'Vie', in *Oeuvres de Rigord et de Guillaume le Breton*, ed. H-F. Delaborde, 2 vols, SHF, vols 210, 224 (Paris, 1882–85) I, p. 197; William the Breton, 'Philippide', in *Oeuvres* ed. Delaborde, II, pp. 118–20, ll. 545–8: 'scripta tributorum fiscique cyrographa; nec non/Cum

Shortly afterwards we find records in a permanent home, with the development of a royal archive, but this does not prove that nothing existed before. Louis VII had already made use of the palace on the Ile-de-la-Cité in Paris as a base for government. We are told that after Fréteval there was an attempt to reconstruct the records which had been lost, but from extant records it is not easy to be sure what form this reconstruction took.

The crux of this matter are the registers. They are a particularly interesting and important section of the surviving material, recently re-edited, and the foundation of much of the interpretative work by historians such as John W. Baldwin and M. Nortier. It is certainly, through their efforts, clearer now what is the nature of the registers, but a number of puzzles remain, and perhaps always will. The relationship of the registers to each other is difficult to disentangle, and the purpose of them is far from certain.

Philip's age was one in which more was recorded in writing than had previously been the case, and one consequence was the proliferation and collection of charters. Many existing rights and customs were now first recorded, and the recording underlined and demonstrated the king's position. Thus now the customs of Hainault were recorded, and the lists of those obliged in one way or another to the king were drawn up in the registers.

. . .

PHILIP'S ADMINISTRATION

The surviving records allow us to see the working of Philip's administration in some detail, its nature and its functions;

---

reliquis rapitur rebus regale sigillum;/Tantaque passus ibi rex est dispendia, vicum/Ut vere dicas a bello et fraude vocatum'; ll. 561–8: 'sed scripta quibus prenosse dabatur/Quid deberetur fisco, que, quanta tributa,/Nomine quid census, que vectigalia, quantum/Quisque teneretur feodali solvere jure,/Qui sint exempti, vel quos angaria damnet,/Qui sint vel glebe servi, vel conditionis,/Quove manumissus patrono jure ligetur,/Non nisi cum summo poterit nescire labore'. William the Breton, *La Philippide, Poème*, ed. M. Guizot (Paris, 1825) pp. 118–20; William the Breton, 'Vie', in *Vie de Philippe Auguste par Rigord*, ed. M. Guizot (Paris, 1825) p. 211; Roger of Howden, *The Annals of Roger de Hoveden*, ed. H.T. Riley, 2 vols (London, 1853) II, p. 328; Roger of Howden, *Chronica*, ed. W. Stubbs, 4 vols, RS no. 51 (London, 1868–71) II, p. 256: 'et cartae universorum hominum regis Angliae, qui se dederant regi Franciae'.

and the records are themselves also a product of that administration, so that their very existence is evidence too. Philip was the first Capetian king, so far as we know, to make a clear effort to preserve registers, together with governmental records for finance and justice, in a royal archive. Charters were collected from the 1190s, and the record of inquests begun by Guérin de Glapion in 1220 was made 'on the order of our lord king'.[2] We have already seen something of the government's general structure. Philip depended primarily on a small group of close counsellors who held offices with particular, if not always specialized, functions. Philip also employed royal agents in the demesne, and outside, to carry on the routine work of government and to enforce the changes which he introduced.

We speak of departments, and we know of the existence of a chancery and a chamber, but we should be mistaken to see these as entirely separated organizations. Household departments do not emerge until the reign of St Louis, but they were in the process of formation in Philip's time. The close counsellors and the clerks could still move from one area of the administration to another, and often did; which fluidity is a likely sign of experimentation, and the officials probably did not see their work as compartmentalized.

Central government was organized under a few major officials: the chancellor, the seneschal, the butler, the chamberlain and the constable. These originated as household officials with specific functions. By the beginning of the twelfth century these offices had been taken over by leading magnates. Under Philip, one or two magnates held such titles, for example Matthew count of Beaumont was chamberlain, and Philip made some use of his noble relatives, notably his mother and Archbishop William of Reims as regents. In the early reign the archbishop had been called his 'watchful eye in council, his right hand in business'.[3] But the trend was to pass office, and sometimes title, to more humble men and their professional staff, for example marshals assisting the constables.

2. C. Petit-Dutaillis, *The Feudal Monarchy in France and England from the Tenth to the Thirteenth Centuries*, trans. E.D. Hunt (London, 1936) p. 301.
3. *Recueil des Actes de Philippe Auguste*, ed. H-F. Delaborde, 4 vols (Paris, 1916–79) I, pp. 136–8, no. 109. p. 137: 'in consiliis nostris oculus vigilans, in negociis dextra manus'.

The writing office was the chancery. It employed a handful of scribes at any one time, two or three, sometimes half a dozen, and seventeen individuals have so far been identified for the whole reign. The scribes were responsible for writing the diplomas, charters and letters of the king. At first the chancellor was a magnate, but after the death of Hugh du Puiset in 1185 no one replaced him until 1223, and the task without the title was taken on by lesser men, *viles personae.* The use of humbler men was not entirely new, but as has been said, Philip 'made a system out of a trend'.[4] Most notable of these men was Brother Guérin de Glapion, for whom the title of chancellor was eventually revived.

Some 2,000 royal acts of the reign are known, including about 440 originals, and this is only a small proportion, perhaps 1 per cent, of the total issued. Not all chancery acts were enrolled, and the chancery did not retain duplicates. Those known to us contain grants, commands and instructions, letters and notifications. The reign also saw a change in the style of handwriting of official documents, with the introduction of Gothic cursive.

Three types of seal were used: the great pendant seal for solemn charters, with lesser seals for letters patent and close. The king also possessed a small personal seal for certain more private letters, the seal after all was the representation of the king's authority. One finds in many acts reference to the use of a seal, for example on an 1180 act issued at Sens: 'this present page with the authority of our seal'.[5]

There were also tax accounts, mentioned by William the Breton as being lost at Fréteval, along with charters and a seal: 'writings of regular payments, and cash, chirographs, and with the rest was captured the royal seal'. Walter the

4. J.W. Baldwin, *The Government of Philip Augustus* (Berkeley, CA, 1986) p. 404; E.M. Hallam, *Capetian France, 987–1328* (Harlow, 1980) p. 160; A. Luchaire, 'Philippe Auguste'; 'Louis VIII' in E. Lavisse, ed., *Histoire de France depuis les Origines jusqu'à la Révolution*, III, Pt I (Paris, 1911) pp. 233–4.

5. M. Nortier, 'Les actes de Philippe Auguste: notes critiques sur les sources diplomatiques du règne', pp. 429–53 in R-H. Bautier, ed., *La France de Philippe Auguste, le Temps des Mutations* (Paris, 1982) p. 431; E. Poulle, 'La cursive gothique à la chancellerie de Philippe Auguste', pp. 455–67 in Bautier, pp. 458, 464; B.B. Reyah, 'Les sceaux de Philippe Auguste', pp. 721–36 in Bautier, p. 723; *Recueil*, e.g. I, p. 13, no. 9, 1180 Sens: 'presentam paginam sigilli nostri auctoritate'.

Young was given the task of reassembling the lost material; and, although it is impossible to verify the statement, it was said that: 'he restored everything in its previous state correctly'.[6]

The Capetians had been used to taking advice from magnates who performed functions at court: the seneschal, the chamberlain, the constable and the chancellor. Early on Philip used a small number of magnates to fill such offices: Ralph count of Clermont was constable, Theobald count of Blois was seneschal. The form of some of Philip's acts suggests that a certain small group of officials was expected to witness them. On the whole we know of officers more than of functions: of constables such as Matthew de Montmorency; of butlers like Henry de Sully; of chamberlains like Bartholomew de Roye. They are generally found as witnesses to the king's acts. Possibly there was a form to be followed by the scribes, with an expected list of witnesses. Why otherwise should many charters give not only the witnesses but also note that a certain official was *not* present, for example: 'no butler'?[7]

Increasingly Philip employed men from the lesser nobility of the demesne as his officials, men whose main task in life was not to look after great principalities but to serve the king as administrators. These men came to dominate the royal entourage, the main instrument of government under the king. The two main elements in the entourage were the clerks employed by the king, and his household knights. Professor Baldwin further divides the knights into military and administrative knights, but the division was probably not a clear one. It is true that, for example, Bartholomew de Roye was more involved with administration than fighting; but even the clerks who were close to the king in administrative work were also involved in his warfare, as at Bouvines, where we find for example Bartholomew and Walter the Young.

6. R. Fawtier, *The Capetian Kings of France*, trans. L. Butler and R.J. Adam (London, 1964) p. 7: William the Breton, 'Philippide', ed. Delaborde, pp. 118–20, ll. 545–6; see n. 5 above; p. 120, ll. 569–73: 'Prefuit huic operi Galterus junior; ille/Hoc grave sumpsit onus in se, qui cuncta reduxit/Ingenio naturali sensusque vigore/In solitum rectumque statum, prestructus ab illo/Esdram qui docuit reparare volumina legis . . .'. *Layettes du Trésor des Chartes*, 5 vols (Paris, 1863–1909) vols I and II ed. A. Teulet, I, p. xxv; *Grandes Chroniques de Saint-Denis*, ed. J. Viard, 9 vols (Paris, 1920–37).
7. *Recueil*, II, no. 477, p. 1, 1194, Vitry-aux-Loges: 'dapifero nullo'.

The king had, on more or less immediate call, some 250 knights, about the same number of horse sergeants, almost a hundred mounted crossbowmen, 133 crossbowmen on foot, 2,000 foot sergeants and 300 mercenaries. To this, at need, could be added the forces due from obligations of military service.[8]

When Theobald count of Blois died, his office as seneschal was left vacant. The men Philip turned to were such as Walter de Nemours the chamberlain and his sons. It was his son, Walter the Young, who had the task of restoring the archives lost at Fréteval. Even the patronymic of Nemours came through marriage not birth. Another major figure in the administration was Bartholomew de Roye, who became chamberlain in 1208. He was a younger son from a middling knightly family in the Vermandois. Unlike most of these lesser nobles, Bartholomew married into a major family, taking as his wife the daughter of the count of Évreux. The Clément family, a moderate landed family of the Gâtinais, held several official posts. Two members of the new military orders were also employed in the king's work: Brother Guérin de Glapion, a Hospitaller, who through the later reign was probably the dominant figure in the administration, particularly in the chancery, and who came from such obscure origins that no one knows them now; and Brother Haymard, the Templar, who was the king's treasurer in Paris from 1219, and who has been seen as a 'banker'. Among others used by Philip were William des Barres, William Garlande, Philip de Nanteuil, Aubert de Hangest, Guy le Bouteilleur, Peter Tristan and Matthew de Montmorency; nearly all of whom came from knightly families of the royal demesne, and in particular from the Ile-de-France.

Guérin de Glapion was seen as the king's 'special counsellor, because of his wisdom in the royal hall, and his incomparable gift at advising . . . second to the king . . . the special friend of the king, who with the king handled the difficult business of the kingdom'. The Béthune Chronicle speaks of an inner circle of advisers, called on when the decision to invade England was made, mentioning Guérin, Bartholomew de Roye, Henry Clément, and a fourth who was probably

---

8. Baldwin, *Government*, pp. 109–10; J-F. Finó, 'Quelques aspects de l'art militaire sous Philippe Auguste', *Gladius*, VI, 1967, pp. 19–36, p. 28.

Walter the Young. The chronicler did not approve, since these were 'lesser men . . . the only people to whom the king was accustomed on all occasions to open his soul and reveal his secret thoughts'. One notes that the sensitive document of Philip's will was to be executed by Guérin, Haymard and Bartholomew.[9]

The French kings had come to use prévôts to administer the demesne directly, and usually employed their own castellans for the purpose. Philip did not abandon this system, but he extended it and supervised it more closely. At the start of the reign there were some forty-one prévôtés in the royal demesne; by 1190 there were fifty-two and by 1203 this had risen to sixty-two. That Philip increased efficiency as well as numbers is clear from the increase in revenues which resulted, a 22 per cent increase in the first decade, and 72 per cent altogether through the reign.[10] Supervision was carried out by newly introduced officials, again royal agents, the baillis. These officials are given instructions time after time in Philip's acts, for example in 1187, to the constable of the Vexin and the relevant prévôts and baillis to guard the possessions of the monks of Notre-Dame de Valle Beate Marie.[11]

The extension of responsibilities to a broader social range of men is also clear in Philip's attitude to town government. Communes were generally encouraged, and the king's designs for government while on crusade included the employment of six leading citizens of Paris. This may have been a temporary experiment, but is none the less significant, and the functions of this group were not confined to Parisian affairs.

Philip did not usually reward his servants with great estates and marriages, though a few obtained such gains, and some were promoted to high office in the Church. By and large

9. Baldwin, *Government*, pp. 119, 123; *Recueil des Historiens des Gaules et de la France (RHF)*, ed. M. Bouquet and L. Delisle 24 vols (Paris, 1869–1904) XXIV, Anonymous of Béthune, pp. 750–75; William the Breton, 'Philippide', ed. Delaborde, II, pp. 311–12; p. 312, l. 731: 'regis specialis amicus'; William the Breton, 'Vie', ed. Delaborde, p. 256: 'specialis consiliarius effectus in aula regia propter prudentiam et incomparabilem consilii virtutum . . . quod quasi secundum a rege negotia regni'.
10. William the Breton 'Vie', ed. Guizot, p. 267; William the Breton 'Philippide', ed. Delaborde, pp. 271, 304; Baldwin, *Government*, p. 100.
11. *Recueil*, I, no. 216, p. 261, 1187, Saint-Léger.

rewards were modest: small estates, small gifts, clothing; but for relatively humble men there was always hope of some gift or promotion, and there was a regular salary. The test of the system is loyalty, and Philip received almost invariable fidelity from all his men.

One of the major developments of the reign was the move towards a more permanent home for government in Paris, which had begun before Philip's reign but made progress under him. This was done partly by Philip making it a regular base, and partly by his promotion of the interests of Paris as a capital. His itinerary shows that even in years of military campaigns he would return regularly to his capital, often for visits in the middle of campaigns which were mostly not that distant. His gifts to the city and grants of privileges ensured that he was a welcome resident, and that together with his work on the fortifications also made Paris a secure base for him. It was moreover under Philip that Paris became the home of a more stable centre for administration, with the keeping of archives, and the establishment of a permanent treasury at the Temple.

There were abuses and failures, as in any governmental system. Officials did not always act honourably. Gilles de Paris speaks of people 'tortured by the agents of the royal fisc'; and Parisian theologians criticized the collection of tax in the demesne as 'robbery'. As we have suggested earlier, the burden of taxation tended to fall more heavily upon lesser men than on the nobility. There were accusations against royal agents of extortionate treatment of the monasteries in newly conquered Normandy.[12]

Philip's officials were not pristine pure, and there is a concrete example of the activity of at least one official who abused his power. He coveted the land (or in one version the mine) of a certain knight, and on the man's death forced his widow to sell it to him. The official tried to make the transfer look legal by dragging the knight's neighbours to the cemetery and disinterring the corpse. He stood the dead man on his feet to 'swear' before witnesses that he would

---

12. Petit-Dutaillis, p. 191; *RHF*, XVII, the 'Carolinus' of Gilles de Paris, pp. 288–301, p. 291, ll. 108–9: 'Forsitan et crebro fisci exactore juvandi/Difficiles leges et tempora dura tulisti'; J.W. Baldwin, *Masters, Princes and Merchants: The Social Views of Peter the Chanter and his Circle*, 2 vols (Princeton, 1970) I, p. 236; A. Luchaire in E. Lavisse, p. 141.

sell, proclaiming: 'who does not speak, consents'. Naturally there was silence; the official then pressed the cash for the purchase into the corpse's hand and reburied him. But the widow complained and brought the case before Philip. The king's official produced his 'witnesses', but Philip insisted on questioning them individually. He made one recite the Paternoster, and then told the others that the man had confessed as truly as he had recited the Lord's prayer. The others duly admitted their fault, and the official threw himself at the king's feet, begging for mercy. He was banished (or hanged or buried alive in variant versions) and his house and demesne were handed to the widow; it was 'a judgement worthy of Solomon'.

This story comes from an *exemplum,* and sounds embroidered, perhaps invented, but it demonstrates a view of Philip as fair-minded and observant over the activities of his officials, even if he had to resort to dirty tricks in the process.[13] The overall picture of the nearly 2,000 acts in the collected *Recueil* is of a deliberate attempt at fairness in government: if something is taken something is given in exchange, if someone has served well there is reward, if there is a dispute there is an attempt to find a just settlement.

. . .

THE REGISTERS

Much attention has recently been given to one group of the surviving documents of the reign, the registers. They are the first documents of the kind to survive in France. The basis of scholarly use of these records was the work of Delisle, and they are now being published in a modern edition. Their significance can hardly be overstated. Bautier has called them 'without doubt the documentary source of the greatest importance which we have from this period'.[14] We must be careful to know what we mean when we call them 'registers':

13. Luchaire in Lavisse, pp. 237–8; J. Le Goff, 'Philippe Auguste dans les exempla', pp. 145–55 in Bautier, p. 149, who refers to the official as a bailli.
14. See D.R. Bates, 'Léopold Delisle', in H. Damico and J.B. Zavadil, eds, *Medieval Scholarship: Biographical Studies on the Formation of a Discipline,* I, History (New York and London, 1995) pp. 101–13; L.V. Delisle, *Catalogue des Actes de Philippe Auguste* (Paris, 1856). The first published

they do not contain an all-inclusive registration of any particular series of royal acts; they are rather a selection of documents, often in the form of lists, and at first sight apparently random.[15]

There is uncertainty about the purpose of the registers and their use. But a simple explanation of the registers is that they work exactly like a filing system. All state documents had to be copied out by hand, and for some purposes there would be a need to abbreviate and systematize, as well as to make exact copies. The registers contain abbreviations of various government measures, and lists which were useful for immediate government action. This was a way of setting out major state measures for reference, for gaining information which was necessary for government, starting with material as it existed at the time, and leaving space for additions relevant to the same measure or category over the years. For example, one might list towns which currently owed certain dues, and add to the list as circumstances altered.

What then happened will be easily understood by anyone who has set up a database. However carefully one sets out the definitions, with use one will find there were omissions in the original concept, and ways in which it could be improved. When therefore it is necessary to make a new start, in the case of the registers as the space allowed was filled, one would reconsider the parameters and redefine the database. So with the registers, when on two occasions it was time to begin again, the categories under which information was stored were reorganized.

The documents are labelled as Register A, Register B and so on to Register E. It is not the most clear classification, but is so well used by now that it would be counter-productive to alter it. Delisle provided this lettering system; he labelled fourteenth-century copies of A as B, and of C as D; so that only A, C and E are the important original registers, B and D being late copies.

Scribe N is identified as responsible for the original part of Register A, begun in about 1204, consisting of some ninety-

---

part of the new work is J.W. Baldwin with F. Gasparri, M. Nortier and E. Lalou, eds, *Les Registres de Philippe Auguste*, VII, Texte (Paris, 1992); quote from preface, p. 1.
15. Baldwin, *Government*, pp. 415, 418.

six folios. Five other scribes made additions to Register A over the next eight years. The sheer volume of Capetian government by the thirteenth century is made clear by the very size of the register. It was designed for ease of access to necessary information, but ended with ninety-six folios to flick through. There was not much space left to fill with additional information, and in less than a decade it was decided to make a new start. In 1212 three different scribes seem to have shared the task of beginning the new register, copying material from Register A to what we know as Register C. This was also redesigned in more formal divisions, under ten headings, such as fees, alms and communes. These sections were then added to by about ten scribes up until 1220.

At this point Stephen de Gallardon took on the task allotted to him by Brother Guérin of making another new start, copying Register C into the new register, known to us as E. The number of sections was expanded to eighteen; and these in turn were added to by some dozen scribes until 1247. The new sections included divisions for particular individuals and groups with whom the government had frequent dealings, including bishops, abbots and the pope. Each register was a small 'manual of information . . . a source of ready reference', and easy to carry about.[16] They were working documents, with regular additions made, and with a periodic need to update, reorganize and make more space, so that the current register was kept up to date and remained useful.

One difficult question about Register A is whether it is the first ever compiled, or simply the first to survive. This is made more rather than less problematic by the certainty that it uses material from earlier sources. One such source, referred to in Register A, was the Rouen Roll: 'which was read to us and was transcribed in our register', according to a charter granted to Falaise in 1204.[17] Whether or not this indicates a previous register remains uncertain. It does seem possible that the beginning of Register A is made up

16. Baldwin, *Government*, p. 418.
17. *Recueil*, II, no. 790, pp. 368–9, p. 369: 'sicut continetur in rotulo qui coram nobis lectus fuit et in registro nostro transcriptus'; no. 806, pp. 385–6, p. 386: 'sicut in rotulo Rothomagensi continetur et in nostro similiter regesto continetur expressum'; no. 809, pp. 388–9, p. 389: 'que continentur in regesto nostro'; no. 828, pp. 405–7, p. 406: 'in registro nostro'.

of material copied from a previous register. It would then be like all the later ones, which were opened when new organization or more space was required, each copying what was still useful from its predecessor. Historians have been divided over this issue. Several have considered there to be a previous but now lost register, and some have made attempts to reconstruct it. Delisle, for example, argued that the earlier register had been kept from 1200 to 1204. Tuety agreed, and believed that Register A even mentioned its predecessor. He thought it possible to see that the added documents were all in chronological order. This school of thought also points to references in Philip's other acts of 'registro nostro' and similar phrases.[18]

But Delaborde and Baldwin have thought that all the references in Register A to a previous document are to the *Établissements* of Rouen. Baldwin's conclusion is that 'as yet, there is no compelling reason to hypothesize a lost register'.[19] Indeed the most obvious reading of Register A on this point is that the *Établissements* of Rouen were entered into the register as an example of significance for the granting of commune status, and that this was then referred to when a commune was granted to Niort three months later, hence demonstrating the usefulness of the register. So the new commune was granted on the same terms as those already written down: 'the customs of the commune of Rouen, which are contained in our register'.[20]

There has also been a debate over the nature of the registers. What exactly was being recorded? They seem to be an abbreviation of more complete documents, perhaps summarizing fuller documents in a speedy way for government use, picking out significant points. Delisle thought the scribes were working from minutes, copying up from abbreviated versions of material incorporated into fuller documents. Other historians have noted abbreviations and differences from the complete documents, but have considered this was simply a case of copyists using an existing register and making

18. Baldwin, *Government*, pp. 418, 588 n. 66, and see previous note.
19. Baldwin, *Government*, pp. 418, 586 n. 46.
20. *Recueil*, II, no. 789, pp. 362–7, the Rouen terms, at Falaise, May 1204; no. 828, pp. 405–7 for the later grant, at Poitiers in August 1204, p. 406: 'ut communiam suam habeant ad puncta et consuetudines communie Rothomagensis que continentur in registro nostro'.

errors in the process. However, the fact that some of the 'copies' have dates which the 'originals' lack rather undermines such an interpretation.[21] Recently one of the editors of the registers, Nortier, has argued that they are not copies, not minutes, and not the originals either, but 'a first redaction . . . a first draft containing the essence of the act'.[22] This, he argued, was then polished up in content and style as a finished act by trained notaries. He also postulates a reconstructed lost register, as 'Primitive A'.

Bisson on the other hand has hinted that the registers may have begun as the reconstruction of records after Fréteval. He believes that what William the Breton describes as lost is 'a good resumé' of Register A.[23] In the sixteenth century the guardian of the records, Jean du Tillet, took the registers home and failed to return them; his son, who made copies, says that he had seen *five* registers. This has been taken by some to suggest that another actual register, an earlier one, did then exist, but the evidence is shaky.

There is also the problem of the lengthy gap between the loss of documents at Fréteval in 1194 and the beginning of Register A in 1204. Although the reconstruction would not have been easy and would have taken some time, if the document was required for current and continued use, it would hardly have been ten years in the making. Also, none of the material in Register A seems to date from earlier than 1200, so by that argument we would need not only a Primitive A, but a Primitive 'proto A' as well; and although not impossible, that seems to be taking us too far away from an interpretation based on surviving documents.

All of these views are possible, none of them are proven. On the whole it seems likely that Register A was based on some existing documents used by the government for administration of the royal demesne. It seems likely that the existing document or documents used were not in the form of registers, as Nortier and Baldwin have already suggested.[24]

21. Nortier in Bautier, pp. 439, 440, who disagrees; *Recueil*, p. xviii.
22. Nortier in Bautier, pp. 440–1.
23. T.N. Bisson, 'Les comptes des domaines au temps de Philippe-Auguste: essai comparatif', pp. 521–39 in Bautier, p. 528; he also notes some exceptions.
24. Nortier in Bautier, p. 451; Baldwin, *Government*, p. 586, n. 46.

Coming in the early thirteenth century, when the great expansion was under way, the register could indicate the need then for a review of the position in the old demesne, with preparations for a new survey in new circumstances. The most likely conclusion is that Register A was an innovatory effort begun after 1200.

Our preference is therefore for the view that Register A represents some sort of new beginning in government records in the early thirteenth century. This view is not proven either, but seems a possible interpretation of the documents without having to stretch probability far. Register A would then be a new style of survey of what the king could obtain from the demesne, especially with regard to military service, in the period when that service was most needed against the Plantagenets. A date in the early thirteenth century for the actual origin of the registers could also be argued from the parallel development of a similar trend in governmental record-keeping in England at about the same time. The reign of King John and the keepership of Hubert Walter see the beginnings of English register-keeping, though it must be said not of the same nature as the Capetian registers, so that neither is directly derived from the other.[25]

The later registers inevitably took account of the new demesne lands and the new conquests in general, along with the broadening scope of royal government, but still with a dominating interest in military gain from towns, castles, knights and sergeants. Register C introduced a heading for military obligations from the recently acquired Normandy.[26] Virtually all the material has this military focus, since the entries mainly relate to the crown obtaining service and money in one way or another, even for example from the royal regalian rights, most of which could be used for warfare. The gaps and omissions argue for a new style of record, which had to be gradually put together, and was always being filled in as the omissions were realized.

The contents of the registers vary. Professor Baldwin makes the point that over 80 per cent of the inquests in the registers relate to ancient demesne lands and rights, but at the same time they introduce royal claims over the newly conquered

25. J. Gillingham, *The Angevin Empire* (London, 1984) pp. 50–1.
26. *Recueil*, p. xxiv; heading 4 is 'servitia militum Normannie'.

lands. Lists of nobles may be, as Baldwin suggests, related to the setting down of a hierarchy, but it seems more likely that they are there for the same reason as the lists of churches, to show royal rights not only in the demesne, but over individuals in the kingdom as a whole.[27]

Claims on military service form an important part of the register material. They cover a whole range of topics where the king had rights from which he could benefit: in towns, over forests, tolls, justice, castles, as well as regalian rights over churches. The registers also list some royal obligations to others, for example to pay *fiefs-rentes*, and they include matters of the moment which might bring immediate gain, such as lists of prisoners and hostages.

As we have seen, of the five registers labelled A to E, there are three originals: A, C and E; B and D being copies.[28] Register A contains lists of towns and castles in the demesne, and of men who owe services to the king. Its dominant theme is what military value the demesne has for the king. It dates from 1204 to 1206 and belongs to the key period of expansion, the conquest of the Plantagenet territories. It is held now in the Vatican. Additions were made to the initial lists as new information came in. It was kept in use until 1211 and contains 255 royal acts.

Register C, the second original, like all the registers except possibly the first, begins by copying from its predecessor any material which was still relevant. It was begun in 1211 and was redesigned under ten headings, new entries being made not in order of date only, but also according to category. The chapter headings included 'fees', 'alms', 'communes' and so on. Under the main headings are various subheadings, for example under 'fees' come 'fees of the lord king', these in turn were further subdivided, for instance the 'fees of the bailli of Rouen'. Register C remained open until 1220 and has 178 new acts entered in it.[29]

Register E, the third original, was made for Guérin de Glapion. It was begun in 1220 and copies all the still useful

27. Baldwin, *Government*, p. 250.
28. *Recueil*, pp. x, xxvi, xxxix; Baldwin, *Government*, pp. 585–6, n. 45; *Registres*, p. 6: the manuscripts are A (Vatican Ottoboni lat 2796; C (Archives nationales JJ7); E (Archives nationales JJ26).
29. *Registres*, p. 575; 'Feoda I, Elemosine II ... Communie V'; 'Capitula Feodorum Domini Regis ... Feoda ballivie Rothomagi'.

material from C. Again there were headings, which were reorganized with some additions, to make fourteen in total. Blank leaves were left for continuations. It contains 676 acts, 243 of which are new.[30] Some 463 of these acts are not known from other sources, so about a quarter of the known acts of Philip survive only because of the registers, which makes them an important source for this reason alone.

The major contents of the registers, as analysed by Baldwin, are: inquisitions, accounts, fees and services, chancery documents, securities, diverse charters, and miscellaneous material. Not only did they include such obvious documents as major charters, peace agreements, the legitimization of Philip's children by Agnes de Méran and judicial decisions, and such clearly necessary information as who owed what military service, but they also provided information likely to be useful in daily routine administration, such as lists of the names of kings, popes and cardinals; the genealogical connections of Queen Ingeborg; or an analysis of those with claims to the throne of England: a sort of handy encyclopedia for royal administrators.[31]

One persuasive suggestion about the function of the registers is that they became necessary once government found a fixed home for its records after the loss of existing records at Fréteval. The king's government was still largely itinerant, even if the records were not, so it became necessary to carry about certain vital information; therefore a copy of significant acts kept in the permanent archive was made, and travelled around with the king and his officials for their immediate reference.

Alternatively it might have been that full copies were made for the travelling government, and the register was a record, not complete, of what had been copied and taken. It is difficult to reach a conclusion, but our tentative preference is for the former thesis, that is to see the registers as working documents made for use by a travelling king when the originals were left in Paris for safety after the lesson of Fréteval. The lesson was always keep a copy! The publication in print of the text of the registers makes clear the

---

30. Nortier in Bautier, p. 436.
31. *Registres*, pp. 345–51, lists of rulers; pp. 549–53 the genealogical information; pp. 554–5 on the descendants of William the Conqueror.

enormous detail they contained, and in the words of Bautier, we can now see what Philip's government had to hand for working purposes.[32]

We have also noted a military emphasis in the registers, which is not surprising since war, law and order, and defence would commonly be the dominant concern of Philip on his travels. In our view the main function of the registers was to keep the king informed of the resources, in men, money and kind, which were available to him, and in particular to provide a ready reference for the military resources on which he could call.

We therefore postulate that the initial thrust behind the making of Register A was an urgent need for governmental information on resources for military use, and represents Philip's aggressive intentions with regard to the Angevin Empire. Certainly the registers reflect the significance of military matters to Philip's government, not only in terms of what men, resources and transport should be available, but also with regard to such matters as listing the arms and armaments handed over in the course of his wars with the Angevins, the hostages taken in order to try and keep the Flemish towns secure, and the names of the prisoners taken at Bouvines.[33]

. . .

FINANCIAL ADMINISTRATION

The surviving records make it possible to examine Capetian finance in this period in a manner not possible earlier. Even so, those records are incomplete, often fragmentary, and leave many awkward questions. The existing records were lost at Fréteval in 1194, though there was an attempt to reconstruct them, and financial records of a kind begin from 1190, the Testament of that year giving at least an outline of financial administration. There was a fire in 1737 when further vital records were destroyed. Fortunately Brussel

---

32. *Registres*, p. 3.
33. *Registres*, p. 518, for example, lists arms and armaments handed over in 1213 to Guy of Dampierre in the Tower of Riom, including bows, hauberks, helmets and shields. The hostage lists are pp. 558–61; the prisoners pp. 561–6.

had before then published important extracts from the records for 1202–3, 1217 and 1219, on which modern study largely depends. Nortier, in 1978, discovered a new financial account from 1221, which is especially valuable for hinting at development late in the reign. According to the Testament, accounts were to be rendered in Paris three times a year. There they would be inspected by six named citizens of Paris and by Adam the Clerk. Adam was to make a record of the transactions and the treasure was to be stored in the Temple in locked chests. The first accounts to survive are from 1202–3, which are also the most complete set for the reign, giving the transactions of the prévôts and baillis.[34] There are also fragmentary surviving accounts from 1212, 1217, 1218, 1219, 1220 and 1222. Although incomplete, they confirm the thrice annual accounting at Purification, Ascension and All Saints, but the Templars now took over the role given to the Parisian citizens in 1190. The accounts were presented under main headings, a mix of territorial, military and official topics: under payments from prévôts, baillis, sergeants and the marches.[35]

Accounts by themselves are insufficient to give a full picture of royal finance if they lack a balance of receipt and expenditure, as these do. From a comparison with later records, it seems likely that various sources of income, including cash revenues, are not recorded under Philip, though they probably existed. It means that although we can give a picture of royal finance, can see it increasing, and something of the methods employed in collecting and accounting, still we cannot give an accurate view of the entire budget. Bisson has pointed out the importance of combining our information from smaller ancient accounts, and from the *prisia*, together with the financial information in the registers, and other not specifically financial documents.[36]

The comments on finance made by Conon of Béthune reveal the uncertainties that remain in this area. He was the prévôt of the cathedral of Lausanne and, after Philip's death, he claimed to have overheard Philip's officials talking among

34. These are the accounts called 'the first budget' by Lot and Fawtier, but as Bautier comments, 'misguidedly' (*abusivement*) so-called, *Registres*, p. 2.
35. Bisson in Bautier, p. 528; Hallam, p. 165.
36. Bisson in Bautier, pp. 525–7.

themselves about royal finances. He reported them as saying that Philip had inherited £19,000 from Louis VII. But no one is certain what the amount refers to. Is it the ordinary income for a year? for a month? Is it income only from the demesne? Conon thought that Philip had increased royal income 'beyond what can be believed'; and this reaction is possibly the most significant aspect of what he says. We may not know exactly what his figures refer to, but we know what someone who lived at the time thought about the results of Philip's financial policies. What we have does demonstrate an effective financial administration, an increase in the efficiency of record-keeping, and an increase in revenues coming to the crown.

The usual method of examining the finances of Philip is to make a division between regular fixed income on the one hand, and occasional and extraordinary income on the other. This makes sense, because the records themselves make this distinction, and the officials were often associated respectively with one or the other: the prévôts with the regular income, the baillis with the extraordinary. It has been calculated that 30 per cent of revenue came from regular income, and as much as 70 per cent from occasional income.

The main sources of regular income were the royal demesne, justice, and the towns. The registers include headings for particular kinds of regular income: fixed revenues, census accounts, revenues from agriculture, woods, meadows, fish, mills, markets, rents; revenues from rights over patronage, from tolls, mints, customs and so on. Often agreements were made to commute services for payments, for instance instead of *gîte* or the obligation to give hospitality to the king the bishop of Beauvais agreed to pay £200 per annum instead of standing the cost of three royal visits each year.

All such due payments had to be collected. In the same way the regalian rights over vacant churches meant that collections must be made; sometimes an agreement was made to remit rights in exchange for regular payment. Hence the need for lists of places to which the collecting agents needed to go. By the later registers there are listed some seventy-three places which owed *gîte*, and seventy others which owed a payment in lieu of *gîte*. There are records of what had to be paid out in expenses by the prévôts: to towns, in alms, as *fiefs-rentes* and salaries.

One of the problems in calculating royal income is the extent of the occasional payments. These varied tremendously, some were very valuable, but often the amounts are difficult to know. Sometimes a chronicler makes reference to a large payment, but even then one is uncertain of the accuracy from such a source. There were reliefs on succession which Philip was assiduous in collecting, such as 5,000 marks from Baldwin of Flanders in 1191; 7,000 marks from Renaud of Boulogne in 1192; 20,000 marks from King John in 1200; and possibly the 24,000 marks promised by Richard the Lionheart in 1189.[37]

The attack on the Jews was another lucrative policy which brought in a great deal for a short time, though some of this wealth was diverted to other beneficiaries, including the Church. The Jews were accused of various crimes, including torture of Christian debtors, and usury which the Church condemned. In Brie-Comte-Robert, ninety-nine Jews were burnt to death. In the royal demesne they were dispossessed in 1180, then ransomed and expelled in 1182: 'ejected from his [Philip's] own towns and castles', their property being confiscated and redistributed. Christians who were liberated from their debts had to make a contribution of one-fifth to the treasury for 'the protection of the realm'; 'from which expulsion he received an immense sum of money from French Christians'. This raised immediate amounts for the king, as well as allowing gifts to be made to the Church and others. Thus in 1183 Philip granted to the bishop of Paris the synagogue in the city, 'in which the Jews are wont to pray', to turn into a church. While to the marshal, Matthew de Bourges, went 'a house at Bourges which had belonged to a Jew called Isaac Uradis'. Then in 1198 the Jews were allowed to return, though it was 'against the general wish, and despite his own edict'.[38] They were able to continue making profits for the royal benefit: some £1,200 in 1203, £7,550 in 1217.

37. Baldwin, *Government*, pp. 171, 50–1.
38. William the Breton, *Philippide*, ed. Guizot, p. 35; 'Philippide', ed. Delaborde, II, p. 37, l. 766: 'nonaginta novem'; II, pp. 22–5, p. 22, l. 376: 'parte sibe quinta pro regni jure tuendo'; Giselbert of Mons *La Chronique de Gislebert de Mons*, ed. L. Vanderkindere, Recueil des textes pour servir à l'étude de l'histoire de Belgique (Brussels, 1904) p. 163; Rigord, ed. Guizot, p. 140; Rigord, ed. Delaborde, I, p. 141: 'contra omnium hominum opinionem'.

Philip's marriages brought in additional occasional cash, not least 21,000 marks from the unhappy Danes for his marriage to Ingeborg. Some taxes were occasional rather than regular, for example those in support of crusades. The heavy and arbitrary nature of these, such as the demand of a tithe for the Third Crusade, led to resistance, which in this case proved successful. It was the high rate of the Saladin Tithe, as well as its broad application, which aroused so much concern; but from 1215 ecclesiastical tenths were tried on other occasions, and not always with papal permission. Vacancies in bishoprics were fairly regular, and though not very numerous, they could bring in a considerable amount of money to the crown.

The main knowledge of detailed finance must come from an examination of the surviving accounts. One problem is that they do not give total income, only an account of what was received under certain headings. But total ordinary revenue for a year has been calculated to have been about £115,000, from the 1202–3 record. This did not include certain known payments during that year, such as the relief of 20,000 marks paid by King John as a result of the agreement at Le Goulet, or the *prisée des sergeants* for the year.

The latter was mainly a means of obtaining money in lieu of personal military service, levied generally upon the greater towns such as Paris, which alone paid something like £4,000. The *prisée des sergeants* was a list of quotas of the military service, commuted payments and related obligations, owed from the *prévôtés*: from the towns, villages, abbeys and communes of the demesne. The earliest known of these is from 1194 and was revised in 1204. By then, from eighty-three named places came over 8,000 sergeants and 138 carts, to the value of £11,693.[39]

Even from the fragmentary records it is clear that royal income was increasing progressively through the reign and at a considerable rate, a rise of 72 per cent between the beginning of the reign and 1203. It is also clear that it was a successful operation and more was collected than spent. A good deal came from better management of existing resources, for example a considerable improvement of income

---

39. G. Duby, *France in the Middle Ages, 987–1460*, trans. J. Vale (Oxford, 1991) p. 176.

from the forests of the demesne, something like a 350 per cent increase. The large surplus was stored in the Temple, a balance of at least £60,000 on the one year. Of course Philip had his major expenses, not least in the frequent warfare in the earlier half of the reign, but it is not easy to point to a sounder financial system in the period than his. The 1221 record suggests an overall ordinary income of almost £195,000, a 69 per cent increase since 1203.[40]

It was the chamber which received these payments and recorded them. The chamberlains were the principal financial officials and dealt with money matters at court, but the establishment of the Temple meant that a permanent treasury was separated off from the court. From 1210 this was under the care of the Templar, Brother Haymard, who also took charge of the Norman exchequer for Philip later.[41]

It is not at all sure, as is usually stated, that French development was far behind that of Flanders and the Plantagenet lands. The only evidence for this is that the French records appear later, but that does not mean they started later. When they do survive, they show at least some facets in advance of neighbouring systems: Flanders for example accounted far more in kind than did the Capetian system; Philip's administration in Normandy seems an advance over the seneschal system of organization which it replaced. In fact many of the new developments seem to have occurred at about the same time in all these parts of north-western Europe.

Philip was cautious in his approach to finance, prepared to drop the Saladin Tithe when it aroused strong opposition, careful not to spend more than he could afford in largesse, patronage or gifts – even to the Church. This aroused criticism: the troubadours and poets moaned about his meanness. As Bertran de Born said, 'a rich young man who doesn't like spending on courts, and war, cannot gain glory'. Philip saved surpluses since, as he said, his 'predecessors were too poor'. According to Rigord, he was able to amass treasure because his expenses were modest.[42] In the record for 1221,

40. Baldwin, *Government*, pp. 155, 256, 247.
41. Luchaire in Lavisse, p. 244.
42. Bertran de Born, *The Poems of the Troubadour Bertran de Born*, ed. W.D. Paden Jr, T. Sankovitch and P.H. Stäblein (Berkeley, CA, 1986) p. 193, ll. 12–13; R-H. Bautier, 'La place du règne de Philippe Auguste dans l'histoire de la France médiévale', pp. 11–27 in Bautier, p. 23.

covering one term, the income recorded in this late stage of the reign was £73,000, the expenditure £44,000, which left a very fair balance. Thus Philip could provide for the exceptional expenses of warfare and emerge triumphant. In his will he left some £600,000.

The changes of the reign are significant: the appearance of a new bureau of accounts in Paris, along with a permanent treasury, and regular accounting by prévôts and baillis preserved in archives.[43] The accounting system for the demesne was altered and the revenue increased, allowing for checks and for better control. Royal and Parisian domination increased. There was a move towards unification of the currency; and, though it was not fully achieved, the Parisian pound became more widely used. In the newly acquired Angevin lands the pound Tournois was retained, also gaining ascendancy over other units in that area. In the end the Parisian currency would win everywhere.[44]

. . .

THE ADMINISTRATION OF JUSTICE

As with finance, so with Capetian justice, surviving records allow a better view of this aspect of royal government than is possible at any previous period. The earliest records come from Capetian Normandy, though again records which are not specifically judicial provide some earlier information.

Royal officials had a function as judges as well as in other spheres. Many royal acts were judicial decisions, often given in the form of an agreement or concord. The royal court was an actual judicial court as well as a social group. Many vital judgements against the great were made in it, as against King John, or Renaud count of Boulogne. The king was pressing to become the arbiter in all judgements concerning the great men of the land.

Philip's entourage became more legally expert than had previously been possible. A growth in the use of notaries and lawyers led to the formation of what was virtually a new profession.[45] There were now professionally trained men com-

43. Bisson in Bautier, pp. 529–30.
44. F. Dumas, 'La monnaie dans le royaume au temps de Philippe-Auguste', pp. 541–74 in Bautier, pp. 546–8.
45. Duby, *France*, p. 174.

ing from the schools and the new universities, and their part in Philip's government was considerable. Philip himself had a legalistic mind, and invariably in his major invasions or aggressions took care to find a legal defence for his actions, whether it be from papal approval or from a relevant decision of his own court. In France the decision-making aspect of the court, and of assemblies, was primarily judicial; the process of making important political decisions which involved consultation with the nation was judicial in origin.

In Philip's reign we see assemblies for example at Chinon in 1205, Soissons in 1213 or Melun in 1216. They have been called the 'embryo' of the Estates General. They were not so much regional assemblies as national assemblies carrying out regional business. It was a legally minded age, in which customs were written down, judgements recorded and collected. It was, as a result, the age when French customary law emerged: the law not so much of local lords, but the law 'of the land'.[46]

The king delegated royal authority, especially to his baillis, who were in one sense royal itinerant justices, holding assizes to give justice and receive appeals. In his absence, Philip allowed complaints against the baillis to be heard by the regents in Paris; in his presence, he himself was the final arbiter. It was also true at lower levels. On occasion the king would defer judgement, and leave to named persons the task of arbitrating the solution to a problem, he himself promising to guarantee the decision. According to Baldwin, this became 'the preferred method for resolving disputes in the royal courts' by the latter part of the reign. Sworn inquests also became common practice, used for 22 per cent of decisions.[47]

Justice was an important source of revenue, accounting for at least 7 per cent of the total royal income, and probably more. This gave Philip a financial as well as a power-seeking motive to extend royal justice. Another obvious aim of justice was to maintain law and order. Settling disputes was one way of attaining this, and preventing men from turning to violence in order to get their way. If the king's justice was

46. Petit-Dutaillis, pp. 237–8, 241; P. Ourliac, 'Législation, coutumes et coutumiers au temps de Philippe Auguste', pp. 471–88, in Bautier, p. 471.
47. Baldwin, *Government*, pp. 43, 42.

enforced, it became respected, and if it was respected it would be resorted to and become even more effective. Philip encouraged the use of royal justice beyond what had previously been the case, both in geographical jurisdiction and in juridical competence.

Law and order was not always easy to maintain. In a land where famine occurred on average every fourth year, where warfare was common and destructive, where lords were used to turning to private war for their rights, where mercenary bands demanded ransoms from travellers on the highway, the king's task was difficult. At least one lord and his wife abused their power, employing it to penalize peasants by various mutilations: blinding, slitting breasts, tearing out nails.

It was a common sight to see peasants fleeing from their homes, driving flocks into the woods in the hope of saving them, watching their crops burned and destroyed in war: 'the smoke spreads, the flames rise'. A troubadour wrote ironically of the warrior class: 'honour lies in stealing cattle, sheep and lambs'. While Jacques de Vitry declared: 'all that the peasant amasses in a year ... the knight, the noble, devours in an hour ... the fruit of their years of pain and sorrow is extorted from them'. He added that knights made soothing promises in church, but in practice 'they do the opposite'.[48]

Increasingly the Church condemned mercenaries, who were often labelled as heretics, but they were also vital in royal and magnate armies and were even, for example, employed by the crusaders against the Albigensian heretics. Unemployed roaming bands, or those used in private war, were the biggest threat to order. There was a mass reaction against noble and mercenary abuses (as noted in Chapter 2), which erupted in a peasant movement led by the carpenter Durand, partly inspired by the Church's peace movement, a reaction which the king needed to harness. The peasants were angered by the failure of the authorities to keep order, and took the task upon themselves. They formed a sworn brotherhood, and wore a white uniform as well as a scarf with a motto on it; they even proved strong enough to defeat

48. A. Luchaire, *Social France at the Time of Philip Augustus*, trans. E.B. Krehbiel (New York, 1912) p. 261 from 'Lorrains', p. 253 from the troubadour Giraud de Borneil, pp. 254, 274 from a letter of Peter of Blois.

mercenary bands. The movement got out of hand, and the gentry and the local Church preferred a system of royal justice and keeping order to one which allowed power in peasant hands. The brotherhood was crushed by 1184, but it had demonstrated the strong yearning of the ordinary population for better order.

Our previous argument, that Philip sought peace through diplomacy, is relevant also to the keeping of order. Warfare was perhaps the most damaging of all events for the peasant and the citizen, for crops and trade; bringing peace was of benefit to the nation. Philip's long reign was in general a period of political stability, and the eventual defeat of his enemies with his triumph at Bouvines resulted in a stronger peace than France had known for many a year. Philip may not always have been successful in keeping order, but he was assiduous and determined in his efforts. When his own hired troops rebelled over pay, he summoned them to Bourges as if they were about to be paid, and then arrested and fined them for their offences. And he was always intent on increasing royal control over the activities of the warrior class. When Philip was able to, for example, he carefully tied up deals over castles in a legally binding manner, so that castle-holding came 'within the protection of the law', and private war went into decline.[49]

When Burgundian lords were charged with stopping merchants on the highway and robbing them, Philip responded by leading an expedition against them. Such action both pleased the Church and the populace, and increased the prestige of royal authority. The defence of the Church often involved dealing with lords who were taking the law into their own hands, often seizing Church property, and we have seen how frequently the Church turned to Philip for aid, and how consistently he gave it.

There was some rationalization of the judicial process. In France, as in England and at Rome, the practice of ordeal and trial by battle was losing favour. Decisions by inquest and the use of sworn juries were replacements. Peter the Chanter led the criticism of what he saw as barbaric and Germanic

49. C. Coulson, 'Fortress-policy in Capetian tradition and Angevin practice: aspects of the conquest of Normandy by Philip II', *ANS*, VI, 1983, pp. 13–38, pp. 34–5, though the quote is from Charles Coulson's own synopsis of this paper provided for members of the Battle conference.

practice, deriding those who expected God to judge in this manner: 'thou shalt not tempt the Lord thy God'. He quoted an example of a priest found guilty by ordeal of murder and hanged, only for the victim to turn up alive and well. It is an argument familiar in modern times over the death penalty. As Peter said, why, if they believed that God truly gave a judgement in the trial by battle, did they trouble to choose the best fighter as their representative? And if they believed in the efficacy of ordeal by water, why only use it on lesser folk and not on everyone? The reforming attitude for the replacement of the crude process of the ordeal was pursued by Philip in his own lands, and was also imposed on Normandy after the conquest.[50]

The count of Flanders claimed the right to trial by his peers in 1216, but this does not mean that the later idea of an exclusive and definable number of noble individuals was intended; more likely he meant right to trial in the royal court. The demand probably also implied a criticism of the employment of any but great nobles in positions of importance at court, seeing lesser men as unworthy to be in authority over greater. But in judgements over princes by the court, and in judgements over the populace by royal representatives, with royal justice also extending beyond the demesne, something akin to a national system of law was emerging.

Although Philip was prepared to give the Church courts their place, he was insistent on the rights of secular justice. Despite ecclesiastical protest, Philip Augustus was not averse to using churchmen trained in the law to supervise his own secular courts. And even bishops, such as Manasses of Orléans, were called to answer before his courts in Paris. In 1221 the bishop of Paris complained that the king's court was dealing with a case which should belong to the Church; but Philip told him that a bishop had no right to interfere and the prelate, albeit under protest, left the court to its business. As Innocent III used the argument of 'reason of sin' to claim jurisdiction over many matters which had once been thought secular, so Philip used the argument that matters relating to lands and secular duties were his sphere, even if they involved clerics. Philip was a good defender of what he

50. Baldwin, *Masters*, pp. 326, 324–32; William the Breton, *Philippide*, ed. Guizot, p. 222; 'Philippide', ed. Delaborde, II, pp. 218–19.

agreed were the rights of the Church, but he was an even tougher defender of what he claimed as royal rights.

It is interesting that in the *exempla*, one of the major images of Philip was that of the just king. Philip's acts contained a great deal on the definition of rights, not only of the king but of his subjects, including for example the rights of widows.[51] This too was a great contribution to the system of law, because by defining what the king's justice was protecting, Philip was also stating the main purposes of justice. At the same time as a local, territorial, customary law was being recognized, the king was producing a series of acts which went beyond the localities and offered an overall national protection in certain matters.

. . .

THE EFFECTS OF EXPANSION ON GOVERNMENT

There is no question but that the position of the crown was dramatically improved during the reign of Philip Augustus. He 'increased and wondrously multiplied the kingdom of France', and his administration and his justice grew too.[52] The demesne was perhaps four times larger than it had been. Not only that, but the power of the great princes had been severely reduced, and the monarchy's role throughout the realm was more influential.

In any discussion of the changes in methods of government, the effect of territorial expansion has always loomed large. Many historians have argued that it was the main factor in initiating change. Of course the added lands did require change in government: there was a greater area to administer, there was a need to expand the administration in order to cope, there were problems in dealing with regions more distant from Paris. But our argument has been that the changes were of degree rather than kind: that existing Capetian methods were introduced into new areas, rather than that either the traditions of those areas altered Capetian methods, or that the new situation caused revolutionary change in France as a whole.

51. Le Goff in Bautier, p. 148; Ourliac in Bautier, p. 495.
52. Duby, *France*, p. 227, from 'Grandes Chroniques de France'.

It has generally been assumed that Plantagenet and even Flemish methods were well ahead of the Capetian. This is because of the survival of financial records in those areas before they survive for the Capetians. But, as suggested earlier, this is more probably because of the loss and destruction of French royal records for the earlier period. The more likely scenario is that changes in financial method were fairly common to neighbouring states, and were proceeding at much the same pace throughout north-western Europe. Again, as suggested, one finds that although the *Gros Bref* of Flanders is earlier than any similar French royal record, it is also more ancient in style, with its accounting in kind, than is the case when the earliest Capetian records do appear.

It has also been proposed that the most significant administrative change under Philip, the employment of baillis, was borrowed from the Anglo-Norman itinerant justices, but this too is uncertain, and the baillis had a different and broader function than the itinerant justices. Baldwin believes that it was the expansion which 'created the need for inventories and registers', and it cannot be denied that the broader the area the greater the need.[53] But the first register possibly predates the major expansion in Normandy, or at least is co-existent with it. Probably the initial spur was the need for military support in order to achieve the expansion, rather than the expansion itself.

The question then remains, what changes did occur in the areas into which Philip expanded? Did he borrow methods from them, or did he impose his own system? The key area is Normandy, where Philip shaped the region to fit existing Capetian methods: the Plantagenet seneschalcy was abolished, his own baillis were brought in, and no Norman was used as a bailli until 1243. Philip never took the title of duke in Normandy, abolished the former central institutions, including its treasury, and integrated the duchy into France.[54] In the Church in Normandy too, the major new appointments were of men from outside the duchy. But it was a gradual business, with a certain amount of backtracking when thought necessary, for example the Exchequer

---

53. Baldwin, *Government*, p. 394; cf. pp. 220, 250, 260.
54. L. Musset, 'Quelques problèmes posés par l'annexion de la Normandie au domaine royale français', pp. 291–309 in Bautier, pp. 297–8, 303–4, 300; Baldwin, *Government*, pp. 359, 280.

was re-established in 1207, and survived at Falaise to 1220, though always under direct Capetian supervision.

In other Plantagenet lands, change was less drastic and Philip was prepared to accept existing magnate seneschals to act for him. This was true of Poitou and Anjou, where Aimery de Thouars and William des Roches were retained. But they were instructed on how to proceed with their accounting and, according to William the Breton, their powers – at least of William des Roches – were reduced. This almost certainly was a result of Philip's relative political weakness in those areas, rather than of long-term administrative intent. It was also a consequence of the decentralized nature of power in those regions under the previous regime; Poitou for example has been seen as made up of regional lordships.[55] In the southern Plantagenet lands royal or external power had never been great, whether operated by the Capetians or the Plantagenets.

Normandy, much of which he brought directly into the royal demesne, and to which he always gave priority, is the key to Philip's intentions. He took over directly the larger estates whose lords had stayed with King John, including those of the earls of Warenne, Arundel, Leicester and Clare, and declared that: 'all other lands of knights who are in England, are equally our demesne'.[56] A number of his loyal servants were planted in Normandy on magnate estates, including Peter de Thillai and Cadoc, who was granted the Tosny lands and whose daughter married a Norman knight; both these men incidentally were also to become baillis; Henry Clément, Bartholomew de Roye, and Walter the Young were also among those given Norman lands.

One interesting change in Normandy, after the conquest and the immediate introduction of Capetian baillis, was a reorganization of that system itself in the former duchy. At the time of the first royal register, there were some thirteen baillages; by 1220 this had been cut to eight, and a year later to six. This is so drastic and consistent a change that it must be deliberate. The baillis were reduced in number,

55. Gillingham, *Angevin Empire*, p. 56; William the Breton, *Philippide*, ed. Guizot, p. 224; R. Hajdu, 'Castles, castellans and the structure of politics in Poitou', *JMH*, IV, 1978, pp. 27–53, pp. 34, 37, 43; R.V. Turner, *King John* (Harlow, 1994) p. 83.
56. Musset in Bautier, p. 297.

and therefore each individual bailli became more powerful.[57] What it seems to represent is the change from Plantagenet to Capetian methods. Plantagenet divisions for administration survived for a time but were soon adapted to fit the system of powerful baillis used already in Philip's demesne.

In Flanders there was not the same need for change, since baillis had been introduced by Count Philip of Alsace at about the same time they were being employed in his own territories by Philip Augustus. But in Flanders their role was not quite as dominant as in France, since they tended to be under the authority of noble castellans. One change which occurred was to merge the county of Flanders into the broader French system, so that 'in effect, Flanders was ruled from Paris'.[58]

One major result of the expansion was an increase in revenue, and this occurrence cannot be questioned. There may have also been an increase in expenditure, but income expanded as well as turnover. It has been calculated that royal income more than doubled as a result of the expansion.[59] Normandy was a significant contributor, and it has been reckoned that income from Anjou, Aquitaine and Normandy totalled about £27,000 a year.

There was also a political effect of the expansion. The new monarchy was more powerful than the old. Philip ruled more land, and he ruled it more effectively. He could call more certainly on a greater military service or money in lieu of service. Philip's rule may not have always been light – he was too careful a monarch for that – but it often proved less burdensome and less hated than that of John. The speed with which many of the barons transferred their allegiance from King John to Philip Augustus was a sign of that. Instability had begun under John, with his massive confiscations of land, before the conquest ever occurred. Some in due course would wish to back away from Philip too, but his regime never earned as evil a reputation as John's.

There was a transfer in landholding, not far from revolutionary in its proportions. A third of the land of the lay lords changed hands, yet Philip's management was good

57. Baldwin, *Government*, p. 224.
58. D. Nicholas, *Medieval Flanders* (Harlow, 1992) pp. 87, 154.
59. Baldwin, *Government*, p. 243.

enough to cope without arousing any large-scale reaction or rebellion, though William the Breton suggests that there was certainly some resentment.[60] And, for the new lands, Philip also brought one great benefit, peace; in the main they would now prosper.

It is clear that the transformation of the Capetian monarchy which Philip was able to achieve, depended to a large extent on a greater royal control over administration in general, and finance and justice in particular. The registers and other surviving documents give a clearer picture of Philip's government at work than it is possible to paint for any of his predecessors. This evidence also shows the king's personal influence upon his officials and upon the structure of offices. It was part of his achievement that this structure was built and that the monarchy could profit from it. The subject matter of this chapter is not at first sight exciting or earth-shattering: the daily routine of administration. To some it might seem the rather boring detail on which all bureaucracy depends. But it is from such work that all great governments, rulers and leaders derive their power. And Philip not only used his administration to good advantage, but also guided its development.

In the end perhaps Philip's reputation and significance depend even more upon such things as registers, charters and finance records than upon the more dramatic events of Château-Gaillard or Bouvines. The transformation of Capetian kingship rested upon a secure financial system and a judicial system which was growing in its range and authority. The territorial expansion which Philip achieved did not fundamentally alter the Capetian system, but it moved it on to a new scale. Taken together, the transformation and the expansion make the reign of Philip Augustus one of the most crucial periods in French history.

---

60. Musset in Bautier, pp. 294, 300; William the Breton, *Philippide*, ed. Guizot, p. 221; 'Philippide', ed. Delaborde, II, pp. 218–19.

Chapter 10

TRIUMPH AT BOUVINES

Philip Augustus confirmed the reputation which he had earned in Normandy of Philip the Conqueror, by an even more dramatic victory against a combination of his enemies in the battle of Bouvines in 1214. Philip has in the past been given the reputation of a wily, rather tricky manipulator, timid, even cowardly. The tendency of English historians has been to point out that William the Breton was eulogizing Philip, and to make this sufficient excuse for ignoring what after all is our best source for Philip's character. We do not, in a similar case, normally ignore the views of the chroniclers closest to English kings. It still is necessary to revive these close views of Philip in order to balance the image in many modern minds. If Philip was such a feeble, unpleasant figure, how did he keep so many men loyal to him, and how did he win the greatest battle of his age? We do not claim that Philip was a perfect human being, only that he was an effective and able king, a warrior and leader as well as a diplomat and administrator.

William the Breton gives the most detailed account of the battle of Bouvines, but it is also well covered by other sources, and better reported than the great majority of medieval battles. It was a great military victory, and it was a great political triumph. Oman thought it the victory to which 'modern France owes its existence'.[1] The significance of Bouvines is a European one, it perhaps affected the history of more regions than any other western medieval battle: the security of France; the fate of the Angevin Empire, the downfall of

1. C. Oman, *A History of the Art of War in the Middle Ages*, 2 vols (London, 1924) I, p. 467.

King John before the English barons; the fall of the Holy
Roman Emperor, Otto IV (1209–14), and the accession of
his successor Frederick II (1215–50); the fate of Flanders,
Hainault and Boulogne, and of their respective counts; more
indirectly the fate of Poitou. Above all it left Philip as the
dominant ruler in western Europe.

. . .

PHILIP'S ARMY

By the early years of the thirteenth century Philip already
had considerable military success to his name and a long
experience of warfare. He had been on the Third Crusade
and fought against Richard the Lionheart in the West. He
had survived a long and bruising war against the Plantagenets. His army was therefore a well-tried instrument, the
means of raising and maintaining it having been lubricated
by years of practice.

Success, especially against John, brought additional wealth,
and this was demonstrated in the military power now at his
call. Philip had already threatened, though not carried out,
an invasion of England. His services were in demand from
the Church for its own purposes, not least to assist further
crusades and to deal with the Cathars. But Philip's priority
was to maintain control of his conquests, and further to sub-
due Flanders. The crushing of the latter had been a gradual
and cumulative process. Philip's intentions had been made
clear in 1213, when he used the redundant force prepared
against England to inflict punishment on Flanders. The
campaign was not a great success, but it showed both his
priority and his readiness for action in that quarter.

Like all forces of the period, Philip's army relied on a variety of resources: feudal, hired, and negotiated. Philip could
call on in total some 3,000 knights, 9,000 sergeants, 6,000
men from urban militias, and as many thousands of foot
sergeants as he was prepared to hire.[2] In a large and increasing realm, it was not practicable to call on all the possible
resources on every occasion. But Philip, like others, had a

2. J.F. Verbruggen, *The Art of Warfare in Western Europe During the Middle
Ages*, trans. S. Willard and S.C.M. Southern (Amsterdam, 1977)
pp. 142–3, is the basis for the given figures, which are, however, my
own estimates.

permanent force around him in his household troops, and
the means of raising such other forces as were needed for
garrisons or campaigns. Feudal levies were relatively lightly
used, and usually called upon from regions closely related
to the area of conflict.

A part of the victory against King John in Normandy had
been in the conflict between their purses, and between their
pull as attractive lords to serve. Both, for example, had sought
to win soldiers from areas such as Flanders who were keen
to fight for pay, whether for direct cash through captains, or
for rewards such as lands or *fiefs-rentes*. The registers show
Philip's activities in this respect, in winning over men in sensitive areas such as the borders of Normandy and the Loire
Valley. Philip was not, however, an extravagant paymaster; he
paid only for what he felt was needed at the time. Nevertheless the role of such hired troops had become invaluable.

The increasingly professional attitude of armies is partly
due to this development, at command level as well as in
fighting terms. Richard and John, as well as Philip, placed
great reliance on the advice of professional captains, usually
called mercenaries. In Philip's case, the role of Cadoc was
of great value, and he was rewarded accordingly, becoming
lord of Gaillon. But Cadoc was no longer on hand by the
time of Bouvines.

By this time, however, Philip's well of advice was perhaps
a little broader and deeper than most. At Bouvines it was no
mercenary captain who appeared as the king's chief adviser,
but a cleric, none other than the bishop-elect of Senlis,
Guérin de Glapion. It may be true that the latter owed his
promotion in the Church more to his usefulness than to his
saintliness, and he was a member of Philip's close circle in
the household, but he was obviously experienced and shrewd
in matters of war. Professor Baldwin saw the initial move
at Bouvines as 'Guérin's strategy', perhaps better called his
tactics. Verbruggen refers to the tactical command of the
cleric; while one historian considers that Philip left the
command to Guérin, and another that the bishop-elect was
'the strategist of Bouvines'.[3] We shall need to review these

3. J.W. Baldwin, *The Government of Philip Augustus* (Berkeley, CA, 1986)
   p. 219; Verbruggen, p. 198; G. Bordonove, *Philip Augustus* (Paris, 1986)
   p. 239; A. Luchaire, *Social France at the Time of Philip Augustus*, trans.
   E.B. Krehbiel (New York, 1912) p. 160.

opinions in due course, but in general they seem to give too large a role to the cleric who was Philip's adviser rather than his general.

At the heart of Philip's force, as we have seen, were the troops culled from the royal demesne, who owed a particular allegiance to him. This focus on men coming from the demesne has been shown by analyses of the troops actually serving to be true both of the commanders who were drawn from the household and of the men fighting in the field. The army, as we noted earlier, has been called 'a domanial affair'.[4] This is taking it too far, certainly for major campaigns and conflicts such as Bouvines, but it contains more than a grain of truth.

Many of the records Philip kept, as we have stressed, related to military matters. The lists he was so keen on keeping most frequently contained resources for the army, whether it be in military service owed or items of military value such as wagons or pack horses, and also included newly acquired military assets. Philip could, for example, now call on some thirty knights from the Vexin and sixty from Ponthieu. Like Henry II and the count of Flanders, the French king had also streamlined and rationalized the military service owed to him. If we follow Susan Reynolds, the working out of a system to raise what we call 'feudal' forces was largely developed by Philip himself and his contemporaries.[5]

In looking at Bouvines, we must not forget the fact that Philip's army was not geared primarily to fighting battles. Like all great contemporary commanders, Philip generally avoided battle. What he sought was dominance and control, most often achieved through negotiation and by siege warfare. What he mainly needed was sufficient force to guarantee his desired effect, to employ for immediate action when required, and also adequate troops for permanent garrison work. However, the same resources could be galvanized, if need be, for larger-scale campaigns and for battle by organic expansion from those permanently in arms on his behalf.

The army employed at Bouvines was only a part of the forces which could be available to the king. Even during such

4. Baldwin, *Government*, pp. 280–1, and see above ch. 8 n. 64.
5. Baldwin, *Government*, pp. 280–1; S. Reynolds, *Fiefs and Vassals* (Oxford, 1994) p. 320.

a vital campaign, garrisons had to be maintained, at least in skeletal form, for key strongholds throughout the realm. The attack by King John in the south, deliberately intended to coincide with the northern war, also on this occasion required a second large Capetian force in the field, whose command was given to Prince Louis. The army at Bouvines was therefore probably a relatively small army for such a crucial conflict.

Estimates of the army's size vary considerably and can hardly be more than informed guesses at the best. Even recent suggestions still show a wide range of difference, from 5,000 to 50,000 men. The number of knights can be more closely worked out, and probably did not exceed 2,000, some 750 or so of whom came from the royal demesne. There were also about the same number of mounted warriors obtained by other means, and generally referred to as mounted sergeants. These it would seem were 'armed as knights'.[6] Some crossbowmen were also mounted, but these were probably still not in very large numbers.

Verbruggen thought that cavalry was 'scarce on both sides', but it seems likely that the cavalry was in normal proportion for an army of the times. The 'scarceness' was probably no more than a reflection of the modest size of the armies involved.[7] Horsemen were well armoured, one reason for the relatively small number of deaths recorded in the conflicts of the age. William the Breton thought that 'modern men take much more care to protect themselves than did the ancients'.[8] Their horses were also barded or protected. The accounts of the fighting at Bouvines make it clear that actually to kill a horse, and even more a knight, required some deft yanking at metal protection or careful aiming through narrow spaces such as eye-slits.

The feudal forces incorporated their own infantry, and additional infantry forces were hired. At Bouvines one of the increasingly important factors in manpower for war became

---

6. Baldwin, *Government*, pp. 285, 287; Oman, p. 467; Bordonove, pp. 207, 222; P. Contamine, 'L'armée de Philippe Auguste', in R-H. Bautier, *La France de Philippe Auguste, le Temps des Mutations* (Paris, 1982) pp. 577–94, p. 588.
7. Verbruggen, p. 233.
8. G. Duby, *The Legend of Bouvines*, trans. C. Tihanyi (Cambridge, 1990) p. 200.

apparent, the use of urban militias. On both sides, these forces were numerically important. Overall, it has been pointed out, by this period armies relied more on urban forces of one kind or another than on any other source.[9]

The French seem to have possessed more of the best quality cavalry, their opponents more infantry, but the respective sizes are difficult to assess with any precision. Verbruggen makes a sound point to argue that Philip may have had the smaller army, since he had to risk a single line in order to extend his front and prevent outflanking. But this could relate to the area which had to be covered, and does not necessarily demonstrate a larger allied army. However, the fact that Otto IV thought he was in a winning position suggests that he believed he had a larger army, and the two points together seem enough to argue the case. At any rate the French cannot be said to have won because of overwhelming superiority in numbers.

. . .

FLANDERS BEFORE BOUVINES

Philip's mind was undoubtedly more exercised over the control of Flanders than over winning southern France. His whole reign was marked with regular efforts in the northern direction. He had early on thrown off Philip count of Flanders' attempt at domination. Philip had then outmanoeuvred Count Baldwin IX, who went on to become Latin emperor. The Emperor Baldwin's capture at Adrianople and subsequent death in captivity left Flanders at Philip's mercy. From 1202 to 1226 Flanders suffered a 'double interregnum'.[10] Philip easily dominated the regent, Baldwin's brother Philip of Namur, calling for a meeting at Pont de l'Arche in 1206 to make suitable arrangements for Flanders. The French king won control of the two surviving daughters, Joan and Margaret, as his wards. He arranged the marriage of his own daughter, Marie, to his 'dear friend' the regent Philip of Namur, which took place in 1211. He had obtained

9. Reynolds, p. 309.
10. G. Duby, *France in the Middle Ages, 987–1460*, trans. J. Vale (Oxford, 1991) p. 32; the quote is from G.G. Dept.

possession of the two heiresses and transferred them to Paris in 1208. It was said that Philip of Namur later regretted his actions and went through the streets of Valenciennes with a rope round his neck, proclaiming 'I ought to die as a dog', but that did little to remove the controlling power which the French king had obtained by that time.[11]

Philip Augustus also countered efforts by King John to win over the Flemish nobility to an English alliance by cash payments. Philip responded by efforts to establish a pro-French party, which flourished. Some 49 per cent of Philip's *fiefs-rentes* were expended in Flanders, and included payment to the regent himself, until his death in 1212, as well as to some of the most powerful figures in the county, such as the three main household officers and the key castellans at St-Omer, Bruges, Ghent, Cassel and Lille.[12]

Philip had imposed upon Flanders, through marriage, the choice of Ferrand of Portugal as count. Ferrand, son of Sancho I king of Portugal, was married to the Flemish heiress Joan in Paris in 1212, when Philip also favoured the Portuguese prince by knighting him, and Ferrand in return did homage to the king. The idea had first been put to Philip Augustus by Count Philip of Flanders' widow, Matilda of Portugal, who was Ferrand's aunt. Philip even gained £50,000 from the arrangement, but the move backfired when Philip's son, Louis, took advantage of the weakness of the new count to seize Aire and St-Omer, which he claimed as his mother's dowry.

This seizure was the first of several aggressive moves by Prince Louis which were at odds with his father's policies, and which had unfortunate consequences. Philip is usually said to have encouraged these actions, but their frequency, and Philip's consistent failure to support them, suggest that they sprang directly from the impulsive nature of Louis, and were not approved by his more diplomatic father. Philip was clearly fond of his son and protected him from the worst repercussions of his own follies, but that is not to say that he either encouraged or approved them.

11. A. Luchaire in E. Lavisse, ed., *Histoire de France depuis les Origines jusqu'à la Révolution*, III, Pt I (Paris, 1911) pp. 170–1.
12. D. Nicholas, *Medieval Flanders* (Harlow, 1992) p. 151; G.G. Dept, *Les Influences Anglaise et Française dans le comté de Flandre au début du troisième siècle* (Ghent and Paris, 1928) p. 83.

Ferrand of Portugal was reluctantly forced to accept the loss of Aire and St-Omer, which blighted his accession to Flanders and brought taunts from his new subjects, who accused him of being the 'serf' of the French king and told him to go home.[13] Ferrand, needing to regain the respect of his subjects, then sought to show his independence of Philip. He moved reluctantly but gradually into the only possible alternative sphere of influence, that of Otto of Brunswick and John of England, exiling pro-French nobles from Flanders to gain John and Otto's favour. From 1212 the pro-English nobility in Flanders revived, supported by Ferrand, fed by John's cash and fertilized by the need of the towns to retain the considerable English trade – especially in wool.

When Philip planned to invade England in 1213, Ferrand count of Flanders refused to take part or to contribute, thus formally breaking any agreement made when Philip had manoeuvred him into his county. Instead Count Ferrand formed an alliance with King John, going to England in December 1213 to cement it. When Philip's invasion of England was frustrated, the French king used the ready-made force to avenge himself on Ferrand, and invaded Flanders.

The attack proved inconclusive: Philip won a number of towns and strongholds, including Tournai, Cassel, Lille, Bruges and Ghent, and took hostages from them, while Ferrand was forced for a time to seek refuge in Zeeland. A broad swathe of Flanders was put to sword and fire, but the French in their turn suffered a major disaster when their fleet was attacked and destroyed at Damme, the port for Bruges, by the Flemings in alliance with the earl of Salisbury and the count of Boulogne.

William the Breton blamed Cadoc for the failure to protect the French fleet, and it is possible that the mercenary captain was killed in the conflict. Those ships the English and Flemish did not destroy, Philip was forced to burn himself in order to deny their use to his enemies. Philip had to abandon most of what he had won during the campaign, and John now flooded Flanders with cash, ambassadors and promises, in what became 'the golden age' of English influence. Pro-French castellans fled to the safety of the French court. Not only was Ferrand now firmly in alliance with

13. Luchaire in Lavisse, p. 172.

John, but practically all of Flanders was 'ranged on the side of Ferrand' against Philip Augustus.[14]

War continued through the winter of 1213 and the spring of 1214. Much of Flanders was devastated by one side or the other. Philip burned several towns, including Lille, and captured Douai, but Ferrand gained some compensation against Louis by destroying Aire, and seemed to be establishing his authority over his new subjects.

. . .

KING JOHN, 1206–1214

Flanders was the focus and centre of the trouble that boiled up into the crisis of Bouvines, but always behind the troubles for Philip, and always at the real heart of them, was King John of England. John had lost Normandy, but in the years before Bouvines he saved the remnants of his continental empire, survived a crisis with the Church, and then began to mastermind a coalition against Philip of the sort that had served Richard so well, combining the Holy Roman Empire, Flanders, and those with reason to be hostile to Philip both within France and just outside its borders. And John had the resources to make this a genuine threat to Philip's very existence.

The loss of Normandy and other continental lands in the early part of the thirteenth century had been a tremendous blow to John, but he had made enough effort to save Poitou and Gascony from Philip's control. John could always find some dissident figure with whom to ally, whether Guy de Thouars, Renaud count of Boulogne, or Hugh de Boves. In Britain John had sufficient success to renew his hopes. He had forced William de Braose into exile, and had at least minor victories against both the Welsh and the Scots.

Although Philip's planned invasion of England in 1213 was abandoned, one should not overlook the part played by Philip in England during this year. John was a threat to him, but perhaps always the French king was a greater threat to John. Dissident English barons made their way to Philip, including Robert Fitz Walter, whose lands Philip promised to

14. Dept, pp. 107, 125.

restore when England was conquered. The fact that William Marshal had done homage to Philip for his Norman lands had made John suspicious and worried. In 1209 Philip wrote to John de Lacy, ordering him to keep an agreement to make war on John, which shows that Philip was indeed involved in stirring the baronial reform movement in England. The barons of England even sent a charter to Philip, promising him the crown. Prince Louis also married Blanche of Castile, the grand-daughter of Henry II, and thus developed a genuine claim to the English throne. Because of the dispute over Canterbury, Innocent III declared that John should be deposed, and promised that Philip and his successors should 'hold possession of the kingdom of England for ever'.[15] King John had good reason to fear the French threat and see an urgent need for action against Philip.

John's dispute with the papacy over the election to Canterbury was damaging for the English king. The dispute had begun with the death of Archbishop Hubert Walter in 1205, when a group of the Canterbury monks chose their own prior, Reginald, in opposition to John's preferred candidate, John de Gray. Innocent III had examined the case and rejected both choices. In 1207 he simply informed John that Stephen Langton's consecration had taken place, at Viterbo. Langton, although English, had been many years in Paris, and was accused by John of being Philip's 'trusted adviser and friend'.[16] It was not surprising that John refused to accept Langton in England, but it was perhaps surprising that he was able to outface the papal blast of interdict in 1208, and excommunication in 1209, for some five years.

When John did yield over the matter, he had five years' worth of ecclesiastical cash to tide him over, and used the act to halt a projected French invasion of England with papal encouragement in 1213. John ended up actually gaining papal support against France. Yet the dispute had left its mark on John's prestige, and on the attitude of ordinary folk, as well as on Church and barons in England. The

15. Roger of Wendover, *Flowers of History*, ed. and trans. J.A. Giles, 2 vols (London, 1899) II, p. 259; Roger of Wendover, *Chronica*, ed. H.O. Coxe, 4 vols (London, 1841–44) III, p. 242: 'ipse et successores sui regnum Angliae jure perpetuo possiderent'.
16. J.T. Appleby, *John, King of England* (London, 1958) p. 146.

Barnwell chronicler saw John as a 'pillager' of the Church, while Wendover thought that he had 'almost as many enemies as he had barons'.[17]

The surrender of the English crown to the papacy, recognizing overlordship as if the kingdom were a fief, seemed at the time a humiliation. John also had to pay 1,000 marks a year and accept Stephen Langton, who proceeded to aid the baronial reform movement which resulted in Magna Carta. But if hardly the triumph some historians have believed, it still seemed as if the king had wriggled out of a desperate position with hopes of recovery.

Philip's plans before John submitted to the Church were real enough; he spent some £60,000 on the intended campaign. The invasion came very near to being put into execution, when Philip embarked in his assembled fleet at Boulogne on 10 May 1213, reaching Gravelines by 22 May. John's submission to the papacy really was a last minute act; but when he did yield, the papacy at once forbade the French invasion. Philip was naturally furious, and blustered: 'great anger and fury were in the heart of the king of France'.[18] But with his usual political sense, Philip contained his anger and called off the crossing. He used the assembled force, as we have seen, to try and take out his anger on Ferrand of Flanders for allying with John.

In 1213 King John was hoping to recover his continental losses. Once Philip's invasion had been diverted against Flanders, John prepared an expedition for Poitou, but he found little enthusiasm from the English barons. The English king was finally able to assemble a force in 1214, despite refusal by many lords, especially those in the north, to pay the scutage tax.

At first the expedition to France had remarkable success. Many of the previously near-independent lords had become alarmed at increasing French royal authority in their region, many were prepared to return to John's allegiance, at least for a time. According to William the Breton, 'affection will

17. The Barnwell Chronicle in Walter of Coventry, *Memoriale*, ed. W. Stubbs, 2 vols, RS no. 58 (London, 1872–73) II, p. 232: 'depraedator'; K. Norgate, *John Lackland* (London, 1902) p. 171; Roger of Wendover, ed. Coxe, III, p. 241: 'rex tot fere habuit hostes, quot habuit magnates'.
18. Luchaire in Lavisse, p. 164.

no more hold a Poitevin than chains will bind a Protean'.[19]
For John, it was at first a procession of triumph, and he was
able to re-enter the old family capital of Angers on 17 June.
Philip and Louis were forced to march against him. But
then came news of Otto IV's activities in the north, so Philip
had to split his forces. He himself headed northwards to
deal with Otto, leaving his son to cope with John. There was
all to play for, and the outcome at this stage was by no
means certain.

. . .

THE COALITION AGAINST PHILIP

John was the puppeteer, Flanders the main theatre, but the
coalition which had built up against Philip Augustus by 1214
was very broad indeed, spreading to such potential enemies
as Raymond of Toulouse and the viscount of Thouars. Philip
himself had need of allies, and at various times made agreements with Philip of Swabia, Henry of Brabant, the count of
Holland, the elector of the Palatinate, the duke of Austria,
and Boniface of Montferrat, while also putting himself on
good terms with a number of leading churchmen in Germany
and the Netherlands.

Perhaps the most enthusiastic member of the coalition
against Philip was Renaud de Dammartin, the count of Boulogne. So often former friends make the worst enemies. By
1214 Philip could accuse Renaud of numerous betrayals and
of ingratitude. Renaud's family had been castellans in the
Ile-de-France and royal officials, while he himself had been
brought up with Philip at the French court and knighted by
Louis VII. When Renaud repudiated his wife and seized the
widowed heiress, Ida of Boulogne, Philip had defended the act
and recognized his claims to the county. As William the
Breton put it: 'the king had given him the countess and the
county of Boulogne'.[20] It is probable that Philip's generosity

19. William the Breton, *La Philippide, Poème*, ed. M. Guizot (Paris, 1825)
   p. 231; William the Breton, 'Philippide', in *Oeuvres de Rigord et de
   Guillaume le Breton*, ed. H-F. Delaborde, SHF, vols 210, 224 (Paris,
   1882–85) II, p. 227, ll. 450–1: 'Sed que firma satis innexio Protea
   nectat?/Nec Pictas constringit amor, nec Protea nexus'.
20. William the Breton, *Philippide*, ed. Guizot, pp. 120–1; 'Philippide',
   ed. Delaborde, p. 121, ll. 583–5; l. 585: 'Boloniam toto comitissam
   cum comitatu'.

towards Renaud in the first place sprang not from trust, but from the knowledge that Renaud's support would need to be bought. A quarrel at court with the count of St-Pol led to Renaud's first defection to the Plantagenets. But in 1201 the king had arranged the marriage of his favoured illegitimate son, Philip Hurepel, to Renaud's daughter Matilda. Also, through the king's support, Renaud's brother was married to the daughter of the count of Ponthieu, Philip's niece.

The main split with Renaud occurred when the latter became embroiled in private war with the king's cousin, Philip of Dreux the bishop of Beauvais, and hence found himself at odds with the king. The king ordered Renaud to surrender the castle of Mortain, which the count refused to do. Philip then acted promptly and captured the castle after a brief siege, storming it on the fourth day. Renaud took himself into exile, and in 1212 did homage to King John, who had been wooing his support for some time.

Renaud was the link man in the coalition against Philip Augustus, frantically travelling about to stoke up support. He has been called 'the moving force' behind the alliance, and 'the inspirer and organizer of the coalition'.[21] Renaud brought Theobald of Bar into the alliance, kept contact with Henry of Brabant and, using King John's cash, attracted many leading nobles from Flanders and Hainault to join them. He also helped to bring King John and Otto IV together. William the Breton has Renaud de Dammartin organizing the conference at which the ringleaders of the continental coalition agreed to share out France between them after their anticipated victory. According to the writer, Renaud was both living in sin with a courtesan and suggesting a sort of Reformation seizure of Church property from the 'idle race' of clerics, whom he castigated for 'their useless lives, whose sole occupation is to devote themselves to Bacchus and Venus and fill their stomachs'.[22] Renaud became one of the leaders of the group paid by John which campaigned

21. Bordonove, p. 210; C. Petit-Dutaillis, *The Feudal Monarchy in France and England from the Tenth to the Thirteenth Centuries*, trans. E.D. Hunt (London, 1936) p. 223.
22. William the Breton, *Philippide*, ed. Guizot, pp. 308, 310; 'Philippide', ed. Delaborde, II, p. 308, ll. 629–31: 'Qui frustra vivunt, quorum labor omnis in hoc est/Ut Baccho Venerique vacent'; II, p. 305, on sharing the realm: ll. 563, p. 306, l. 584; cf. II, p. 299, l. 422.

against Philip, sailing with the earl of Salisbury from Dover in 1213.

Another leading figure in the coalition, and of military value to it, was Hugh de Boves, a younger son from a noble family in Picardy. Like some of the other allies, he had a rather unsavoury reputation. In his case he had killed a prévôt of Philip's and then fled to King John, who hired his services. Like Renaud, Hugh de Boves was among the companions of William of Salisbury who fought against the French king at Bouvines.

King John's chief representative at Bouvines was to be William earl of Salisbury. He was an illegitimate son of Henry II, and therefore a half brother of John, a large, powerful and tall man, hence his nickname of Longsword. He became a respected soldier and the commander of John's troops in the Bouvines campaign. By then, however, Duby perhaps too harshly sees him as an ageing 'blusterer'.[23]

On the surface the greatest coup for the allies was to bring in Otto IV, the Holy Roman Emperor. But it was not quite so great a coup as it looked. Otto was not a very admirable ruler; modern historians have called him 'glib in tongue, lavish in promises, big in size, and somewhat stupid'; 'arrogant'; 'a worthless, inefficient, bungling, totally unreliable braggart'.[24] As had been the case in the Holy Land, Philip's political choice was the better man. Even Innocent III, when disillusioned by Otto's ingratitude, admitted his mistake to Philip. Otto's position in Germany by 1214 was becoming uncertain, and he badly needed success against Philip in order to survive.

After the early death of Henry VI in 1198, there had been a conflict for the Holy Roman Empire between Otto of Saxony and Philip of Swabia, brother to the deceased emperor. Otto had been born in Normandy, a grandson of Henry II and nephew of both Richard and John, who sided with him, so that almost inevitably Philip Augustus favoured Philip of Swabia. The latter had been crowned in 1205, but was assassinated three years later, so that Otto recovered the crown.

23. Duby, *Bouvines*, p. 28.
24. Jane Sayers, *Innocent III* (Harlow, 1994) p. 52; Duby, *Bouvines*, p. 27; W. Ullmann, *A Short History of the Papacy in the Middle Ages* (London, 1972) p. 212.

For a brief period Philip Augustus sought to oppose Otto through Henry of Brabant, but then began to encourage the claims of Henry VI's son, Frederick of Hohenstaufen. In the meantime Otto IV had lost the papacy's favour by his invasion of Italy, and been excommunicated in 1210. Innocent also turned now to Frederick. In 1212 an exploratory meeting took place between the young Frederick and Prince Louis near Toulouse. Then at Vaucouleurs Philip himself met Frederick and made an agreement.

Events in Flanders, as we have seen, turned Philip's 'puppet' count, Ferrand, into an enemy. When Philip planned to invade England in 1213, Ferrand refused to give the military service he owed and failed to arrive at the assembly point. Philip then invaded Flanders though, as we have seen, he failed to defeat the count. Ferrand was now firmly in the opposition camp. Many lesser northern lords were also brought within the influence of the coalition against Philip Augustus.

. . .

LA ROCHE-AU-MOINE

The coalition against Philip put itself into the field in 1214, presenting the French king with the greatest threat he was to face throughout his long reign. Large field armies were now operating against him simultaneously to the north and the south. This activity of the coalition has always been presented by historians as a 'broad and far-reaching plan'; a 'grand strategy' according to one of our most respected military historians.[25] This is to place more on the evidence than it can bear. There was a certain amount of previous planning and a mutual arrangement that Otto would attack in the north and John in the south. But there is no evidence for anything more subtle than that.

To what extent King John ever planned to march right through France from south to north is sheer guesswork. If it was planned, it seems grand fantasy more than grand strategy, given the problems that were posed even by the

25. Oman, I, p. 469; J. Gillingham, *The Angevin Empire* (London, 1984) p. 77.

modest defences of La Roche-au-Moine. It seems more likely that the coalition plan was simply for John to do as much damage as he could in the south, while his friends did much the same in the north, and then wait upon events. John did succeed in drawing off a considerable proportion of the forces available to Philip, but any success in the early stages of his campaign was soon neutralized.

John left Portsmouth in February 1214, early in the year for such a campaign. He arrived at La Rochelle by 15 or 16 February. Within a few weeks the king wrote back to William Marshal: 'hardly had I appeared when twenty-six castles and fortified places opened their gates to me'. A variety of lords were prepared to accept him once he appeared before them, including Savaric de Mauléon and the viscount of Limoges. The latter wrote to Philip to explain his predicament: 'my natural lord has entered my fief in such force that I can neither resist nor wait for your help'.[26]

King John arranged a match between his daughter Joan and Hugh Lusignan count of La Marche in an attempt to heal old wounds, though the marriage was not destined to take place. John's progress through Saintonge, Poitou, Angoulême and the Limousin was apparently triumphant: towns surrendered, lords did homage to him. But Brittany proved less welcoming, suspicious still over John's part in the death of its young ruler, Arthur. Nevertheless John took Ancenis on the border, and Nantes on 13 June. Moving westwards along the river, he entered the ancient Plantagenet capital of Angers on the Loire on 17 June, and then attacked the French-held castle at La Roche-au-Moine on 19 June.

La Roche-au-Moine had been built by William des Roches and defended the route to Le Mans and Maine. With success in the south behind him, King John's ambitions were clearly moving northwards and for the recovery of all the old Angevin lands. At La Roche he set up his engines, but the garrison, including the giant crossbowman Pons, resisted, knowing that royal forces were coming to its aid. John besieged the place for two weeks. He built a gallows and threatened to hang the garrison if it did not surrender, but it bravely continued to defy him.

26. Appleby, p. 15; R.V. Turner, *King John* (Harlow, 1994) p. 16; Luchaire in Lavisse, p. 180.

It is not clear if John knew exactly the arrangements made by the Capetians to cope with the present crisis. Both Philip and Louis had at first come south against John, but on hearing of the activities of Otto IV and the coalition in the north, Philip decided he must go and deal with that threat. He left a considerable proportion of his forces behind under his son, Louis. John may have thought that the whole French force had gone, and rediscovered his aggression.

Louis, with inferior forces, was uncertain whether to risk a fight against the English king, but received an order from his father to relieve La Roche.[27] The prince then advanced from Chinon against John, who declared his intention of fighting but in fact slunk away on 2 July. He abandoned his engines and tents, together with all the baggage, and fled, leaving some of his men to drown in a hasty crossing of the Loire. There was no battle, though Louis pursued the enemy as far as Thouars.

John probably thought the whole French army had returned, and it seems certain that his new Poitevin allies 'said that they were not ready for a fight in the open field' against the Capetians, but it was still a panic move.[28] He moved off so fast, he was at St-Maixent within two days. John's southern campaign petered out, and he returned tamely to La Rochelle. The English king's recent gains were lost and his new friends soon deserted again to make their peace with Philip. In September Philip agreed a truce with John, on relatively generous terms, but Philip could now afford generosity. In October King John sailed back to England, his campaign and his reign in tatters.

. . .

THE PRELIMINARIES TO BOUVINES

While John's hopes came to grief in the south, even more dramatic events were happening on what is now the northern border of France with Belgium, and was then the border between the Capetian lands and the county of Flanders. The news that brought Philip back from the south was that

27. William the Breton, *Philippide*, ed. Guizot, p. 293; 'Philippide', ed. Delaborde, II, p. 289.
28. Norgate, *John*, p. 201; Roger of Wendover, ed. Coxe, III, p. 286.

his enemies were massing in that region. Otto IV assembled first at Aachen on 23 March, taking a long time to progress further which, as Sir Charles Oman once suggested, probably damaged his hopes.[29]

There were negotiations by the Holy Roman Emperor with the princes of the region, resulting in Otto IV's marriage to Mary, the daughter of the duke of Brabant, but there was also a long delay. Otto eventually moved on to Maastricht, and then on 12 July to Nivelles in Brabant (just south of Brussels), and so to Valenciennes in Hainault, where he waited to assemble his forces, apparently with the aim of moving against Paris itself. With the emperor came the dukes of Brabant and Limbourg, the lord of Mechelin, while to him came the counts of Flanders, Boulogne and Boves, and the earl of Salisbury.

Philip reached Péronne, which he left on 23 July, moving on to Tournai on 25 July. The difficulties of communication for medieval armies is made apparent by the Bouvines campaign. Both sides sent out their spies and their scouts, both sides contained men with good local knowledge, and it is notable how many of the leading figures had their estates in the region: Audenarde, Namur, Beaumont, Mechelen, St-Pol. Most of the urban militias were also drawn from nearby towns. But neither army found it easy to keep in touch with the enemy.

Both sides made somewhat unexpected moves. From conflicting reports, Otto and Philip had to make what might be decisive or fatal decisions on the basis of incomplete information. Philip marched from Cambrai, not directly towards Valenciennes and his opponents, but in a westwards wheel, probably intending to take the enemy by surprise from the north. But in the meantime the allied force moved southwards, perhaps aiming at where they thought the French force would be. As it happened, the two forces passed by each other without realizing it, so that now the French army was to the north and the allied army to the south. Both sides were therefore in some danger of having their natural retreat cut off, and Philip's danger appeared the greater. Otto moved on to Mortagne, where the rivers Scarpe and Escaut meet, apparently seeking battle, believing himself to have

29. Oman, I, p. 471.

the superior force, and knowing that only victory could really save his position in Germany.

Philip was assisted by a traitor in the opposing camp. Even the favourable marriage granted to the duke of Brabant had failed to win him over entirely to the coalition. He attended Otto's assembly, but he feared Philip's anger. He therefore sent secret information to the king of France about the allied force and its movements. Another of Philip's motives for choosing to move was the nature of the country in which he found himself. He was not eager for battle, but even less was he keen to fight on unsuitable ground dominated by marshes and woodland. So he aimed for Lille and the Cambrésis.

Philip certainly did not seek battle at Bouvines while on this march. It is just possible that he made the feigned flight, said to have been advised by Gerard la Truie, to tempt the enemy into closer contact, but it does not seem likely.[30] Philip had learned that Otto IV was at Valenciennes and in Hainault, and knew that in order to evade him he would have to keep to the west, hence the need to move westwards across the Marcq before heading south. Escape from the coalition army in that location was his obvious intention.

The allies seem to have believed that it was a panic retreat, such as King John made from La Roche-au-Moine. William the Breton said that one of Otto's spies told him so, though Renaud de Dammartin argued against it being so, and he knew the mind of Philip as a commander better than most of his allies in the coalition. The spirits of the allies were dampened by this disagreement among themselves, with Hugh de Boves calling Renaud a traitor for wishing to avoid battle. Otto probably expected that he was going to catch the French in a much greater state of disarray than would prove to be the case. The allies still tried to convince themselves of the rightness of their cause and had crosses sewn on their coats of arms at front and back, as if they were crusaders.

The French thought they were safe for the day, a Sunday, not believing that the enemy would break the Christian tradition against fighting on the sabbath. Tournai did not seem a safe place to remain, its defences had recently been destroyed. So on 27 July, in the freshness of dawn, Philip set

30. Bordonove, p. 226.

out from Tournai, heading for Lille, Douai and Cambrai, countryside where cavalry could operate better, and where Philip said he would see 'the fields of his birth' and would know the lie of the land. It was a fine, hot day, which probably slowed his march.

Before the allies set out to catch the French, it was said that the confident Count Ferrand of Flanders distributed ropes to be used in tying up the prisoners they would capture. When Otto IV learned of the actual position of his opponents, and the direction of their march, he decided to make pursuit and seek battle, believing himself to have all the advantages. According to William the Breton, Otto reminded his men that the French had only one-third as many knights as themselves, and that they would not like the feel of cold steel. [31]

The French army reached the little River Marcq, secured their crossing, and began to make their way over the bridge near the village of Bouvines. Philip had clearly already planned his march and had noted how narrow the bridge was. We are told that he therefore had it widened to take twelve men abreast, and the necessary four-wheeled carts, more speedily. How well Philip knew the 'fields of his birth' is not certain, but he probably knew then pretty well. There were men with local knowledge in his force, and also his wife, Ingeborg, had for a time been kept in the nearby religious house at Cysoing. Philip let the army go forward and, as it was noon, took the opportunity for lunch and a rest on a height from which any movements of the enemy could be observed. He took off his armour, found a shady spot under an ash tree, and swallowed some lumps of bread dipped in wine.

At the rear of the French army, however, the action soon began. Otto, learning of Philip's move, wrongly believing him to be in a panic retreat, aimed to catch the force half way over the river and destroy it. The allied force then rushed into the fields 'like a plague of locusts'. [32] The pursuing troops caught the French rear in a wood near Tournai and began

31. William the Breton, *Philippide*, ed. Guizot, pp. 313, 312; 'Philippide', ed. Delaborde, II, pp. 308–9; p. 310, l. 690: 'ut videam natalia rura'.
32. William the Breton, *Philippide*, ed. Guizot, p. 314; 'Philippide', ed. Delaborde, II, p. 311, ll. 711–12: 'egrediens exercitus unique densis,/ More locustarum, legionibus occulit agros'.

to harass their march. Several times the French rear had to turn about and fight them off before continuing. It was reminiscent of the march of Richard the Lionheart's forces before his victory at Jaffa. The harassment became increasingly difficult to cope with and messages went out for immediate aid.

At the rear of the French army, some 3 miles separated from it, was a party of scouts, with Guérin de Glapion bishop-elect of Senlis and Adam viscount of Melun at its head. Although a churchman, Guérin was practised in matters of war and had a shrewd military mind. The group reached a mound in the middle of the plain, from where they could see the enemy, their 'shields like stars at nights, their helmed heads reflecting the sun'.[33] Guérin took in the picture from his observation point and realized the implications. He noted that the enemy banners were unfurled, and their cavalry horses were barded, in other words that the imperial army was ready for battle, with its horses armoured as they would only be for a fight, especially on such a hot day. Philip must be informed urgently.

Guérin told the viscount to stay put and work out the enemy's numbers and dispositions and, while the rear held off the initial attacks, he himself rode apace to find his master, who was still lunching under the ash. The bishop-elect explained the situation concisely saying that, although it was Sunday, the enemy was intending battle. Most historians prefer to credit Guérin with such military decisions as the French made. This is perverse, and in effect discredits Philip. The episode just described makes perfectly clear who was the commander. Guérin could not make the vital decision, he could only advise. And Philip, once informed, reached a quick and bold decision. He entered the nearby church, dedicated to St Peter, and offered a brief prayer: 'Lord, I am but a man, but I am king.'[34]

Then he armed and ordered the French army to prepare for battle, which meant it must turn on its tracks. The

33. William the Breton, *Philippide*, ed. Guizot, p. 315; 'Philippide', ed. Delaborde, II, p. 312, ll. 743–4: 'Tot clypeos preferri astris splendoribus ausos,/Tegmina tot capitum solis replicantia lucem'.
34. W.H. Hutton, *Philip Augustus* (London, 1896) p. 101; Philip Mouskes, *Chronique Rimée*, ed. Baron de Reiffenberg, 2 vols (Brussels, 1836–38) II, p. 359.

main decision Philip made was to stop the march and fight. Although his intention had almost certainly been to retreat, he saw that a fight was almost inevitable now, so made the best of what must be done. Philip told Guérin that this was the chance he had been waiting for, exclaiming: 'the Lord gives me what I desire'. He gave instructions for the van, which included the main infantry forces in his army, to return over the bridge.

Meanwhile Philip re-armed himself for the fight, jumped on his horse shouting 'Allons!', and told his men that they must go to the aid of their friends. Then he rode to the front of the army to deploy the troops on his side of the river.[35] It was Philip himself who made the vital decisions of the day and should be credited with the victory. That he employed able advisers and took good advice only enhances his reputation. After all, Richard the Lionheart was advised by such experts as Mercadier, but we do not credit the captain with the king's successes. It is just part of the revision that needs to be done on the way in which Philip is remembered.

Philip made a battle speech, criticizing his opponents as enemies of the Church, which he and his force was defending. As so often, Philip liked to present a case of justification for his actions, putting himself in the right. A number of the enemy, he reminded his men, were excommunicate. Worst of all their opponents were all defying the Church and their Christian belief by choosing to fight on a Sunday; the French could not be to blame for defending themselves.

Philip had acted smartly enough to allow time for proper disposition of his forces. He did not wait for those crossing back over the bridge, they must take their places as they arrived. He formed three main divisions, as did the enemy, whose plans he had been informed of by Henry duke of Brabant. The French right consisted largely of the forces who had been fighting the rearguard action, and was commanded by the duke of Burgundy, with Guérin by his side. It is interesting that Philip thought Burgundy might need that assistance more than he himself. The duke of Burgundy

35. William the Breton, *Philippide*, ed. Guizot, pp. 316, 318; 'Philippide', ed. Delaborde, II, p. 313, l. 759: 'quod optabam Dominus mihi contulit ultro'; p. 315, l. 826–7: 'euntes/Festinemus'.

was a large man, with an impassive expression; perhaps Philip needed to be sure he would not make any false decisions. With Burgundy were the counts of Beaumont, Melun, St-Pol, Montmorency and Sancerre.

Philip was in the centre, surrounded by his trusted household knights, mostly from the Ile-de-France, such as Walter the Young, Gerard la Truie, Peter Tristan, William de Garlande, Bartholomew de Roye and William des Barres, who was famed 'as far away as Syria'. William the Breton's description of Philip at Bouvines is generally ignored so that it comes as a surprise to read it. To him Philip made an imposing figure: 'a tall body on a tall horse'.[36] One must remember though that Philip lacked some of his normal company: many trusted men, including many from the Ile-de-France, had stayed with Prince Louis in the south. But the king and his men still made an imposing picture. At their head the king's banner was carried by Galon de Montigny. The scarlet oriflamme had yet to return with the troops from over the river, but Philip had his own standard with the fleur-de-lys emblazoned upon it, silver on blue. Also in the centre with the king were the count of Bar and William des Roches.

On the French left were Philip's Dreux relatives, including Philip the bishop of Beauvais, along with 'Old Robert' the count of Dreux, and the counts of Ponthieu and Auxerre.[37] Philip had arrayed his available cavalry forces and Otto IV was surprised to find an army so well prepared. In fact, the French had moved so rapidly in the time given, a sign of good discipline, that virtually all the troops across the river were back and in place before the battle commenced. In their initial deployment, Philip's men had left spaces so that the infantry van could return through the lines and re-form at the front, including the commune troops from Corbie, Amiens, Beauvais and Compiègne. Now too the famous and legendary standard from St-Denis, the vivid red oriflamme, took its accustomed place. Otto had not managed to catch

36. Duby, *Bouvines*, p. 196, from the Anonymous of Béthune; p. 199; William the Breton, 'Philippide', ed. Delaborde, II, p. 316, ll. 836–7: 'alto/Insilit altus equo'.
37. William the Breton, *Philippide*, ed. Guizot, p. 304; 'Philippide', ed. Delaborde, II, p. 301, l. 476: 'senior Robertus', more correctly 'Robert the Elder'.

his enemy by surprise after all, nor would he fight half an army, as he had hoped.

Otto IV's disposition of the allied army was similarly in three, and this formation determined the pattern of the battle. On the allied left was Ferrand count of Flanders and lords who were his neighbours, including the count of Holland, together with some of the German cavalry. In the centre was Otto himself, with his standard of the dragon with fierce teeth, whose tail and wings seemed to fly in the wind, attached to a pole on which was carved the imperial eagle with golden wings. It was dramatically set on a cart, itself covered in gold, the *carroccio* now familiar from Italy. The emperor was resplendent, in gold with imperial ornaments, bearing a black and gold shield. With Otto were the dukes of Brabant, Louvain and Limbourg, the counts of Holland and Namur, and his most trusted German lieutenants such as Bernard Horstmann, Otto von Tecklenburg and William von Dortmund. In front of Otto ranged his infantry, in three ranks.

The allied right consisted chiefly of the forces loyal to, or paid by, King John. They were led by the earl of Salisbury, 'a man of incredible strength', along with Renaud de Dammartin and Hugh de Boves. The latter is described by Roger of Wendover as 'a brave soldier, but a cruel and proud man'.[38] In this group were the few English present, including Ralph Bigod. Here also were the hired Brabançon infantry, which would figure in the last dramatic stages of the fight. All along the allied front were lined strong infantry forces, mostly provided by the northern communes, many carrying pikes. The surprise of finding Philip and the French advancing towards him, subsequent to Philip's hasty ride to the front, made Otto hesitate and draw back his left wing, allowing the French that much more time. The emperor asked querulously: 'who told me that the king of France was in flight?'.[39]

Philip was worried by the numbers of the enemy and, on the advice of Guérin de Glapion, extended his line to the

38. William the Breton, 'Philippide', ed. Delaborde, II, p. 340; Roger of Wendover, ed. Coxe, III, p. 287: 'miles strenuus sed crudelis et superbus'; Roger of Wendover, ed. Giles, II, p. 298; Duby, *Bouvines*, p. 200.
39. Oman, I, p. 479; Luchaire in Lavisse, p. 189.

north-west. This was at the cost of lessening his army in depth, but achieved the more vital task of preventing outflanking.[40] Guérin is said to have encouraged the knights in their thinner ranks by exhorting them to knightly valour, saying that no knight should make another his shield.[41] This explanation is no modern construction upon the actions, but is made clear in William the Breton's account. Otto seems to have simply followed Philip's example, and also deployed his force in that direction.

. . .

THE SITE

And so the two sides faced each other. They were placed in the centre of a triangle with its points at Douai, Tournai and Valenciennes. Three small settlements were nearer at hand: the village of Bouvines to the east, Gruson to the north, and the settlement around the abbey of Cysoing to the south. The ancient Roman road for Tournai, a raised road across the marsh, led to the bridge at Bouvines on its way to Lille and was followed by both armies as they headed towards the crossing. It was a region of rivers: the Escaut, the Scarpe, the Deule and the Marcq; and much of the surrounding area was dense with willows and covered with muddy marshland. This had been worsened by a wet winter and spring. But immediately to the east of the river was a flat plateau, cultivated for grain, just then being harvested: 'a beautiful plain, blooming with Ceres' grains'.[42] It was about a mile wide and suitable for cavalry, which must have encouraged Philip in making his decision to turn and fight. One can see why a chronicler might hazard the guess that Philip had planned a feigned flight to bring the enemy to battle at this point, but we cannot credit Philip with quite that degree of foresight. If that were the case, he would hardly have allowed so great a proportion of the army to cross the bridge, and then been forced to bring it back.

The river formed a barrier behind the French, keeping them in position, but depriving them of easy retreat in case

40. William the Breton, *Philippide*, ed. Guizot, p. 321.
41. Oman, II, p. 480.
42. Duby, *Bouvines*, p. 198; William the Breton, 'Philippide', ed. Delaborde, II, p. 314.

of defeat. It suggests that Philip was prepared for an all-out throw, victory or nothing. Wendover reinforces this idea, describing how the French king had the bridge broken behind him, thus deliberately denying his men the chance of flight.[43] One disadvantage of the position to the French was the slope of the plain which ran gently downwards towards the river, but it was not steep enough to play a significant part in the battle. To their advantage was the time of the day, with the sun behind the French shoulders, shining and reflecting in the faces of the allies. The other concern about his position for Philip was his left flank: the right was covered by marshy ground, but the left was vulnerable, given that Otto possessed a larger force. But it was as good a position as could be obtained, occupying the available high ground.

. . .

THE BATTLE OF BOUVINES

On the afternoon of 27 July 1214 was fought one of the most decisive and significant battles in European history. At stake were the futures of France and the Holy Roman Empire, and indirectly of England and the Angevin Empire, as well as the counties of Flanders and Boulogne. As with all medieval battles, one relies on partial and sometimes biased accounts, but at least there are a variety of sources for Bouvines. It is also, on the whole, not a battle which has aroused historical controversy over its course. The main accounts, and the main modern interpretations, are largely in agreement.

The only serious point to be raised is the role of Philip Augustus, which has mostly been undervalued. Oman, for example, believed that he acted 'as a good knight, not as a general'; 'we cannot ascribe much influence on the fate of the day to the French king', which seems an extraordinary remark given that historian's lucid account of the battle.[44]

The armies faced each other about an arrow shot apart. A silence descended in which at first no one spoke. Then, after making a speech, Philip embraced those around him, proclaiming: 'In God is all our hope.' Behind Philip throughout

43. Roger of Wendover, ed. Giles, p. 300; Roger of Wendover, ed. Coxe, III, p. 290.
44. Oman, II, p. 489.

the battle stood the household clergy, including William the Breton, chanting psalms and prayers while their knees knocked. The battle began at a command from Guérin de Glapion on the right, which is strongly suggestive of Philip's motive for placing him there. Philip had initially been mostly concerned about being outflanked on the more exposed left flank.[45] He began the battle by driving the enemy left into its centre, and turning attention away from his own left.

The trumpets sounded and Guérin ordered the 300 horse sergeants from Soissons on his side of the field to charge against the enemy. This may well have been because of the unusually late arrival of the French infantry, coming back from across the bridge, and may also have been intended to gain a little time by causing the enemy to draw back once more. In the event the Flemish cavalry who faced this first attack were contemptuous of it, because it was made by men of lower social rank and not by nobles of equal standing to themselves. Apparently they therefore refused to charge forward as they normally would, and resisted only from a stationary position.

After surviving the first attack, three Flemish knights rode forward and issued a challenge to the enemy knights of Champagne. One of their number, Eustace de Mechelen, was rash enough to cry repeatedly in a great voice: 'death to the French!' He was surrounded and killed by Michel de Harnes, who found a gap in his enemy's armour. Michel exulted: 'he has now received the death he promised to the French'.[46]

Only gradually, as Burgundy's knights became involved, did it become a more general conflict; the chroniclers concentrated on individual incidents, described as though they were jousting combats. There was a certain amount of confusion: one man fell with his legs pointing to the sky, one fell with his head buried in the mud, loose horses charged about the field, some with hocks severed, some 'vomiting

45. Luchaire in Lavisse, p. 191; William the Breton, 'Vie' in *Vie de Philippe Auguste*, ed. M. Guizot (Paris, 1825) p. 281; 'Vie' in *Oeuvres*, ed. Delaborde, I, pp. 273–4: 'stabant retro regem, non procul ab ipso, capellanus qui scripsit hec, et quidam clericus . . .'.
46. William the Breton, *Philippide*, ed. Guizot, p. 326; 'Philippide', ed. Delaborde, II, p. 324, l. 150: 'Mortem quam Francis inclamas accipe, dixit'.

entrails', while bodies accumulated on the field: 'many a shiny shield and helmet could then be seen lying there'.[47] The duke of Burgundy himself, like many other of the leaders in this battle, was unhorsed at one point, but was saved and able to return to the fray. The count of St-Pol charged right through the allied line and had enough control over his men to rally them and attack again from the rear, bringing disorder to the Flemish knights. The count of Melun accomplished a similar feat. As the battle spread along the rest of the line, gradually the French gained the upper hand on their own left. Ferrand count of Flanders was unhorsed and captured. Half dead from wounds and exhausted, he surrendered to the brothers Mareuil.

Otto IV initiated the next major stage in the battle, by ordering his own centre to advance and engage the section of the enemy where Philip himself was placed. Attack on the enemy commander was a common and often successful ploy. Infantry had filed through the cavalry to be at the fore in Philip's central division. They were proud militia from the communes for the most part, but they proved no match for Otto's onslaught. It is often said that Bouvines was an early battle to demonstrate the power of commune infantry. In a sense this is true, because it showed the potential of such forces, but in the major phases of the conflict in which they were engaged, they were always defeated. To save the situation, Philip and his cavalry in the centre had to charge forward themselves. This halted the allied advance, but left Philip and those with him in a forward and isolated position.

Philip himself was unhorsed by a halberd aimed between chest and head, and fell with the lance still hanging from his mail tunic. He had been saved by his armour, and then by the courage and loyalty of his household knights: Peter Tristan stood over the king for a while, and then mounted him on his own horse, which Philip jumped on with 'surprising agility', while Galon de Montigny raised and lowered the royal banner in such a way as to attract attention to the need for urgent aid.[48]

47. Duby, *Bouvines*, p. 200.
48. William the Breton, 'Vie', ed. Guizot, p. 286; 'Vie', ed. Delaborde, I, p. 283: 'spe citius a terra surgens inopinata levitate equum ascendit'.

One of the few major figures in Philip's army to be killed was Stephen Longchamp, a household knight, felled by a dagger pushed through the opening in his helmet. William the Breton says the enemy were using long thin knives, sharpened on three sides, that is of a triangular section, no doubt intended especially to pierce through gaps in armour. Here and there allied knights were surrounded and captured, caught 'like little birds in a trap'.[49]

Meanwhile the French left wing had become engaged at much the same time as the centre. Philip had felt most concern over this sector, but in the event it proved the decisive one for the French victory. The primary allied tactic proved not to be an outflanking attempt, which Guérin and Philip had feared or perhaps prevented, but the reverse – an attempt to break straight through the centre of the French. The allied right now advanced at an angle, aiming in towards the centre and Philip. The response of the French was correct and successful. We do not know who was responsible, but probably the credit should go to the bishop of Beauvais, who 'happened by chance to have a mace in his hand'.[50] At any rate the French left moved across to block the advance from the allied right, and successfully halted the threatening move. They also delivered the first really decisive blow in the battle.

Most of the moves to this point had been countered, but now the allied left was smashed. The bishop of Beauvais, in most unbishoply manner, clubbed down William Longsword earl of Salisbury, breaking his helmet. Like Odo of Bayeux at Hastings, the bishop was armed with a mace, or perhaps a baton, rather than a sword, which seems in the latter's case at least to have honoured the word but not the intention of the Church ban on the drawing of blood by clerics.[51] The English earl was captured. Hugh de Boves, who had taunted others with cowardice before the battle, took to flight. The determination of the forces fighting in response

49. Duby, *Bouvines*, p. 211, from Philip Mouskes.
50. Duby, *Bouvines*, p. 201, from William the Breton.
51. See R.A. Brown, 'The battle of Hastings', *ANS*, III, 1980, pp. 1–21, in n. 15, who thought that Odo's mace was only for use as a baton, though in the Bayeux Tapestry he certainly looks aggressive enough to be using it as a weapon.

to the glitter of money from King John's purse had not proved very great. The imperial right melted away.

Only Renaud de Dammartin, for whom nothing but victory would do, fought on with the support of mercenary infantry and his own knights. Their resistance survived all the other conflicts across the field, but it did not engage all of the French left. The capture and flight of the bulk of the allied forces on this wing resulted in surplus troops remaining on the French left, who again were well commanded and not allowed to pursue or drift away, but were turned in against the enemy centre. Throughout the battle the discipline of the French army, and the ability to transfer its impetus as desired, was superior. The Béthune chronicler says the allies 'did not ride as well or in as orderly a fashion as the French'.[52]

Along the line the French had success after success. Philip was still sorely pressed in the centre, but on his left Ferrand of Flanders joined the list of noble prisoners. Gradually it became clear that the likely outcome in the centre was the capture not of Philip, but of Otto IV. Gerard la Truie said that Otto could be recognized by his gold shield with the black eagle upon it.[53] William des Barres, a knight of great renown, with a group of other household men managed to ride around the central infantry force and chase after Otto. Peter Mauvoisin grabbed the emperor's bridle, while Gerard la Truie twice delivered blows upon the emperor's body, the second sliding off his armour to strike his mount in the eye. Otto's horse was seriously wounded and plunged away to its death. Bernard Horstmann handed his own horse to the emperor, and once more William des Barres gave chase after Otto until the Saxons halted the pursuer's progress by stabbing his horse. Thomas of St-Valery was able to save William's life. Otto IV managed to leave the field. Fighting continued, but the battle was as good as over. Philip realized this, exulting over the emperor's disappearance: 'you will not see his face again today'.[54] The allied *carroccio* was smashed to pieces with axes, the imperial eagle standard was carried to Philip with its wings broken off.

52. Duby, *Bouvines*, p. 195, from the Anonymous of Béthune.
53. Philip Mouskes, p. 369.
54. Baldwin, *Government*, p. 217.

Only Renaud de Dammartin of Boulogne fought on. This episode is of more interest for technical military development, and as a subject worthy of chivalric praise, than for its effect on the battle. It was a last ditch fight by a desperate man. He carried a great ash lance and was a skilled horseman, but according to William the Breton he was also a womanizer, and it was Venus who inspired him with new fire.[55] Renaud's fears for the future should he be defeated proved justified; he would never be free again. On the day of Bouvines, he at least showed that the taunts of cowardice for wishing to avoid battle were false, and that his warnings against fighting might have been better heeded than scorned.

What is of technical military interest is the manner in which Renaud fought on, and the reason his troops survived so long. He formed the 700 infantrymen with him into a circle, two ranks deep. They were chiefly pikemen, their pikes long enough to hold horses at bay. He and his cavalry then used this pike ring like a castle wall. Indeed it was described as 'a kind of living tower', a 'fortress of pikes', 'a rampart of men at arms'.[56] The knights issued out in sorties, and when tired or under great pressure retreated back inside the ring for a breather. It proved very effective, but in the end as their friends around them were captured or fled the field, the sheer weight of numbers against them told, and Thomas of St-Valery was sent in by Philip to finish them off.

Renaud by this time was left with only some half dozen knights around him. In a final sortie the count was brought down. An unhorsed sergeant, Peter de la Tournelle, got under his horse, lifted its armour and wounded it. The horse fell on its master, and Renaud's leg was trapped. A boy tried to knife the fallen count, and Renaud's life was only saved by the protection of his armour and the intervention of Guérin, to whom he surrendered. The circle of Brabançons was hewed down, killed to the last man, as was the customary fate for those who were not knights.

It was said that the battle lasted three hours, though some modern historians have doubted this. Delbrück thought it was

55. William the Breton, 'Philippide', ed. Delaborde, p. 332, l. 331: 'Annua quando novis Venus incitat ignibus illum'.
56. Luchaire in Lavisse, p. 195; William the Breton, 'Vie', ed. Guizot, p. 288; William the Breton, 'Vie', ed. Delaborde, I, p. 285: 'duplici serie in modum rote ad instar castri obsessi'.

'decided almost at the first clash'; but our description of the details shows this not to be the case. If someone who was there thought it lasted three hours, there seems no good reason to doubt it.[57] Philip ordered that the pursuit should only be over the restricted distance of one or two miles, because the country was difficult and unfamiliar. After a while, trumpets sounded the recall. Philip stayed put on the battlefield and remained at Bouvines for the night. This did allow some of the allied force to escape along the Tournai road, and Otto IV to make his getaway, but he would no longer be a threat to anyone. The dead were buried in the grounds of the abbey of Cysoing, the wounded taken off to Douai.

Comments on the tactics of the battle are generally contemptuous and dismissive. Luchaire wrote: 'nothing was more elementary than the battle tactics of a king of France at the end of the twelfth century'. Oman thought it no more than 'a colossal tilting match', with little manoeuvring by either side. Warren wrote that 'tactically it was a crude affair', made up of confused mêlées; and Petit-Dutaillis thought 'the battles of those days were not a matter of science'. This last point has now been countered in general terms by modern military historians, but few have had much to say in praise of the tactics at Bouvines.[58]

It is hoped that our brief account demonstrates that Philip, if not one of the great commanders of the Middle Ages, was at least a competent one. He had deployed his troops successfully, despite the pressure of time and circumstances. Forced into battle against his will, he had selected an adequate site, protected at the rear by the river and to the left and right by marshes and woodland. The placing of Guérin de Glapion and his role suggests that the opening move of the battle was a planned tactic. The operation of the French left was shrewd and effective in blocking the chief tactical ploy of the allies, when they attempted to move their right wing eastwards against the enemy centre. The French troops showed good discipline throughout, as for example the return to the fight of those who broke through the allied

57. H. Delbrück, *History of the Art of War*, III, trans. W.J. Renfroe Jr (Westport, CT, 1982) p. 417.
58. Luchaire in Lavisse, p. 248; Oman, I, p. 489; W.L. Warren, *King John*, 2nd edn (London, 1978) p. 223; Petit-Dutaillis, p. 225.

ranks, and that is always a sign of good command. Infantry and pike forces might be the arm of the future, but they had been successfully dealt with by Philip in 1214. Otto may have escaped, but the haul of prisoners was an impressive one. The threat which Bouvines had posed to Philip Augustus and to France had been decisively answered by a triumph in the field. Philip deserves the credit for successfully commanding one of the great victories of the Middle Ages.

. . .

THE IMMEDIATE EFFECTS OF THE BATTLE

There was immediate reward for the victors: booty, armour and weapons were seized, carts were captured full of gold vases and clothes; there were lucrative ransoms to be claimed for the prisoners. Peasants cavorted about in the abandoned imperial silks. Philip did not forget his debt to God. He gave praise at once in the nearby chapel for the success he had been granted. Victory in battle was a judgement of God, and Philip became now the beloved of the Church. His wishes were far more difficult to gainsay. He was soon to found a chapel in commemoration of his victory. Not only the Church now accepted the increased authority of the king, he was 'feared and respected all over the land'.[59]

In the battle, the French had captured some 130 knights and five counts or earls, those of Boulogne, Flanders, Salisbury, Dortmund and Tecklenburg. Some 110 of the knights were taken to Paris in carts. Most were held in the two fortresses at either end of the bridge over the Seine in Paris; others were kept in secure royal towns. Some were put into the hands of magnates, some into those of household men, so that they could benefit from the ransoms. In general Philip was not vindictive. Most of the prisoners were ransomed and none was executed. As he said of Arnoul d'Audenarde: 'if he has done me wrong in order to serve his lord, I hold no ill toward him on that account'.[60] Only those whom Philip believed to have betrayed his trust had much to fear.

59. Duby, *Bouvines*, p. 216; from the Minstrel of Reims, *MGH*, XXVI, pp. 538–41.
60. Duby, *Bouvines*, p. 197; from the Anonymous of Béthune, *RHF*, XXIV, pp. 768–70.

As Philip surveyed the battlefield on the evening of 27 July when it was lit by French candles, as he set about preparing the army to move on, as he made his way back to Paris, the extent of his triumph must have dawned on him. He had almost another decade to reign, and its tenor would be entirely different from the years which preceded Bouvines. At a stroke Philip had become the most successful royal commander in French history. Not one enemy, but virtually all his enemies, had been either destroyed or seriously weakened by his great victory.

Otto IV had escaped, but to what? His defeat was the last straw in his decline from power. He had alienated the papacy, which had already turned towards his young rival Frederick of Hohenstaufen. Frederick had always been a stronger candidate by his descent than Otto, and there was every excuse now to accept the son of Henry VI. Few in Germany could any longer be in doubt as to where the future lay, and the nobles hastened to make their peace with the young Frederick, soon to be their new emperor. As a symbol of the outcome of the battle, Philip had the captured imperial standard, or at least its broken remains, sent on to Frederick of Hohenstaufen. The latter was crowned at Aachen in 1215. Otto retired to Brunswick and died in 1218 from an overdose of medicine, 'poor and miserable' and in a mean house, his fate sealed by the defeat at Bouvines.[61]

Philip had already, through his military and diplomatic efforts throughout the reign, caused a deterioration in the power of the county of Flanders. Whereas Flanders had been a powerful and virtually independent principality when Philip first came to the throne, ruled by a count who sought to dominate the young king, the county had now become dependent upon the king's will. Its heiresses had been under his wardship, and it was the king who had arranged the marriage of Joan to Ferrand of Portugal, and his succession to Flanders. Ferrand, however, had proved unwilling to subordinate himself to the French monarchy, and had with some reluctance moved into the influence of the German emperor and the English king, with the backing of most of his subjects. Now the pro-English party had been destroyed and pro-French castellans had been restored. Now, after Bouvines,

61. Duby, *Bouvines*, p. 216, from the Minstrel of Reims.

Ferrand was Philip's prisoner. For the rest of Philip's reign Flanders proved no threat. In the end, only the parts of Flanders which Philip had already acquired before Bouvines remained under the rule of the French monarchy, but in 1214 it seemed that the county must come inevitably to France. Even though that did not happen, Bouvines played a large part in dictating that Flanders would not come entirely under imperial control either, and that Philip would retain his earlier gains.

Count Ferrand of Flanders suffered humiliation. He was chained and placed upon a cart, pulled by two iron grey horses which were called by the same name as himself. Two *ferrands* pulling a third, taunted the peasants who lined the route as victors and captives passed. The sad count was to spend many years imprisoned; only after the deaths of Philip and his son Louis VIII was Ferrand finally released in 1227. He died six years later of an illness contracted in prison, a broken man.

Renaud de Dammartin of Boulogne was a less powerful count than Ferrand, but in many ways a stronger personality. Once a comrade of the king of France, and much favoured by him, he had turned against the king and gone into bitter exile. His intention in fighting at Bouvines was to bring down Philip and to recover his county. Philip now told the captive Renaud: 'after all you have done against me, I give you your life'.[62] But the king was furious when he learned that Renaud had continued to act against him by sending a secret message to Otto IV to renew the fight. Philip kept his word and Renaud his life, but it was made too painful an existence to be enjoyed. On one occasion the king climbed the stairs of the tower where Renaud was imprisoned, and to his face listed his betrayals and treacheries, which he promised never to forget. Renaud languished in prison, and in pitiful conditions. He was chained to a heavy log, which two men had to lift every time he wanted to go to the toilet. Unaided, he could only move half a pace in his chains. His county was granted to Philip's illegitimate son, Philip Hurepel, who saw to it that Renaud would never regain his lands. All those years later, when Ferrand was released, Renaud's hopes of

62. William the Breton, 'Philippide', ed. Delaborde, II, p. 353, ll. 125, 132–3.

freedom were again dashed. He realized he was to remain in prison for ever. It was too much. He could take no more and committed suicide.

Hugh de Boves had fled the field at Bouvines and escaped. He made for safety in England, but drowned after being caught in a storm out of Calais, and his body was washed ashore at Yarmouth. William Longsword, the earl of Salisbury, had been captured in the battle, but Philip had no grudge against him such as he had against Ferrand and Renaud. Salisbury had simply been loyal to his royal master, John, and Philip allowed the earl to be exchanged by the count of Dreux for his captured son. John refused this offer, but the earl was soon released. He had yet a distinguished career ahead of him, and would die as a valiant crusader.

As for King John, he had not been at Bouvines, but he suffered much by its outcome. His patient years of rebuilding a coalition against Philip, his hopes of recovering the continental lands of the Angevin Empire, all were ended on that day of battle. Louis once again was able to make progress south of the Loire and recover what John had recently gained. La Roche-au-Moine had been a humiliation for the Plantagenets, but Bouvines was an absolute disaster.

King John had saved Poitou and Gascony, but now the days of Angevin control of Poitou were numbered, though John would not live to see its final loss. In addition, as for Normandy, Brittany, Maine and Anjou, they were all gone. In fact Philip was relatively generous to John and agreed a six-year truce at Chinon in 1214. But there were repercussions to Bouvines in England also. As one modern historian has it: 'the road from Bouvines to Runnymede was a short one'.[63] In 1213 Philip had been planning an invasion of England; his son Louis was now to revive the plan and claim the English throne, encouraged by discontented English barons.

There were many causes of complaint against King John: his treatment of the Church, his tax demands, his ruthless, cruel and inconsistent conduct, his losses abroad. Bouvines brought them to a head. The barons met on their own and discussed how the kingdom should be governed. Some invited the French to rule them. They drew up demands for

63. D.A. Carpenter, *The Minority of Henry III* (London, 1990) p. 9.

constitutional and political change. John had temporarily to accept the humiliation of agreeing to Magna Carta, with all its restraints upon his powers. He tried to fight back, but died within the year, leaving behind a divided land, with French invaders and baronial rebels in arms against him. It was many years before England could recover from the crisis brought closer by the defeat of his friends and paid men at Bouvines.

Philip's return to Paris was a triumphal procession, with the prisoners on show, including Ferrand chained in a cage. Bells were rung along the route, branches and flowers laid before the victors. Peasants left their labours in the fields and came to stare and to cheer, sickles in hand, pitchforks on shoulders. The day after the battle Philip came to Douai, and the following day to Bapaume. When he reached Paris, the citizens came out to rejoice, and the revels continued for a whole week, night becoming day in the brightness of the torches, with singing and dancing and feasting.

Chapter 11

THE LAST YEARS

There is a story that messengers carrying the news from Prince Louis of King John's flight at La Roche-au-Moine in one direction, and from Philip of victory in the battle of Bouvines in the other direction, met at a spot near Senlis, where afterwards an abbey was built to commemorate the event. This being the case, Louis's messenger had not exactly hurried, but certainly there was good cause for thanking God and rejoicing at the double triumph for the Capetians.[1] There were yet nine years of the reign to run after the triumph at Bouvines, and as a result of the battle they were to be relatively quiet years. France gloried in the victory, few cared to oppose the king now, and peace and prosperity resulted. Professor Baldwin has seen the period as 'a tranquil epilogue', though it was perhaps a little more than that.[2]

We have briefly considered the immediate effects of the great battle, but there were longer-term effects as well, and this chapter sees the working out of them in France and elsewhere. Philip had never been a demonstrative king, and he did not become so now. He had always preferred negotiation and diplomacy to war, further demonstrated by the fact that once triumphant he did not lead a major campaign again. In many ways his son, Louis, emerged as a more prominent figure than the king during the last decade of the reign. There was to be a certain tension between the youthful and aggressive designs of Louis, and the caution and

1. La Roche-au-Moine was on 1 July, Bouvines on 27 July, 1214.
2. J.W. Baldwin, *The Government of Philip Augustus* (Berkeley, CA, 1986) p. xix.

restraints of his father. Philip's caution, though, was more than inactivity, he was eager to retain his extensive gains and feared losing them by precipitate aggression. His government was now well practised, and his chosen servants, men such as Guérin de Glapion and Bartholomew de Roye, dominated administration during the last years. Philip allowed more rein for Louis's activities, but he never let his own restraining hand lose ultimate control.

For King John, Bouvines had been a terrible disaster. His efforts to bolster the imperial forces in 1214 had utterly failed. In effect Bouvines confirmed the collapse of the Angevin Empire which Philip had brought about ten years before. It was the English barons who offered the crown to Louis in order to encourage French involvement in their cause. Even the previously loyal and reliable William of Salisbury turned away from John for a time. It was said that he had been antagonized by John's seduction of his wife during the earl's imprisonment after Bouvines.

Philip concentrated on introducing his own system of government into the lands which had once been under John's rule. The wisdom of Philip as a ruler is nowhere better demonstrated. He ruled firmly, he sought to integrate the new areas, for example by using baillis, but he was prepared to compromise. In the southern areas, where a different system had existed under the Angevins too, he relied on the local nobility to represent him. In Normandy, after initial reforms, he allowed some relaxation back towards the former Norman system.

. . .

PRINCE LOUIS IN ENGLAND

In the last years of his father's reign, Prince Louis undertook two major aggressive campaigns. The first of these was an invasion of England. Considering its impact, this campaign has been given surprisingly little attention, probably because it can now be viewed with the knowledge that it failed. But it came very close to success. We shall never know for certain what was Philip's attitude to the project. It cannot be said that he was entirely opposed to such a venture, since he had himself planned invasion in 1213 and only called it off under papal threat of excommunication after John had submitted to the Church. Had he been resolutely opposed it would surely never have occurred.

In 1215 the Church again made threats against Philip, since John, now having taken the cross, was even more firmly under ecclesiastical protection. But John's position in England was frail; virtually the whole of the baronage favoured the demands incorporated into Magna Carta. It was only the Church's censure again, the pope calling the charter 'vile and shameful . . . unjust and illegal', which caused some of them to hesitate.[3] Even so, many English barons were prepared to risk the Church's ban and proceeded to force John into accepting the charter. The same barons were ready to invite Louis to take the throne. Wendover says they were 'unanimously determined to appoint Louis', though this is clearly an exaggeration.

A group of English barons came to join Louis in France, including Robert Fitz Walter and Eustace de Vesci. They treated their opposition to John as something of a crusade, and the backing of Stephen Langton gave that some credence. Robert Fitz Walter called himself the 'Marshal of the host of God and Holy Church'.[4] Louis had already made a claim for the English throne, based on his marriage to Blanche of Castile, grand-daughter of Henry II. The claim was now repeated and it was asserted, as in 1213, that John had been deposed for the killing of Arthur of Brittany.

At the assembly at Melun on 24 April 1216, it was proclaimed: 'the throne of England is vacant, since King John has been condemned in our court'.[5] Philip was present and the papal legate, Gualo, begged him to call off the invasion. Louis arrived and sat beside his father, turning to scowl at the legate. Philip agreed when his son said he had a just claim, though he would not go so far as to promise aid for Louis. Philip told Gualo that he had always been a devoted and faithful ally of the pope, and promised not to assist the

---

3. A. Luchaire in E. Lavisse, ed., *Histoire de France depuis les Origines jusqu'à la Révolution*, III, Pt I (Paris, 1911) p. 253.
4. Roger of Wendover, *Flowers of History*, ed. J.A. Giles, 2 vols (London, 1899) II, p. 358; Roger of Wendover, *Chronica*, ed. H.O. Coxe, 5 vols (London, 1841–44) III, p. 299: 'Mareschallum exercitus Dei et sanctae ecclesiae'; R.V. Turner, *King John* (Harlow, 1994) pp. 234–5.
5. Luchaire in Lavisse, p. 255.

expedition. But he said that if his son's claim could be proved: 'let what is right be conceded to him'.

The legate listened as the case for Louis was made out.[6] Louis claimed that the war against John predated the latter's taking the cross, and that the just cause for invasion still remained. The legate refused to accept the argument, and threatened excommunication if he continued with the plan. When Philip's ameliorating influence was sought, Louis turned on him, telling his father: 'it is not up to you to decide matters concerning England . . . I fight for the inheritance of my wife', which sounds more like a petulant son than one in secret conspiracy with his father.[7]

Louis left, and Gualo asked Philip for a safe-conduct. The king promised protection through his lands, but said he could not speak for his son's fleet under Eustace on the seas. It sounds like a reasonable enough proviso, but Gualo was enraged, obviously thinking Philip was not doing enough. The Church's attempt to halt the invasion failed, but it was enough to restrain Philip from giving open support. The excommunication of Louis in the spring of 1216 was a blow to the campaign, though the death of Innocent III shortly afterwards lessened its impact.

What is unclear is whether Philip's stance was simply hypocrisy, in order to avoid Church condemnation, a 'feigned reluctance' as is usually assumed, or whether the king had genuine reservations about it.[8] If anything, after Bouvines, he was in a stronger position than he had been in 1213. In 1213 he had sufficiently heeded the warnings of the Church to halt an invasion in which he personally had been far more involved; it seems likely that the same restraints acted upon him in 1215. Philip never liked proceeding with political and military projects for which he could not claim full legal and moral justification. No doubt he had every wish to defeat John in England, but he did not wish to defy the Church in order to do so. That being the case, he must have had serious reservations about his son's actions. It is our view

6. Roger of Wendover, ed. Giles, II, p. 362; Roger of Wendover, ed. Coxe, III, p. 365: 'torvo vultu'; 'Ergo domino papae et ecclesiae Romanae devotus semper fui et fidelis'; 'et quod justum fuerit concedatur eidem'.
7. Luchaire in Lavisse, p. 256.
8. E.M. Hallam, *Capetian France, 987–1328* (Harlow, 1980) p. 133.

that Philip's refusal to participate, which certainly lessened his son's hopes of success, was genuine albeit reluctant.

When the countess of Champagne and her son were asked to contribute towards the expedition, they refused on the grounds that they did not wish to fight against a king protected by the Church as a crusader. A gang of knights and sergeants then broke in upon her to enforce a contribution. Lavisse believes that Philip allowed this, but it is so untypical of the way that Philip behaved, and so much more in the style of the youthful and aggressive Louis, that there can be little doubt who was responsible. Philip disclaimed any part in it. Indeed the Champagne opposition, and his son's reaction, could only have confirmed his reservations about the whole project.[9]

The Minstrel of Reims has Philip telling his son: 'I believe you should not go', warning that his English friends will not be as good as their word. Louis's response was: 'let the will of God be done'. There is no good reason to discount the evidence of the chronicler best placed to know Philip's mind. William the Breton says that Philip 'refused consent, not wishing to offend the pope'.[10] At the same time Philip was fond of his son, had no sympathy for John, and did not utterly forbid his son's activities. Philip also had serious reservations about the papal claims over England, disputing John's right to hand the kingdom to the papacy: 'the kingdom of England never was the patrimony of St Peter, nor is, nor will be'.[11]

Louis first sent a force with 140 knights to aid the rebel barons in England late in 1215, with others following in January. Louis himself sailed at nine o'clock in the evening of 20 May 1216, in bad weather, so that only seven of the ships, including Louis's, arrived directly at their destination. The prince's early success was dramatic, and shows the

9. Luchaire in Lavisse, p. 257.
10. Luchaire in Lavisse, p. 255; William the Breton, *La Philippide, Poème,* ed. M. Guizot (Paris, 1825) p. 362; William the Breton, 'Philippide' in *Oeuvres de Rigord et Guillaume le Breton,* ed. H-F. Delaborde, SHF, vols 210, 224 (Paris, 1882–85) I, p. 359, l. 304: 'Pontificis nolente offensam incurrere summi'.
11. W.H. Hutton, *Philip Augustus* (London, 1896) p. 200; Roger of Wendover, ed. Giles, II, p. 361; Roger of Wendover, ed. Coxe, III, p. 364: 'Regnum Angliae patrimonium Petri nunquam fuit, nec est, nec erit'.

frailty of John's position. Virtually all the eastern half of England accepted Louis, as did London where bishops, nobles and citizens welcomed the prince as king, and Magna Carta was confirmed. Rochester was captured, Winchester surrendered; Orford, Norwich, Cambridge, Colchester, Guildford, Farnham, Odiham, Marlborough and Worcester were taken. The north had always been hostile to John. Only isolated garrisons offered pockets of real resistance, in powerful castles at Windsor, Lincoln and Dover. Louis naturally made these centres his targets and the war was to revolve around them.

Louis brought with him a powerful force of 1,200 knights, which included some of the great names from France's military past: William des Barres, Gerard la Truie, Enguerand de Coucy, together with the counts of Dreux, Brittany, St-Pol and Perche. This roll of great men suggests that if Philip's support was half-hearted, so was his opposition. There was also support for Louis from John's British neighbours: Scotland, Wales and Ireland. Alexander II king of Scots came to Canterbury and did homage to Louis. Even some of John's hired Flemish mercenaries, mostly unpaid, went over to Louis, as did some of his barons, including the earls of Salisbury, Surrey, York and Arundel, together with William the Marshal's son.

King John was never entirely crushed, but his position was desperate. Louis returned to France to seek reinforcements, which shows that Philip had not provided much direct support for the expedition. Indeed the king now refused to speak to his son. According to William the Breton, Philip had confiscated unspecified lands of his son for going on the expedition.[12] Louis did not return to England until 23 April 1217, a surprisingly long period, once more suggesting little cooperation from Philip, and in the meantime the prince had lost his best chance. Wendover says that during this period Louis forfeited the goodwill of the English barons.[13]

The turning point of the campaign, and the first time when it began to look as if Louis might not succeed, was the

12. William the Breton, 'Vie', in *Vie de Philippe Auguste,* ed. M. Guizot (Paris, 1825) p. 322; William the Breton, 'Vie' ed. H-F. Delaborde, I, p. 307: 'totam terram filii sui et aliorum baronum qui cum eo erant confiscavit'.
13. Roger of Wendover, ed. Giles, II, p. 382; Roger of Wendover, ed. Coxe, IV, p. 10.

death of King John from massive indigestion attributed to the consumption of peaches with new cider on 19 October 1216.[14] It may well have actually been a heart attack. The strength of the baronial opposition to the crown was removed at a blow by the king's death, which Wendover thought 'had stilled war's raging storm'.[15] Virtually all the English barons united now in support of the reforms of Magna Carta, despite the pope's condemnation of it, and most were prepared to accept the succession of John's young son.

Barons who had various reasons for opposing John, had less reason to oppose his nine-year-old son, now crowned as Henry III (1216–72). One by one the English nobles returned to the fold, including major converts such as the earl of Salisbury. Louis's military strength was thereby much weakened. Eleven of the twelve English bishops who had sided with Louis, now returned to support the young monarch. The new English government was weak, and the crown in desperate poverty, but Louis had little hope of taking the throne from the boy who now had nearly universal support within England.[16]

With hope already waning for Louis, now came the two death-blows to his campaign. The new rulers of England, led by William the Marshal in person, decided to try and relieve the long-pressed garrison at Lincoln. Louis had taken over the town of Lincoln in 1216, but was still having to blockade the castle. The Marshal and his comrades managed to get help through to the beleaguered garrison on 20 May 1217. The relief force entered by unblocking the unused west gate, and then made a sortie into the town against the French besiegers. There was a sharp encounter in the steep streets, and the French were 'killed like pigs'.[17] They suffered a severe reverse, and Louis's hope of overall success was virtually destroyed.[18]

14. Baldwin, *Government*, p. 333; Roger of Wendover, ed. Coxe, III, p. 385: 'de fructu persicorum et novi ciceris potatione'.
15. Roger of Wendover, ed. Coxe, III, p. 386: 'Qui moriens multum sedavit in orbe tumultum'; K. Norgate, *John Lackland* (London, 1902) p. 286.
16. D.A. Carpenter, *The Minority of Henry III* (London, 1990) pp. 51, 109, 154.
17. Roger of Wendover, ed. Giles, II, p. 395; Roger of Wendover, ed. Coxe, IV, p. 22: 'telis confossi sunt et ad instar porcorum jugulati'.
18. William the Breton, 'Vie', ed. Guizot, p. 327; William the Breton, 'Vie', ed. Delaborde, I, p. 314: 'tristes et victi'.

This was made even more certain by a second serious defeat, this time at sea. Reinforcements had been raised in France, apparently largely through the efforts of Louis's wife, Blanche. They were sent over the Channel in a fleet under the command of Eustace the Monk, a renegade monk who had once served John for money and was now in the pay of Louis. Despite his experience in sea command, Eustace was trapped by the English fleet under Hubert de Burgh and Richard of Chilham near Sandwich. The boy king, Henry III, and his aged Marshal were able to observe the battle at sea from the cliffs. The English threw lime into the wind which blew in the enemy's faces and blinded them, allowing the English to board. Eustace the Monk was captured and, though he offered riches in return for his life, was beheaded on the spot with a sword. The head was placed on a pike and paraded through the streets of Canterbury.

These two defeats made it clear that Louis would have to give up the campaign. He ended the siege of Dover and went to London to open peace talks. William the Breton says the prince had to abandon the expedition because he did not receive aid from his father.[19] He began to negotiate terms, and agreement was reached between Louis and William the Marshal on an island near Kingston-upon-Thames in September. The demand that Louis should appear in his underwear to receive absolution was withdrawn and he was allowed to wear a mantle to cover his dignity. The peace was confirmed before the end of the year in the treaty of Lambeth, by which Louis secretly received 10,000 marks in compensation for abandoning his claim to the English throne.

Louis had failed, but it had not been an overwhelming humiliation. His reputation was not shattered. The English could offer little threat to the French monarchy for many years to come, and Philip was clearly happy to accept the settlement which his son made, with one exception. Louis had apparently agreed to try and persuade his father to return the Angevin continental lands to England, but it is not hard to guess how Philip received that request! Louis himself also ignored it when he became king. The settlement ended the

19. William the Breton, 'Vie', ed. Guizot, p. 325; William the Breton, 'Vie', ed. Delaborde, I, p. 314.

knife-edge of possible repercussions for defying the Church. Philip still retained all his gains on the continent.

. . .

FLANDERS AFTER BOUVINES

The threat from Philip's enemies in northern Europe faded away with their defeat at Bouvines. Flanders now found itself isolated and under French domination. The count of Flanders, Ferrand, remained in prison. His wife, Joan (d.1244), made efforts to get him released, but with Philip alive she had no success. For a time something like two-thirds of the nobility of Flanders and Hainault, captives from Bouvines, were in French prisons. The payments of their ransoms helped further to impoverish the northern nobility. For Warlop, 'the great period of the old Flemish nobility was definitely over'.[20] French or pro-French castellans were placed in charge of all the main fortifications of Flanders, and there was no hope of real opposition to Philip's wishes for the county.

The settlement for Flanders was drawn up by Philip in the treaty of Paris, imposing on Countess Joan French control of such centres as Ypres, Oudenarde and Cassel, a number of which also had their defences destroyed. New castles were not to be built without French permission. The heir of the duke of Brabant was to be handed into Philip's custody. Gradually Flemish prisoners taken at Bouvines were ransomed and released, but not Ferrand.

Philip arranged for restraints to be placed upon the future behaviour of those Flemish nobles who had opposed him, taking sureties for their future allegiance: as many as sixteen on Heluin de Wavres, twenty-three on Robert de Courtenay, £3,000 on Eustace de Ren should he take arms against Philip or Louis. It would not pay them or their friends to war against Philip again. When men such as Arnoul d'Audenarde were released, they found it wise to become pro-French in their allegiance. Arnoul even accompanied Prince Louis on the Albigensian Crusade in 1219. In Flanders only loyal castellans were appointed, such as Jean de Nesle for Bruges, who also became the bailli for both Flanders and Hainault.

20. H.E. Warlop, *The Flemish Nobility before 1300*, Pt I, Historical Study, I (Courtrai, 1975) p. 328.

The Flemish towns tried to maintain their essential trade with England, but they had to pass through a difficult period, and in general co-operated with the countess. When they submitted to Philip, they found King John taking reprisals against them. But John could no longer support Flemish mercenaries who had previously been in his pay, and they were dismissed. After John's death, the new English regime seemed even more impoverished, and *fiefs-rentes* previously paid to Flemings were halted. The Capetians seemed the only possible paymasters. Many Flemings went with Louis on his invasion of England, including William de St-Omer with a hundred knights.

Countess Joan did resist Philip's efforts to get her to divorce Ferrand and remarry. His candidate for her new husband was Peter Mauclerc of Brittany. It seems that Philip intended to try and repeat the Ferrand experiment of a friendly count under his own authority. But Joan was genuinely fond of her feckless and imprisoned partner, and refused to be divorced. She continued her efforts to have Ferrand released, eventually succeeding after the deaths of both Philip and his son Louis VIII, in 1227.

Nominally Countess Joan ruled Flanders, but in practice she was in the hands of the pro-French nobility, which itself was directed by Philip. She did have some success in opposing the ambitions of her brother-in-law. Bouchard d'Avesnes had married her younger sister, Margaret, in 1212. He was a Hainaulter, and had hopes of securing a stronger position in Flanders, perhaps of becoming count. Joan failed to get the marriage stopped, though she found support from both Innocent III and Honorius III (1216–27), so that Bouchard was excommunicated. He took arms against Joan, but was captured in 1219 and remained a prisoner until 1221. Then Joan forced him to separate from her sister, and Margaret was married to William de Dampierre in 1223. The Church, however, refused to recognize the new match, despite the fact that it produced a son, and in the end Bouchard was allowed to return to his wife.

Flanders was never to become entirely French, but some areas which had been Flemish did move permanently under the control of the crown: what became known as Artois, with the Amiénois, Valois and Vermandois. Philip had also, for the foreseeable future, destroyed English political influence in

Flanders. The government, the nobility, the main strongholds, all were under his sway. Flanders had become 'an annex of the Capetian monarchy'.[21]

. . .

THE EFFECT OF BOUVINES ON FRANCE

Not least of the beneficial effects of Bouvines for Philip was the impact of the battle on France itself. It confirmed all his previous gains, particularly those at the expense of John, which had provided an important expansion of the demesne, as well as of the income and authority of the French crown. These former Plantagenet territories, after Bouvines, accepted that the change was likely to be permanent. By now, the extension of royal demands was becoming established.

The following decade of peace underwrote all this; it was a period of relative ease and growth. The survival of one account from the later reign shows how, in this period, Philip had been increasing his revenue from the established sources. There was time to improve the efficiency of administration and to produce a budget with a balance, such as England would not possess for twenty years. In 1221, one-third of the crown's income was saved, giving a very healthy balance indeed.

And within France, the unrivalled power of the crown had to be respected. Philip had now been king for well over thirty years. He had seen off all potentially dangerous enemies. There was no dividend to be had from opposing such a powerful monarch. Philip had already been steadily extending the scope of royal justice; its progress now seemed inevitable. The peace coincided with an economic growth of France, whose cities prospered, and whose trade grew. A chronicler commented that 'the whole land was at peace for a long while'.[22]

The greatest threat to France and to the monarchy over the previous years had been not so much from foreign powers as from the great principalities within or bordering upon

---

21. G.G. Dept, *Les Influences Anglaise et Française dans le comté de Flandre au début du XIIIe siècle* (Ghent and Paris, 1928) p. 140.
22. G. Duby, *France in the Making, 987–1460*, trans. J. Vale (Oxford, 1991) p. 226; G. Duby, *The Legend of Bouvines*, trans. C. Tihanyi (Oxford, 1990) p. 197, from the Anonymous of Béthune, *RHF*, XXIV, pp. 768–70.

'France' and connected with it, from such as Flanders, Normandy, Toulouse, Champagne and Blois. Philip had steadily reduced the threat from all the principalities throughout his reign; Bouvines not only confirmed this progress, but marked the point beyond which there could be no return. Royal power and prestige now so much outdistanced that of any individual noble, that opposition began to seem hopeless or even foolish. Only coalition had made it seem possible in 1214, now there was no one to turn to. Bouvines was 'the victory which God had given', and Philip was now 'a hero-king'.[23]

The victory at Bouvines allowed Philip to become the ruler he wished to be. Many of the great figures of the past were ever hungry for further conquest, so that in the end their achievements outgrew the bounds of reality and their successors could not keep together the conquests they made: from Alexander the Great to Charlemagne and Henry II there is at least some truth in that.

Philip had never sought war, he had never sought battle. He had forbidden his son to attend, let alone to take part in, tournaments. Why had he done this? He did not forbid Louis from leading armies in campaigns. One concludes that Philip accepted the Church's teaching about tournaments. Philip is rarely seen as a devout Christian monarch, nearly always as a two-faced one. The criticisms of enemy chroniclers are usually accepted by historians, the comments of those who were close to him neglected. Philip had his flaws, but it is quite possible that he was genuine in his religious belief, and in his obedience to the rulings of the Church on spiritual matters. He kept a sober court, was opposed to tournaments, reluctant to fight a battle on a Sunday. He prayed in advance of that battle, and had priests chanting prayers behind him during the course of it, afterwards giving thanks to God for the victory.

Now that Philip was in an unassailable position he chose virtually to retire from a military life. Such war as occurred was led by his son. Philip did not retire from active life, but he concentrated on the peaceful pursuits, running the administration, conducting negotiations, mending bridges with the papacy. The only military activity to which he gave

23. Hallam, p. 179.

any approval in the last part of the reign, and that reluctantly, was the Albigensian Crusade.

. . .

PRINCE LOUIS IN THE SOUTH

It was the destiny of Philip's son to complete one part of his father's work, and to fit in place one piece of the jigsaw of provinces which would be drawn into the boundaries of modern France. Philip himself, after making considerable efforts to combat Angevin ambitions in southern France, once those ambitions had been thoroughly blunted by the outcome of Bouvines, showed little wish to continue activities in the south.

It was Louis rather than his father who displayed any aggressive intent. In this case, Philip was as unenthusiastic as he had been about the English invasion by his son, but for quite different reasons; though there was one point in common. Philip liked to have legal and moral support for his aggression. Over the invasion of England in 1216 there had been irremovable opposition from the Church. In the south the Church gave every encouragement, and pressured Philip to act by making various promises and offers. He had already failed to respond to appeals in 1201 and 1205, and had given but a brief explanation of his inaction in 1207.

As we have seen, Philip was prepared to deal with the problem of heresy in his realm. Nor was he uninterested in royal rights and peaceful action in the south; the trend of his charters shows the increase in that interest through the reign after 1209.[24] But for Philip, in the south, there was a different stumbling block to the legality of military action. He was reluctant to attack and disinherit the count of Toulouse.

Raymond count of Toulouse was subject to the king of France and, regarding that relationship, Philip felt that he himself, and not the Church, had the power of decision. When first appealed to for action against Raymond, Philip pointed out that the Church had not yet condemned Raymond as a heretic, and exclaimed: 'you are putting the cart

24. C. Higounet, 'Problèmes du Midi au temps de Philippe Auguste', in R-H. Bautier, ed., *La France de Philippe Auguste, le Temps des Mutations* (Paris, 1982) pp. 311–21, p. 319.

before the oxen'.[25] The more one looks at the evidence, the more it seems that Raymond VI (count 1194–1215, d.1222) was never himself a Cathar, and was always prepared, once there was a threat against him, to compromise and offer the Church what was required. He did public penance and took an oath that he was not a heretic. This was the sort of man with whom Philip could usually do business and reach an arrangement. Unfortunately for Count Raymond, his ecclesiastical opponents showed less willingness to compromise or show mercy.

Philip had allowed knights to participate in the southern crusade called by the pope, but never himself contemplated going. He did not even show much enthusiasm for his son's participation. The success of Simon de Montfort required some royal response. But for many years Philip was unwilling to assist in bringing down the count of Toulouse. Even the excommunication of Raymond VI in 1211, which cleared the way for royal intervention, did not spur Philip to action, nor did the enthusiastic preaching for the Albigensian Crusade by such as Jacques de Vitry in 1213.

In 1213 Prince Louis took the crusading vow, but Philip actually forbade his son to undertake a southern expedition. Louis, however, became increasingly interested in the south, encouraged by his wife Blanche of Castile with her southern background, and he was more free for activity there after the defeat of the coalition in 1214. Philip seems only to have been prepared for direct activity in the area when the balance of power was threatened by a third force. There was concern for a time over the involvement of Aragon, but the death of Pedro of Aragon at Muret in 1213 lessened that danger.

In 1215 Louis made his first expedition, passing through Montpellier, Narbonne and reaching Toulouse, which he entered in the company of Simon de Montfort. The defences of both the latter towns were destroyed. Raymond of Toulouse had suffered as a result of Simon's victory at Muret, and in 1215 was dispossessed in Simon's favour, though his son Raymond VII (1215–49) did not abandon hope and was to retain a reduced territory to the north of Toulouse.

Again, at first, Philip refused even to agree to Simon's desire to receive the county from him. He seems to have

25. G. Bordonove, *Philippe Auguste* (Paris, 1986) p. 268.

shared Innocent III's reservations about raising up a new powerful figure in Toulouse. Certainly Philip was never reluctant to receive homage from the lesser lords who held lands in the south. But in the end Simon was permitted to do homage to the king in 1216 for the county of Toulouse, the duchy of Narbonne, and the viscomtés of Béziers and Carcassonne.

Raymond was able to recover to some extent by 1217, with aid from Spain, and he re-entered Toulouse, where the local people 'fell on their knees and kissed his clothes, his feet, his legs, his arms and his fingers. It was with tears of joy that he was received.'[26] The southerners' hopes of a return to the old position seemed further increased when, in 1218, Simon de Montfort was killed while besieging Toulouse. Honorius III again appealed to Philip to send aid to the south, but the king seemed no keener than before.

Amaury de Montfort, Simon's son, found the going hard, and was soon prepared to cede his rights to the French crown. Again Philip was not enthusiastic about receiving them, and refused, while Raymond VII recovered many of the losses sustained by his father, including Carcassonne and Béziers. Raymond VI lived on till 1222, but his son now took charge of their interests. The war in the south became a war of the sons.

In 1219 Louis made his second expedition to the area, seeing possibly a consolation in efforts there for his failure in England. Perhaps it was this failure that caused him to vent his anger on the southern opposition; at Marmande, even though the garrison surrendered, dreadful atrocities were executed upon them: 'the earth, the soil, the streets were red with blood', and 5,000 people were killed.[27] Toulouse was besieged on 14 June, but after six weeks Louis had to burn his engines and abandon the attempt, probably because those members of his force under a forty-day agreement were ready to leave.

In 1222 an official army was sent by King Philip, with his blessing. This contained 200 knights, and it was said 10,000 infantry, under the count of La Marche and the archbishop of Bourges. It was not a particularly successful or important

26. J.R. Strayer, *The Albigensian Crusades* (Michigan, 1971) p. 114.
27. William the Breton, 'Vie', ed. Delaborde, I, p. 319: 'missus a patre suo'; Luchaire in Lavisse, p. 278.

expedition as such, but it marked a significant turning point in the history of the south. At last Philip was prepared openly to take part in the southern war.

Louis's opinion was undoubtedly of some importance in swaying his decision, but possibly most influential was fear of the intentions of Theobald IV count of Champagne (1201–53), who had a claim to Navarre (king, 1234–53). Theobald had shown increasing interest in the southern area and may have been planning to turn himself into a second and more powerful Simon de Montfort. At any rate, now at last there was genuine royal intervention. The Albigensian Crusade was no great success, but in the long run the political gain for the monarchy would be enormous. Eventually intervention led to the region coming directly under Capetian rule.

. . .

THE END OF AN ERA

From September 1222 Philip had been ill, 'suffering the common fate of humanity'. In that year, says William the Breton, there was an awesome comet which presaged the king's death and 'the decadence of the realm of France'. Philip made his will at St-Germain-en-Laye. By it, a good deal of cash was to be set aside for helping the Christian cause in the Holy Land, with money for the Templars, the Hospitallers and the king of Jerusalem. There was also money or jewels for the abbey of St-Denis, and gifts for the poor, orphans, widows and lepers.

For Ingeborg, now 'his own very dear wife', there was no bitter reference to their past differences, and she was to have £5,000. She lived on in comfort till 1236. In addition to his normal inheritance as the heir, a sum was set aside for his son Louis to use either for the defence of the realm or for an expedition to the Holy Land. Philip Hurepel, son of Agnes de Méran, in addition to his existing lands, was to be given the county of Clermont, and the Beauvaisis.[28]

28. William the Breton, 'Vie', ed. Guizot, pp. 345–6; William the Breton, *Philippide*, ed. Guizot, p. 371; William the Breton, 'Vie', ed. Delaborde, I, p. 322: 'si funus haberet amicum'; pp. 325–6; pp. 322–3: 'pretendens signum mortis ejusdem et debilitatem regni Francorum'; p. 319; William the Breton, 'Philippide', ed. Delaborde, II, pp. 373, 367–8, 366.

To the last Philip refused to stop working, and insisted on continuing with his itinerary. But in July 1223 he clearly knew himself to be failing, and called Prince Louis to him at Pacy-sur-Eure, where he had summoned a council. Here Philip imparted final words of wisdom to his son: that he should fear God and protect the poor and humble. According to Joinville, Philip also gave advice to his young grandson, the future St Louis, which clearly made a lasting impact on the boy.

According to William the Breton, Philip had a quartan ague, one of those fevers which was felt every fourth day.[29] The fever grew worse as the weather became hotter. Briefly he felt better, and wanted to go on to Paris, against the advice of his physician. But the following day, 14 July 1223, having reached Mantes, he felt worse again, and it was in that city he died. Philip Augustus was fifty-eight and had ruled France for forty-three years. A citizen of Segni at the papal court claimed to have received a vision in which he saw Philip going to heaven in the company of St Denis, together with angels clothed in white; after which he heard that Philip had died.[30]

Philip Augustus was the first French king to be buried in the fashion of the Angevins, in full regalia with crown and sceptre. He had died at Mantes, but the body was taken to Paris on a bier. At the point where the bearers rested and changed over, on entering the city, a church was to be built.[31] It was said that the lame and the blind were healed at the tomb. There was a procession to the abbey of St-Denis, where the king was buried in the presence of his son and heir Louis, together with his illegitimate son Philip Hurepel, and John de Brienne the king of Jerusalem.

According to William the Breton, 'he who had made a good beginning and a good middle had made a happy end'.[32] St Louis encapsulated his view of the royal past by having tombs built for Dagobert, Charles the Bald, and his own

29. William the Breton, *Philippide*, ed. Guizot, p. 370; 'Philippide', ed. Delaborde, II, p. 366, l. 493: 'Invadit febris regis quartanica corpus'.
30. R. Foreville, 'L'image de Philippe Auguste dans les sources contemporaines', in Bautier, pp. 115–32, p. 127.
31. Baldwin, *Government*, p. 391.
32. William the Breton, *Philippide*, ed. Guizot, p. 376; 'Philippide', ed. Delaborde, II, p. 372, l. 642: 'Est sortita bonum, finiri fine beato'.

immediate ancestors, Philip Augustus and Louis VIII, to be covered in gold and silver. The tombs for the ancient kings were built to the north of the choir, those for the Capetians to the south. There was a vacant place reserved for Louis IX himself. The whole thing was obviously meant to glorify the Capetian dynasty.

There can surely be no doubt that Philip II had been a great king, and unlike many who ruled for so long, he did not lose his powers or his authority at all in old age. There had been differences with his son Louis, and undoubtedly they had disagreed over certain policies, but there had been no flare-ups of the kind in which the Plantagenets frequently indulged. On his deathbed, Philip was able to say to his son: 'my son, you have never caused me any trouble'.[33] Philip had allowed Louis an increasing role in the direction of affairs, and the son had responded by voicing his differences and sometimes going his own way, but he was never openly at odds with his father. At his death the son showed nothing but respect.

Philip was not the king we in England have come to think him. He was not feeble, treacherous or double-dealing. He was bluff and hearty, fond of food, wine and women – though not immoderately so, never a glutton, a drunkard or a womanizer. He was a truly brave king, though no great warrior, who risked his life on occasions; a contrast to Richard the Lionheart, who to modern minds would appear as a kind of maniac, frequently risking his life for the least cause, and who eventually not surprisingly perished as a result of carelessness. Philip was the sort of man the modern world should admire: intelligent, diplomatic, effective, successful, but generally modest, peace-loving and hardworking. It is ironic that, thanks to historians, the general modern appreciation is something less than admiration.

Philip's chief clash with the papacy was over how or if his second and unsatisfactory marriage should have ended. He was only defiant to the extent that, for whatever reason, he could not stomach marriage to Ingeborg, and because he had a strong affection for Agnes, whom he treated and saw as his wife. He was a fond father to all his children,

33. Luchaire in Lavisse, p. 265; R. Pernoud, *Blanche of Castile*, trans. H. Noel (London, 1975) p. 90.

and their futures were carefully protected. Nor did Philip treat any of them unfairly, and there was no great malice between them.

. . .

EPILOGUE

The reign of Louis VIII (1223–26) seems little more than a postscript to that of his father. This was not because Louis lacked ability or energy, but simply because he lived only a further three years. In such a short time he nevertheless managed to make a significant contribution to French history. Described as small and thin, often ill, rather coldly pious, he was crowned with Blanche at Reims on 6 August 1223.

Louis VIII retained royal authority in Flanders, needing to assist Countess Joan through the strange episode of the False Baldwin, when a man turned up claiming to be Baldwin IX (1195–1206) the former count of Flanders who had become Latin emperor (1204–6). The latter had been killed by his captives after being taken in battle, but the impostor bathed in a brief period of glory, until he was shown up by those who had really known the dead emperor, and by questions put to him by Louis VIII himself at Péronne. The False Baldwin had been the excuse for popular revolt in Flanders, before his execution at Lille in October 1225. The episode had required direct intervention by Louis to restore order and showed the true political situation in the county. After that episode, however, Louis could begin to relax over Flanders and was even ready to release the long-imprisoned Count Ferrand. Louis VIII died before the count's freedom occurred, but Queen Blanche saw it through. Ferrand was set free for a ransom of £25,000, half of which Blanche returned in a gesture of generosity. The humbled count repaid it by remaining loyal to the crown for the rest of his life.

Appropriately the region where Louis VIII made most impact was the one where his actions had been more positive than those of Philip for several years. In the south Louis made two notable advances: he added Poitou to the areas taken over by the Capetians from the Plantagenets; and he ensured that the foremost beneficiary from the Albigensian Crusade was the French monarchy.

In 1224 Louis employed the army intended for the Albigensian Crusade against Poitou. He besieged and took Niort from Savaric de Mauléon, St-Jean d'Angely surrendered, and Louis finally won the prize ocean port of La Rochelle after a three-week siege. Poitou became an *apanage* for Louis's son Alphonse, henceforward known as Alphonse of Poitiers. Louis moved into Gascony, the last bastion of the continental Plantagenet empire, but Henry III's minority government was finally able to raise enough energy to save it in 1225. Henry III was keen on continental adventure, and twice attempted invasions of France, in 1230 and 1242, but both were complete disasters and easily resisted by the French government.

Louis VIII as king sent money to aid Amaury de Montfort and undertook his third expedition on the Albigensian Crusade. Raymond VII had just been excommunicated, which prepared the way. Unlike Philip, Louis was happy to accept the surrender to himself of Amaury's rights in the Languedoc, which Honorius III recognized. The pope also favoured an ecclesiastical tax to support the new crusade, which he had refused in the previous year. Louis showed more ruthlessness than his father, and agreed to an ordinance in 1226 which sanctioned the burning to death of heretics.

The crusade of 1226 saw the formation of the largest army the Capetians had ever assembled, but it was not a great success. After Louis thought he had arranged for his journey via Avignon, which was still considered as part of the imperial territory of Provence, that city decided to oppose him. Angered by this about-turn, Louis VIII sat down to besiege Avignon, thus losing precious time that might otherwise have been spent further south. He had to set up throwing engines, dig trenches, and build a bridge of boats. Food ran short, dysentery spread and there was a plague of enormous black flies. The count of St-Pol was killed by a stone from an engine, and Theobald of Champagne returned home.

In the end Avignon surrendered on terms, but from then on the royal expedition achieved little, apart from the surrender once again of Carcassonne. It may have been at the siege of Avignon that Louis contracted his fatal illness. By the time he arrived at Montpensier in the Auvergne, on his return journey, he was seriously ill, apparently suffering from dysentery, though one chronicler thought the cause of his

335

ill health was excessive chastity. Louis VIII died on 8 November 1226.[34]

Even the unexpectedly early death of Louis VIII in 1226 did not seriously undermine his own or Philip's work. There were difficulties during the minority of Louis IX (1226–70), which did not end until 1234, including serious baronial revolt. But Louis VIII's widow Blanche of Castile, and the structures of government established over the previous half century, proved sufficient to cope. The frail blond youth, surely one of the most pious monarchs ever to rule, yet from Joinville's portrait a likeable and charming person, survived the dangers of minority.

The outlook on the treatment of the poor and the Church, which Philip had imbibed from his own predecessors, and notably from his father Louis VII, was passed on to his own descendants. The deathbed advice to son and grandson was remembered for years. The royal role as protector of the Church and the poor was the foundation of the reputation of Louis IX. This is not the place, and indeed it would prove a rather pointless exercise, to argue the respective merits of Philip and his grandson. Certainly St Louis in no way saw himself as competing with his grandfather's reputation, only as emulating it.

Louis IX brought to fulfilment the geographical expansion of France in north and south. He made two major treaties which settled the political changes of the past into a more permanent pattern. The treaty of Paris made with Henry III in 1258, and confirmed in the following year, recognized the Plantagenet loss of Normandy, Maine, Anjou and Poitou to the French crown. The treaty of Corbeil, made with James I of Aragon in 1258, did much the same for the south, recognizing the Pyrenees as the border between France and Aragon. In both cases some territories were allowed to the foreign monarchs, for which they agreed to do homage to Louis. Henry III performed his homage in the garden of the royal palace in Paris.

In 1242 Louis IX recognized Raymond VII of Toulouse and restored some of his lands, following an agreement made during the minority with Blanche, who was the count's

34. Strayer, p. 135; J. Sumption, *The Albigensian Crusade* (London, 1978) p. 222, from William of Puylaurens.

cousin. Raymond had briefly joined the Plantagenets in the 1242 war, but was pardoned again. Raymond's daughter and heiress, Joan of Toulouse, was to marry Louis's brother Alphonse, and on Raymond's death the county of Toulouse was to pass to them, as indeed it did in 1249. The marriage took place in 1237, and when both partners died without children in 1271, Toulouse eventually reverted to the French crown.

The Inquisition began its work against the Cathars with the support of Louis IX. The old status of the heresy in the south altered; Cathar strongholds were captured, notably Montségur in 1244, when over 200 heretics were burnt alive on a great pyre. The castle was destroyed and it remains as an imposing ruin on its sheer height. But Catharism was not entirely wiped out and the heresy lingered on for many years. The last Cathar 'bishop' of Toulouse was burnt in 1273, the last Cathar, the *perfectus* William Belibasta, in 1321. As one historian puts it: 'everyone, from Innocent III on, had worked, struggled and suffered, without realizing it, for the benefit of the king of France'.[35] The French crown took over the Trencavel lands in 1226 and those of the count of Toulouse in 1271. Louis IX's own marriage, to Margaret daughter of the count of Provence, at Sens in 1234, further strengthened the royal position in the south. Louis is said to have prayed for three nights before the marriage, though the content of the prayers is unknown.

The risky policy of allowing broad estates, known as *apanages*, to members of the royal family did not in fact cause major upsets, indeed the crown benefited further. Philip Hurepel's lands, which in effect made up an early *apanage*, reverted to the crown when he joined the abortive coalition against Blanche, and died without heirs. The marriage of Alphonse had a similarly fortunate outcome for the crown.

Much of what was achieved by Louis IX was founded on the policy and work of his grandfather, Philip Augustus. His administrative interest paralleled that of Philip, and saw the flourishing of new kinds of documents and new systems of government. The additional revenue from the increased demesne, and from the greater territory now ruled, helped to lubricate the mechanism of administration under an able

---

35. Strayer, p. 142, quoting Luchaire.

monarch. France continued to flourish in economic terms too, and led Europe culturally. France, as a great European power, owes an enduring debt to Philip and St Louis, the two great rulers of the Capetian dynasty. Louis, like Philip, was eager to crusade, though his expeditions were less successful than his grandfather's; he was captured at Damietta in 1250, and eventually died on his venture to Africa in 1270 muttering 'Jerusalem, Jerusalem'.[36] Even the death of Louis IX is not the last page in the roll of Capetian achievement, but perhaps its greatest days were by then in the past.

36. S. Runciman, *A History of the Crusades*, 3 vols (Cambridge, 1954) III, p. 292, from William of St-Pathus.

BIBLIOGRAPHY

ABBREVIATIONS

ANS	*Anglo-Norman Studies*
Bautier	R-H. Bautier, ed., *La France de Philippe Auguste, le Temps des Mutations*, Actes du Colloque International organisé par le Centre National de la Recherche Scientifique, 1980 (Paris, 1982)
BSAN	*Bulletin de la Société des Antiquaires de Normandie*
Cartellieri	A. Cartellieri, *Phillip II. August, König von Frankreich*, 4 vols (Leipzig, 1899–1922)
CHF	Classiques de l'Histoire de France
CG	*Château-Gaillard, Études de Castellologie Medievale*
EHR	*English Historical Review*
EHS	English Historical Society
Howlett	R. Howlett, ed., *Chronicles of the Reigns of Stephen, Henry II and Richard I*, 4 vols, RS no. 82 (London, 1884–89)
GRH2	*Gesta Regis Henrici Secundi*
JMH	*Journal of Medieval History*
Lavisse	E. Lavisse, ed., *Histoire de France depuis les Origines jusqu'à la Révolution*, III, Pt. I (Paris, 1911)
MGH	*Monumenta Germaniae Historica*
RAB	*Studies in Medieval History presented to R. Allen Brown*, ed. C. Harper-Bill, C.J. Holdsworth and J.L. Nelson (Woodbridge, 1989)
Recueil	*Recueil des Actes de Philippe Auguste*, ed. H-F. Delaborde, 4 vols (Paris, 1916–79)

RHF	*Recueil des Historiens des Gaules et de la France*, ed. M. Bouquet and L. Delisle, 24 vols (Paris, 1869–1904)
Regesta	'Die Register Innocenz III', ed. O. Hageneder and A. Haidacher, 2 vols (Graz and Cologne, 1964, 1979), in *Patrologiae Cursus Completus, Latina*, ed. J.P. Migne, 221 vols (Paris, 1844–1903), vols 214, 217
RS	Rolls Series
SHF	Société de l'Histoire de France
Spec	*Speculum*
Stevenson	J. Stevenson, ed. and trans., *The Church Historians of England*, 5 vols (London, 1853–58)

. . .

PRIMARY SOURCES

Ambroise, *L'Estoire de la Guerre Sainte*, ed. G. Paris (Paris, 1897)

Ambroise, *The Crusade of Richard Lionheart*, ed. and trans. M.J. Hubert and J.L. La Monte (New York, 1976)

Archer, T.A., *The Crusade of Richard I, 1189–92* (London, 1888)

Barnwell Chronicle, The, in Walter of Coventry, *Memoriale*, ed. W. Stubbs, RS no. 58, 2 vols (London, 1872–73)

Becket, Thomas, in J.C. Robertson, ed., *Materials for the History of Thomas Becket, Archbishop of Canterbury*, RS no. 67, 7 vols (London, 1875–85)

Béthune, the Anonymous of, 'Histoire des Ducs de Normandie et des Rois d'Angleterre', ed. L.V. Delisle, *RHF*, XXIV, Pt II

Born, Bertran de, *The Poems of the Troubadour Bertran de Born*, ed. W.D. Paden Jr, T. Sankovitch and P.H. Stäblein (Berkeley, CA, 1986)

Breton, William the, 'Philippide', in *Oeuvres de Rigord et de Guillaume le Breton*, ed. H-F. Delaborde, SHF, vols 210, 224 (Paris, 1882–85)

Breton, William the, 'Vie de Philippe Auguste', in *Oeuvres de Rigord et de Guillaume le Breton*, ed. H-F. Delaborde, SHF, vols 210, 224 (Paris, 1882–85)

Breton, William the, *La Philippide, Poème*, ed. and trans. M. Guizot (Paris, 1825)

Budget, *Le Premier Budget de la Monarchie Française*, ed. F. Lot and R. Fawtier (Paris, 1932)

Canterbury, Gervase of, *Opera Historica*, ed. W. Stubbs, 2 vols, RS no. 73 (London, 1879–80)

Chanson de la Croisade Albigeoise, ed. E. Martin-Chabot, 3 vols (Paris, 1931–61)

'Chronique de St Martin de Tours', *RHF*, XVIII

Clari, Robert de, *La Conquête de Constantinople*, ed. P. Lauer (Paris, 1924)

Clari, Robert de, *The Conquest of Constantinople*, ed. and trans. E.H. McNeal (New York, 1936)

Coggeshall, Ralph of, *Chronicon Anglicanum*, ed. J. Stevenson, RS no. 66 (London, 1875)

Delisle, L.V., *Catalogue des Actes de Philippe Auguste* (Paris, 1856)

Devizes, Richard of, *The Chronicle of Richard of Devizes of the Time of Richard I*, ed. and trans. J.T. Appleby (Edinburgh, 1963)

Diceto, Ralph of, *Opera Historica*, ed. W. Stubbs, RS no. 68, 2 vols (London, 1876)

Exuviae Sacrae Constantinopolitanae, ed. P. Riant (Geneva, 1877)

Fantosme, Jordan, *Chronicle*, ed. and trans. R.C. Johnston (Oxford, 1981)

Gabrieli, F., ed., *Arab Historians of the Crusades*, trans. E.J. Costello (London, 1969)

Gesta Regis Henrici Secundi, commonly known as 'Benedict of Peterborough', ed. W. Stubbs, RS no. 49, 2 vols (London, 1867)

Grammaticus, Saxo, *Pontificorum Romanorum Vitae*, ed. Watterich (Leipzig, 1862)

Grandes Chroniques de Saint-Denis, ed. J. Viard, 9 vols (Paris, 1920–37)

Gros Bref, in A. Verhulst and M. Gysseling, eds, *Le Compte Général de 1187, connu sous le nom de 'Gros Brief'* (Brussels, 1962)

Howden, Roger of, *Chronica*, ed. W. Stubbs, RS no. 51, 4 vols (London, 1868–71)

Howden, Roger of, *The Annals of Roger de Hoveden*, ed. and trans. H.T. Riley, 2 vols (London, 1853)

Howlett, R., ed., *Chronicles of the Reigns of Stephen, Henry II and Richard I*, RS no. 82, 4 vols (London, 1884–89)

Innocent III, *Selected Letters of Pope Innocent III concerning England, 1198–1216*, ed. and trans. C.R. Cheney and W.H. Semple (Edinburgh, 1953)

'Itinerarium', in W. Stubbs, ed., *Chronicles and Memorials of the Reign of Richard I*, RS no. 38, 2 vols (London, 1864–65)

'Itinerarium', in K. Fenwick, ed. and trans., *The Third Crusade* (London, 1958)

Joinville, Jean de, *Histoire de Saint Louis*, ed. N. de Wailly (Paris, 1964)

Joinville, Jean de, *La Vie de Saint Louis*, ed. N.L. Corbett (Québec, 1977)

Joinville, Jean de, 'History of Saint Louis', in *Joinville and Villehardouin, Chronicles of the Crusades*, ed. and trans. M.R.B. Shaw (Harmondsworth, 1963)

Layettes du Trésor des Chartes, 5 vols (Paris, 1863–1909), vols I and II ed. A. Teulet

Lincoln, Hugh of, *The Life of Saint Hugh of Lincoln*, ed. and trans. D.L. Douie and H. Farmer, 2 vols (Edinburgh, 1962)

Map, Walter, *De Nugis Curialium*, ed. M.R. James, C.N.L. Brooke and R.A. Mynors (Oxford, 1983)

Map, Walter, *De Nugis Curialium*, ed. and trans. F. Tupper and M.B. Ogle (London, 1924)

'Margam Annal', in *Annales Monastici*, ed. H.R. Luard, RS no. 36, 5 vols (London, 1864–69)

Marshall, William the, *L'Histoire de Guillaume le Maréchal*, ed. P. Meyer, 3 vols, SHF nos 255, 268, 304 (Paris, 1891–1901)

Mons, Giselbert of, *La Chronique de Gislebert de Mons*, ed. L. Vanderkindere, Recueil des textes pour servir à l'étude de l'histoire de Belgique (Brussels, 1904)

Morea Chronicle, *Crusaders as Conquerors: The Chronicle of the Morea*, ed. and trans. H.E. Lurier (New York, 1964)

Mouskes, Philip, *Chronique rimée*, ed. Baron de Reiffenberg, 2 vols (Brussels, 1836–38)

Nogent, Guibert of, *Self and Society in Medieval France: The Memoirs of Abbot Guibert of Nogent*, ed. and trans. J.F. Benton (Toronto, 1984)

Pairis, Gunther of, 'Historia Constantinopolitana', in *Exuviae*, pp. 104–6

Paris, Gilles de, 'Carolinus', *RHF*, XVII, pp. 288–301

Paris, Matthew, *Chronica Majora*, ed. H.R. Luard, RS no. 57, 7 vols (London, 1872–83)

Paris, Matthew, *Chronicles*, ed. R. Vaughan (Gloucester, 1986)

Paris, Matthew, *English History*, ed. and trans. J.A. Giles, 3 vols (London, 1852)

Paris, Matthew, *Historia Anglorum*, ed. F. Madden, RS no. 44, 3 vols (London, 1866–69)

Paris, Matthew, *The Illustrated Chronicles of Matthew Paris*, ed. and trans. R. Vaughan (Stroud, 1993)

Recueil des Actes de Philippe Auguste, ed. H-F. Delaborde, C. Petit-Dutaillis, J. Boussard and M. Nortier, 4 vols (Paris, 1916–79)

Recueil des Historiens des Gaules et de la France, ed. M. Bouquet and L. Delisle, 24 vols (Paris, 1734–1904)

Register Innocenz III, Die, ed. O. Hageneder (Rome, 1964)

Register, *Le Premier Registre de Philippe-Auguste*, ed. L.V. Delisle, reproduction héliotypique (Paris, 1883)

Registres de Philippe Auguste, Les, ed. J.W. Baldwin, with F. Gasparri, M. Nortier and E. Lalou, *RHF*, Documents financiers et administratifs, VII, Texte (Paris, 1992)

Rigord, 'Vie de Philippe Auguste', in *Oeuvres de Rigord et de Guillaume le Breton*, ed. H-F. Delaborde, SHF, vols 210, 224 (Paris, 1882–85)

Rigord, and William the Breton, *Vie de Philippe Auguste*, ed. and trans. M. Guizot (Paris, 1825)

Riley-Smith, L. and J., *The Crusades, Idea and Reality, 1095–1274* (London, 1981)

St-Pathus, William de, *Vie de Saint Louis*, ed. H-F. Delaborde (Paris, 1899)

Salisbury, John of, *Historia Pontificalis*, ed. and trans. M. Chibnall (Edinburgh, 1956)

Suger, *Vie de Louis VI, le Gros*, CHF, ed. H. Waquet (Paris, 1929)

Suger, *Vie de Louis VI, le Gros, suivie de le Histoire de Roi Louis VII*, ed. A. Molinier (Paris, 1887)

Torigny, Robert of, 'Chronicle', in Stevenson, IV, Pt. II

Torigny, Robert of, 'Chronicle', in Howlett, IV

Tyre, William of, *Chronicon*, ed. R.B.C. Huygens, 2 vols (Brepols, 1986)

Tyre, William of, *A History of Deeds Done Beyond the Sea*, ed. E.A. Babcock and A.C. Krey, 2 vols (New York, 1943)

Vaux-de-Cernay, Peter of, *Hystoria Albigensis*, ed. P. Guébin and E. Lyon (Paris, 1826–1939)

Vaux-de-Cernay, Peter of, *Hystoria Albigensis*, ed. and trans. P. Guébin (Paris, 1951)

Villehardouin, Geoffrey de, *La Conquête de Constantinople*, ed. E. Faral, 2 vols (Paris, 1938–39)

Villehardouin, Geoffrey de, 'The Conquest of Constantinople', in *Joinville and Villehardouin*, ed. and trans. M.R.B. Shaw (Harmondsworth, 1963)

Vitalis, Orderic, *The Ecclesiastical History*, ed. M. Chibnall, 6 vols (Oxford, 1969–81)

Wales, Gerald of, *Opera*, ed. J.S. Brewer, J.F. Dimock and G.F. Warner, RS no. 21, 8 vols (London, 1861–91)

Wendover, Roger of, *Flores Historiarum*, ed. H.G. Hewlett, RS no. 84, 3 vols (London, 1886–89)

Wendover, Roger of, *Chronicon sive Flores Historiarum*, ed. H.O. Coxe, EHS, 5 vols (1841–44)

Wendover, Roger of, *Flowers of History*, ed. and trans. J.A. Giles, 2 vols (London, 1899)

. . .

SECONDARY SOURCES

Appleby, J.T., *England Without Richard, 1188–99* (London, 1965)

Appleby, J.T., *John, King of England* (London, 1958)

Audouin, E., *Essai sur l'armée royale au temps de Philippe Auguste* (Paris, 1913)

Baldwin, J.W., *The Government of Philip Augustus* (Berkeley, CA, 1986)

Baldwin, J.W., *Masters, Princes and Merchants: The Social Views of Peter the Chanter and his Circle*, 2 vols (Princeton, 1970)

Barratt, N., 'The revenue of King John', *EHR*, CXI, 1996, pp. 835–55

Bates, D.R., 'Léopold Delisle (1826–1910)', in H. Damico and J.B. Zavadil, eds, *Medieval Scholarship: Biographical Studies on the Formation of a Discipline*, I: History (New York and London, 1995), pp. 101–13

Bautier, R-H., ed., *La France de Philippe Auguste, le Temps des Mutations*, Actes du Colloque International organisé par le CNRS, 1980 (Paris, 1982)

Benjamin, R., 'A forty years war: Toulouse and the Plantagenets, 1156–96', *Historical Research*, LXI, 1988, pp. 270–85.

Benjamin, R., 'The Angevin Empire', *History Today*, XXXVI, 1986, pp. 17–22

Benton, J.F., 'The revenue of Louis VII', *Spec*, XLII, 1967, pp. 84–91

Bolton, B., 'Philip Augustus and John: two sons in Innocent III's vineyard', *The Church and Sovereignty c.590–1918: Essays in Honour of Michael Wilks*, ed. D. Wood (Oxford, 1991) pp. 113–34

Bordonove, G., *Philippe Auguste, le Conquérant* (Paris, 1986)

Bournazel, É., *Le Gouvernement capétien au XIIe siècle, 1108–1180* (Limoges, 1975)

Boussard, J., *Le comté d'Anjou sous Henri Plantagenêt et ses fils, 1151–1204* (Paris, 1938)

Boussard, J., *Le Gouvernement d'Henri II Plantagenêt* (Paris, 1956)

Bradbury, J., *The Medieval Siege* (Woodbridge, 1992)

Bridge, A., *Richard the Lionheart* (London, 1989)

Brown, R.A., 'The battle of Hastings', *ANS*, III, 1980, pp. 1–21

Butler, H.E., *The Autobiography of Giraldus Cambrensis* (London, 1937)

Carpenter, D.A., *The Minority of Henry III* (London, 1990)

Cartellieri, A., *Phillip II. August, König von Frankreich*, 4 vols (Leipzig, 1899–1922)

Cheney, C.R., *Pope Innocent III and England* (Stuttgart, 1976)

Church, S.D., 'The knights of the household of King John: a question of numbers', in P.R. Coss and S.D. Lloyd, eds, *Thirteenth-Century England*, IV, pp. 151–65

Constable, G., 'The Second Crusade as seen by contemporaries', *Traditio*, IX, 1953, pp. 213–79

Contamine, P., *War in the Middle Ages*, trans. M. Jones (Oxford, 1984)

Coulson, C., 'Fortress-policy in Capetian tradition and Angevin practice: aspects of the conquest of Normandy by Philip II', *ANS*, VI, 1983, pp. 13–38

Coutil, L., *Le Château-Gaillard* (Paris, 1906)

Crouch, D., *The Image of Aristocracy in Britain, 1000–1300* (London, 1992)

Crouch, D., *William Marshal* (Harlow, 1990)

Davidsohn, R., *Philipp II. August von Frankreich und Ingeborg* (Stuttgart, 1888)

Delbrück, H., *History of the Art of War*, III, trans. W.J. Renfroe Jr, (Westport, CT, 1982)

Dept, G.G., *Les Influences Anglaise et Française dans le comté de Flandre au début du XIIIe siècle* (Ghent and Paris, 1928)

Deville, A., *Histoire du Château-Gaillard* (Rouen, 1829)

Druon, M., *The History of Paris, from Caesar to Saint Louis* (London, 1969)

Duby, G., *France in the Middle Ages, 987–1460*, trans. J. Vale (Oxford, 1991)

Duby, G., *William Marshal, the Flower of Chivalry*, trans. R. Howard (London, 1986)

Duby, G., *The Legend of Bouvines*, trans. C. Tihanyi (Cambridge, 1990)

Duby, G., *The Knight, the Lady and the Priest*, trans. B. Bray (London, 1983)

Dunbabin, J., *France in the Making, 843–1180* (Oxford, 1985)

Dutton, C.M., 'Aspects of the institutional history of the Albigensian Crusades, 1198–1229', unpublished Ph.D. thesis (London, 1993)

Fawtier, R., *The Capetian Kings of France*, trans. L. Butler and R.J. Adam (London, 1964)

Finó, J-F., 'Quelques aspects de l'art militaire sous Philippe Auguste', *Gladius*, VI, 1967, pp. 19–36

Garnett, G., and J. Hudson, eds, *Law and Government in Medieval England and Normandy* (Cambridge, 1994)

Garnett, G., ' "Ducal" succession in early Normandy', in G. Garnett and J. Hudson, eds, *Law and Government in Medieval England and Normandy* (Cambridge, 1994) pp. 80–110

Gauthiez, B., 'Paris, un Rouen capétien? Developpements comparés de Rouen et Paris sous les règnes de Henri II et Philippe-Auguste', *ANS*, XVI, 1993, pp. 117–36

Gibbon, E., *The History of the Decline and Fall of the Roman Empire*, ed. F. Fernández-Armesto, 8 vols (London, 1989)

Gillingham, J., *Richard Coeur de Lion: Kingship, Chivalry and War in the Twelfth Century* (London, 1994)

Gillingham, J., 'Richard I, galley-warfare and Portsmouth: beginnings of a royal navy', *13th Century England*, VI, 1997, pp. 1–15.

Gillingham, J., *Richard the Lionheart*, 2nd edn (London, 1989)

Gillingham, J., *The Angevin Empire* (London, 1984)

Gillingham, J., and J.C. Holt, eds, *War and Government in the Middle Ages* (Woodbridge, 1984)

Godfrey, J., *1204, The Unholy Crusade* (Oxford, 1980)

Grabois, A., 'The crusade of King Louis VII: a reconsideration', in P.W. Edbury, ed., *Crusade and Settlement* (Cardiff, 1985) pp. 94–104

Gransden, A., *Historical Writing in England c.550 to c.1307* (London, 1974)

Green, J., 'Lords of the Norman Vexin', in J. Gillingham and J.C. Holt, eds, *War and Government in the Middle Ages* (Woodbridge, 1984) pp. 47–63

Hajdu, R., 'Castles, castellans and the structure of politics in Poitou', *JMH*, IV, 1978, pp. 27–53

Hallam, E.M., *Capetian France, 987–1328* (Harlow, 1980)

Hamilton, B., *The Albigensian Crusade*, Historical Association (London, 1974)

Hardengue, Antoine, *Philippe Auguste et Bouvines: Bouvines, victorie créatrice* (Paris, 1935, reprint 1978)

Héliot, P., 'Le Château-Gaillard et les forteresses des XIIe et XIIIe siècles en Europe occidentale', *CG*, I, 1964, pp. 53–75

Henderson, P., *Richard Coeur de Lion* (New York, 1958)

Hollister, C.W., and J.W. Baldwin, 'The rise of administrative kingship: Henry I and Philip Augustus', *American Historical Review*, LXXXVIII, 1978, pp. 867–905

Holt, J.C., *Magna Carta* (Cambridge, 1965)

Hutton, W.H., *Philip Augustus* (London, 1896)

Jordan, W.C., *Louis IX and the Challenge of the Crusade* (Princeton, 1979)

Jordan, W.C., *The French Monarchy and the Jews, from Philip Augustus to the Last Capetians* (1989)

Kedar, B.Z., ed., *The Horns of Hattin* (Jerusalem and London, 1992)

Labarge, M.W., *Gascony, England's First Colony, 1204–1453* (London, 1980)

Labarge, M.W., *Saint Louis: The Life of Louis IX of France* (London, 1968)

Lambert, M., *Medieval Heresy* (London, 1977)

Lewis, A.W., *Royal Succession in Capetian France: Studies in Familial Order and the State* (Cambridge, MA, 1981)

Lewis, P.N., 'The wars of Richard I in the West', unpublished M. Phil. thesis (London, 1977)

Leyser, K.J., *Medieval Germany and its Neighbours, 900–1250* (London, 1982)

Lot, F., *L'Art militaire et les armées au Moyen Age en Europe et dans le Proche Orient*, 2 vols (Paris, 1946)

Luchaire, A., *Études sur les actes de Louis VII* (Paris, 1885)

Luchaire, A., *Innocent III, la Croisade des Albigeois* (Paris, 1911)

Luchaire, A., 'Philippe Auguste' and 'Louis VIII', in Lavisse, III, Pt. I (Paris, 1911)

Luchaire, A., *Social France at the Time of Philip Augustus*, trans. E.B. Krehbiel (New York, 1912)

Maalouf, A., *The Crusades through Arab Eyes* (London, 1984)

Madaule, J., *The Albigensian Crusade*, trans. B. Wall (London, 1967)

Mayer, H.E., *The Crusades*, trans. J. Gillingham (Oxford, 1972)

Moore, R.I., *The Formation of a Persecuting Society* (Oxford, 1987)

Moore, R.I., *The Origins of European Dissent* (London, 1977)

Morris, C., *The Papal Monarchy: The Western Church from 1050 to 1250* (Oxford, 1989)

Nelson, J.L., ed., *Richard Coeur de Lion in History and Myth* (London, 1992)

Newby, P.H., *Saladin in his Time* (London, 1983)

Nicholas, D., *Medieval Flanders* (Harlow, 1992)

Nicholson, R.L., *Joscelyn III and the Fall of the Crusader States, 1134–99* (Leiden, 1973)

Nicol, D.M., *The End of the Byzantine Empire* (London, 1979)

Norgate, K., *England under the Angevin Kings*, 2 vols (London, 1887)

Norgate, K., *John Lackland* (London, 1902)

Norgate, K., *Richard the Lionheart* (London, 1924)

Norgate, K., *The Minority of Henry III* (London, 1912)

Oman, C.W.C., *A History of the Art of War in the Middle Ages*, 2 vols (London, 1924)

Owen, D.D.R., *Eleanor of Aquitaine, Queen and Legend* (Oxford, 1993)

Owen, D.D.R., 'The prince and the churl: the traumatic experience of Philip Augustus', *JMH*, XVIII, 1992, pp. 141–4

Pacaut, M., *Louis VII et son royaume* (Paris, 1967)

Pacaut, M., 'Conon de Lausanne et les revenus de Louis VII', *Revue historique*, CCXXXIX, 1968, pp. 29–32

Painter, S., *The Reign of John* (Baltimore, 1949)

Painter, S., *William Marshal* (Baltimore, 1933)

Pernoud, R., *Blanche of Castile*, trans. H. Noel (London, 1975)

Perry, F., *Saint Louis, the Most Christian King* (London, 1902)

Petit-Dutaillis, C., *Étude sur la vie et le règne de Louis VIII, 1187–1226* (Paris, 1894)

Petit-Dutaillis, C., *The Feudal Monarchy in France and England from the Tenth to the Thirteenth Centuries*, trans. E.D. Hunt (London, 1936)

Pirie-Gordon, C.H.C., *Innocent the Great: An Essay on his Life and Times* (London, 1907)

Poly, J-P., and E. Bournazel, *The Feudal Transformation, 900–1200*, trans. C. Higgitt (New York, 1991)

Power, D.J., 'What did the frontier of Angevin Normandy comprise?', *ANS*, XVII, 1994, pp. 181–201

Powicke, F.M., *The Loss of Normandy*, 2nd edn (Manchester, 1960, revised 1961)

Powicke, F.M., *The Thirteenth Century, 1215–1307* (Oxford, 1953)

Prawer, J., *The Latin Kingdom of Jerusalem* (London, 1972)

Pryor, J.H., *Geography, Technology and War: Studies in the Maritime History of the Mediterranean, 649–1571* (Cambridge, 1988)

Queller, D.E., *The Fourth Crusade, the Conquest of Constantinople, 1201–4* (Leicester, 1978)

Reynolds, S., *Fiefs and Vassals* (Oxford, 1994)

Richard, A., *Histoire des comtes de Poitou, 778–1204*, 2 vols (Paris, 1903)

Richard, J., *Saint Louis, roi d'une France féodale, soutien de la Terre sainte* (Paris, 1983)

Richard, J., *The Latin Kingdom of Jerusalem*, 2 vols (Amsterdam, 1979)

Riley-Smith, J., *The Crusades, a Short History* (London, 1987)

Riley-Smith, L. and J., *The Crusades, Idea and Reality, 1095–1274* (London, 1981)

Robinson, I.S., *The Papacy, 1073–1198: Continuity and Innovation* (Cambridge, 1990)

Rogers, R., *Latin Siege Warfare in the Twelfth Century* (Oxford, 1992)

Rowlands, I.W., 'King John, Stephen Langton and Rochester Castle, 1213–15', *RAB*, pp. 267–80

Runciman, S., *A History of the Crusades*, III, The Kingdom of Acre (Cambridge, 1955)

Russell, F.H., *The Just War in the Middle Ages* (Cambridge, 1975)

Sassier, Y., *Louis VII* (Paris, 1991)

Sayers, J., *Innocent III, Leader of Europe, 1198–1216* (Harlow, 1994)

Setton, K.M., ed., *A History of the Crusades*, 6 vols (Wisconsin, 1955–89); II, The Later Crusades, 1189–1311, ed. R.L. Wolff and H.W. Hazard (Philadelphia, 1962)

Seward, D., *Eleanor of Aquitaine* (Newton Abbot, 1978)

Smail, R.C., *Crusading Warfare, 1097–1193* (Cambridge, 1956)

Smith, J.B., 'The Treaty of Lambeth, 1217', *EHR*, XCIV, 1979, pp. 562–79

Strayer, J.R., *The Albigensian Crusades* (Michigan, 1971)

Sumption, J., *The Albigensian Crusade* (London, 1978)

Tillmann, H., *Pope Innocent III*, trans. W. Sax (Amsterdam, 1980)

Tout, T.F., *The Empire and the Papacy, 918–1273* (London, 1924)

Turner, R.V., *King John* (Harlow, 1994)

Ullmann, W., *A Short History of the Papacy in the Middle Ages* (London, 1972)

Verbruggen, J.F., *The Art of Warfare in Western Europe during the Middle Ages*, trans. S. Willard and S.C.M. Southern (Amsterdam, 1977)

Warlop, H.E., *The Flemish Nobility before 1300*, 4 vols, pt I, Historical Study, I, Text (Courtrai, 1975)

Warren, W.L., *Henry II* (London, 1973)

Warren, W.L., *King John*, 2nd edn (London, 1978)

Werveke, H. van, *Een Vlaamse Graaf van Europees formaat. Filips van de Elzas* (Haarlem, 1976)

Werveke, H. van, 'La contribution de la Flandre et du Hainaut à la troisième croisade', *Moyen Age*, LXXVIII, 1972

Wolff, R.L., 'Baldwin of Flanders and Hainault, first Latin emperor of Constantinople: his life, death and resurrection, 1172–1225', *Spec*, XXVII, 1955, pp. 281–332

Yver, J., 'Philippe Auguste et les châteaux normands: la frontière orientale du duché', *BSAN*, LIX, 1967–89, pp. 309–48

GENEALOGICAL TABLES
AND MAPS

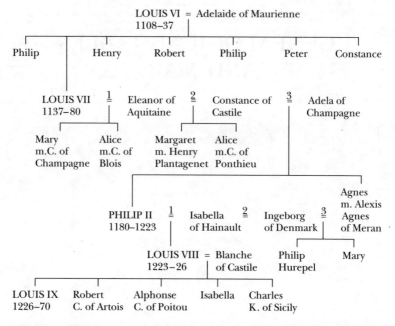

Table 1: The French royal house

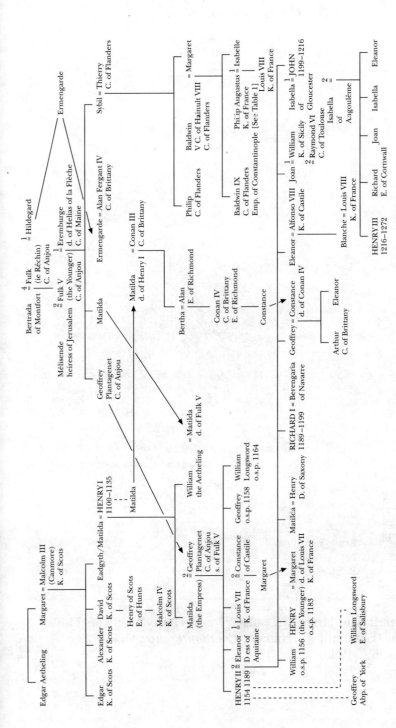

Table 2: The Angevin kings

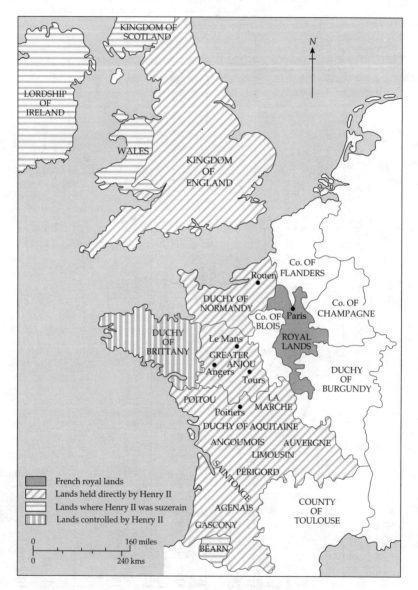

Map 1: The lands of Louis VII and Henry II in the 1170s
After Elizabeth M. Hallam, *Capetian France, 987–1328*
(Harlow, 1980)

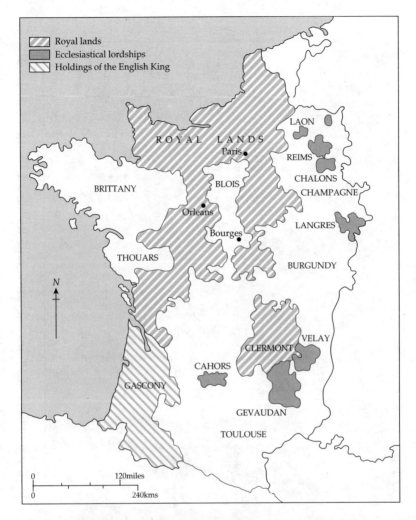

Map 2: The royal lands in 1223
After Elizabeth M. Hallam, *Capetian France, 987–1328*
(Harlow, 1980)

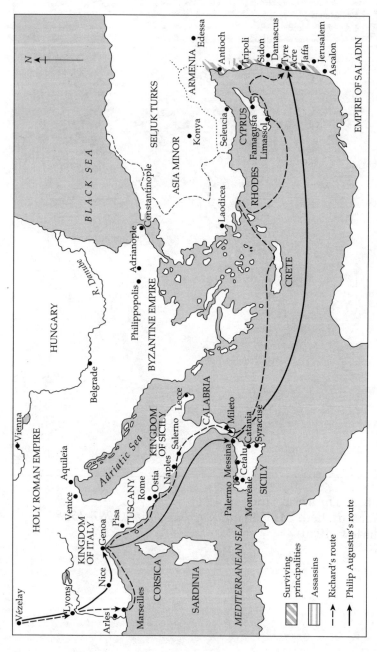

Map 3: The Third Crusade: the journeys of Philip Augustus and Richard I to the Holy Land

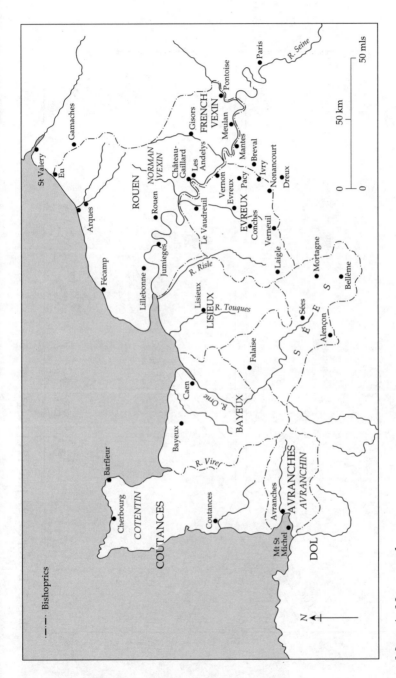

Map 4: Normandy

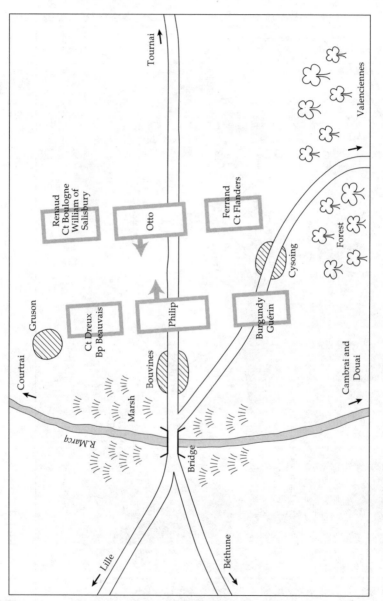

Map 5: Bouvines, 27 July 1214

INDEX